THE HOLY SPIRIT:
GROWTH OF A BIBLICAL TRADITION

THE HOLY SPIRIT:

Growth of a Biblical Tradition

George T. Montague, S.M.

Paulist Press
New York/Paramus/Toronto

ACKNOWLEDGMENTS

Scripture texts marked (NAB) are taken from the *New American Bible*, copyright © 1970 by the Confraternity of Christian Doctrine, Washington, D.C. and are used by permission of said copyright owner. No part of the *New American Bible* may be reproduced in any form without permission in writing from the Confraternity of Christian Doctrine, Washington, D.C.

Scripture texts marked (RSV) are taken from the *Revised Standard Version Bible* copyrighted 1965 and 1966 by the Division of Christian Education of the National Council of Churches of Christ in the U.S.A.

Translations from the Dead Sea Scrolls are taken from *The Dead Sea Scrolls in English* by G. Vermes (©1962, reprinted with revisions 1965, 1968) and is used by permission of Penguin Books, Ltd.

Library of Congress
Catalog Card Number: 76-4691

ISBN: 0-8091-1950-1

Published by Paulist Press
Editorial Office: 1865 Broadway, N.Y., N.Y. 10023
Business Office: 400 Sette Drive, Paramus, N.J. 07652

Printed and bound in the
United States of America

Contents

The Mountain
Seen from the Valley

"If you only knew the gift of God. . ." (John 4:10).

These words of Jesus to the woman at the well have been taken by Christians of all centuries as an invitation to know better the divine gift they have already received and to drink more deeply of the living water offered by the Lord. This water, John tells us, is the Spirit (Jn 7:37).

This book is the fruit of a search to know that gift of the Spirit better through another of the Lord's gifts, his word. That word is timeless, and yet wherever it appears in the Bible, it is always, like Jesus Christ himself, incarnated in a given time and place and culture. It meets men and women where they are. For this reason the scientific study of the Bible, situating the texts in the context of their time and the development of the revelation-tradition, offers an immense enrichment to our understanding of the word, even a necessary preamble to discovering what that word might be saying to us today.

Fundamentalism makes the mistake of thinking there is no distance between the biblical times and ours, and it distrusts the help of historical and literary sciences to bridge that distance. To some extent this reaction is understandable, for biblical criticism of the rationalist variety has not always avoided imposing its own philosophical presuppositions on the material and on the student. Somehow the truth of the matter must lie between these extremes. This book seeks to avoid fundamentalism on the one hand and purely rational exegesis on the other, using the contributions of biblical scholarship without burdening the reader with excessive academic detail. It stands, hopefully, at the confluence of two great and respected rivers of the Christian tradition—scholarship and spirituality. If by not being totally one nor the other it runs the risk of not satisfying either the norms of "pure scholarship" or the expectations of unenlightened piety, the risk is nonetheless worth taking, for the purpose of the scientific study of theology is to support faith's seeking of understanding, and a faith that never seeks understanding never grows.

The method used here may be new to those readers who have not been accustomed to think of the Bible as a gradual revelation. No father can tell his child everything at once, and neither can the Lord his people. If the study of biblical history has anything to tell us, it is that only gradually did the understanding of Yahweh and his expectations dawn upon the consciousness of his people. From the viewpoint of the Lord, this meant that his revelation was a progressive pedagogy. For example, we must not expect that when the author of Genesis 1:2 spoke of the spirit of God hovering over the waters at the cosmic creation he was thinking of the person of the Holy Spirit as understood, say, by the evangelist John, much less as understood by the theologians at the council of Nicea. If this were the case in biblical revelation there would be no room for surprise or for fulfillment beyond expectations. But what is the New Testament if not just that?

The reader will notice that we strive not merely to understand a given passage in its immediate context but also to discover the intention of the biblical author in the light of his overall theological outlook. Since God chose not parrots but persons as the conveyers of his word, to get inside the author's way of thinking is to understand better the message. On the other hand, in studying the material we have preferred to stick close to the biblical texts themselves, so that the reader may be in constant touch with the original source which we simply try to elucidate.

To study any biblical tradition in this way is like climbing a mountain. At the start of the journey what looms before us may be the brook we cross or the crest immediately before us. We would never pretend we could judge the whole lay of the mountainous area on the basis of the limited view at the beginning. But each stage is enjoyable in its own right. As we climb, new vistas appear and the old ones, while never completely lost from view, recede into a broader perspective, our earlier impressions being corrected by what we later see. When finally we reach the top, we find that nothing of what we saw along the way has been lost, but it is now only part of a vast panorama in which we see the parts in terms of the whole. To climb the mountain may take effort, but it is rewarded by the surprise of new discovery at every step, and at the summit a splendid vision.

Although I have streamlined the text by avoiding footnotes and bibliography, I must acknowledge from the outset my debt to hundreds of scholars whose works have made this book possible. Likewise my special thanks go to those friends and colleagues who read portions of the manuscript and helped with their comments: Fathers Aloysius M. Ambrozic (since made Auxiliary Bishop of Toronto), Raymond E. Brown,

S.S., Bertrand Buby, S.M., Dennis Hamm, S.J., William H. Irwin, C.S.B., and Anthony Saldarini, S.J. And to those who helped with the typing and the material preparation of the typescript: Mss. Silvia Bustamante, Melba Fisher, Alma Sternik and Sister Anne Carter, R.S.C.J.

George T. Montague, S.M.

PART I
THE OLD TESTAMENT

1
Life-Breath
and Prophetic Impulse:
The Earliest Traditions

The Yahwist

When Israel was still a collection of tribes, before she knew the centralizing power of a king, her religious traditions were handed on largely by word of mouth from parent to child and, in a more formal and organized way, at the shrines to which the tribes came regularly in pilgrimage. When Solomon acceded to the throne of David, he was determined to set up his court in a way that could rival the royal houses of Egypt and his other neighbors. That meant, among other things, that he would establish a school of scribes to research and put down in writing the traditions which were the foundation of the monarchy. For some of the scribes that meant recording the more recent tribal history. But for at least one of them it meant going back to the very origins of mankind and tracing the story from there through Abraham and the patriarchs down through the exodus and the period of the desert wanderings.

This author is called the Yahwist, not because that was his real name (we don't know what it was) but because his favorite name for God is Yahweh, the same name revealed to Moses at the burning bush (Ex 3:14). Turning out to be as much a critic of the monarchy as an advocate of it, he wanted to show that Israel's present history—its agonies and its ecstasies, its blessedness and its sin—is only the current chapter of a love-story that began with the very dawn of human consciousness, the creation of man. What happened then, as well as what is happening now, the Yahwist wanted to say, concerns not just Israel but all of mankind. Throughout it all Yahweh appears as a God who loves with a concerned love. And because he loves, he chooses to give life freely to whom he will. He is the Lord of all life and fertility, and he has chosen Israel and the Davidic dynasty and bound them in a covenant relationship with himself, so that Israel's history is in a mysterious way his history and her future his. Part of that gift is also an awesome freedom,

3

which Israel, as much as Adam, shows she rarely knows how to use. But instead of taking back the gift, the Lord allows man to sin, since he knows that somehow he can use even the evil and weakness of man to save man from himself. This determination of Yahweh never to abandon the sinner but to pursue him with saving love is shown in two ways: punishment and forgiveness. The first is not a vindictive anger, as if the Lord were "upset" or piqued. Rather, it is the "therapy of privation" for man's own good. Man, knowing once the blessings of peace, life and fulfillment that came from the Lord, experiences self-imposed deprivation when he turns away from the Lord. The very deprivation creates in him a realization of how much better it was when he walked in intimacy with his Lord and thus disposes him to accept the forgiveness and the new beginning offered him by the Savior-God.

What is important to remember about the method of this theological artist is that he is doing several things at once. The raw materials he uses are for the most part traditions of great antiquity, some popular, some cultic. Many of the most remote traditions were quite similar to those of other ancient peoples of the Near East. But all of them the author uses in a creative, even an ingenious way, to teach Israel important lessons about God, happiness, sin and redemption, brotherhood, covenant responsibility, and the way to life and happiness. In the same breath he is also addressing the monarchy both to legitimize it in terms of Yahweh's elective love and also to remind the king that his future, as much as Adam's, depends on loyal and loving fidelity to Yahweh and his word. As we examine some of the Yahwist texts it will be important to keep in mind the various levels on which the author is working.

Where do we find the Yahwist's work? Scholars generally agree that it begins at Genesis 2:4 and ends with Numbers 24:25. Not that all the material between these two points is the Yahwist's. Rather his work appears and disappears along with other literary sources in such a way that the books of Genesis, Exodus, and Numbers appear like a vast tapestry where the Yahwist thread has been woven in and out with these other sources by the final editor of the Pentateuch for its publication around 400 B.C. For all its later re-use however, the work of the Yahwist has remained marvelously intact, and so when we try to get inside the Yahwist's mind to discover his teaching, we are really simply confirming the judgment of the Pentateuch's final editor, who thought the Yahwist's work so precious it should be enshrined forever in the written word of God. Though he wrote sometime during the reign of Solomon (965-926 B.C.), the Yahwist not only spoke to Israel meaningfully some 600 years later, but he also speaks to us nearly 3,000 years later about many vital things, including the spirit.

Genesis 2:7: God Gives the Breath of Life

> **4.** At the time when the Lord God made the earth and the
> heavens— 5. while as yet there was no field shrub on earth and
> no grass of the field had sprouted, for the Lord God had sent
> no rain upon the earth and there was no man to till the soil, 6.
> but a stream was welling up out of the earth and was watering
> all the surface of the ground— 7. the Lord God formed man
> out of the clay of the ground and blew into his nostrils the
> breath of life, and so man became a living being. (NAB)

As we find it now in Genesis, this is the second account of creation,
differing considerably in detail from the first (Gen 1:1-2:4a), which is attributed to the Priestly author of a later date. Since we shall examine the
first account in detail further on, we will be content here with pointing
out how this Yahwist account differs. Whereas the first account described creation as a process from the chaos of water to the order of dry
land, the Yahwist describes the process as the reverse—from lifeless
desert to a fertile garden. Land without water is as chaotic as water
without land, and for those desert nomads or semi-desert farmers whose
life depended on water, as was the case with Israel, this image was closer
to their daily experience than the boundless seas. The Yahwist has no interest in the formation of cosmic light (Gen 1:3-5) or the sun, the moon
and the stars (Gen 1:14-19). His view is restricted to the *earth* and the
things that immediately touch human life; water, earth, the sown land,
animals, woman. His interest is centered in man, who is Adam from the
adamah, earthman from the earth.

The word used to describe the Lord's making of man is the same
used in the Bible of a potter who shapes clay. The Yahwist is not at all
concerned here about the theological problem of creation out of nothing.
Nor of course is he aware of the later scientific questions about evolution. What he is concerned with is to show man's essential brotherhood
with the earth. The "raw material" of man is earthy. The earth itself is,
of course, God's gift, but the point here is that of himself man is nothing
but the dust of the earth until the shaping power of God does something
with that earth. He blows into man's nostrils the *breath of life*. The
graphic imagery here befits the telling of a dramatic story. The Jews
who later read this story knew that the Lord did not have lungs like man
and that creation was not an early form of artificial respiration. (The
later creation account in Genesis 1 avoided even the possibility of that
question by attributing the creation of everything, including man, to
God's *word*.) But they also were aware—as the Yahwist certainly was—

that there is no sign of life so visible in man as his breath. What breathes, lives. And man's breath of life is a direct gift of God to him.

It is not said of any other of God's creatures in this account that he gave them the breath of life in this way. He planted a garden (2:8), he made trees grow (2:9), he "formed animals" of all kinds out of the ground (2:19), but it is never said that he breathed the breath of life into their nostrils. This suggests that man's life is a more intimate gift from the Lord than is that of the rest of creation. The Lord puts more of himself into this work, with the result that man is more personally oriented to God than is the rest of the universe. In the Babylonian creation myth *Enuma Elish*, man is made of clay mixed with the blood of the gods. The Priestly account of creation in Gen 1:26-27 describes man's relationship to the divine by saying that man is created "in our image, after our likeness." Here the fellowship with the divine world is described as the breath of life, the effect of man's receiving, in his very bodily life, the spiritual life of the divine world. The result of this inbreathing by God (*in-spiration*) is that man should become a *living being*. The Hebrew *nephesh hayyah* means literally "a living soul," as the Greek translators understood with the words *psychēn zōsan*, "a soul having life." This Greek expression will become very important for Paul in 1 Cor 15 when he seeks to explain how Christ by his resurrection has received the Spirit to impart to all his members.

For the moment, however, let us stick to the horizon of the Yahwist. Man is obviously a living being, he says, but if you want to know the secret of his living-ness, you must know that it comes from the *breath of life* he has from the Lord. The Hebrew word for breath here is *neshamah*. It is not the more familiar *ruah* but is virtually equivalent to it, since the two expressions are elsewhere used equivalently (Job 27:3; Gen 2:17; cf. also Job 33:4; 34:4; Is 57:16). It can be translated, like *ruah*, as "spirit," but if so we must remember it means spirit in the sense of breath. There is no thought here of a communication of the Holy Spirit but rather of the spirit or breath of life which is now in man as his gift from God, relating him to the divine world, on the one hand, and accounting for his human life on the other.

If the question is asked, is the author trying to tell us something about the composition of man, whether, for example, he is made of "body and soul," or whether perhaps he is suggesting that man is made up of body, soul, and spirit (a triad that appears in 1 Thes 5:23-24), we would have to say: Yes, he is teaching something about the make-up of man; but no, we cannot say he is defining man in terms of strictly distinguishable parts. In later Judaism, particularly among those heavily exposed to Greek culture, there was some speculation about this matter and our text was sometimes alluded to. But certainly the Yahwist was

not a theoretician about the essential composition of man in a philosophical sense.

He was greatly interested in showing that man, a living being like
but also above the animals, lives in a twofold relationship—he is brother
to the earth and all that springs from it. But he is also the breath of
Yahweh, or "spirit" if you will, and thus the source of his life not only
in its beginning but in every breath he takes, is God. The author is subtly preparing us for understanding the tragedy of man when he turns
from this source of life. For when God's breath is withdrawn (Ps 104:29-
30; Job 34:14-15) man reverts to lifeless dust (Gen 3:19). It was the lesson of Adam and Eve and the lesson of the flood (Gen 6:1-4; 7:22). It
would be God's word to mankind at every age.

Such seems to be the primary teaching of this verse. But if the
Yahwist was writing in the shadow of Solomon's court, perhaps even at
his request, is it possible that he might be addressing a particular message to the Son of David who was sitting upon the throne? Recently
scholars have turned up a number of pieces of evidence that make this
likely.

In general, each of the sin stories in Genesis 2-11 moves through
sin and its punishment to a surprising climax in the re-affirming of
God's graciousness—all leading up to the call of Abram in chapter 12 as
the Lord's final attempt to deal with the human predicament. Now the
story of David, still fresh in the memory of the Yahwist, was just such a
series of accounts relating David's sins, his punishment and then, in spite
of it all, a surprising reaffirmation of the Lord's love for David. Could it
be that the Yahwist, aware of this wonderful way the Lord had treated
David, expanded his theology of Yahweh-Savior to the canvas of all
mankind in Adam?

It is an interesting suggestion, but unless we had more evidence, it
could only be a guess. A number of notable scholars do find more evidence precisely in the language of our 2:7. In 1 Kings 16:2, reporting the
enthronement of Baasha, the Lord says, "I lifted you up from the dust
and made you ruler of my people Israel." Lifting from the dust here
means to make a nothing into a king, to take a man from obscurity and
invest him with royal power. The poetry of 1 Samuel 2:6-8 (the Song of
Hannah) also associates the "lifting from the dust" with royal accession:

6. The Lord puts to death and gives life;
   he casts down to the nether world;
   he raises up again.
7. The Lord makes poor and makes rich,
   he humbles, he also exalts.
8. *He raises the needy from the dust,*

from the ash heap he lifts up the poor,
to seat them with princes
and make a glorious throne their heritage.
For the pillars of the earth are the Lord's
and he has set the world upon them. (NAB)

Notice the contrast of death and life, bringing down and raising up, making poor and making rich and the theme "from dust to kingship." Note, too, the immediate reference to the stable order of creation, a frequent allusion in the Psalms associated with the accession of a king. For the role of a king is to establish order on the earth, and when he reigns well in obedience to Yahweh, the earth is at peace. In the Genesis account just such a role is prescribed for "the man"—who, raised from the dust, shares in the work of ordering creation—by caring for the garden (described also as a royal park) and naming the animals! Psalm 113:7 has a very similar ring: "He raises up the lowly from the dust: from the dunghill he lifts up the poor, to seat them with princes, with the princes of his own people."

The very word *formed* (in the Hebrew *yisar*) used in Gen 2:7 appears elsewhere in the Old Testament for installation in an office like ordination or enthronement (Jer 1:4-10; Is 44:24-25; cf. Ps 2:6-7). It would be perfectly appropriate to describe the installation of the Davidic king, raised from the dust of the earth to the throne prepared by Yahweh.

The word *ha-adam*, "the man," in Gen 2:7 appears to be the equivalent of the Mesopotamian *lu-gal* (big-man) or "king." (Some American Indian tribes called their chief the "big man" of the tribe.)

Finally, let us look for a moment at those curious "nostrils" in our text. The author of Lamentations bewails the capture of King Zedekiah with the words: "The Lord's messiah, the breath of our nostrils, was taken by their snares" (Lam 4:20). The "breath of our nostrils" is the king. One might object that the Lamentor is writing nearly 400 years after the Yahwist. True, but there are other indications from surrounding peoples that show the antiquity of this association with kingship. In Egypt the god Amon was called "the venerable god who came into being first; he is that breath which stays in all things and through which one lives forever." And in the Luxor temple a design depicts Amon holding the sign of life *(ankh)* toward king Amenhotep III with the words: "My beloved son, receive my likeness in thy nose." The goddess Hathor is also said to "give life to thy nostrils," referring to the king. Even more pertinently for our purposes here, another design from Luxor shows Hathor extending the *ankh* sign of life to king Amenhotep III, while the god Khnum is fashioning the young ruler on the potter's wheel.

All of this, especially the last parallel, suggests very strongly that the Yahwist has used enthronement language to depict the creation of man in Gen 2:7, confirming the ordination to lordship explicitly developed in the sequence. If the author has projected the royal enthronement back into the creation of the universal man, it is also likely that he is subtly issuing a warning to the Solomonic court, which became notorious for its hubris, its arrogant pride (1 Kgs 10-11): "You reign by the breath of Yahweh; if Yahweh takes away his breath, his spirit, you will return, as Adam did, to the dust of your former state."

What we first suspected to be no more than a description of the creation of man turns out to be, in the end, a kind of program for the messiah, the anointed one of Yahweh. Adam is king because of the breath God put in his nostrils. The sons of David are kings by the same gracious but precarious gift of God's favor. When the New Testament comes, Jesus Christ's resurrection from the dead by the "spirit of holiness" (Rom 1:4) is his enthronement as king of heaven and earth (Acts 2:36).

Genesis 6:3: The Limitation of the Life-Breath

1. When men began to multiply on earth and daughters were born to them, 2. the sons of heaven saw how beautiful the daughters of man were, and so they took for their wives as many of them as they chose. 3. Then the Lord said, "My spirit shall not remain in man forever, since he is but flesh. His days shall comprise one hundred and twenty years."

4. At that time the Nephilim appeared on earth (as well as later), after the sons of heaven had intercourse with the daughters of men, who bore them sons. They were the heroes of old, the men of renown. (NAB)

This story is usually confusing to the reader who is not provided with a little background. An artist rarely creates out of nothing. Like the Lord in the "second moment" of cosmic creation (Gen 1:2), the artist generally uses some unshaped material which by his skill he transforms into a thing of beauty. If God bids men beat their swords into plowshares and their spears into pruning hooks (Is 2:4; Mi 4:3), and the beauty of the tools of peace is only enhanced by their creation from the weapons of war, why could not an author, under divine inspiration, use and refashion even an old popular tale to illustrate a divine lesson? This is apparently what the Yahwist has done here. Among the ancient peoples there circulated a myth about the marriage of the astral gods with mortal women resulting in a generation of giants (literally, "Nephilim," "meteors"). As the tale was told it portrayed the amazing grandeur to which the human race once ascended, and the telling of the tale was a toast to man. The sacred author knew the tale, knew that it was popular even among his own people; so he decided to use it, but by reworking it at significant points he changed the tale from a toast to man's power to a satire on his insatiable hubris.

We can tell how the old tale has been reworked by certain ruptures in the story as we have it now in Genesis. By adding the note that these beings took wives "as many of them as they chose" the author is showing how far things had gone from the ideal of monogamy he had portrayed in Gen 2:24. He is, in other words, *pressing* the hubris in the story in order to prepare for the Lord's response which now follows. That response given in vs. 3 really interrupts the old tale, which makes perfect sense as a tale if the verse is omitted. But this verse contains precisely the motive the author has for relating the tale: why does man have only a limited life-span? Because the spirit (breath) of God given in creation is hampered by man being *flesh*—and man's fleshly nature is illustrated supremely by this sin of demonic pride. This requires explanation.

For the first time in the Bible we see the contrast of spirit (*ruah* in Hebrew) with *flesh* (*basar* in Hebrew). We translate "spirit" here instead of "breath," for, though the same Hebrew word means both, it is certainly life in a more general sense that is intended here, and not merely physical breathing. In saying that man is *flesh* here the author does not mean simply that man's being has a material component. *Flesh* here means proneness to evil and sin, the "downward-to-death" tendency in man, his weakness, physical and moral. The tendency of the flesh can be as much to pride as it is to lust—as we see illustrated in the story. What the Lord calls "my spirit in man" is the opposite tendency —to life and especially the source of life, the Lord himself. Spirit and life are thus implicitly connected here as they were in Gen 2:7 and as they will be hereafter in the Bible (e.g., Jn 6:63). Of itself the life of the spirit that comes to man should last forever, but by his sinfulness man allows the flesh to rule him and shows himself to be flesh, as the text says. An important lesson for man of all ages: sin weakens man's hold on life, it limits the power of God's spirit within him.

By setting the story at this point in his primitive history, the Yahwist uses it as the climax of the tide of evil begun with Adam's sin. Having turned against God and lost the divine intimacy (the fall of Adam and Eve), having turned on his fellowman in violence (the Cain story, Gen 4:1-16), having proclaimed violence and revenge without limit in the oath of Lamech (Gen 4:23-24), man shows so much wickedness that he can only be described as being invaded by the demonic. Popular tradition may glorify the super-race that resulted from such a conspiracy with the spirit-world—a situation in which man holds his life not as God's gift but as a semi-angelic "trick." But such a myth now, as then, is a deception, the supreme deception of all. For the Lord has not made man to share in the life of the angelic world but in God's own life, the *ruah* that is his own gift to man. Again an important lesson: If the *ruah*, the spirit in man puts him at the threshold of God himself, it is contrary to man's destiny to seek anything less, even though it be communion with superhuman spirits.

Genesis 7:22: Breath of Life

> Everything on earth with the faintest *breath of life* in its nostrils died out. (NAB)

The story of the flood is told both by the Yahwist and by the Priestly author each with different details, and the first editor of Genesis has interwoven both accounts, so that we find considerable repetitiveness and some difference in details as we follow the long braided narrative in Gen 6-9. For both authors, the flood was God's starting over with a remnant of his faithful ones—and a remnant of animals too—in an earth that had to be washed clean. The text of Gen 7:22 is noted here simply because in it again we find a reference to breath and spirit and life. The Hebrew translated here as "faintest breath of life" is the combined form *nishmath-ruah hayyim*. It simply recalls that living and breathing are synonymous in the Bible. Breath is life.

Numbers 24:2: The Spirit of God on Balaam

> When [Balaam] raised his eyes and saw Israel encamped, tribe by tribe, the spirit of God came upon him, and he gave voice to his oracle: "The utterance of Balaam, son of Beor, the utterance of a man whose eye is true . . ." (NAB)

This passage belongs to the third of the four oracles of Balaam related in the latter part of the book of Numbers. The first two oracles are generally understood to belong to the Elohist tradition (which we discuss later), the third and fourth to the Yahwist. In the Elohist tradition, the Lord is said to put a word (a message, *dabar*) in the mouth of Balaam (Num 23:4, 16) whereas the Yahwist here attributes the prophetic activity to the *spirit* of God rushing upon him. Here for the first time in our sources, prophecy is attributed to the spirit of God. The Elohist tradition, which is slightly later, attributes the activity to the *word* of God being given. At this point in the development of the tradition "word" and "spirit" are not sharply differentiated as they become in the period of classical prophecy.

There is doubt as to how to translate the adjective with which the author describes Balaam's prophetic eye. It could mean "true" as the NAB gives it, or "perfect" or "open" or "closed." If it is to be translated "closed," then it would be an indication of a prophecy delivered in an ecstatic state, but this meaning is not certain.

The Elohist

After Solomon's death his sons disputed the succession, finally precipitating a split of their father's realm into the tribes of the north under the name of Israel and those of the south under the name of Judah. The new kingdom to the north strove to compete in every way with the old southern kingdom that still had the city of David, Jerusalem, as its capital, and the temple and the court of Solomon. Jeroboam, Israel's first king, quickly set up temples and shrines, making Bethel and Dan rivals of the temple of Jerusalem. He also organized priests around these shrines (1 Kgs 12:26-33). We can assume that he fostered the gathering of the traditions of the northern tribes, most of which, of course, went back beyond even the united kingdom to the time of the patriarchs. This literary activity was fostered all the more by Omri's establishing Samaria as the capital city of Israel in 822 B.C. Somewhere during this time, a collection of traditions was made which has since been called the *Elohist*, because the author prefers *El* or *Elohim* as the name of the God of Israel. Around the time of the invasion and destruction of Samaria by the Assyrians (721 B.C.), the priests who fled from the north supposedly brought the Elohist documents with them to Jerusalem, where they were eventually fused with the Yahwist.

Coming from the northern kingdom, the Elohist traditions show little concern for the question of dynastic succession which so occupied the successors to the throne of David in Jerusalem. Heir to the more independent spirit that had characterized the time of the judges ("In those days there was no king in Israel; everyone did what he thought best" Jgs 17:6; 18:1; 19:1; 2:25), they were more open to charismatic than to dynastic leadership, with both the power and the pitfalls of such an orientation.

It is generally agreed that the Elohist source first appears in Genesis 15, the story of the covenant made with Abraham (though already there it is mixed with the Yahwist tradition).

Genesis 41:38: The Wise Joseph and the Spirit of God

"Could we find another like him," Pharaoh asked his officials,
"a man so endowed with the spirit of God?" (NAB)

One of the traits of the Elohist is his remarkable interest in dreams. The covenant made with Abram is done in a dream (Gen 15:12-21). And chapters 40-42, almost entirely Elohist, concern the interpretation of dreams and the first journey to Egypt of Joseph's brothers. Joseph, our text informs us, has shown himself to be full of the spirit of God. In what fashion? The context indicates it has been in the interpretation of dreams, first of Pharaoh's courtiers and then of Pharaoh himself. When Pharaoh then looks for a "wise and discerning man" (vs. 33) to administer the land, his choice falls on Joseph. Now this is interesting for several reasons. (1) To be endowed with the spirit of God refers here to a charismatic gift put at the service of the king and the people, in short a gift of service for the common good. (2) The gift in question is *interpretation*, the first appearance of this "gift of the spirit" in the Bible. Though it refers to dreams as its subject matter, it has many similarities with the gift of interpreting tongues of which Paul speaks in 1 Cor 14. (3) Perception by the king of the gift of interpretation in Joseph leads to constituting him in the office of administration. This is precisely the pattern later followed by the early church (Acts 6:3; Tit 5:22; *Didache*), where as a general rule appointment or ordination to office presupposes either the manifestation of a charism of the Spirit in the candidate or even occasionally a designation for ordination by prophetic discernment (Tit 4:14). The assumption in Joseph's case was that he who had the gift of interpretation would also have that of administration. The church has, for better or worse, often applied the same rule in the appointment of its leaders.

Numbers 11:17, 25-26, 29: The Spirit Comes Upon the Elders

10. When Moses heard the people, family after family, crying at the entrance of their tents, so that the Lord became very

angry, he was grieved. 11. "Why do you treat your servant so badly?" Moses asked the Lord. "Why are you so displeased with me that you burden me with all this people? 12. Was it I who conceived all this people? or was it I who gave them birth, that you tell me to carry them at my bosom, like a foster father carrying an infant, to the land you have promised under oath to their fathers? 13. Where can I get meat to give to all this people? For they are crying to me. 'Give us meat for our food!' 14. I cannot carry all this people by myself, for they are too heavy for me. 15. If this is the way you will deal with me, then please do me the favor of killing me at once, so that I need no longer face this distress."

24. So Moses went out and told the people what the Lord had said. Gathering seventy elders of the people, he had them stand around the tent. 25. The Lord then came down in the cloud and spoke to him. Taking some of the spirit that was on Moses, he bestowed it on the seventy elders; and as the spirit came to rest on them, they prophesied.

26. Now two men, one named Eldad and the other Medad, were not in the gathering but had been left in the camp. They too had been on the list, but had not gone out to the tent; yet the spirit came to rest on them also, and they prophesied in the camp. 27. So, when a young man quickly told Moses, "Eldad and Medad are prophesying in the camp," 28. Joshua, son of Nun, who from his youth had been Moses' aide, said, "Moses, my lord, stop them." 29. But Moses answered him, "Are you jealous for my sake? Would that all the people of the Lord were prophets! Would that the Lord might bestow his spirit on them all!" 30. Then Moses retired to the camp, along with the elders of Israel. (NAB)

The whole of chapter 11 of Numbers is needed as the context for this scene. A mixture probably of the Yahwist and Elohist sources, the story tells of the Israelites in the desert complaining to Moses for food, of Moses lamenting to the Lord that they were becoming an unbearable burden for him, of the solution given to Moses in the sharing of his leadership among the seventy elders, and of the quail given finally to satisfy the people.

The association of Moses' lament with the grumbling about food is only incidental to our interest in the role of the spirit in this passage. It is simply another of many burdens, surely not the greatest, but at the moment it appears as the "last straw." Though it is assumed in vs. 17 that Moses was granted a divine gift whereby he was enabled to fulfill his prophetic leadership, it nonetheless for the moment appears a burden to him, and he wants out, even if it means death.

The Lord's solution to Moses' predicament is remarkable in several ways: (1) If the burden is divided, so the spirit too is "divided," suggesting that in God's way of doing things there is a complete correspondence between "burden" and "spirit." The Lord does not give burdens without also giving the spirit corresponding to them. (2) The spirit given to the elders is not just God's spirit. It is the spirit that is upon Moses. The unity of the office, though shared by many, is thus affirmed. After Jesus' resurrection and Pentecost, the disciples would make a similar claim, that the spirit poured out upon the many was none other than the Spirit that dwelt in Jesus.

In vs. 25 the verbal form "they prophesied" is the only description we are given of the phenomenon. There is no indication of the content of their prophesying, and the sense is therefore probably that of prophetic ecstasy, as in 1 Sam 10:5ff. and 19:20ff. Since there is no more mention of Moses' burden we may assume the author's major interest is the derivation of the prophetic office from Moses, and probably even the kind of prophetic ecstasy that was common in Israel in the early days. Since certain other biblical texts indicate that this form of non-intelligible exaltation was ridiculed, our present text may indicate a concern to legitimize the practice by linking it to Moses.

The addition of the anecdote about Eldad and Medad seems aimed against attempts to restrict the working of the spirit to official channels. Joshua, with a general's passion for order in the ranks, tells Moses to silence these men who apparently did not care enough to come to the community assembly or were somehow prevented (one thinks of people who could not get a ride to a prayer meeting!). But Moses believes in a God who is not limited in his action even to the structures he himself institutes as the channels of the spirit. With the broadmindedness later manifested by David when cursed by Shimei (2 Sam 16:5-14) Moses rejects Joshua's jealousy, and, anticipating by centuries the prophecy of Joel (Joel 3:1), even expresses the wish that the spirit of prophecy would come upon every one of the Lord's people.

The surprising thing about this text is that the spirit of prophecy, understood to be the authentic spirit of Yahweh, here is one of non-rational expression. While prophecy has a long way to go in its development in Israel we should not forget that in this very early stage there is a singular respect for the role of the non-rational in authentic religious experience. On Pentecost day Peter will describe the community's enthusiastic outburst in tongues, which scoffers take for drunkenness, as prophecy (Acts 2:17).

Conclusion

From our examination of the Yahwist and the Elohist traditions we can conclude that the earliest understanding of the spirit was two-fold. On the one hand, it was understood in the anthropological sense as the life-breath received directly from God, the gift and the source of life, calling for a relationship of man with God as the keystone in the arch of his existence. This relationship may have been understood by the Yahwist author as a special lesson for the king who is raised from the dust of the earth and enthroned by the divine favor. On the other hand, spirit was understood to be a divine impulse which came sometimes by way of a word of prophecy (Balaam) or knowledge or wisdom (Joseph) but equally by way of ecstatic exaltation which might have no particular message other than being a sign of the coming of the spirit upon those so touched. This last case is that of the elders who, designated to share Moses' pastoral care for Israel, receive the prophetic spirit in order to do so effectively.

2
The Charismatic Spirit
in the Deuteronomist

At this point it is difficult to decide to which part of the Old Testament to turn next. We choose first to look at the books of Joshua, Judges, Samuel and Kings (what is called the Deuteronomic History) and then Deuteronomy itself because, while their final editing and publication may have been only in the 5th century B.C., the narrative they contain goes all the way back to Israel's conquest of the "Holy Land," and scribes began to write down these traditions during the period of the monarchy long before the Babylonian exile in 587 B.C. In particular, the material that has to do with the *spirit* gives every evidence of belonging to an early stratum of the materials in the Deuteronomic history. Since the *book* of Deuteronomy sets the theological blueprint by which to interpret the historical material in Joshua to Kings, we shall first look at the material on the spirit in those books and then see whether the comprehensive interpretation given in the book of Deuteronomy has anything to add. Keep in mind, once again, that we are tracing a thread through the literary tapestry of the Old Testament.

The Book of Judges

The major contribution of the book of Judges to the understanding of the spirit lies in its very graphic interpretation of the charismatic leadership of this period as the work of the *ruah Yahweh*, the spirit of the Lord. During this period prior to the monarchy, Israel was not even a nation but simply a loose federation of tribes, and its political leadership was carried on by men and women who assumed leadership roles. Though often referred to as "judges" these leaders spent little or none of their time presiding at court. They were "heroes," men and women who brought "justice" to the tribes in the sense of vindicating their cause against their enemies. Those leaders whose movement to act for Israel is explicitly attributed to "the Spirit of the Lord" are: Othniel, a savior

17

given to the Israelites in response to their prayer (3:10); Jephthah, who though born of a harlot, delivered Israel from the Ammonites (11:29); Gideon, who defeated the Midianites and in the process showed that the Lord can do better with a select "remnant" than with the excess of human calculation (6:34; 7:2); and especially Samson, whose legendary feats are attributed to the spirit of the Lord which first stirs Samson (13:25), then gives him unusual bodily powers as he needs them (14:6, 19; 15:15). Though the work of Deborah is not explicitly attributed to the spirit of Yahweh, such attribution seems to be implied in the note that she was a prophetess, one obviously inspired by the spirit of the Lord (4:4).

What is to be retained from this? We should note first that the movement of the *ruah Yahweh* is in every instance directed to the good of the nation as such (though some of Samson's feats may have been so only indirectly). Beyond this, however, there is no connection between the spirit and ethical holiness of individual or people. The motion by the spirit is direct upon the individual and not tied to any institution or rite. We should note, however, that prayer on the part of those who need salvation often precedes the saving motion of the spirit and thus the latter appears clearly as an answer to prayer (3:10; 4:3; 16:28).

1 Sam 9:26-10:13: Saul's Anointing and the Spirit

26. . . . At daybreak Samuel called to Saul on the roof, "Get up, and I will start you on your journey." Saul rose, and he and Samuel went outside the city together. 27. As they were approaching the edge of the town, Samuel said to Saul, "Tell the servant to go on ahead of us, but stay here yourself for the moment, that I may give you a message from God."

10:1. Then, from a flask he had with him, Samuel poured oil on Saul's head; he also kissed him, saying: "The Lord anoints you commander over his heritage. You are to govern the Lord's people Israel, and to save them from the grasp of their enemies roundabout.

"This will be the sign for you that the Lord has anointed you commander over his heritage: 2. When you leave me today, you will meet two men near Rachel's tomb at Zelzah in the territory of Benjamin, who will say to you, 'The asses you went to look for have been found. Your father is no longer worried about the asses, but is anxious about you and says, what shall I do about my son?' 3. Farther on, when you arrive at the terebinth of Tabor, you will be met by three men going up to God at Bethel; one will be bringing three kids, another three loaves of bread, and the third a skin of wine. 4. They will greet you and offer you two wave offerings of bread, which you will take from them. 5. After that you will come to Gibeath-elohim, where there is a garrison of the Philistines. As you enter that city, you will meet a band of prophets, in a prophetic state, coming down from the high place preceded by lyres, tambourines, flutes and harps. 6. The spirit of the Lord will rush upon you, and you will join them in their prophetic state and will be changed into another man. 7. When you see these signs fulfilled, do whatever you judge feasible, because God is with you. 8. Now go down ahead of me to Gilgal, for I shall come down to you, to offer holocausts and to sacrifice peace offerings. Wait seven days until I come to you; I shall then tell you what you must do."

9. As Saul turned to leave Samuel, God gave him another heart. That very day all these signs came to pass . . . 10. When they were going from there to Gibeah, a band of prophets met him, and the spirit of God rushed upon him, so that he joined them in their prophetic state. 11. When all who had known him previously saw him in a prophetic state among the prophets, they said to one another, "What has happened to the son of Kish? Is Saul also among the prophets?" 12. And someone from that district added, "And who is their father?" Thus the proverb arose, "Is Saul also among the prophets?" 13. When he came out of the prophetic state, he went home. (NAB)

For the first time in our sources we encounter a prophet, the "seer" Samuel (1 Sam 9:9, 11, 19), who is enlightened directly by the Lord (9:17) and is gifted repeatedly with a "word of knowledge" for Saul (9:20; 10:2-6). With the story of Saul's anointing by Samuel, the monarchy is linked at its very beginning to the prophetic office, so that kingly authority in Israel is shown from the very beginning to derive from the "spirit of the Lord," not from mere dynastic succession. The account shows both the continuity of Israelite monarchy with the prophetic movement and also the limitation of its power to the spiritual aims of Yahweh—a point which the Deuteronomist makes repeatedly in his history of the kings.

For the first time in our accounts the spirit is joined with anointing. Though the spirit does not immediately rush upon Saul after the rite,

Samuel immediately foretells an event which will confirm the election and consecration ritualized in the anointing: Saul will receive the spirit and "will be changed into another man" (10:6). Samuel gives him no further instructions except that Saul should thereafter follow the spirit's leading (10:7). The conversion already begins as Saul turns to leave Samuel (10:9). It is not yet said that the new heart given Saul is an effect of the spirit; the conversion appears rather as a preliminary to the inrushing of the spirit. This happens when Saul is met by a band of prophets "in a prophetic state" (10:5, 10), that is, in a state of religious and probably ecstatic fervor. The mention of tambourines, flutes and harps shows that from the earliest hour music was used to dispose to prophecy and also to express it ("prophesying" here meaning simply to be caught up in a state of religious fervor). Elisha later will ask for a minstrel to dispose him to prophesy (2 Kgs 3:15), and David will use the harp to chase the evil spirit from Saul (1 Sam 16:14-23).

When Saul, an important and respected civic leader, falls into the prophetic state, there is general wonderment among the populace. The writer considers this event the origin of the proverb, "Is Saul also among the prophets?" And for some it was obviously a contemptuous remark, for the curious expression, "and who is their father?" means that these prophets appeared and functioned in a purely charismatic, non-structural way, and they could point to no particular lineage to give them status in Israelite society. Saul had such status as the son of Kish, but to demean himself by association with such unattached eccentrics made people question his sanity. The writer however assesses the event positively, just as the author of the Acts of the Apostles will later assess the event of the "new wine" on Pentecost, for he sees Saul's seizure by the spirit as the fulfillment of Samuel's prediction and as a distant effect of his consecration.

1 Sam 11:5: The Spirit Rushes on Saul

6. As he listened to this report, the spirit of God rushed upon him and he became very angry. (NAB)

By New Testament standards we are naturally surprised to find anger as an effect of the spirit of God. The context makes clear, however, what kind of anger is meant. Coming in from the field after a day's work, Saul learns that some of his fellow Israelites, besieged by Nahash the Ammonite, have been threatened with the gouging out of every man's right eye as an act of humiliation for all of Israel. Saul's wrath is kindled by the same spirit of God, the text says—and he immediately organizes a campaign of rescue. We learn from this that the spirit Saul has received is one that has bound his heart to all of Israel, and his anger is the blazing up of God's jealous love for his own people, to do them justice. Later Jesus, the man anointed by the Spirit, will flush with anger upon encountering human bondage, physical (Mk 3:5) or cultural (Mk 10:14) or religious (11:15-17). The spirit, then, is not one which encourages passivity but on the contrary one that inspires a holy aggressivity to establish the justice and the kingdom of God.

1 Sam 16:13: The Spirit Rushes on David

Then Samuel, with the horn of oil in hand, anointed him in the midst of his brothers; and from that day on, the spirit of the Lord rushed upon David. (NAB)

Here the coming of the spirit upon David is more clearly a direct effect of the anointing than had been the case with Saul. The superiority of this "ordination" over Saul's appears likewise in the fact that David needs no group of prophets to induce the spirit to manifest itself. The "rushing" of the spirit upon David results immediately from the anointing by the prophet Samuel. However, the spirit received in the anointing does not in fact put David on the throne. The anointing only makes him the rightful king. The actual accession to the throne will depend on a series of mounting successes in which the received spirit becomes manifest. So too, Jesus' later anointing by the Holy Spirit in his baptism readies him for the conflict with the powers of darkness even to death before his actual enthronement as Messiah and Lord through his resurrection (Acts 2:36).

1 Sam 16:14-23: "The Evil Spirit from God"

14. The Spirit of the Lord had departed from Saul, and he was tormented by an evil spirit sent by the Lord. 15. So the servants of Saul said to him: "Please. An evil spirit from God is tormenting you. 16. If your lordship will order it, we, your servants here in attendance on you, will look for a man skilled in playing the harp. When the evil spirit from God comes over you, he will play and you will feel better." 17. Saul then told his servants, "Find me a skillful harpist and bring him to me."

18. A servant spoke up to say: "I have observed that one of the sons of Jesse of Bethlehem is a skillful harpist. He is also a stalwart soldier, besides being an able speaker, and handsome. Moreover, the Lord is with him."

19. Accordingly, Saul dispatched messengers to ask Jesse to send him his son David, who was with the flock. . . . 23. Whenever the spirit from God seized Saul, David would take the harp and play, and Saul would be relieved and feel better, for the evil spirit would leave him. (NAB)

The occasion for the beginning of David's long association with Saul is here given as Saul's need for relief from his melancholy. The spirit of the Lord has departed from Saul, since the Lord has rejected him as king due to his disobedience (1 Sam 15: 4-23). Samuel's separation thereafter from Saul is a kind of outward symbol of this departure of the spirit of the Lord (1 Sam 15:35). Once again it is clear that to be in authority over God's people is not to "manage" the spirit. The spirit remains the gift of the Lord, which he need not give to anybody and may rightly withdraw when confronted by infidelity. Hereafter, the Lord will achieve his purposes through David, the newly anointed one (1 Sam 16:1-13), from whom God's favor will not depart even when David sins. A curious contrast: Saul was not as fortunate. His story shows that God is just in withdrawing his spirit because of Saul's infidelity. David's story shows that the Lord is merciful and may freely decide not to withdraw his gifts and his spirit, though David may fall repeatedly. The two stories of the two leaders reveal the two poles of the same mystery of God's grace. The emergence of David into the kingly role will only be gradual. He begins humbly as Saul's harpist and armor-bearer.

The repeated mention of the evil spirit sent by the Lord (vs. 14) or by God (vss. 15, 16, 23), a thought which recurs elsewhere (Jgs 9:23; 1 Sam 18:10; 19:19; 1 Kgs 22:21), will give the modern reader pause. How can God in any way cause evil? The biblical writers were, for the most part, not that far along in theological sophistication. Their question was rather: "If anything at all happens, how could the Lord not have caused it?" (cf. Amos 3:3-6). In the popular mind in those early days, Yahweh was not thought of as the supreme or the only God. Many Israelites upon finding that Yahweh delayed his answer to their prayers, readily went to the gods of the Canaanites or of other peoples to see "if they couldn't get a better deal." Archaeological excavations in the past decades have repeatedly turned up images and tokens of pagan gods in periods that were officially supposed to be Yahwistic. In short, the planting of faith in the one true God ("besides whom there is no other,"

Is 45:5), was as slow and painful a process as it is today among many primitive peoples, who, though outwardly Christianized, still resort to magic and charms to make sure no possible resource is neglected. So in earliest Israel, Yahweh was often popularly thought to be a God who had to struggle with other supernatural powers outside the domain of his control. One of the ways in which the biblical authors first dealt with this problem was by bringing the activity of all spirits, good and bad, under the dominion of Yahweh. There seemed to be no other way of doing this than to say that the "evil spirit" was also from the Lord. Among a people who at this time did not have the refined theological distinction between God's direct and his permissive will, the *intent* of this teaching was to bring all of human experience, even that of evil, somehow within the pale of God's dominion. The Bible itself will later refine this view. Whereas in the Deuteronomic view Yahweh incites David to take a census, a sinful act (2 Sam 24:1), the author of 1 Chronicles in relating the same story says that a "satan" incited David to do this (1 Chron 21:1). And, of course, even greater clarity comes in James 1:13-14: "Let no one say when he is tempted, 'I am tempted by God': for God cannot be tempted with evil and he himself tempts no one; but each person is tempted when he is lured and enticed by his own desire."

Finally, we should note in this text how music is used to dispel the evil spirit (see above under 1 Sam 9:26-10:13). The author avoids saying that the spirit of the Lord returned to Saul when David played lest the reader think the Lord's rejection of Saul as king no longer held.

1 Sam 19:20, 23: Saul in the Prophetic State

18. Thus David got safely away; he went to Samuel in Ramah, informing him of all that Saul had done to him. Then he and Samuel went to stay in the sheds. 19. When Saul was told that David was in the sheds near Ramah, 20. he sent messengers to arrest David. But when they saw the band of prophets, presided over by Samuel, in a prophetic frenzy, they too fell into the prophetic state. 21. Informed of this, Saul sent other messengers, who also fell into the prophetic state. For the third time Saul sent messengers, but they too fell into the prophetic state.

22. Saul then went to Ramah himself. Arriving at the cistern of the threshing floor on the bare hilltop, he inquired, "Where are Samuel and David?", and was told, "At the sheds near Ramah." 23. As he set out from the hilltop toward the sheds, the spirit of God came upon him also, and he continued

on in a prophetic condition until he reached the spot. At the sheds near Ramah 24. he, too, remained in the prophetic state in the presence of Samuel; all that day and night he lay naked. That is why they say, "Is Saul also among the prophets?" (NAB)

Earlier in this section the author had introduced the jealousy of Saul at the rising success of David (1 Sam 18:6ff.). Saul is now in pursuit of David, and the author is concerned to show how the Lord's protection of David is not only due to such strategems as his wife Michal might devise (19:12-17) but is also due to the direct and manifest intervention of the spirit of God. David is the protegé now of Samuel, who anointed him in the first place. This anointer of kings is here depicted as presiding over a company of prophets who are "in a prophetic frenzy" similar to the state of ecstasy we have already encountered in the band of prophets in 10:10. It is not said that Samuel himself is overcome by this prophetic state, nor that David is. But the phenomenon is, in the author's view, a manifestation of the presence and the spirit of God, as is said specifically in vs. 23. The series of messengers and finally Saul himself find the prophetic experience irresistible. It begins to affect Saul already before he reaches the spot, and when he gets there he rips off his clothes and lies paralyzed by the experience. Without royal regalia he lies before the Lord and before Samuel and David like a slave. The story is another way in which the author explains the origin of the proverb, "Is Saul also among the prophets?" Does he approve of prophetic ecstasy? There is certainly no suggestion that he condemns it. Its meaning here is surely a manifestation of the Lord's presence and power, particularly as an effective shield for David. The spirit surrounds the anointed of Yahweh like a shield (cf. Ps 18:31, 36, 51).

1 Kgs 18:12: The Spirit and the Mobility of the Prophet

"After I leave you, the spirit of the Lord will carry you to some place I do not know, and when I go to inform Ahab and he does not find you, he will kill me." (NAB)

Much narrative color surrounds this statement of Obadiah, King Ahab's servant who in the midst of Queen Jezebel's extermination of the prophets of the Lord had hidden and supplied a hundred of them in caves (18:4). Elijah upon meeting Obadiah tells him to announce the prophet's arrival to Ahab who has been searching for him. Obadiah fears that as soon as he leaves Elijah to tell Ahab, Elijah will pull one of his famous disappearing acts, and Obadiah will have to pay for the disappearance with his life. The text interests us inasmuch as it attributes Elijah's ability to vanish to the "spirit of the Lord." To what does it refer specifically? To the kind of amazing physical endurance that enabled Elijah, after his victory over the prophets of Baal, to run in front of Ahab's chariot as far as the approaches of Jezreel (18:46)? Or does it refer to Elijah's astuteness in avoiding capture? Or in a more general way to the divine wisdom that made his escapes possible? Perhaps all three. When the prophets at Jericho learn of Elijah's strange disappearance (even stranger to Elisha who saw him ascend in the fiery chariot!), they suggest a search party on the grounds that "perhaps the spirit of the Lord has carried him away to some mountain or some valley" (2 Kgs 2:16).

The expression "carried off by the spirit of the Lord" is frequent in Ezekiel to describe his own prophetic flights. Though he may have taken it from the Elijah story, it comes to mean simply spiritual rapture, or a vision such as Jesus' temptations on the pinnacle of the temple and on the mountain seem to have been (see Lk 4:5). However, the vanishing of Philip from the eunuch's side is described in terms reminiscent of the Elijah texts: "The Spirit of the Lord snatched Philip away" (Acts 8:39). We do not necessarily have to posit any more miraculous vanishing of Philip than we do of Elijah. The underlying suggestion is that the messengers of the Lord are endowed with a spiritual subtlety appropriate to their vocation.

1 Kgs 22:24: The Problem of Discerning the Spirit

Thereupon Zedekiah, son of Chenaanah, came up and slapped Micaiah on the cheek, saying, "Has the spirit of the Lord then left me to speak with you?" (NAB)

The entire chapter in which this verse appears should be read to appreciate what is at issue here. King Ahab, who has set it in his heart to undertake a campaign against Ramoth-gilead, gathers the prophets of the land, some four hundred in number, and asks their advice. They promise victory. But on the insistence of King Jehoshaphat of Judah, whose alliance Ahab wishes to have, a neglected prophet, Micaiah ben Imlah is called. He first mockingly mouths what the other prophets have been saying and tells Ahab to go ahead with his plans. When put under oath in the name of the Lord, Micaiah speaks out:

19. . . . "I saw the Lord seated on his throne, with the whole host of heaven standing by to his right and to his left. 20. The Lord asked, 'Who will deceive Ahab, so that he will go up and fall at Ramoth-gilead?' And one said this, another that, 21. until one of the spirits came forth and presented himself to the Lord saying, 'I will deceive him.' The Lord asked, 'How?' 22. He answered, 'I will go forth and become a lying spirit in the mouths of all his prophets.' The Lord replied, 'You shall succeed in deceiving him. Go forth and do this.' 23. So now, the Lord has put a lying spirit in the mouths of all these prophets of yours, but the Lord himself has decreed evil against you."

24. Thereupon Zedekiah, son of Chenaanah, came up and slapped Micaiah on the cheek saying, "Has the spirit of the Lord then left me to speak with you?" (NAB)

We are at a very primitive stage in the development of the relationship of the spirit-world to the world of man. We have already discussed the theological problem involved in the statement that an evil spirit was sent by the Lord (cf. above under 1 Sam 16:14-33). Here the heavenly court is portrayed like an earthly king's royal court. The Lord reigning on his throne is surrounded by the "whole host of heaven," the heavenly spirits elsewhere given the title angels (cf. 1 Kgs 13:18). One of the spirits finally comes forth and agrees to deceive Ahab. The method of the deception is important. He will become a *lying* spirit in the mouth of Ahab's prophets. Now it is significant that only Micaiah perceives that this spirit is a lying spirit. Zedekiah, one of Ahab's prophets, calls the spirit by which he speaks "the spirit of the Lord" (vs. 24). Biblically speaking, when "the spirit of the Lord" is used without qualification it means a good spirit. Note that in 1 Sam 16:14 it is not necessary to say that the spirit of the Lord was good: "The spirit of the Lord had departed from Saul, and he was tormented by an evil spirit sent by the Lord."

Did the Deuteronomist mean by "the spirit of the Lord" simply a good spirit from the Lord's court or did he mean something more akin to the "breath of the Lord," hence something more personally identified with him? We cannot be sure. The function of message-giving is different from the function of giving life, but we do not know how clearly this distinction was felt by the Deuteronomist. At any rate, picturing the heavenly court as a host of spirits distinct from the Lord yet functioning in his sight has a double advantage. On the one hand, it enables the author to speak of "a spirit" *from* the Lord (vs. 23; 1 Sam 16:14), thus bringing all supernatural activity under the Lord's dominion. At the same time, on the other hand, this spirit is not the spirit *of* the Lord, and therefore the good and saving purpose of his own heart, so to speak, is not compromised (see a similar treatment of "an angel" in 1 Kgs 13:18). This is one of the early ways of dealing with the problem of false prophecy and the need for discernment. Not everything that any prophet claims is from "the spirit of the Lord" is necessarily so. As a matter of fact, subsequent events proved that the spirit inspiring Ahab's four-hundred "yes-men" was a lying spirit. Ahab was slain in the battle they urged him to undertake.

We can conclude by retrieving the following points from this story: (1) The fact that one or many may claim to speak in the Lord's name or by his spirit is not an automatic assurance that their prophecy is true and conducive to good (cf. also 1 Kgs 13:18). Some norm of discernment is necessary. (2) Directive prophecy in particular is difficult to discern. "Dogmatic" or "ethical" prophecy—i.e. prophecy that has to do primarily with right teaching about the nature of God or his law—at least can be checked out against the common teaching tradition of the whole community (Deut 13:2-6). But prophecy that suggests political action, doing this or doing that, very often has no other support than the apparent certitude of the prophet himself that he is speaking in the Lord's name. There is the discerning norm of the outcome or the fulfillment of his prophecy (Deut 18:15-20), but this is helpful only in retrospect, and then it is too late to decide whether to act or not. (3) Sheer majority of agreement is not an adequate norm either, as the story amply demonstrates.

The account then raises acutely, without resolving, the problem of discerning prophecy. We can expect to meet this problem again in our journey through the developing biblical tradition.

2 Kgs 2:9, 15: Elisha Receives the Spirit of Elijah

> 9. When they had crossed over, Elijah said to Elisha, "Ask for whatever I may do for you, before I am taken from you." Elisha answered, "May I receive a double portion of your spirit." 10. "You have asked something that is not easy," he replied. "Still, if you see me taken up from you, your wish will be granted; otherwise not." 11. As they walked on conversing, a flaming chariot and flaming horses came between them, and Elijah went up to heaven in a whirlwind. 12. When Elisha saw it happen he cried out, "My father! my father! Israel's chariots and drivers!" But when he could no longer see him, Elisha gripped his own garment and tore it in two.

13. Then he picked up Elijah's mantle which had fallen from him, and went back and stood at the bank of the Jordan. 14. Wielding the mantle which had fallen from Elijah, he struck the water in his turn and said, "Where is the Lord, the God of Elijah?" When Elisha struck the water it divided and he crossed over.

15. The guild prophets in Jericho, who were on the other side, saw him and said, "The spirit of Elijah rests on Elisha." They went to meet him, bowing to the ground before him. (NAB)

This classic story of the transmission of charismatic power from Elijah to his successor Elisha is one whose principal point is often lost by focusing on the problem of the historicity of the flaming chariot. We are not here given a narrative of what happened physically and biologically to Elijah as he passed from this earth. All kinds of alternatives are possible here, and physical death certainly need not be excluded. It is rather a question here of showing how Elisha experienced Elijah's passing and how the prophet's spirit was passed on. The tradition had already described many of the events of Elijah's ministry as meteoric appearance and disappearance because of the action of the spirit of the Lord in him (e.g. 18:7-12). It could only be expected that Elisha, the only one granted to be with the great prophet at the end, should experience his passing as a climactic *raptus*. It is clearly question of a vision by Elisha (his *seeing* the wonder is spoken of three times in the text, vss. 10, 12) by which the meaning of Elijah's life and death and Elisha's own future is conveyed.

Note that the spirit is not only the spirit of the Lord but also the "spirit of Elijah" (vss. 9, 15), the charismatic spirit which rested in a stable way upon Elijah and now comes to rest similarly on Elisha (vs. 15). It was a spirit of wonderworking, after the example of Moses (vss. 8, 14). Elisha asks for a double portion. According to Deut 21:17, the first born son is to inherit a double portion of his father's property. Elijah is spiritual father (vs. 12), and Elisha his principal disciple. As the spirit that rested on Moses was conveyed to the seventy elders (Num 11:17, 25), so the spirit of Elijah is passed on to Elisha, the transfer being confirmed by Elisha's immediate use of Elijah's mantle to part Jordan's waters (vs. 14). The particular meaning of the vision of chariot and driver is probably that Elijah was worth more than all of Israel's armies as far as its welfare and true faith were concerned. King Joash, weeping over Elisha's deathbed years later would apply the same imagery to this esteemed prophet successor to Elijah: "My father! My father! Israel's chariots and horsemen!" (2 Kgs 13:14). The superiority of the spirit of the Lord over military might will be affirmed in a slightly different way later by the prophet Zechariah (Zech 4:6).

The similarities between this account and the events of Jesus' own passing over to the father are worth observing. Elisha requests a double portion of Elijah's wonder-working spirit. Jesus promises his disciples they will do the works he did and even greater ones (Jn 14:12). Elisha sees his master transferred to heavenly glory. The disciples see Jesus in his risen glory (e.g. Acts 7:56; 9:3-6). The theophany experienced by Elisha involves fire and wind. So too does the giving of the spirit on Pentecost (Acts 2:2-3). The disciples go in search of Elijah but do not find him (2 Kgs 2:16-18). The disciples of Jesus search for him but find only an empty tomb (Jn 20:1-10). As the spirit of Elijah falls on Elisha as the master is glorified, the spirit that was upon Jesus is transferred to his disciples as he himself enters his glory (Luke 23:49; Acts 1-2; Jn 7:39; 16:7). Finally a more tenuous detail of comparison: Elijah is taken up on the other side of the Jordan. According to Luke, Jesus' ascension takes place near Bethany, on the other side of the Kedron (Lk 23:50).

The Book of Deuteronomy

The Book of Deuteronomy is the bridge between the Torah or Pentateuch (the first five books which Jewish tradition considered the core of Yahweh's revelation to her) and the Deuteronomic history beginning with the book of Joshua. The book is basically a long homiletical exposition of the law presented as an exhortation by Moses prior to his death in Moab. The actual concern of the book is, however, life in Israel in the later period of the kings. At that time it was keenly felt that Israel's identity as a nation and her future as a people depended on a return heart and soul to the covenant with Yahweh, a revival of the Mosaic spirit, a new rejection of Canaanite religion and even a militant dedication to the political and religious independence of Israel from foreign influence.

Most biblical scholars place the occasion for this revival at the time of the reform initiated by King Josiah (2 Kgs 22:8ff.) and promoted through the renewal of cult in the Jerusalem temple, where the Levites proclaimed anew, with warning and exhortation, the covenant law. Deuteronomy appears to be just such a sermon text.

Deuteronomy differs from the Deuteronomic history not in basic intention or teaching but in materials used and in the method of exposition. Deuteronomy is basically a law-code, God's blueprint for people and king, presented as a homiletical exposition. The Deuteronomic history is basically a chronicle of events presented as a narrative. The two works are related in that as they are now arranged, Deuteronomy appears as the theological prologue giving the blueprint for covenant living, and what follows details Israel's success and failure in doing so. From this we could already suspect an influence of the prophets on this work, for they, more than any, read Israel's daily history in the light of her covenant relationship with Yahweh. Indeed the influence of prophetism becomes apparent from passages like Deut 18:9-14, which reflects the struggle of the prophets of Yahweh against false prophets, or 18:15-20 in which Moses promises that the Lord will raise up a *prophet like himself* to lead the people. The point of the latter passage is that prophecy is to continue to enlighten Israel, but true prophets can be recognized by their adherence to Mosaic faith in Yahweh. In fact this orthodoxy (13:2-6) is a more important sign for discerning the true prophet than is the fulfillment of his prophecy (18:21-22).

With this prophetic influence, then, we would expect Deuteronomy to give great place to the spirit of the Lord, so important for the prophets we have met up till now. Oddly, however, the opposite is the case. There is almost no mention of the spirit in Deuteronomy.

What has happened? We noticed in the texts previously examined the emerging problem Israel's kings and people faced: how to discern true prophecy from false. Fulfillment was helpful only in retrospect, too late for prior discernment. Prophetic trance, frenzy or ecstasy was not sufficient either, for the false prophets were at times in that state too. Among the prophets of the classical period, as we shall see, a significant development took place—an almost total abandonment of reference to the "spirit of the Lord" as the source of their prophecies in favor of the "word of the Lord." The word has the advantage of being clearer, more pointed and therefore more easily tested against the sound tradition of Yahwistic faith. It left less in doubt about the origin and the direction of the inspiration. The word, then, becomes a way in which the spirit can be discerned. And it was on the *word* of the Lord rather than upon his spirit that the classical prophets staked the certainty of their mission and their message.

Now Deuteronomy could be said to be a theological treatise on the *word* of God. This appears from the very opening line of the book: "There are the *words* which Moses spoke. . . ." (1:1). And those words are quite clear in the specific demands they laid upon Israel's daily life: commandments and laws. As for prophetic inspiration, the true prophet, like Moses, is described in terms of word rather than spirit (Deut 18:15-

20), and it is the prophet's *word* which can be checked against authentic tradition (Deut 13:2-6—note the strong *verbal* context).

If the word gives a more objective basis for the Lord's directives for his people, the author wants to reassure his audience that it is not merely an external norm but rather something already within the heart of Israel. To experience its closeness one need only do it:

> "For this command which I enjoin on you today is not too mysterious and remote for you. It is not up in the sky, that you should say, 'Who will go up in the sky to get it for us and tell us of it, that we may carry it out?' No, it is something very near to you, already in your mouths and in your hearts; you have only to carry it out." (Deut 30:11-14, NAB)

We notice in this text both an exalting of the word almost to the point of making it a separate substance from the Lord, and yet at the same time an "intimizing" of it, to make its immanence match its transcendence. Nothing more is apparently necessary for this "understanding of the heart" to take place than the word itself. At a time when Israel's teachers were reacting against undifferentiated spiritual impulse (as Paul himself will later do, 1 Cor 12:1-3), it is understandable that they would say that the word is sufficient of itself. We must remember we are still a long way from the New Testament teaching that the spirit is necessary to understand the word (1 Cor 2:12; Jn 14:26).

There is, however, one text at the very end of Deuteronomy which mentions the spirit, and we must look at it, if only because it is so unique.

Deut 34:9: The Laying On of Hands

> Now Joshua, son of Nun, was filled with the spirit of wisdom.
> since Moses had laid his hands on him. (NAB)

Here for the first time we encounter the conveying of the spirit by the laying on of hands. In Num 11:25, the spirit that was upon Moses was transferred directly by the Lord to the elders in the context of the descending cloud. In Saul's case (1 Sam 10:1-13) and even more clearly in David's (1 Sam 16:13) the movement of the spirit follows upon Samuel's anointing. In Elisha's case the spirit of Elijah was passed on by Elisha's vision and the mantle of Elijah (2 Kgs 2:9-14). The Deuteronomist sees Joshua's "ordination" by Moses as the moment and the instrument of the spirit of wisdom coming upon him. This "sacramental" theology stands in some tension with Num 27:18, which we shall examine further on. The wisdom here is, as the sequence of the Deuteronomic history will bring out, primarily the practical wisdom of military leadership. As the editor prepares the reader for the story of Joshua which is about to begin, he wishes to show that Joshua's charismatic leadership is rooted in the prophetic spirit that was Moses'.

Conclusion

The Deuteronomist tradition understands the spirit of the Lord as a charismatic, wonderworking spirit which at times comes upon the recipient in an ecstatic way either to manifest the divine choice or, in one instance, to shield God's anointed one, David, from harm. In this, the Deuteronomist understanding of the spirit shows its close relationship to the Elohist tradition of the northern kingdom, which was interested in relating leadership to prophecy.

The figure of Samuel functions in a central way to show that Israel's first kings were designated and spirit-filled through the ministry of prophecy and, by implication, must remain faithful to this spirit of which they are not the autonomous lords but humble recipients; at the same time, however, the rite of anointing or of the laying on of hands, tends to put a visible order to the conveying of the spirit upon the leaders of the people. If the prophet Elisha receives Elijah's prophetic and wonderworking spirit by vision and mantle, Saul, David and Joshua receive the spirit of the Lord by the more usual means of visible designation. In each of the latter instances, however, it is a prophet who anoints the king, and a prophet who "ordains" the leader.

So far in our quest the spirit has appeared as life-breath or charismatic power. Its relationship to Israel's ethical life, judgment, purification and holiness, has nowhere been explicitly stated. How did this dimension of the spirit develop? We shall see in the coming chapters.

3
Spirit of Judgment and Salvation: The Pre-Exilic Prophets

Already in the early period of the monarchy we have encountered prophets—Elijah and Elisha in particular and Micaiah ben Imlah whose prophecy would have saved King Ahab's life had it been heeded. There were other prophets in this early period, Nathan, David's court prophet (2 Sam 7:1-17; 12:1-25), Gad (2 Sam 24:12-25), Ahijah (1 Kgs 11:29-39), and an anonymous prophet from Judah (1 Kgs 13:1-32). But in the eighth century B.C. begin to appear the "writing" prophets—so called not because they themselves always wrote out their own prophecies but because their sayings were collected and eventually published under their name. Whereas Elijah and Elisha had been known primarily for their wonderworking, these prophets were remembered primarily for their message.

Amos

In Amos, the first of the classical prophets, the concept of the "spirit" is singularly absent. Amos' view of prophecy is ambivalent. On the one hand he can say, "The Lord God does nothing without revealing his plan to his servants, the prophets" (3:7). The prophet, according to this text, is given to the people in order to interpret for them what the Lord is about in their history. From this time onward till the waning of prophecy in the third century B.C., the prophetic books supply us with an ongoing interpretation of Israel's history in terms of her covenant with the Lord.

Amos also positively views the experience of authentic prophecy as a compelling power from the Lord: "The lion roars—who will not be afraid! The Lord God speaks—who will not prophesy?" (3:8)

Yet when describing his own call and mission, Amos goes so far as

33

to disclaim that he is (or was) a prophet: "I am no prophet, nor have I belonged to a company of prophets: I was a shepherd and a dresser of sycamores. The Lord took me from following the flock, and said to me, 'Go, prophesy to my people Israel. Now hear the word of the Lord!' " (7:14-16). Amos is concerned to dissociate himself from the image of the professional prophets who, for a price, will predict good for anyone. The same reluctance seems to lie behind Amos' avoidance of attributing his inspiration directly to "the spirit of the Lord." Instead he simply says the Lord "took" him and spoke to him. The call is mediated by the divine word and the mission is to proclaim that word (vs. 16). Similarly, the book of Amos begins: "The words of Amos, a shepherd from Tekoa, which he saw. . . ." (1:1). While the word can for Amos be not only something heard but also something seen, the avoidance both of the title "prophet" and any allusion to the spirit of the Lord reflects a reaction to the non-rational seizures or trances with which the professional prophets had come to be identified.

Hosea

Though we find a tinge of negativism about the professional prophets in Hosea (4:5), when he recalls Moses, the ancient hero of the exodus, he simply says, "By a prophet the Lord brought Israel out of Egypt, and by a prophet they were protected" (12:14). Israel's infidelity to this grace of prophetic leadership becomes the cause of her downfall (12:15). The thought is similar to 9:7-9, where to Israel's scorning taunt, "The prophet is a fool, the man of the spirit is mad!" Hosea counters, "A prophet is Israel's watchman with God" (9:8). The prophet here is first of all Hosea himself, who has criticized Israel's empty worship and has been repaid with rejection and humiliation. But Israel has rejected a long line of prophets (Jesus would say the same in Lk 13:34), and her hostility to them can only be explained by her guilt which the prophet reproves (9:7c). Important to note here is the equating of prophet with "the man of the spirit" (*ish ha-ruah*, 9:7b). Though there is a general tendency among the classical prophets to avoid too close an identification with the spirit, for reasons already explained, here is clearly an exception. While the term is part of a taunt placed in the mouth of the prophet's critics, Hosea takes it as applied not incorrectly to himself and to all prophets of reform.

But there is a new emphasis on the word of the Lord, too. The book opens with the title: "The word of the Lord that came to Hosea." The word (singular, unlike the "words" which Amos "saw," Amos 1:1) is the "word of the Lord" and it is described in terms formerly used of the spirit: it *comes* to the prophet. The "man of the spirit" will hereafter be also "the man of the word." Word and spirit are not, however, expressly joined here. Word here has replaced spirit as the way the Lord "comes."

Before leaving Hosea we should note other usages of *ruah* (spirit) in his book. In 8:7, *ruah* has its primitive meaning of wind, and it stands in a pejorative sense for the vanity Israel is pursuing to her own destruction: "When they sow the wind, they shall reap the whirlwind." A similar sense appears in 12:2: "Ephraim chases the wind." A more anthropological sense is found in 5:4: "Their deeds do not allow them to return to their God; for the *spirit* of harlotry is in them, and they do not recognize the Lord." Israel needs purity of heart to know or recognize the Lord acting and speaking in her life. A life-pattern of infidelity makes man deaf to the word of the Lord and blind to his gifts. This is the negative side of what Paul will attribute positively to the Holy Spirit who enables the Christian to recognize the gifts of God (1 Cor 2:12).

Finally, in 4:19 *ruah* for *wind* is used as a symbol of judgment. Like chaff caught in the wings of the wind Israel will be carried off.

Micah

While Amos and Hosea did their work in the northern kingdom of Israel, Micah prophesied in the foothills of Judea and perhaps in Jerusalem itself in the early part of the eighth century B.C. Like Amos he preached social justice, with particular concern for the orphan and the widow. Like Hosea he preached covenant fidelity. The note he added to the message of these predecessors was the need for a humble spirit before God: "You have been told, O man, what is good and what the Lord requires of you: only to live justly, to love loyally, and to walk humbly with your God" (6:8).

In Micah we find the same theology of the invading word that appeared in Hosea: "The word of the Lord which *came* to Micah of Moresheth" (1:1). We find more explicit a condemnation of the false prophets in 2:11 and especially in 3:5-8, which is important because Micah concludes it by an affirmation of his own identity as a prophet who has the spirit of the Lord:

> 5. Thus says the Lord regarding the prophets
>   who lead my people astray,
>   who, when their teeth have something to bite,
>   announce peace,

but when one fails to put something in their mouth,
proclaim war against him.
6. Therefore you shall have night, not vision,
darkness, not divination;
the sun shall go down upon the prophets,
and the day shall be dark for them.
7. Then shall the seers be put to shame,
and the diviners confounded;

they shall cover their lips, all of them,
because there is no answer from God.
8. *But as for me, I am filled with power,*
with the spirit of the Lord,
with authority and with might,
to declare to Jacob his crimes
and to Israel his sins. (NAB)

Micah distinguishes himself from the false prophets not only by being above venal interests but also by the fact that his message is a message of ethical judgment. Here the spirit of the Lord upon the prophet means that he is endowed with power (*koah*), authority like that of a judge (*mishpat*) and might (*geburah*). In this Micah may be simply repeating a sterotyped formula used by the prophets of his day to introduce and accredit their oracles. At any rate even into New Testament times *spirit* is frequently associated, sometimes even identified, with power and authority. What is clearly unique about Micah's message, however, is that this power and authority, this prophetic spirit of Yahweh, is given him not to mouth automatic salvation but on the contrary to expose the sin of Israel. This is new. Until this text the *spirit of the Lord* has been either the principle of life, the means of divine communication or the source of charismatic activity. Now for the first time in our sources there is a clear relationship of the spirit of the Lord to the ethical life of Israel. The Spirit inspires the prophet to pronounce an ethical judgment upon the people. Whereas the preceding prophets had avoided the use of *ruah* because it did not clearly convey an ethical expectation but only charismatic salvation, Micah dared to use it because he felt it could be given a new, ethical meaning.

This new direction was not, however, easily initiated. In a passage notorious for its textual obscurities (2:6-7), the prophet's adversaries disclaim that disaster is a judgment of the Lord upon his people, saying, "Is the *spirit of the Lord* foreshortened?" (7b)—which the NAB takes as idiom as in Job 21:4 and renders, "Is the Lord short of patience?" The point Micah's critics are trying to make by this statement is that the

Lord has only unconditional positive regard for his people, and words of doom could not possibly be inspired by his spirit. To this complacency Micah objects. The Lord's spirit and his words promise good only to him who is willing to walk uprightly (7d).

The spirit, then, in Micah is linked to moral life. We have met a new strand in the tapestry of the spirit in the Old Testament. Later writers will vastly expand its use, but they will be using the thread first introduced by the humble prophet of Moresheth.

Isaiah

Unlike Micah, his contemporary, Isaiah does not use the "spirit of the Lord" (*ruah Yahweh*) to describe his own prophetic experience. But he does advance the objective understanding of the spirit in remarkable ways.

First let us dispatch a text which reflects one of the more ancient usages of *ruah* as a bad spirit sent from the Lord, such as we already met and explained in 1 Sam 16:14-23. In 29:10, where Isaiah is chastising the people for their blindness and spiritual torpor, he says, "For the Lord has poured out on you a spirit of deep sleep." The "deep sleep" here is not the creative deep sleep the Lord cast upon Adam before creating Eve (Gen 2:21) nor the revelatory deep sleep cast upon Abram before his vision (Gen 15:12), though the same Hebrew word is used in each case. It is rather the sleep of unawareness, insensitivity to the Lord and the events of the day through which he is speaking. Isaiah would not of course for a moment deny that his people were responsible for being in this state. But somehow, if that's the way things are, the Lord must have had something to do with it. We touch again the divine causality question discussed in the last chapter.

Is 4:4: Wind of Judgment, Wind of Fire

    2. On that day,
        the branch of the Lord will be luster and glory,
        and the fruit of the earth will be honor and splendor
        for the survivors of Israel.
    3. He who remains in Zion
        and he that is left in Jerusalem
        will be called holy:
        every one marked down for life in Jerusalem.

4. When the Lord washes away
   the filth of the daughters of Zion,
   and purges Jerusalem's blood from her midst
   with a blast of searing judgment,
5. then will the Lord create,
   over the whole site of Mount Zion
   and over her place of assembly,
   a smoking cloud by day
   and a light of flaming fire by night.
6. For over all, his glory will be shelter and protection:
   shade from the parching heat of day,
   refuge and cover from storm and rain.
   (NAB)

The use of *spirit* (*ruah*) here is found in vs. 4, translated by the NAB as "blast of his searing judgment." The Hebrew has literally, "When the Lord . . . purges Jerusalem's blood from her midst with the spirit (*ruah*) of judgment (*mishpat*) and with the spirit (*ruah*) of fire." Here Isaiah sharpens the theme already introduced by Micah 3:8, namely the relation of *ruah* to judgment (*mishpat*) and moral purification. *Ruah* here could mean the Lord's *breath* annihilating his enemies and purifying his people, a sense in which Isaiah uses it of the Messiah in 11:4. Later tradition would use the images of the Lord's *breath* for the ease with which he extinguishes his enemies (Wis 11:20; 2 Thes 2:8). More likely however, *ruah* here means *wind* as an image of the Lord blowing away the chaff from his threshing floor and burning it, as becomes clear in Is 30:28 where Isaiah describes God's judgment on Assyria: "His breath (wind), like a flood in a ravine that reaches suddenly to the neck, will winnow the nations with a destructive winnowing . . ." A similar image is used in the apocalypse of Isaiah for the purification of the Lord's own people in the very midst of his coming to save them (Is 27:4, 8). This is the primitive imagery that lies behind the eschatological preaching of John the Baptist (Mk 3:12).

What is significant and new about our Isaian text is however the association of the spirit with the promise of God's coming salvation. The prophecy begins with a description of what is going to happen "on that day" (vs. 2). The Lord is going to restore the remnant of his people in Jerusalem to their glory, and he is going to renew the saving marvels of the exodus—a leading cloud by day and a pillar of fire by night (vs. 6). The "branch of the Lord" who "will be luster and glory" is the Davidic king. So we have here an oracle of coming salvation that concerns both people and king. What role does the "spirit" have in this coming event?

It appears as the element of purification. The prophet, of course, does not call the spirit, wind or breath, *holy*, but its function is clearly to sanctify, since the washing away of filth and blood (menstrual on the level of the image, moral on the level of the meaning) was a necessary preliminary for participation in the holy cultic community (cf. Lev 15:16-27), and that is precisely what the Lord is creating anew on Mount Zion (vs. 3).

Is 28:5-6: A Spirit of Justice

5. On that day the Lord of hosts
   will be a glorious crown
   and a brilliant diadem to the remnant of his people,
6. a spirit of justice
   to him who sits in judgment,
   and strength to those
   who turn back the battle at the gate. (NAB)

Here again is an eschatological oracle incorporating the spirit. The expression "spirit of justice" (*ruah mishpat*) is the same we met in Is 4:4 and Mi 3:8. Here, however, the spirit is not the external cleansing agent, as in 4:4, nor the spirit of authority as in Micah, but rather the ability and the will in the magistrate to declare just judgment and strength to the soldier defending the city. Given the repeated complaint of the prophets about the venal judges of their day, this promise of ethical renewal is all the more important. We should note, for future reference, the way this renewing presence is expressed. It is not said that "the spirit of the Lord" will do this, but rather "The Lord . . . will be . . . a spirit. . . ." The spirit here is far from being made a separate being from the Lord. Rather it is the Lord himself whose presence is manifested by the gift of this new spirit in men.

Is 32:15: The Spirit Poured Out

15. . . . until the spirit from on high
    is poured out on us.
    Then will the desert become an orchard
    and the orchard be regarded as a forest.
16. Right will dwell in the desert
    and justice abide in the orchard.

17. Justice will bring about peace;
    right will produce calm and security.
18. My people will live in peaceful country,
    in secure dwellings and quiet resting places.
20. Happy are you who sow beside every stream,
    and let the ox and the ass go freely! (NAB)

This text is the high point in Isaiah's theology of the spirit. It comes immediately after a prediction of disaster. The period of humiliation will not last forever. It will be replaced by a time of salvation introduced by the outpouring of the "spirit from on high." This spirit of the Lord is seen as the source of all the eschatological blessings that follow. Each word of the text is important. The spirit is *poured out*. Though the image of "pouring out" was used in 29:10 of the "spirit of deep sleep," this is the first time it is used of the spirit in the positive sense of salvation—the beginning of a theme that hereafter will appear frequently in the Bible, especially in the New Testament. Though retaining its etymological meaning of breath or wind, the spirit here draws to itself the function of a stream of water, thus picking up a relationship introduced already in 30:28: "His breath (*ruah*), like a flood in a ravine that reaches suddenly to the neck, will winnow the nations with a destructive winnowing, and with repeated winnowings will he battle against them." There, however, the context is that of judgment upon Assyria. Here the first effect of the spirit as water poured out is to produce fruitfulness in the land. The desert blooms and the sown land thrives marvelously. But this fruitfulness of the land is clearly only an image of the moral renewal of the nation. The spirit poured out is a spirit of right and justice, which in turn will bring peace and security. This is the first clear and positive association of the spirit of the Lord with the new ethical life that is part of the coming salvation. Micah had, of course, pronounced an ethical judgment upon the people under the inspiration of the spirit (Mi 3:8); and Isaiah himself in previously cited texts has attributed the coming purifying judgment to the spirit. But here the spirit *is* the eschatological ethical salvation itself, not merely wind of judgment but water of life.

Is 11:2: The Spirit on the Messiah

1. But a shoot shall sprout from the stump of Jesse,
   and from his roots a bud shall blossom.
2. The spirit of the Lord shall rest upon him:
   a spirit of wisdom and of understanding,

a spirit of counsel and of strength,
a spirit of knowledge and of fear of the Lord,
3. and his delight shall be the fear of the Lord. (NAB)

For Isaiah the coming salvation was to be mediated to men in a special way through the king who sat on the throne of David. His title would be *Emmanuel* because his reign would be so full of divine blessings that it would be obvious to the entire people that "God is with us." Unfortunately the great things Isaiah promised to come through the Davidic kings (cf. chs. 7 and 9) never really came about in Isaiah's lifetime with the intensity he had expected. Even his hero, King Hezekiah, toward the end of his reign showed himself too much of a human politician for Isaiah to be satisfied that the earlier oracles had really been fulfilled. And so Isaiah seemed to turn to the more distant future for the realization of his (and the Lord's) dream of Israel's ideal (Is 11:1-9). The kingdom would be one of perfect cosmic peace like that of paradise (11:6-9), and the king introducing it would be one on whom the spirit of the Lord rested in a perfect way (11:2). This text, in which "the spirit" appears four times and six different qualities are listed, is the source of the traditional "gifts of the Holy Spirit" in the Christian tradition. In the Greek text and the Vulgate which followed it, the word "piety" was found instead of "the fear of the Lord" in its first occurrence, thus bringing the "gifts" to seven. The Hebrew text, however, lists only six. Thomas Aquinas and the scholastic theologians worked out a very elaborate correlation of these gifts with the infused virtues given to every Christian. It should not be forgotten, however, that these traits in our text are given to the king to assure his inspired rule over the people of God, not just after the fashion of Joshua and David, but to bring about the perfect kingdom, the new paradise. Since Isaiah had applied them to the ideal king of the future, the anointed one, the messiah, this text is most appropriately evoked in the New Testament description of the baptism of Jesus (Mt 3:16; Mk 1:10).

Before leaving Isaiah three other minor texts should be glanced at. In 31:4 we read, "The Egyptians are men, not God, their horses are flesh, not spirit." Here Isaiah builds on the opposition between flesh and spirit of Gen 6:3, to show that the power men rely on is nothing compared to the might of the Lord. The opposition between spirit and flesh will become a cardinal point in Paul's theology.

In 30:1, another warning against alliances with Egypt, the expression "by my spirit" means simply "by me" and the NAB appropriately translates, "webs that are not inspired by me."

Finally, in 34:16, we may simply note how the Lord's *spirit* gathering is parallel to his mouth commanding—thus opening the possibility of the association of word and spirit that will become important for Second Isaiah.

We may summarize Isaiah's contributions to the development of the theology of the spirit as three, all of them concerned with eschatology: (1) The spirit is associated clearly with the coming event of judgment and salvation; (2) the spirit of the Lord is associated with the coming messiah who will establish the kingdom of eschatological peace; (3) the spirit is poured out to assure a new ethical life for Israel.

Jeremiah

Between the age of Isaiah and that of Jeremiah a century later the stage of history changed considerably. If Isaiah had to struggle to establish Israel's faith in her own election by Yahweh, in Jerusalem as the city of his glory and the Davidic king as the instrument chosen by the Lord to establish the kingdom of peace, Jeremiah now had to cope with the degeneration of that election faith into complacency and blindness to the implications of the covenant. If Zion was the city of the Lord and the temple the sanctuary of his choice, then surely he would not allow it to be destroyed (Jer 7). He had saved it once miraculously from the Assyrians; he would now do the same from the Babylonians! Not so, countered Jeremiah, for neither king nor people are paying any attention to the moral will of Yahweh. They count on automatic salvation, no matter what. Perhaps the highest dramatization of this attitude came when Jehoiakim took the throne. In the midst of national peril, when Judah was already under heavy tribute, Jehoiakim launched a building spree, remodeling his own house in the most lavish way—and using forced labor to do it. Jeremiah's stinging rebuke is found in Jer 22:13-18.

Most of the prophets of Judah supported this attitude of blatant presumption, probably under the pretext that to predict doom for the city of the Lord was to lack trust in him. Jeremiah stood alone against them—and history proved him right. As might be expected in such a situation, Jeremiah had no use for these supposed "men of the spirit." The texts of Jeremiah's tirades against the false prophets are too numerous and long to reproduce here, but they should be read at this point to get the full impact of the struggle: 2:8; 5:13, 31; 6:13; 14:11-16; 23:9-40 (especially vss. 25-32); 28:1-17. These seers have dreams (23:25), "lying visions, foolish divinations" (14:11). We may assume that they also attributed these non-rational attempts to decode the future to the spirit. Jeremiah mocks them: "The prophets have become *wind (ruah)*, the *word* is not in them" (5:13). This text gives us the key to Jeremiah's view of the prophetic experience. Because of the abuse to which these prophets put the non-rational in the service of their presumption, Jeremiah avoids any mention of the *spirit* in relation to his own prophecies. When he uses *spirit* of the prophetic experience it is only in the pejorative sense of wind, that is, vanity: the men of the spirit have become men of wind. Jeremiah is not a man of the spirit but a man of the *word*—that is, the clear, discernible message of the Lord rooted in the covenant revelation of his will.

The same contrast between the non-rational media and the word appears in 23:25-29:

> 25. I have heard the prophets who prophesy lies in my name say, "I had a dream! I had a dream!" 26. How long will this continue? Is my name in the hearts of the prophets who prophesy lies and their own deceitful fancies? 27. By their dreams which they recount to each other, they think to make my people forget my name, just as their fathers forgot my name for Baal. 28. Let the prophet who has a dream recount his dream; let him who has my word speak my word truthfully! What has straw to do with the wheat? says the Lord. 29. Is not my word like fire, says the Lord, like a hammer shattering rocks? (NAB)

Never before have we met such a strong opposition of word to spirit —and never again will we meet it so strongly. Later in Paul we will find a trace of this Jeremian reaction when he urges that the work of the spirit in tongues is fruitless for the community unless it be brought to its completion by conceptualization in the word (1 Cor 14:13-19). But for Jeremiah, the medium of God's revelation is his *word*, pure and simple. This appears throughout his ministry, from his inaugural vision ("See I put my words in your mouth," 1:9; "I am watching to fulfill my word," 1:12) to the end of his ministry (28:12). It is always the *word* of the Lord that comes to Jeremiah (2:1; 7:1; 14:1; 18:1, etc.).

However to be complete we must observe that in spite of Jeremiah's consistent attack upon the dreams and fantasies of the false prophets, he was himself granted visions (1:11-14) and in the chapter on the restoration there is one slight hint of a revelation he received in sleep: "Upon this I awoke and opened my eyes; but my sleep was sweet to me" (31:26).

In the objective sense, Jeremiah uses *ruah* only for the wind or blast of judgment (4:12) as Hosea and Isaiah had done before him. This is not to say that Jeremiah never had a word of consolation or promise. In chapter 31, he prophesies the ultimate return from exile and the making of a new covenant relationship with the Lord. But in that prophecy (31:31-34), there is not the slightest hint that the reconstitution of the nation would involve an outpouring of the spirit. For this we shall have to turn to Ezekiel.

4
Spirit and Covenant: The Prophets of the Exile and the Return

Ezekiel

With Ezekiel an entirely new "wind" is blowing, one that fits his vocation to rally the hopes of the exiles and prepare this remnant to become the new and purified people of the restoration. The spirit now appears everywhere, both as the author of the prophet's own experience and as the objective agent of renewal. From the opening lines of the book, Ezekiel's vision of the living creatures is full of movement and power. The spirit of the Lord is the force behind the moving cherubim: "Wherever the spirit wished to go, there they went . . . (1:12). Wherever the spirit wished to go, there the wheels went . . . for the spirit of the living creatures was in the wheels" (1:20). The bizarre imagery of this vision is meant to convey the glory of the Lord (1:28) in a setting of intense dynamism, implying that God is not dead but alive and well among his people in Babylon.

Especially does the spirit return as the instigator and the animator of prophecy. The spirit sets the prophet on his feet (2:2; 3:2f), lifts him up and carries him away in vision (3:12; 8:3; 11:1; 43:5). The spirit and the hand of the Lord are associated to the point of identification: "The spirit which had lifted me up seized me, and I went off spiritually stirred, while the hand of the Lord rested heavily upon me" (3:14). Or: "The hand of the Lord came upon me, and he led me out in the spirit of the Lord. . . ." (37:1). The *word* of the Lord comes to the prophet through the spirit falling on him (11:5).

It is of special significance here to note how the expression "the spirit" can stand independently when it means divine action or inspiration, without having to be qualified, as it most often was in Isaiah and Jeremiah, as "the spirit of the Lord." This is in itself indicative of the more congenial atmosphere for pneumatology in this animator of a depressed people.

The coming salvation too is described not only in terms of the spirit, but in terms of a *new* spirit and a *new* heart. It is the Lord's gift (11:19) but the people have the responsibility to make it their own (18:31). The high point of Ezekiel's theology of the spirit comes in chapters 36 and 37. The whole section 36:1-37:14 merits attentive reading. We shall look closely at two sections of this long passage.

Ez 36:23-31: The Spirit and the New Covenant

23. I will prove the holiness of my great name, profaned among the nations, in whose midst you have profaned it. Thus the nations shall know that I am the Lord, says the Lord God, when in their sight I prove my holiness through you. 24. For I will take you away from among the nations, gather you from all the foreign lands, and bring you back to your own. 25. I will sprinkle clean water upon you to cleanse you from all your impurities, and from all your idols I will cleanse you. 26. I will give you a new heart and place a new spirit within you, taking from your bodies your stony hearts and giving you natural hearts. 27. I will put my spirit within you and make you live by my statutes, careful to observe my decrees. 28. You shall live in the land I gave your fathers; you shall be my people, and I will be your God. 29. I will save you from all your impurities; I will order the grain to be abundant, and I will not send famine against you. 30. I will increase the fruit on your trees and the crops in your fields; thus you shall no longer bear among the nations the reproach of famine. 31. Then you shall remember your evil conduct, and that your deeds were not good; you shall loathe yourselves for your sins and your abominations. (NAB)

The Lord intends to prove his holiness—that is, to manifest his power in the sight of the nations—by an act of redemption. (This is the sense in which the Lord's prayer asks that God's name be hallowed— that God "sanctify his name," that is, manifest himself actively in history to bring about his kingdom.) This will involve restoring the people to their land, but much more. It will be first of all a cleansing from sins, especially from Israel's contamination with idols, contracted by living among a pagan people and at times aping their ways. The cleansing associated with water and followed by the gift of a new spirit and a new heart is unprecedented in the pneumatology of the Old Testament. The need for a washing clean had of course already been stressed by the prophets (cf. Is 4:4) but the *ruah* or "spirit" there was the agent of the cleansing itself. Here the new spirit appears as the positive life which *follows* the cleansing. The "new spirit" (vs. 26) is the Lord's own spirit (vs. 27) and that is why it manifests itself in a willing observance of the Lord's mind for his people, the law (36:27).

This text lies behind much of the theology of the Acts of the Apostles which tends to distinguish two moments in Christian initiation—that of water baptism and that of receiving the Spirit (Acts 2:38; 8:15-17). Although Ezekiel does not use the term "new covenant" as Jeremiah did (Jer 31:31) covenant renewal is implicit from the language used in vs. 28: "You shall be my people, and I will be your God" (cf. Ex 19:5; Hos 2:20, 25). Our present text later was a favorite of the Qumran community by the Dead Sea, which engaged in many ritual washings as part of the program of being a reformed covenant community.

The culminating effects of this saving action of God are fruitfulness of the land (vs. 29-30) and then—surprisingly in the climactic point!—an acute awareness on Israel's part, of her sinful past. It would seem that this awareness should logically come in verse 25 which speaks of the Lord cleansing his people from their impurities. But for Ezekiel, who has a keen sense of human depravity, Israel cannot, by simply deciding to do so, return to full life with the Lord. Her awareness of her sinfulness comes *after* she experiences God's redeeming act and the gift of his spirit, not before. This view of the psychology of the new creation agrees with Ezekiel's long allegory in chapter 16, which begins with the Lord's finding the baby girl weltering in blood; he rescues her, raises her, marries her, only to see her turn harlot. But then the Lord loves her anyway, performs saving acts for her, renews his covenant with her and forgives her. And it is *this* incredible act of forgiving love, after her ever graver infidelities, that makes her blush for shame (Ez 16:60-63).

Ez 37:1-14: The Dry Bones Awaken to the Spirit

1. The hand of the Lord came upon me, and he led me out in the spirit of the Lord and set me in the center of the plain, which was now filled with bones. 2. He made me walk among them in every direction so that I saw how many they were on the surface of the plain. How dry they were! 3. He asked me: Son of man, can these bones come to life? "Lord God," I answered, "you alone know that." 4. Then he said to me: Prophesy over these bones, and say to them: Dry bones, hear the word of the Lord! 5. Thus says the Lord God to these bones:

See! I will bring spirit into you, that you may come to life. 6. I will put sinews upon you, make flesh grow over you, cover you with skin, and put spirit in you so that you may come to life and know that I am the Lord. 7. I prophesied as I had been told, and even as I was prophesying I heard a noise; it was a rattling as the bones came together, bone joining bone. 8. I saw the sinews and the flesh come upon them, and the skin cover them, but there was no spirit in them. 9. Then he said to me: Prophesy to the spirit, prophesy, son of man, and say to the spirit: Thus says the Lord God: From the four winds come, O spirit, and breathe into these slain that they may come to life. 10. I prophesied as he told me, and the spirit came into them; they came alive and stood upright, a vast army. 11. Then he said to me: Son of man, these bones are the whole house of Israel. They have been saying, "Our bones are dried up, our hope is lost, and we are cut off." 12. Therefore, prophesy and say to them: Thus says the Lord God: O my people, I will open your graves and have you rise from them, and bring you back to the land of Israel. 13. Then you shall know that I am the Lord, when I open your graves and have you rise from them, O my people! 14. I will put my spirit in you that you may live, and I will settle you upon your land; thus you shall know that I am the Lord. I have promised, and I will do it, says the Lord. (NAB)

This classic picture of the restoration in terms of a resuscitation of the dead bones is not, in the author's view, a prophecy of bodily resurrection as it was understood in the New Testament. But it is a graphic symbol for the rebirth of the nation, and the relation of the spirit to this symbolic resurrection prepares for the New Testament association of the Holy Spirit with the resurrection of Jesus (Rom 1:4) and of Christians (Rom 8:11).

The spirit is here obviously related to life (vss. 5, 6, 14), and the gift of the spirit results in knowing "that I am the Lord" (vs. 6). What does that mean?

"To know that I am the Lord" is not quite the same as the expression "to know the Lord." The latter means to acknowledge the Lord and to do his will (Jer 22:16). To "know that I am the Lord" is to experience the Lord's power in a manifest saving act. Though it is the restoration that is at issue here, the broader relationship of the spirit to the experience of God's reality in one's life has at least been broached. In the New Testament it is the Holy Spirit that brings the experience and the confession that Jesus, by his resurrection, is Lord (1 Cor 12:3). The thought in Ezekiel reappears in 39:28f.: "Thus they shall know that I, the Lord, am their God . . . no longer will I hide my face from them, for I have poured out my spirit upon the house of Israel, says the Lord God." Pouring out his spirit is here equivalent to revealing his face, and this expression means conveying the fulness of his blessings (cf. Num 6:20).

In 37:9 the spirit is poetically summoned, not from the side of God, but from the four winds. This is no courting of polytheism; it is simply a way of magnifying the power of the spirit and giving the whole scene a cosmic magnification.

The concluding verse 14 sums up the threefold effect of this action of the spirit. The spirit gives life, it leads the people back to their homeland and it renews in them a conviction of the reality of the Lord. Ezekiel builds boldly on the foundation laid by Isaiah 32:15-20. Never before in the biblical tradition had the whole saving action of the Lord been so clearly and thoroughly attributed to the spirit.

Second Isaiah

Israel was in exile in Babylon for half a century. Despite the promises of Jeremiah and the glowing visions of Ezekiel, time wore on and the words of the prophets were still unfulfilled. The Jews settled down for a long stay, and many had given up all hope of ever returning. Then there appeared in their midst a poet who had pored long hours over the prophecies of Isaiah and now began to move among the people with songs of a coming victory of the Lord over the gods of Babylon. Babylon would soon fall, and Israel would return to her homeland. That is, in fact, what happened, as the mighty city and empire fell to the Persian Cyrus, and the Jews were allowed to return to Judea.

This poet is called Second Isaiah, for want of a better name. His work, sometimes called "The Book of Consolation," begins with chapter 40 of Isaiah and goes down to 55:13. It has a beautifully developed theology of God's *word,* especially its power and even its autonomy (Is 55:10-11). It is primarily the word of promise, the past prophetic word which is now being fulfilled. God's word is making history, and in its presence even such a vaunted empire as Babylon is like grass: "All mankind is grass, and all their glory like the flower of the field. The grass withers, the flower wilts, when the breath of the Lord blows upon it. Though the grass withers and the flower wilts, the word of our God stands forever" (Is 40:6-8). We note immediately that spirit (breath) and word are here teamed together in a way quite unknown to Jeremiah 5:13. The *ruah* of the Lord is the wind or the breath of his judgment (a theme of the earlier prophets) by which he annihilates, effortlessly, his enemies. The *word* of the Lord is principally his promise through the prophets to restore his people. So too, it is likely that the *ruah* of Yahweh here is the spirit that moved the prophets, seen here as the Lord's breath withering Babylon (see also 40:24). God's word and his spirit are in Second Isaiah congenial elements through which the Lord's power is shown.

That power is the power of renewing in the present time the wonders of the exodus (43:2-3, 16-21) and more: it will be like a new creation (45:7, 8, 11-13, 18-19). The poet's interest in creation is remarkable. He had lived among the Babylonians who each new year celebrated the creation myth hailing the god Marduk as the primordial champion over the primeval chaos. Now Marduk was defeated, shown to be nothing but vanity and waste (*ruah wabohu* 41:29; cf. 40:17; 44:9; 34:11) by the prophetic word of Yahweh which has now come true (46:10-11). Consequently, the historical God of Israel, the God who promises and fulfills, has shown that he, not Marduk, is master of creation. We are not yet at the stage of describing cosmic creation as the work of God's spirit and word but the basic tools for that insight have been fashioned and tried out successfully in terms of historical creation. We are now prepared to look at the next text.

Is 40:13: The Spirit and God's Wisdom

12. Who has cupped in his hand the waters of the sea,
    and marked off the heavens with a span?
    Who has held in a measure the dust of the earth,
    weighed the mountains in scales
    and the hills in a balance?
13. Who has directed the spirit of the Lord,
    or has instructed him as his counselor?
14. Whom did he consult to gain knowledge?
    Who taught him the path of judgment,
    or showed him the way of understanding? (NAB)

The "spirit of the Lord" is here specifically associated for the first time in our sources with God's infinite power and wisdom as creator.

Yahweh is not a lesser god illumined by a greater one. He depends on no one else for knowledge. The form of questioning is the same as that used in Job 38:1ff., with a similar meaning. Paul uses this text in 1 Cor 2:16 and Rom 11:34.

Is 44:3: The Spirit and Covenant Renewal

1. Hear then, O Jacob, my servant,
   Israel, whom I have chosen.
2. Thus says the Lord who made you,
   your help, who formed you from the womb:
   Fear not, O Jacob, my servant,
   the darling whom I have chosen.
3. I will pour out water upon the thirsty ground,
   and streams upon the dry land;
   I will pour out my spirit upon your offspring,
   and my blessing upon your descendants.
4. They shall spring up amid the verdure
   like poplars beside the flowing waters.
5. One shall say, "I am the Lord's,"
   another shall be named after Jacob,
   And this one shall write on his hand, "The Lord's,"
   and Israel shall be his surname. (NAB)

This oracle of salvation, addressed to the nation whom the Lord "formed from the womb" (terminology used elsewhere for the election of a prophet, Jer 1:5), introduces the spirit of the Lord with the imagery of water poured out in the desert. We have already seen this imagery used by Is 32:15. Here "my spirit" is equivalent to "my blessing," which means not just delight of the one blessing in the one blessed, but the bestowal of the goods of salvation. In this case it is not only marvelous fecundity but a renewal of the covenant union of Israel with the Lord. The universal outpouring of the spirit leads the individual Israelite to tatoo the name of the Lord on his hand, thus incorporating the Babylonian custom by which a master would tatoo his name on his servant's hand. This relation of the gift of the spirit to covenant renewal should be noted for future reference.

Is 42:1, 5: The Spirit upon the Servant

1. Here is my servant whom I uphold,

my chosen one with whom I am pleased,
upon whom I have put my spirit;
he shall bring forth justice to the nations,

2. not crying out, not shouting,
   not making his voice heard in the street.

3. A bruised reed he shall not break,
   and a smoldering wick he shall not quench,

4. until he establishes justice on the earth;
   the coastlands will wait for the teaching.

5. Thus says God, the Lord,
   who created the heavens and stretched them out,
   who spreads out the earth with its crops,
   who gives breath to its people
   and spirit to those who walk on it:

6. I, the Lord, have called you for the victory of justice,
   I have grasped you by the hand;
   I formed you, and set you
   as a covenant of the people,
   a light for the nations,

7. to open the eyes of the blind,
   to bring out prisoners from confinement,
   and from the dungeon, those who live in darkness. (NAB)

This is the first of the so-called "servant songs" in Second Isaiah. Scholars debate whether vss. 5-9 belong to this song. We have supplied the text up to vs. 7 because of the interesting parallel in vs. 5 of *neshamah* (breath) and *ruah* (spirit), obviously meaning the same thing, life.

The text is important because this *servant* is endowed with the spirit of the Lord for a mission of *mishpat*, an act of judgment or justice. The idea of justice appears three times in the text as the mission of this servant (1, 4, 6). The probable meaning is that he will vindicate the cause of Israel in the sight of the nations by returning Israel to her homeland. This leads some scholars to identify the servant with the Persian king Cyrus who freed the Jews for repatriation. Indeed Cyrus was an astute humanitarian ruler, and he took Babylon without having to do battle (a fact alluded to perhaps in vss. 2 and 3). But the servant is also a *teacher*, and teaching is never done by kings but only by prophets (Is 8:16; Zech 7:12) and priests (Jer 2:8; 18:18; Ez 7:26). And so the mystery remains as to the person Second Isaiah had in mind. The writers of the gospels certainly intended to see this prophecy fulfilled in the baptism of Jesus (Mt 3:16-17; Mk 1:10-11; Lk 3:21-22).

Third Isaiah

Some scholars attribute all of Is 40-66 to Second Isaiah. Most, however, see the section from 55:13 to the end of the book as the work of a later hand of the Isaian school. However the question of authorship is settled, some of the richest theology of the spirit is found embedded here, as the writer develops his favorite themes of the rebuilding of the city, the change from darkness to light, and the Lord's stirring call to salvation.

Is 61:1-3: The Spirit, Anointing, and Salvation

1. The spirit of the Lord God is upon me,
   because the Lord has anointed me;
   he has sent me to bring glad tidings to the lowly,
   to heal the brokenhearted,
   to proclaim liberty to the captives
   and release to the prisoners,
2. to announce a year of favor from the Lord
   and a day of vindication by our God,
   to comfort all who mourn;
3. to place on those who mourn in Zion
   a diadem instead of ashes,
   to give them oil of gladness in place of mourning,
   a glorious mantle instead of a listless spirit.
   They will be called oaks of justice,
   planted by the Lord to show his glory. (NAB)

The opening line of this song recalls Is 42:1, where the servant was described as the one "upon whom I have put my spirit." Even more clearly however it evokes Micah 3:8, "But as for me, I am filled with power, with the spirit of the Lord . . ." We probably have here a pre-exilic formula of a prophecy in connection with a call; but whereas Micah used the formula to introduce a condemnation of Israel for its sins, here the formula introduces an oracle of salvation. The possession of the spirit is attributed to the divine anointing, and it evokes the anointing of Saul (1 Sam 10:1-13) and David (1 Sam 16:13; cf. 2 Sam 23:1-7) both of whom received the spirit as its effect. Until after the exile, the rite of anointing was reserved to kings, who had the mission of establishing God's justice in the realm. Here however the anointing is for a role of proclamation, healing, liberation, comforting and glorification. Is it a prophetic role? Yes, and for that reason we can assume that the prophet is speaking symbolically of his call as an anointing—particularly necessary at a period when Israel lacked the leadership of an anointed king. But the speaker is more than a prophet. He is the announcer and introducer of the time of salvation. It seems that all he has to do is to announce the day of salvation and it begins. The *glad tidings* were those first announced in Is 40:9; 41:7, the good tidings of the return. Here to the people already returned and perhaps dejected at the sight of the temple in ruins, the prophet proclaims a kind of sabbatical or jubilee year (Deut 15:1-18; Lev 25:8-12), the time of the cancelling of debts and of release of those imprisoned or enslaved because of them. The time of the return was one in which this kind of fraternal freedom was needed (Is 58:6).

By juxtaposing "year" and "day" in vs. 2, the announcer shows that he is not thinking of any particular event but rather of a new era. Describing it as a time of vindication ("vengeance," "revenge") does not really mean anything greatly different from "favor," with which it is parallel. It does not even mean vengeance upon Israel's enemies—of which there is not even a hint in the text. It means a vindication *for* the restoration, thus picking up the primitive meaning of the word as it was used in the days prior to Israel's becoming a state. It meant simply, "the restoration of wholeness."

Luke describes Jesus as the prophet (Lk 4:24) who uses this text in his inaugural speech in the synagogue at Nazareth to open the "time of salvation" (4:16-22) and to set the program for his ministry of preaching, delivering, and healing. Luke adroitly cuts the citation just before "a day of vindication" would have been read, out of sensitivity to his gentile readers who could not have understood it as just another way of saying the age of restoration.

In vs. 3 "oaks of justice" probably does not refer to the ethical character of the new people of God but rather to the Lord's saving justice which the restoration will glorify. The oracle actually does not end here. Verses 4 to 9 show how this salvation is to come about: through the rebuilding of the city (vs. 4) and the restoration of her honor (vs. 7). Both of these things the Lord accomplishes for her (vs. 8) and the whole world must acknowledge it (vs. 9).

Is 63:10, 11, 14: "Grieving His Holy Spirit"

> 9. . . . It was not a messenger or an angel,
>   but he himself who saved them.

Because of his love and pity
he redeemed them himself,
lifting them and carrying them
all the days of old.
10. But they rebelled, and grieved
his holy spirit;
so he turned on them like an enemy,
and fought against them.
11. Then they remembered the days of old
and Moses, his servant;
where is he who brought up out of the sea
the shepherd of his flock?
Where is he who put his holy spirit
in their midst;
12. whose glorious arm
was the guide at Moses' right;
who divided the waters before them,
winning for himself eternal renown;
13. who led them without stumbling through the depths
like horses in the open country,
14. like cattle going down into the plain,
the spirit of the Lord guiding them?
Thus you led your people,
bringing glory to your name. (NAB)

The long passage to which this section belongs (63:7-64:11) is a community lament in a psalm form. It could have been placed among the psalms, and in many ways it reminds us of the Lamentations. A traditional part of the community lament was a review of God's earlier saving acts. Unique about this psalm is the way the author has expanded the review into an almost independent historical psalm in 63:7-14. It reminds us very much of Psalm 44 and even more so of Psalm 89, which begins with the same formula: "The favors of the Lord I will sing forever." Scholars think it likely the three psalms were composed about the same time, not long after the fall of Jerusalem in 587. It is not impossible, however, that our psalm was later reworked into Third Isaiah at this point. Why this incorporation was made is only a matter of conjecture. In any case, the expression "the spirit of the Lord" appears once in the text and "his holy spirit" twice.

In vs. 10, after a long recital of the "favors of the Lord," one would expect an outburst of praise or an exhortation to serve and follow the Lord. Instead there is the recounting of Israel's sinful rebellion (cf. Num

20:10; Ez 2:8). The effect of this rebellion was to "grieve his holy spirit."
What does this expression mean? We must at the outset be careful not
to read back into this text the fuller meaning we find in the expression
"to grieve the Holy Spirit" as it appears in Eph 4:30. There is every indication that the author here was thinking of the Exodus tradition about
the angel of the Lord sent before the desert pilgrims:

> 20. "See, I am sending an angel before you, to guard you on
> the way, and bring you to the place I have prepared. 21. Be at-
> tentive to him and heed his voice. Do not rebel against him, for
> he will not forgive your sin. My authority resides in him. 22. If
> you heed his voice and carry out all I tell you, I will be an
> enemy to your enemies and a foe to your foes. 23. My angel
> will go before you to the Amorites, Hittites, Perizzites, Can-
> aanites, Hivites and Jebusites; and I will wipe them out." (Ex
> 23:20-23 NAB)

One will note immediately the expression *rebel* in vs. 21, the same verb
used in Is 63:10. Instead of "his holy spirit," we have an *angel*. Could
the term here have the simple sense of "messenger" and refer to Moses?
This has been suggested, but it runs into the major difficulty that Moses
did not lead Israel against all the groups listed in vs. 23, and moreover
in Ex 32:34 and 33:2 the angel is promised to Moses as well as to the
people. Ex 23:20-23 is generally understood to be a Deuteronomistic in-
terpolation. In this tradition (though not uniquely there), the angel of
the Lord appears often as a friendly messenger of God (2 Sam 14:17, 20;
1 Sam 29:10) in whom one may confide (2 Sam 19:28), one who inspires
and helps the prophet (2 Kgs 1:3, 15; 1 Kgs 19:7), announces the birth of
a hero (Jgs 13:3-23), commissions leaders (Jgs 6:11-24), and fights for
Israel against her enemies and protects her (2 Kgs 19:35; cf. Ex 14:19).
A similar meaning is surely intended here.

But now, returning to the text of Is 63:10, 11, the crucial question is
this: Is "his holy spirit" simply the equivalent of "the angel" mentioned
in vs. 9—or is it something different, perhaps even in contrast with the
angel of the Exodus tradition? The Hebrew text of vs. 9 is no help at all,
because, depending on how the identical Hebrew letters are pointed, one
can derive the translation, "the angel of his presence saved them" (RSV)
or the opposite, "It was not a messenger or an angel, but he himself who
saved them" (NAB). The latter reading has the support of the Septuagint. Fortunately, too, there is another passage in the book of Exodus
which helps us decide between these alternatives. In Ex 32:30-33:6, to
Moses' prayer asking forgiveness for the molten-calf sin of his people,

the Lord answers, among other things, that he will send his angel before the Israelites (32:34; 33:2), but he adds that he himself will not go because he might exterminate the people on the way (33:3-5). In 33:12 the dialogue between Moses and the Lord continues and Moses tells the Lord, "You have not let me know whom you will send with me." Obviously Moses is not satisfied with the angel as a companion. As a result of Moses' intensified prayer, the Lord relents and agrees to go personally with Moses and the Israelites: "I myself will go along to give you rest" (33:14). And Moses then insists that if the Lord himself will not go, neither will Moses or the people (vs. 15). Now the word translated here *myself* in the Hebrew is literally, "my face," i.e., my personal presence, as distinct from the angel. Moses is aware that this *panim*, this "face" or "presence" of the Lord will be a much more dangerous kind of presence—as already indicated in 33:3, 5 and as also indicated by the fact that *panim* sometimes means the wrath of God (cf. W. F. Albright, *Yahweh and the Gods of Canaan*, Anchor Book edition 1969, p. 135). But Moses would prefer this kind of presence, because it would show him that he is the Lord's intimate friend (33:17).

Now we are in a position to bring all of the above to bear on our text in Is 63. The word *panim* is precisely the word used in vs. 9 to mean "presence." The NAB translation is more faithful to the entire context of Ex 33, in which there is a tension between "the angel" and the *panim*, the intimate presence of God. Similarly, then, it does not seem that we can identify "his holy spirit" in vss. 10, 11, and 14 with the angel. Rather it must be seen as something more akin to the *panim*. That the Lord's spirit (*ruah*) can stand for his *panim* is shown clearly by the parallels in Psalm 139:7: "Where can I go from your spirit (*ruah*)? from your presence (*panim*) where can I flee?"; in Psalm 104:29: "If you hide your face (*panim*), they are dismayed; if you take away their (your?) breath (*ruah*), they perish"; and even more clearly in Psalm 51:13, where "your holy spirit" stands in equivalent parallelism with "your *panim*" (and in the same order as in Is 63:9-10): "Cast me not out from your presence, and your holy spirit take not from me." A third confirmation of the virtual equivalence of "holy spirit" in Is 63 with the *panim* of vs. 9 is the fact that the identical function is ascribed, in the Exodus passage to the Lord's *panim*, and in Isaiah 63 to the "Spirit of the Lord." Thus Ex 33:14 reads, "My *panim* will go and I will give you rest," which is echoed in Is 63:14, "the spirit of the Lord gave them rest" (RSV; the same Hebrew verb is used in both passages).

In Is 63:10, the word "holy" qualifying "spirit" brings out one of the qualities of the *panim*, namely the danger of destruction if one comes too close or sins (cf. Ex 19:21-24 and 33:20). In fact, this is exactly what happens when the people rebel against his holy spirit—he turns on them like an enemy (Is 63:10).

But that is not the primary purpose of God's holiness, nor of his holy spirit, nor of his presence. If there is risk for his own people, there is utter terror and confusion for their enemies, for, by the covenant union with the holy God, they have become a holy people (Ex 19:6). Thus God's holiness is like a blessed shield that protects against enemies from without and, as long as his people are faithful, assures favor to those within. By rebellion Israel withdraws from the sacred enclosure and is thus exposed not only to the dangers from without but also now to danger from the holy shield from which it has defected.

"To grieve" God's holy spirit is thus not only to make it withdraw but also to expose oneself to experiencing the events of life as counter-forces. For the Lord, who is master of nature and history, considers his people's relationship with him the most important in the hierarchy of values ("Seek me and you will live," Amos 5:4) and his "holy spirit" will not allow his people to live long in the deception that they can experience the blessings of life while they are in rebellion against the Source of life. Creation and the events of history marshal against the rebel in the rebel's own interest, to bring him to his senses, as happened to the prodigal son (Lk 15:17) and to make him remember how much better it was in the "days of old" when the Lord first put his holy spirit in his servant's life (vs. 11). "The spirit of the Lord" in vs. 14, to which is attributed the entire guidance of the people during the desert wandering, is equivalent to the "holy spirit" of vss. 10 and 11.

This text represents an advance over the preceding ones in still another way. Until now only a few quite specific activities were attributed to the spirit of the Lord. These were either the inspiration of charismatic leaders, or the blast of judgment, or the restoration of fidelity and fecundity to the nation. Here the Lord's "holy spirit" is seen as the universal director of sacred history. Particularly the question is raised of how the future opens to Israel. It is the work either of God's holy spirit leading and showering with blessing upon blessing—or it is the experience of God's "wrath," the reversal of the sacred shield experienced in counterforces aimed at restoring order in his people's value-system.

What we have discovered in analyzing this text is a mine for understanding many difficult passages of the New Testament concerning the Spirit. It helps us to understand why Ananias and Sapphira fall dead for lying to the Holy Spirit (Acts 5:3, 9), and why the sin against the Holy Spirit is unforgivable (Mk 3:29; Mt 12:31-32; Lk 12:10). For if the guiding angel of Exodus would not forgive the sin of rebellion (Ex 23:21), what is to be said of that Holy Spirit who is the divine presence itself?

Is 59:21: The Covenant of the Everlasting Spirit

19. Those in the west shall fear the name of the Lord,
    and those in the east, his glory;
    for it shall come like a pent-up river
    which the breath of the Lord drives on.
20. He shall come to Zion a redeemer
    to those of Jacob who turn from sin, says the Lord.
21. This is the covenant with them
    which I myself have made, says the Lord:
    my spirit which is upon you
    and my words that I have put into your mouth
    shall never leave your mouth,
    nor the mouths of your children
    nor the mouths of your children's children
    from now on and forever, says the Lord. (NAB)

This passage, most commentators agree, belongs to the latest stratum of Third Isaiah and is really the summit of the book's theology of the spirit. It is the conclusion of a long prophetic liturgy beginning at 59:1: "Lo, the hand of the Lord is not too short to save, nor his ear too dull to hear. Rather it is your crimes that separate you from God, it is your sins that make him hide his face so that he will not hear you." The text continues with a long recital of sins that are presently widespread in the community (vss. 3-8). "That is why right is far from us and justice does not reach us. We look for light and lo, darkness; for brightness, but we walk in gloom!" (vs. 9). The lament continues as a confession of the community's guilt before the Lord. Then in vs. 15, "The Lord saw this, and was aggrieved that right did not exist. He saw that there was no one, and was appalled that there was none to intervene: so his own arm brought about the victory . . ." The dreadful moral situation in the community which no human being can remedy (cf. Rom 3:10-12), is resolved by God's own action. We have no hint as to what that means on the plane of history, whether the author is thinking of a recent event or whether he is simply giving a prophetic description of a redemption yet to come. The latter seems more probable. This victory involves a triumph over the Lord's enemies, who in this instance are not foreign powers but the wicked within the community: "He repays his enemies their deserts and requites his foes with wrath" (vs. 18). This eschatological separation of the wicked from the just is described like the flood of a pent-up river which the breath of the Lord drives on (vs. 19). The *ruah Yahweh* appears here as the driving force behind a mighty flooding river that both cleanses and restores, like the flood in the time of Noah. The image had first appeared in Is 30:28.

Then the positive, restoring effects of this act of redemption are depicted. Though not described as a "new covenant," it is clearly the covenant of the spirit (cf. Ez 36:27). But it is also a covenant of the "words" of the Lord, so that here we have a perfect coincidence of "spirit" and "word." In the context of the mention of sin in vs. 20 (more literally, transgression), the "words" of the Lord here have the Deuteronomic meaning of the Lord's revelation of his will in the Torah. Because, however, only the prophets seemed to have had the perfect integration of "spirit" and "word" (they were totally dedicated to the words of the covenant because they were "men of the spirit") the picture of this "community of the future" is not unlike Joel's prophecy of a community of prophets (Joel 3, which we shall see later). As God's spirit and his word are the promise of blessing, the future goods of salvation are assured—though, interestingly enough, they are not detailed. The essence of the future is that Yahweh's people possess his spirit and his words.

The final seal of this covenant of spirit and word is its eternal nature. Enduringness was, for the Israelite, the mark of perfection.

Conclusion

Beginning with Ezekiel there is a vibrant reawakening of pneumatology. The new covenant of the heart promised by Jeremiah will be a covenant of a new spirit. It will mean the resurrection of the nation as the spirit enters the dry bones. With Second Isaiah a beautiful harmony of word and spirit is poetically dramatized, but more importantly the spirit of the Lord is seen to be an important agent of the new creation. This new creation is concretely the restoration of Jerusalem, but there is a universality about it that indicates a prophetic dream far beyond the political Israel. The spirit upon the Servant of the Lord anoints him to be the special instrument in bringing about the reign of God's saving justice in the sight of the nations. With Third Isaiah the spirit of the Lord is again depicted as resting upon the announcer of the period of salvation, and the promised covenant of the spirit is given the added note of everlastingness. The Lord's "holy spirit" appears as an awesome power more closely linked to the divine presence than the guiding angel and for that reason more dreadful when "grieved" by infidelity or disobedience but also a greater sign of friendship with the Lord.

5
The Spirit and Cosmic Order:
The Priestly Tradition

After the high point reached in the preceding chapter it may seem a regression to go back to the Pentateuch. But actually these first five books of the Bible received their final form and were published only after the return from Babylon—somewhere around 400 B.C. Those responsible for the final layer of tradition and for the overall framework belonged to the priests upon whom, in the absence of a king, most of the leadership of the community now devolved. Like the other traditions in the Pentateuch, the priestly tradition had roots going back deep into Israel's pre-exilic history. We shall therefore uncover ancient elements as well as more recent ones in our search for the priestly understanding of the spirit. To use once again the mountain-climbing image, in the ascent one often reaches a crest only to discover there is another crest farther away which can be reached only by first descending to its base.

The priestly tradition contained a primitive history, a patriarchal history, a desert history, and a code which is now the entire book of Leviticus. Charged with cult, sacrifice and instruction, the priests were naturally concerned with anything pertaining to worship. Their image of God is of the all-holy one who is encountered in the cult (Lev. 19:2). The ages of time are tied together by "generations" and genealogies. The age of perfection is not future (as it was for the prophets) but past, and sinful man, through cult, does the best he can to regain the lost perfection of his union with the Lord. For the priestly author, the primordial sin was not the eating of the forbidden fruit but the fashioning of the golden calf (Ex 32:1-35).

Because the "spirit" came primarily out of the prophetic tradition we may well expect to find little attention given to it in the priestly tradition, less open than the prophetic to the spontaneous and the political. However, Ezekiel the prophet was also a priest, and at the last stage of the development of the priestly tradition, due, in our opinion, to his influence, a summit was reached in the priestly author's understanding of the role of the spirit in cosmic creation. But let us start humbly at the bottom and work to the top.

61

Exodus 31:3: A Spirit of Skill

> 1. The Lord said to Moses, 2. "See, I have chosen Bezalel, son
> of Uri, son of Hur, of the tribe of Judah, 3. and I have filled
> him with a divine spirit of skill and understanding and knowl-
> edge in every craft: 4. in the production of embroidery, in mak-
> ing things of gold, silver or bronze, 5. in cutting and mounting
> precious stones, in carving wood, and in every other craft.
> (NAB)

The whole section 25:1-31:18 is post-exilic in its present form and
reflects as much present directives for the Jerusalem cult as it does
desert recollections. Some elements, however, are clearly ancient, and
this text seems to be one of them.

The "divine spirit" with which the Lord has filled Bezalel is, in the
Hebrew *ruah elohim*, "a spirit of the gods" or "a spirit of God." The
translation "a divine spirit" is a good one. Although detailed in four different ways this spirit is really quite limited to artistic skill, as each of
the four words in the Hebrew indicates: *hokmah* is wisdom (here, the
practical wisdom of artistry), *tebunah* is insight, *da'ath* is artistic sense,
and *mela'kah* skill. The same description is found in 35:31. This text is
interesting for the relationship it affirms between what today we might
call "natural talent" and charism. The movement of the spirit here is
certainly far removed from the kind of spiritual invasion we saw in early
prophecy. It appears as a stable quality identified with daily work for
the sake of the liturgical assembly. In New Testament times we shall see
a similar spectrum in the charismatic gifts between the miraculous at
one end and the ordinary at the other. Even artistic skill, directed toward the upbuilding of the cultic community, is a divine gift.

Num 16:22: God of Spirits

> But they fell prostrate and cried out, "God of spirits and of all
> mankind, will one man's sin make you angry with the whole
> community?" (NAB)

God is here addressed, literally, as the "God of spirits and of all
flesh." It is obviously a title meant to exalt the transcendence and universal dominion of the Lord. The world of "the spirits" is obviously the
heavenly world, the world of the *elohim*, in primitive thought conceived
as the council of the gods and later refined as angels or spirits. In con-

trast, "flesh" stands for all that is on earth, mankind in particular. Here we encounter once again ideas which will be used in the New Testament: the contrast of flesh and spirit, and the relation of the world of the angels and the world of men under one single lordship. The same expression recurs in the next passage we shall examine.

Num 27:18: Joshua, a Man of Spirit

16. . . . "May the Lord, the God of the spirits of all mankind, set over the community a man 17. who shall act as their leader in all things, to guide them in all their actions; that the Lord's community may not be like sheep without a shepherd." 18. And the Lord replied to Moses, "Take Joshua, son of Nun, a man of spirit, and lay your hand upon him. 19. Have him stand in the presence of the priest Eleazar and of the whole community, and commission him before their eyes. 20. Invest him with some of your own dignity, that the whole Israelite community may obey him. 21. He shall present himself to the priest Eleazar, to have him seek out for him the decisions of the Urim in the Lord's presence; and as he directs, Joshua, all the Israelites with him, and the community as a whole shall perform all their actions." 22. Moses did as the Lord had commanded him. Taking Joshua and having him stand in the presence of the priest Eleazar and of the whole community, 23. he laid his hands on him and gave him his commission, as the Lord had directed through Moses. (NAB)

The priestly account of Joshua's succession to leadership describes him as "a man of spirit" (*ish asher ruah*). The leadership of Israel is thus thought of, in this view of the desert scene, not as hereditary but as charismatic. What is even more surprising in this priestly text is that Joshua is a man of spirit prior to and not resultant from his ordination. What is passed on to Joshua by the laying on of hands is not Moses' *ruah* (as in Deut 34:9) but his *hod*, translated "dignity" in the NAB. The meaning of this word, which appears only here in the whole Pentateuch, is difficult to specify. Usually translated "majesty," it is frequently applied to a king and then, by transfer and analogy, to God. Since it is meant to describe something effective and perhaps even visible, it might be translated "vitality." Since only part of Moses' *hod* is to pass to Joshua, Joshua's relationship to the high priest Eleazar will be different from Moses' relationship to him, as vs. 21 makes clear. Moses needed no priestly mediator to find out the will of the Lord. But Joshua, and by implication all subsequent leaders, will. Here we find a justification of the authority of the priests in matters of discernment. The priest's word was to be sought especially in matters pertaining to military undertakings. We have then, here, an institutionalization of the process of receiving a "word of the Lord." Joshua's and the people's ordinary way of receiving guidance is not through direct revelations from the Lord (as was the case with Moses) but through the mediation of the priests.

The New Testament picture shows both continuity and discontinuity with this priestly view. Discontinuity in the sense that by the gift of the spirit God reveals himself directly to the heart of each disciple (Joel 3; Acts 2; 1 Cor 2:12; Eph 1:17), providing him also with the gift of inner guidance and discernment (Phil 1:9-10; Rom 8:14; Gal 5:16, 18) and yet it is equally obvious that the ultimate authority for discerning the spirit is the apostles and their representatives.

Gen 1:2: The Spirit of God over the Waters

> 1. In the beginning *God created the heavens and the earth.* 2. The earth was without form and void, and darkness was on the face of the deep; and *the Spirit of God* was moving over the face of the waters. 3. And God said, "Let there be light;" and there was light. (RSV)

> 1. In the beginning *when God created the heavens and the earth*, 2. the earth was formless wasteland, and darkness covered the abyss, while a *mighty wind* swept over the waters. 3. Then God said, "Let there be light," and there was light. (NAB)

This final text of the priestly author, which provides the preface to the Pentateuch and now opens our whole Bible, is a key one to understanding his theology of the spirit. The whole passage 1:1-2:4a is priestly Torah, instruction. Creation of cosmos and man and the rest following it are narrated in the framework of a liturgical week, six days of work climaxed by the sabbath rest. The reader will pardon, we trust, our reflection on this text in reverse, in order to reach the beginning passage which interests us. God's seventh day has no closing refrain as do the other days, "Evening came and morning came." His rest is everlasting and it is holy, and in the world of man the sabbath is the way provided to "enter into his rest." But there is more here than an etiology founding the sabbath. God's "work week" has established a hierarchy. At its pinnacle is man, the last work of God, the creature who bears his image and likeness, to whose creation God gave special deliberation (1:26). Beneath him and under his dominion are the animals, fish and fowl, which are, like man, the object of God's creative act (in the narration, after the opening title, the word "create"—*bara'*—is used only of animals and man 1:21). Beneath them are the plants, related directly to the earth, indirectly to God (1:11-12). The earth in turn has resulted from a separation of the watery chaos into the waters above the earth and the waters beneath. The night and the seas are the effect of God's ordering, but only the first effect, for they are closest to the primeval chaos, which is the dark watery abyss. We thus arrive, by descent from the pinnacle of the pyramid, to the opening scene of creation, at which the *ruah of God* is present.

But immediately we encounter a crucial problem of translation, as the two versions supplied above illustrate. The two most significant divergences appear in italics. The opening verse can be considered either as a title to the entire narrative, as in the RSV, or as a "when" clause introducing vs. 2. The difference of meaning is only one of emphasis. If the first, then the emphasis is upon God's creation of everything—period! If the second, then the stress is upon how our universe came to be ordered—the real point of the whole instruction. The author's main concern here is not to show that God made the world from *nothing* (a doctrinal statement that does not appear clearly in biblical literature until 2 Macc 7:28) but to show how God brought chaos to cosmos. And that leads us to vs. 2, the second and major difficulty in translation.

The problem is not with the first part of the verse. The "earth"— here certainly not the "dry land" which has not yet been formed but a general name for whatever was "there"—was *tohu wabohu*, two Hebrew words meant to convey both disorder and emptiness (Deut 32:10; Ps 107:40; Jer 4:23; Is 34:11). The second word is related etymologically to *Baau*, the nocturnal mother goddess in Phoenician mythology. The "deep" or the "abyss" over which darkness lies is *tehom*, the primeval sea of chaos. It is related to *Tiamat*, the primeval sea goddess in the Babylonian creation epic. The combination of all this imagery, some of it borrowed from the general mythology of the ancient near East and carefully purified of polytheism, results in a description of absolute formlessness and chaos.

The difficulty comes in the last part of this vs. 2. Over the chaos hovers or moves the *ruah elohim*. The NAB, following a number of eminent scholars, takes it in the sense of "a storm of God," or a "mighty wind," hence as a further description of the chaos. Technically, such a translation is possible, since *ruah* can mean storm-wind and *elohim* can at times be used to describe something "of divine proportions." If this is the author's understanding of the expression here, then he is certainly using a very primitive tradition.

But such, we believe, is not the case. This whole section is a magnificent composition of a poet-theologian written, in its present form, no earlier than the exile, and really responding with authentic Yahwistic faith to the vaunted claims of the Babylonian creation myths, to which the exiles were constantly exposed. (The disproportionate amount of attention given to the creation of the stars, sun and moon on the fourth day, vss. 14-19, confirms the subtle anti-Babylonian polemic underlying the account.) By this time the priest Ezekiel, who would have a great influence on the priestly theology which developed during and after the exile, had already re-introduced and creatively advanced a theology of the spirit breathing life into the bones strewn on a boundless plain (Ez 37:1-2), and making possible the realization of the *word* of the covenant to which the promise of land and fertility was attached (Ez 36:26-27). Whether Second Isaiah preceded or followed or was a contemporary of the priestly author who wrote Genesis 1, much of the creation imagery and theology of the two is the same. And Second Isaiah, as we have seen, not only had a keen conviction of God's creation by his word, but he also attributed the Lord's action to his *ruah*, his breath or spirit. It seems more likely, then, that the priestly author took the insights about God's spirit and word, which Ezekiel and Second Isaiah had applied primarily to the Lord's creation of history, and creatively expanded them to the dimensions of the great act of cosmic creation. Such an expansion was in any case done in Ps 33:6: "By the *word* of the Lord the heavens were made; by the *breath* of his mouth all their host," and even more clearly in the postexilic book of Judith 16:14: "Let every creature serve you; for you *spoke* and they were made. You sent forth your *spirit* and they were created; no one can resist your *word*." The most plausible origin of this association is in the insights of Ezekiel and Second Isaiah, brought to bear on cosmic creation by Genesis 1.

However, there is more here than simply an association of spirit with God's creative word. There is an important relationship of the spirit of God to the primeval chaos on the one hand and to the subsequent word of God on the other, and this relationship we must now examine. On the assumption that *ruah elohim* means the *spirit of God*, the meaning of the rare verb used to describe what this spirit is doing over the waters is easier to ascertain. It has now been determined that the Hebrew word is related to the Ugaritic *rhp*, used in the *Tale of Aqhat* to describe the soaring of vultures over their prey (*Aqhat B* iv, 20, 22, 31, 33; ANET[3] 152-153). In Deut 33:11 the Hebrew verb is used for an eagle hovering over its little ones and beating its wings to teach them to fly. The image in Aqhat suggests a conquest, that in Deuteronomy a parental encouragement to risk. If it is permitted to transfer from these usages anything more than the image of "flying above," it would be the note of expectation. If, then, we translate "hover" ("brood" will certainly not do, and "moving over" in the RSV is too general), then we must remember that it is an active hovering. One might be tempted to say, "The spirit of God was 'swooshing' over the waters," or "the spirit of God was beating its wings over the water." As a prelude to his creative act, it is an image most apt to describe the attitude of God toward the chaos. The fact that it is unformed does not mean that it is evil. If it does not yet merit the epithet "good," it soon will. Because God's spirit is hovering over it, chaos becomes promise.

The *spirit* of God thus disposes the chaos to hear in obedience the *word* of God. Because the chaos has been readied by the spirit, when God says, "Let there be light," there *is* light. Scholars often contrast the effortlessness of the biblical creation story with the pagan creation myths wherein the universe emerges as the result of a bitter struggle among the gods. These scholars point out the difference as lying in God's creation by his *word*. While this is certainly the most obvious contrast, they have not given perhaps sufficient attention to the adroit way the author has dealt with the theme of the process preceding the moment of the word. This is handled in vs. 2 by bringing the chaos under the influence of the spirit. There is of course no hint of cosmic struggle. The chaos here is not an enemy to be overcome and trampled upon, it is rather raw material to be lovingly yet powerfully blown into life. In the Babylonian creation myth, chaos is the goddess Tiamat, whom Marduk, the male hero, slays and splits in two, putting half of her up as sky. If there is a feminine element in the Genesis story, it belongs to the *ruah elohim* (feminine in the Hebrew) which proceeds from God himself and prepares, in natural fashion, the primeval womb-dark formlessness to hear the cosmifying word of God.

Some of my biblical colleagues may think I have seen much more here than the author ever intended. Perhaps. But it should be remembered that in the entire history of salvation contained in the Pentateuch, the priestly author is concerned with matters far beyond scientific curiosity as to how the world began. The priestly creation story is a prototype for man's experience of order and chaos in his life and in this world. That this is the author's intention appears from the way he presents the flood in Noah's time (Gen 6-9). It is the return of the primeval watery chaos precipitated by the rebellion of man. God's word drove the waters of chaos into the boundaries of order. When man obeys God's

word he enjoys the protection of God's order, his cosmos. When he dis-
obeys, he breaks the cosmic dam and the floods overrun his world once
again.

We said above that the priestly theology is much more past-orient-
ed than future oriented. It thinks of the future in terms of regaining the
past. Inasmuch as Genesis 1 presents God's blueprint for man and the
universe it is in some way even now the goal of man's striving. For a
tradition that has known the cosmic views of Ezekiel and probably Second Isaiah, it is not too much to say that the role of the spirit and the
word, seen here as the source of all creation, is the prototype for all life
known to man, and especially his religious life. Man, like the universe,
lives and knows peace when God's spirit breathes over his chaos and
God's word orders his life.

6
The Spirit in Israel's Songs: The Psalms

The Psalter is Israel's song-book, compiled bit by bit over the centuries. Perhaps it would help to fancy what a church song book would look like today if its first songs were written in the middle ages, its latest only a year ago, and in between were songs composed over the intervening centuries—songs originally composed for a specific occasion or celebration but then reused time and again for other occasions and celebrations—with a verse or two added occasionally to make an appropriate application to the later situation. Scholars do their best to situate each psalm in the context of its original composition, judging by the language used, historical allusions, development of the theology, and so on. But they confess how notoriously difficult it is to date precisely the composition of most of the psalms, and that their *meaning* for Israel, enriched over centuries of reuse, really transcends any particular historical situation. The singing of our national anthem 200 years after its composition expresses not only what the author felt the night Fort Sumter was attacked but the whole experience of the nation over two centuries, concretized and rendered present as we open a ball game or bury the war dead. So the psalms tied past and present, memory and experience, into an ongoing unity that also fired hopes for the future. The psalms, then, more than any of the rest of the Bible, had a past, a present, and a future meaning, no matter at what stage of Israel's history we find them reaching their final form.

According to the popular view, the whole Psalter is the work of David. But he could not possibly have composed all the psalms unless he had been miraculously supplied with minute foreknowledge of Israel's future centuries and also the implausible ability to imitate the literary style and reproduce the new vocabulary of later ages. That David was a harpist and a song-writer is an ancient biblical tradition, and he thus became the patron saint of all psalmody, just as Solomon became the great patron of all the wisdom literature. This tradition is reflected in the "testament of David" in 2 Sam 23:1-7, where we find the words: "The spirit of the Lord spoke through me; his word was on my tongue" (23:2). David here is shown to have the spirit not only because he is the anointed leader (cf. 1 Sam 16:13) but also because he is a man skilled in poetry. We notice in this text not only the pairing of spirit and word which we have already met elsewhere, but the statement that the *spirit spoke*. Hence, there is no question here of prophetic ecstasy either by itself alone or even as a preliminary to intelligible communication. The speech itself is directly inspired. This poem is composed in the spirit of the wisdom writers, but it reflects the sense in which Israel viewed all of the psalms as inspired by the spirit.

Psalm 31:6: Man's Spirit

Into your hands I commend my spirit;
you will redeem me, O Lord, O faithful God. (NAB)

Ruah is used here of man's spirit rather than God's. It really stands for "myself," but especially for the source of life in the self, or simply "my life." We recognize here the final words of Jesus on the cross as related by Luke (23:46).

Psalm 33:6: Spirit and Word in Creation

6. By the word of the Lord the heavens were made;
   by the breath of his mouth all their host.
7. He gathers the waters of the sea as in a flask;
   in cellars he confines the deep. (NAB)

Psalm 33 is a festival hymn, appointed to be recited in the worship of the cult community to the accompaniment of cither, harp and loud shouts of joy. It would have been appropriate certainly for a renewal of the covenant on the New Year's feast, for it reviews and gives thanks to the Lord for the great works he has done for Israel. Verse 6 begins with creation. We note the association of word and spirit (breath) again. The verse reflects the theology of Gen 1:1-3, where the spirit and the word are both associated in the cosmifying of creation. Here, however, the poet does not seem to distinguish the moment of the spirit from that of the word but considers them equivalent expression for the same act—in fact word precedes spirit here. The primeval sea, symbol of chaos, is limited and put into order by the cosmifying word and spirit of the Lord.

Psalm 104:27-30: The Spirit and Renewal of the Earth

27. They all look to you
    to give them food in due time.
28. When you give it to them, they gather it;
    when you open your hand, they are filled with good things.
29. If you hide your face, they are dismayed;
    if you take away their breath, they perish
    and return to their dust.
30. When you send forth your spirit, they are created,
    and you renew the face of the earth. (NAB)

This psalm, a magnificent praise of God the creator, is rooted in the same cultic tradition as Genesis 1. The theme introduced in vs. 27 is that of the preservation and renewal of creation. First the host of creatures gather periodically around the Lord's table and he gives food to each according to its need. But then there is the mystery of death and passing in creation, and the mystery of new life. Life is the breath of God (Gen 2:7). For the first time in the Bible a poet dares to describe the breathing of all living things as the breathing of God himself. When God holds his breath, what is alive turns to dust. When he breathes out, new life comes into being. This is a poet's view, of course, and poets are allowed liberties that carefully speaking theologians are not. But what a magnificent vision of the intimate presence of God to all living things of which he is creator! The rhythm of creation's birth and death, its seasons of growth and decline, are the very breathing of God!

One of the fascinating things about this text is the relationship of God's face (*panim*) to his spirit (*ruah*), a relationship we first discovered in Is 63:10-14. Here not only are the expressions parallel, but there is a chiastic arrangement leading from God's face to the face of creation via a double mention of the spirit: "If you hide your face (*panim*) . . . if you take away their breath (*ruah*—Dahood would read "your breath" here) . . . When you send forth your spirit (*ruah*) . . . you renew the face (*panim*) of the earth." In this case, as in Is 63, the spirit or breath of the Lord is meant to convey a personal and active presence of the Lord.

This text would one day supply the Christian liturgy with the words for its prayer for the renewing of the recreating power of the Holy Spirit: "Send forth thy Spirit and they shall be created: and thou shalt renew the face of the earth."

Psalm 106:33: Embittering Moses' Spirit

32. They angered him at the waters of Meribah,
    and Moses fared ill on their account,
33. For they embittered his spirit,
    and the rash utterance passed his lips. (NAB)

The one whose spirit was "embittered" is not the Lord but Moses, who was led to speak rashly and thus forfeit the privilege of entering the promised land. The fact that the author wishes to place more of the responsibility for this sin upon the people who provoked Moses than upon the great national leader himself, has perhaps a deeper abiding lesson for the community of the Lord. The life, physical and spiritual, of each member and particularly of the leader, is not merely his own. It somehow belongs to all. The community can either support and promote the *ruah*, the life-breath, of each, or, on the contrary, choke it or "embitter it" and thus frustrate its full development. When one member sins, all in some way bear the burden of that sin, not only by experiencing its effect (cf. 2 Cor 11:29) but often in having created the atmosphere which occasioned it.

Psalm 139:7: God's Spirit, God's Presence

Where can I go from your spirit?
From your presence where can I flee? (NAB)

This remarkable psalm opens with a description of the psalmist's personal experience of God. Verses 1-6 sing of the Lord's all-pervading knowledge, not of the universe but of the psalmist himself. Verses 7-12 sing of the Lord's presence everywhere, but again in terms of the psalmist's personal experience. Verses 13-16 chant the Lord's all-pervading action, likewise not in terms of his presence in the cosmos but rather of his total involvement in every significant event that touches the individual. This leads on the one hand, to a confession of the psalmist's inability to comprehend God's greatness (vss. 17-18), and, on the other, to a twofold prayer—that he may share in the triumph of God's justice (vs. 19-

22) and, since only God knows the secrets of one's heart, that he may be led by this all-knowing God "in the ways of old." The latter expression is a request to be brought back to the fidelity of ancient times, like that of Abraham and Moses (cf. Jer 6:16).

Returning now to the section that contemplates God's all-encompassing presence (vs. 7-12), the text that interests us is its opening line, verse 7. It is the reaction not of a sinner seeking to escape God, but of a just man overwhelmed by God's omnipresence. "Your spirit" here can be just a grandiose poetic way of saying "you." But we should note the parallelism again of "your spirit" with "your presence." We first met and discussed this relationship in Is 63:10-14; we saw it in Ps 104:29; and we will meet it again in Ps 51:13. All four psalms reflect a common understanding related, we believe, to the tradition of Ex 33. God's spirit is not an angel but a way of speaking of his own intimate presence, which is both life-giving and awesome. This text differs from the others in that it does not envisage the divine presence as something that can be lost. Quite the contrary, it is something that is present everywhere, and thus there is no escaping it, should the psalmist even want to.

Psalm 143:10: God's Spirit, Moral Guide

> Teach me to do your will,
> for you are my God.
> May your good spirit guide me
> on level ground. (NAB)

Psalm 143 is the last of the seven psalms the Church has adopted as the "penitential psalms." The personal and private character of the psalm without any historical allusions makes it impossible to date. It is the lament of a man oppressed by his enemies (vss. 3, 9, 12) and in a state of helplessness. Keenly aware of his own sinfulness (vs. 2), he casts himself on God's grace (vs. 8).

This is truly a high point of Old Testament spirituality, standing out, along with Ps 51:11 (see below), as a unique Old Testament affirmation of grace. The psalmist asks for the gift of God's spirit because his own spirit fails him:

> 7. Hasten to answer me, O Lord,
>   for my spirit fails me.
>   Hide not your face from me,
>   lest I become like those who go down into the pit.

8. At dawn let me hear of your kindness,
for in you I trust.
Show me the way in which I should walk,
for to you I lift up my soul.
9. Rescue me from my enemies, O Lord,
for in you I hope. (NAB)

Then follows our verse 10. God's spirit is described for the first time as *ruah tobah*, his "good spirit." It is not likely that the psalmist is living still in the fear that, according to the primitive view we saw in studying the texts about Saul, God could send an evil spirit. "Your good spirit" is here contrasted with "my spirit" which is failing (vs. 7). The psalmist knows that all good things will come to him through God's spirit and through no other source (a distant preparation for Mt 7:11 and Lk 11:13). The specific grace asked is that of guidance (cf. Is 63:14). The psalmist needs God's spirit in order to know how to accomplish God's will. Thus he prays for the fulfillment in his own life of the promise made in Ez 36:26-27, that the gift of God's spirit would issue in an ability to live according to his will.

Psalm 51:12-14: God's Holy Spirit and Inner Renewal

12. A clean heart create for me, O God,
and a steadfast spirit renew within me.
13. Cast me not out from your presence,
and your holy spirit take not from me.
14. Give me back the joy of your salvation,
and a willing spirit sustain in me. (NAB)

One would do well to have Bible in hand as we look at this psalm, which could be aptly described as the summit of the spirituality of the psalter. It is the most important of the penitential psalms. In it the description of the material sufferings of the penitent, so common in the laments of the Old Testament, recedes to the background in order to give central place to the worshipper's spiritual affliction. Again the psalm is hard to date. The last two verses (20-21) are taken by most authorities as a later addition reflecting the post-exilic concern for the rebuilding of the temple. But the original form probably dates to the time of the exile, and some would even push the date farther back. The superscript (vs. 1) giving the occasion for the psalm as David's confession of his adultery with Bathsheba (2 Sam 11-12) comes from the hand of a later scribe and, like most of the historical references in these superscripts, is to be thought of more as a fitting *literary* setting rather than an historical one.

The psalm has a beautiful, almost logical structure. After an invocation (vss. 3-4), there is a confession (vss. 5-7), a prayer for forgiveness (vss. 8-11), a prayer for renewal (vss. 12-14), and finally an act of praise and thanksgiving (vss. 15-19).

Most significant about this comprehensive poetic theology of the stages of conversion is the work of renewal and restoration which follows God's forgiveness. And it is here that the psalmist introduces the spirit.

The psalmist is keenly aware that his offense (vs. 5) has simply been the surfacing of a sinfulness that is deep and radical: "In guilt I was born, and in sin my mother conceived me" (vs. 7). This is not a reference to the psalmist's conception by illicit intercourse. It is simply a poet's way of saying how all-pervasive is his sinfulness, going back to the very beginning of his life. It means that if he is to experience new life, God will have to create anew (the Hebrew verb *bara'* is not "form" but "create," as at the beginning of the world in Gen 1). What the prophets said God would do in the future for his people—bring about a change of heart (Jer 31:31-34; Ez 11:19-20; 36:26-27) is here grasped and believed out of personal experience.

The *ruah* here is something within man, and it is described as "steadfast" (*nakon*). The Hebrew verb commonly means "to be set up, established, fixed," as a house upon pillars (Jgs 16:26, 29) or the temple mount (Is 2:2; Mi 4:1). Used to describe the firmness of the earth, established by the Lord not to be moved (Ps 93:1; 96:10; 1 Chron 16:30), the verb is used in the same breath to describe the enduring stability God has given to the throne of David (Ps 93:2; cf. 2 Sam 7:16; 1 Kgs 2:45; Ps 89:38) or to the king himself (1 Sam 20:31; 2 Sam 7:26). Used of persons, it may mean to be prepared or ready, especially for divine revelation (Ex 19:11, 15; 34:2) or for the holy war (Jos 8:4). In the psalms it appears frequently as a readiness to sing the praise of the Lord (Ps 108:2-7), even in the face of the most adverse circumstances (Ps 57:8 in context of the whole psalm), certain of victory because of trust in the Lord (Ps 112:7). Here in Psalm 51, however, the word has a strong moral sense because of its parallelism with "a clean heart," suggesting sincerity and fidelity to the covenant union with the Lord (Ps 78:37; 119:5; 5:10). Keenly aware of his sin and weakness, the psalmist prays for perseverance in the covenant union to which the Lord will restore him.

From the inner sources of renewal the psalmist now in vs. 13 looks to the divine sources of it, the Lord's presence and his holy spirit. The first reflects, we believe, the tradition of Ex 33 where the Lord, in response to the sin of worshipping the golden calf, refused to accompany the Israelites except through an angel and then, upon Moses' entreaty, agreed to accompany them with his presence (*panim*). In Is 63:9-11 we saw the presence re-expressed as "his holy spirit" (cf. also Ps 104:29; 137:7). The psalmist is keenly aware that both of these are God's gifts, not something that can be taken for granted. He knows that for disobedience the spirit of the Lord departed from Saul (1 Sam 16:14). Thus he implores that his sin and weakness may not cause the Lord to "hide his face forever," but that he may be reintroduced and maintained in the divine presence. The Exodus imagery is enriched with that of the cult. As in the temple, only what is pure and holy may enter the divine presence (Ps 15), the spirit which enables entry to that presence is called "holy."

In vs. 14, the author gives his final description of the restoration he seeks from the Lord. He develops its experiential dimension. The new life will not be servile observance. Surely the penitent could keep some of the Lord's commandments out of fear of punishment. This he knows is not what the Lord wants, nor would it give the psalmist joy. The *spirit* requested here is a "willing" spirit, a spirit that does not find God's will a burden (1 Jn 5:3) but a joy: "In your law, O Lord, is my delight" (Ps 40:9; 119:16). The renewed life will allow the psalmist to experience his service of the Lord as a joy. Centuries later Paul will identify the Lord's will as love and describe joy as one of the fruits of the Holy Spirit (Gal 5:22).

This psalm, then, brings us to a summit of the Old Testament theology of the spirit. As far as the personal and experiential dimensions of the "holy spirit" are concerned it will be surpassed only in the New Testament, which will, nonetheless, build on the deep foundation laid by this obscure Psalmist who sang of his longing for the new life which only God's spirit could create in his heart.

7
The Spirit, the Temple and the Past: Voices of the Restoration

In restoring the nation after the exiles returned from Babylon the chief project was the reconstruction of the temple. One would imagine that the excitement of Second and Third Isaiah about the New Jerusalem would have fired a widespread eagerness to restore the temple to its original Solomonic glory. Such was not the case. Many repatriates felt that all their energies were sapped sufficiently by the difficult work of getting themselves reestablished and reviving the economy of the country. Into this situation came two prophets whose major function was to stimulate the fervor of the people to rebuild the temple. They were Haggai and Zechariah. Both speak of the spirit as related to the task of temple building.

Haggai 2:5: Spirit, Covenant and the Temple

> 3. Who is left among you
>   that saw this house in its former glory?
>   And how do you see it now?
>   Does it not seem like nothing in your eyes?
> 4. But now take courage, Zerubbabel, says the Lord,
>   and take courage, Joshua, high priest, son of Jehozadak,
>   and take courage, all you people of the land,
>   says the Lord, and work!
>   For I am with you, says the Lord of hosts.
> 5. This is the pact that I made with you
>   when you came out of Egypt,
>   and my spirit continues in your midst;
>   do not fear! (NAB)

The meaning of this passage is sufficiently clear. The covenant of

77

With Zechariah we begin to see a development of the visionary and even the bizarre which has marked his predecessor Ezekiel. The meaning of the whole passage to which this verse belongs is obscure, and it is particularly difficult to know whether *ruah* here means a spirit of wrath or a spirit of promise and blessing.

Zech 7:12: The Spirit of the Past

"And they made their hearts diamond-hard so as not to hear the teaching and the message that the Lord of hosts had sent by his spirit through the former prophets." (NAB)

Here the author looks back on sacred history and views it as a gift of God's word and spirit that was not accepted by the people. The prophets of the past are here seen as the mouthpieces of the Lord's spirit, an expression not particularly popular among the classical prophets themselves, as we saw, because of the climate of the times. The use of the term "former prophets" may signal for us a growing feeling in post-exilic times that prophecy is now largely a thing of the past, a view with which the next text agrees.

Before leaving Zechariah we should note an important development in the manner of communicating divine revelation. The "angel of the Lord" communicates prophecy to Zechariah (3:1-9), and he does this in opposition to Satan (3:1-2). Now communication of divine messages by the angel of the Lord is quite an ancient tradition (Jgs 13:3-23; 1 Kgs 13:18; 2 Kgs 1:3, 15), but despite the connection of "the spirit of the Lord" with the spirits of the heavenly court in 1 Kgs 22:24, the explicit connection of angel and spirit appears quite late. The role of angels in the communication of divine messages becomes increasingly frequent in the post-exilic period and angelic dualism (that is, the contrast of the good and the bad angel) becomes more pronounced. Angelology and pneumatology seem at first to have developed along independent paths. It is nonetheless important to watch what is happening in the angel tradition because it will eventually enrich the tradition about the spirit of God.

Nehemiah 9:20, 30: The Spirit in the Desert and the Prophets

20. "Your good spirit you bestowed on them,
       to give them understanding;

your manna you **did** not withhold from their mouths,
and you gave them water in their thirst."

30. "You were patient with them
for many years,
bearing witness against them through your spirit,
by means of your prophets;
still they would not listen." (NAB)

The first of these texts views the Lord's spirit as one of the important gifts of the desert period, along with the manna and the water. To
what is it referring? The mention of *good* spirit (a term we have already
met in Ps 143:10) might suggest the good spirit from the angelic court
given as guide and leader (Ex 23:20-23; 32:34; 33:2-5) in contrast to the
"evil spirit" (1 Sam 16:14) or a "lying spirit" (1 Kgs 19:19-24). However, it is clear from vs. 30 that the spirit is the spirit that spoke through
the prophets. The only account of a bestowal of the prophetic spirit in
the desert was the one we examined in Num 11, where the spirit upon
Moses was apportioned out to the seventy elders. If so, then the Lord's
"good spirit" (an expression we have already met in Ps 143:10) given
here "to instruct them" refers to the charismatic leadership provided in
the desert in order to help his people understand the meaning of the
marvels worked in their behalf. It is not, apparently, a question of interi-
or teaching of the heart, but of exterior instruction by Moses or other
teachers, prototypes for the kind of teaching activity which Ezra and
Nehemiah were providing for post-exilic Israel.

The second passage, which belongs to the same prayer, sees the
preaching of the prophets as the activity of the spirit. Though spirit-
inspired prophecy is here considered largely past (as above, Zech 7:12),
we notice how the spirit of the Lord is appearing more and more as a
universal dynamic activity. While surely still identified with the Lord
himself, the spirit of the Lord is being freighted with so many attributes
that it could almost be conceived as something in itself. But we still have
a long way to go before distinctions of this sort become clear.

The Chronicler's Review of History

One of the works of the post-exilic restoration was that of the
Chronicler. He used the earlier sources known to him (Genesis, Exodus,
Numbers, Joshua, Ruth, and especially the books of Samuel and Kings)
and tried, by reviewing Israel's early history, to show the relevance of

that past for the present community trying to define its identity in an age in which the political hopes of Israel's past seemed unrealizable. The Chronicler consequently focused on the spiritual lesson of the past and even in treating his ideal monarch David, he shows much more interest in the King's spiritual contribution than in his political achievement. The few brief references to the spirit in this work all have to do with inspired speech. Thus the spirit of God came upon Amasai (1 Chron 12:19), Azariah (2 Chron 15:1), Jehaziel (2 Chron 20:14) and Zechariah (2 Chron 24:20), in each case to enable them to make an inspired discourse, which is then given. One highly significant detail is the fact that Azariah's speech is called prophecy (2 Chron 15:8), though its content is only exhortation. This broad usage of prophecy for any inspired utterance reappears in the New Testament (Luke 1:67).

The Decline of Prophecy

In the later post-exilic period prophecy began to decline as a vital force in the life of Judaism. Three other traditions were beginning to replace it: the law, wisdom, and apocalyptic. This surprising development needs some explanation.

The Law

The great monument of the fourth century B.C. was the publication of the Pentateuch under the careful editorship of the priests of the restoration. Every effort was made to solidify Israel's identity, to mark her distinctiveness from other nations and to ensure her purity from every foreign contamination. Religious tradition and law became the great forces of this work of reconstruction.

Is this not something over which the prophets of old would rejoice? Was it not their great concern to bring Israel back to her covenant with the Lord? Obviously this was the case. But for that very reason, Israel began to think of her covenant message as now adequately contained in the codified law. And the living voice was not the prophet in the street but the expositor from the pulpit. If one wanted guidance for the present, one should look to what was written. The prophets were revered but more and more as heroes of the past, not as a phenomenon that might happily erupt at any moment. Charismatic activity was thought to belong to the sacred, unrepeatable past which could now be entered only through memory, teaching and cult. Thus the Chronicler sees in the singers of the post-exilic temple the successors of the pre-exilic prophets or at least of those ancient singers "who used to prophesy" (1 Chron 24:2, 3), one of whom was the "seer" of the King (25:5). Prophecy thus declined because the past, now become normative for the present and the future, is sufficiently accessible through the law and the cult. The rabbis will greatly develop this approach, especially as regards the law. Not everyone in Israel agreed with it, but the proponents of alternatives did not generate a revival of classical prophecy. What emerged instead were two other ways of dealing with contemporary experience—wisdom and apocalyptic.

Wisdom

The wisdom tradition had of course pre-exilic roots. It originated in the popular folk-tradition of the family or the secular tradition of the royal court. In either case it had strong roots in daily experience, from which it spun its proverbs and sayings, and its practical rules for successful living. Though later wisdom texts, probably under the influence of the prophetic movement, spoke of wisdom as a gift of God, the tradition never lost its strong ties with daily experience. It was even in some tension with the "inspirational," as Elihu's speech to Job (Job 32:6-8) demonstrates. Elihu had to protest, against the mainstream of tradition, that his youth was not an obstacle to his being wise and worthy of a hearing, because he could receive as gift of God what others took a lifetime to acquire.

As the wisdom tradition developed, it sought to build a bridge between the religious faith of Israel and man's life as he experienced it and as wise men, even non-Jews, philosophized about it. At times the concern to do justice to the humdrum rhythms of life could lead to the "anti-surprise" polemic of Qoheleth: "There is nothing new under the sun!" (Eccles 1:9).

Now the prophets too had a great interest in the present. The prophetic word, engendered by the spirit, was always related in some way to the present historical scene. It was provoked by contemporary events, and if the prophets recalled the Lord's past favors or looked to the future to threaten judgment or promise salvation, it was always an attempt to give a Yahwistic meaning to the present historical situation.

But prophet and wiseman did not view the present in the same way. The prophet's way of dealing with the present came from inspiration, the wise man's from experience. And that meant also a different understanding of time. If the prophet was concerned that Israel meet God in the hour of her visitation, it was because he viewed time as *kairos*—as "moment," "hour," "opportunity," the discrete irruption of God in event and word. If the wise man wanted Israel to find God in the dusty run of normal living, it was because he viewed time rather as *chronos*, a continuum of days and seasons and years. This too, he felt, has something to say about life and about God. And in an age when no great change of the political situation of Israel seemed possible, it is understandable that a great number of its reflecting people were attracted to a theology which would help them make sense of their present existence in the world.

Apocalyptic

But there were men of another cloth who still had the prophetic fire in them. They believed strongly as did the prophets that God's arm was not too short to save, that he would intervene on behalf of his people. But they had also come to realize that the stage of history on which they experienced prophetic judgment never adequately balanced rewards and punishments. In spite of all that the prophets and Deuteronomy said about the good man being blessed and the wicked man falling into his own trap, the contrary all too often proved to be the case, particularly when the faithful Israelites underwent persecution and even martyrdom precisely because of their fidelity to the Lord. The only way the Lord could adequately manifest his justice would be through one final cosmic act which would in fact annihilate this present age and replace it with a new age, the "age to come," sometimes called the rule or the kingdom of God. The literature which develops this theme is called *apocalyptic*, meaning *revelational*. It is characterized often by bizarre visions and cosmic scenarios and a language that is highly symbolic, even "coded," containing the "mystery" of God's victory plan. To it belong passages of the prophets which have to do with the final end-time—the last six chapters of Zechariah, parts of the book of Joel, and the book of Daniel, to speak only of apocalyptic portions of the canonical Old Testament. Many other noncanonical writings of the last two centuries B.C. developed apocalyptic themes.

The law, wisdom, and apocalyptic—such were the three successors to prophecy. If the prophetic tradition had been the principal bearer of the understanding of the spirit until now, what effect will the decline of prophecy have upon it, and will it survive in any form in these traditions that now dominate the scene? Such is the question which we shall pursue in the next three chapters, looking first at apocalyptic, then at wisdom, and finally at the law as developed in the rabbinic tradition.

8
The Spirit
in Apocalyptic

Joel 3:1-5: The Spirit Poured on All Flesh

1. Then afterward I will pour out
   my spirit upon all mankind.
   Your sons and daughters shall prophesy,
   your old men shall dream dreams,
   your young men shall see visions;
2. even upon the servants and the handmaids,
   in those days, I will pour out my spirit.
3. And I will work wonders in the heavens and on the earth,
   blood, fire, and columns of smoke;
4. the sun will be turned to darkness,
   and the moon to blood,
   at the coming of the day of the Lord,
   the great and terrible day.
5. Then everyone shall be rescued
   who calls on the name of the Lord;
   for on Mount Zion there shall be a remnant,
   as the Lord has said,
   and in Jerusalem survivors
   whom the Lord shall call. (NAB)

This passage from Joel, written probably in the fourth century B.C., stands on the divide between classical prophecy and apocalyptic or "end-time" prophecy. Although the immediate occasion for the prophecy seems to have been a plague of locusts, Joel sees the event as a symbol of the coming "day of the Lord." In the face of this threatening plague, the prophet in the classical style summons the people to repent, to turn to the Lord with fasting and weeping. At this urging a solemn assembly was convoked and the priests led the people in prayer for deliverance. In response to this turning to the Lord, the Lord through Joel promises to banish the locusts and to bless the land with peace and prosperity (2:18-27). Then follows our text, but it is only loosely attached to the historical situation which precedes: "Then afterward . . . in those days" (vs. 1). With verse 3 we are clearly in a final cosmic cataclysm, "the day of the Lord" (vs. 4). Alluding to Ezekiel 39:29, Joel refers to the pouring out of the Lord's spirit, but whereas Ezekiel had said "on the house of Israel" Joel has "on all flesh." The meaning however is probably not all mankind in general, for the immediate addition of "your sons and daughters . . . your old men . . . your young men" obviously refers to the Jewish community addressed in the prophecy. The spirit that is poured out is, amazingly, the spirit of prophecy—and in this Joel goes beyond the general statement of Ezekiel, for whom the outpouring of the spirit was to be given so that the people could live faithful to the covenant (cf. Ez 36:27). The spirit of prophecy, clearly identified here with its less conceptual elements of dreams and visions, will be given to all the people, from the least to the greatest and not to a mere select number of prophets. This "democratization" of prophecy, as well as its non-rational elements, connects this passage with Numbers 11:25-29, where Moses expressed the wish that the Lord would bestow the spirit of prophecy on all the people. As there, so here, there is no indication of any specific message given in the prophesying. The spirit here has regained ascendency over the word.

Another particularity about this text is that such a measureless outpouring spirit is not given, as in Ezekiel, for the reconstitution of the people in their homeland but rather as a sign of the final day of the Lord with its cosmic upheavals. What is the meaning of this scenario? Does it mean the end of the world, the collapse of the universe, as we know it today? A closer reading shows that the cosmic manifestations are "wonders" of the Lord. Earlier prophets had used just such cosmic language to describe "earth-shaking" historical events such as the fall of Babylon (Is 13:10) or the death of Pharaoh (Ez 32:7-8). The apocalypses pick up this language and apply it, without a specific historical instrument or reference, to God's ultimate triumph over evil (Is 24:23 and here). We are not obliged to see the poetic imagery as describing the end of the world in a physical sense, for this was not the original biblical meaning. The imagery does underline the cosmic significance of this event.

However it is to be manifested, the event is both judgment and salvation. Thus, although the outpouring of the spirit is primarily presented as one of the wonders of the Lord, closely connected with the cosmic signs, the ethical element is not totally absent, for the remnant to be saved will be those who call on the Lord on Mount Zion (3:5) and these are the ones who will have entrance to the heavenly city (4:17).

It was to this prophecy, according to Acts 2:16-21, that Peter appealed to explain the event of Pentecost, harbinger of the coming "day of the Lord."

Zechariah 12:10: A Spirit of Grace and Petition

> I will pour out on the house of David and on the inhabitants of Jerusalem a spirit of grace and petition; and they shall look on him whom they have thrust through, and they shall mourn for him as one mourns for an only son, and they shall grieve over him as one grieves over a first born. (NAB)

The section immediately preceding our passage (Zech 12:1-9) represents the end-time conflict in which the Lord will establish Jerusalem victorious over the nations. Since it does not refer to any historical event on the apparent horizon, it is classified, like the passage from Joel, as apocalyptic. This victory is to be followed, our text informs us, by an outpouring of the spirit—a concept inspired by such texts as Ez 39:29; 36:25-27; Is 44:3. Here however the spirit is defined as one of grace and petition. "Grace" (Heb. *hen*) here probably means, as in 4:7, favor in the sight of God. To understand what "petition" and the combined expression "spirit of grace and petition" means we are helped by Daniel 9:3, 17, 23. Daniel's supplications include an admission of guilt, expressions of sorrow and petitions for deliverance from the just anger of God. Dan 9:3 also links the prayer with fasting and penitential garb. In our text, the gift of the spirit results in a changed attitude. The people repent of their former conduct and mourn particularly for one who has suffered from their misdeeds.

Who is this person "thrust through"? He must be a person of some importance, since a national lamentation is called for. His work was in some way the work of the Lord which provoked opposition, since the lament for his death meant a return to the Lord's way of thinking. Even after his death, one is left with the impression that the people looked on him expectantly, hoping to receive some benefits. This is suggested by the use of the verb *nabat*, used elsewhere in the Bible for the kind of suppliant "looking to" which a poor or afflicted man does toward a benefactor, often the Lord himself (Num 21:9; Ps 34:6; 119:6). That a deceased prophet could intercede for his people was a belief reflected in 2 Macc 15:14, a work generally dated in the later second century B.C. One is led to think of the suffering servant of Is 52-53. Though the no-

tions of redemptive death and vicarious satisfaction are missing in Zechariah, yet in Is 52-53 those who rejected the servant do not expressly
look to him for favor, as is the case here.

Is Zechariah speaking symbolically of one of the traits of the final
times—rejection of one or more of the Lord's messengers and conversion resulting from his or their death? The broad eschatological setting
suggests that the event is meant to be symbolic or typical. On the other
hand, the concrete way in which this servant's role is depicted may be
drawn from a contemporary experience. It is possible that a true charismatic prophet of the Lord had recently suffered violent death at the
hand of cult or professional prophets in league with the royal house, the
priests and the people (cf. Zech 12:12, 13 and 13:7-9). It is clear from
13:2-6 that there were false prophets associated with the idolatry and the
unclean spirit that filled the country (13:2). They were responsible for
misleading the people. A prophet of the Lord would necessarily be opposed to them (as was Zechariah himself), and it may be that their
hatred of him (cf. 10:8, 11) drove them to kill him. The case would be
not unlike that of Jeremiah who opposed the professional prophets (Jer
6:13; 23:9-11) only to be at length physically attacked by them (Jer
26:8). So the most plausible situation to which our text is alluding is
this: A messenger of the Lord appeared proclaiming his work and received a violent reaction from the people, abetted by the professional
prophets. Through the merciful outpouring of the Lord's spirit, the people come to realize what they have done, and (in 13:1-6) they turn upon
the professional prophets and are tempted to treat them in the same way
they treated the true prophet. "If anyone asks him, 'What are these
wounds on your chest?' he shall answer, 'With these I was wounded in
the house of my dear ones' " (13:6). The chest wounds are probably of
the false prophet who engaged, like the prophets of Baal in 1 Kgs 18, in
the practice of gashing himself. In the day when false prophecy is rooted
out of the land, if false prophets are gashed, it will be by members of
their own household who seek to rid the land of their falsehood.

We can retain from the beautiful passage that there was a prophecy
long before Jesus Christ, about a prophet who would be put to death for
doing God's work, but that his death would be followed by an outpouring of a spirit of "grace and petition" turning the violent into mourners
and penitents. The parallels with the New Testament are obvious, one of
which appears in Acts 3:17-19: "Yet I know, my brothers, that you
acted out of ignorance, just as your leaders did. God has brought to fulfillment by this means what he announced long ago through all the
prophets: that his Messiah would suffer. Therefore, reform your lives!
Turn to God, that your sins may be wiped away!"

Daniel, Maccabees, and the Later Apocalypses:
The Two Ages, Immortality and Resurrection

The apocalyptic tradition was given its greatest impetus by the persecution under the Greek Seleucid king Antiochus IV in the second century B.C. During this period there was intense pressure from without, and many of the ancient, vibrant resources of national strength were missing. There was no prince or leader and what was worse, prophecy seemed to be dead. This appears particularly in the view of the first book of Maccabees which describes the situation of the times (1 Macc 4:46; 9:27; 14:41) and in Dan 3:38.

In the midst of this persecution the Book of Daniel was written. Though classified in our editions among the prophetic books, it really is of a different literary type. Daniel, who is never called a prophet, is the hero of the book rather than its author. The first six chapters look back to a time when, in the author's view, the spirit of prophecy was alive and active, at least in his hero Daniel. The latter's charismatic gifts were primarily those of interpreting dreams and mysterious events (chs. 1-2; 4-5) through unusual knowledge and wisdom (5:4) and, in the Susanna incident, of manifesting knowledge of the elders' guilt prior to public evidence of it: "As she was being led to execution, God stirred up the holy spirit of a young boy named Daniel, and he cried aloud: 'I will have no part in the death of this woman' " (Dan 13:45-46). Holding up Daniel as a model of witnessing to the faith fearlessly in the presence of the Babylonian monarch, the author is really admonishing those being persecuted by Antiochus to remain faithful.

The second half of the book of Daniel looks to the future and sees the glorious manifestation of God's reign when he triumphs over all his enemies. It is here that we encounter the major contributions of the book of Daniel (to be followed by other apocalypses) in the distinction it introduces on the one hand between the present age and the age to come and on the other hand the association of resurrection and immortality with the future saving act of God. The spirit will play an important role in both these elements.

The present age is the age of imperfection, the age of sin and suffering, the age when evil often triumphs. The age to come is the age of perfection, for it is the period of God's rule or kingdom. Israel has had so much to suffer she is no longer interested in the piecemeal or temporary political salvation promised at different times by the prophets. She is asking the question about a definitive salvation, and she sees that it can only belong to an entirely different age, a different epoch, the heavenly epoch. The decision which the faithful Israelite must face in this age is to live in such a way that he will partake in the heavenly age to come.

It had already been said by Habakkuk centuries earlier (Hab 2:4) that the just man because of his fidelity, will have the fullness of life. But what does "the fullness of life" mean? And where does physical death fit into the picture?—for obviously just men die as universally as unjust men. The question became even more acute in the death of Israel's martyrs—those who died precisely in order to remain faithful to the covenant. Could the covenant union, often spoken of as "justice," be thwarted of its promise by the very act of fidelity to it?

The problem thus raised triggered a development that took various paths. The image of resurrection which earlier texts had used in a purely figurative way for the restoration of the nation after the exile (Is 26:19; Ez 37) Daniel took literally as a promise of bodily resurrection for those who had died for their faith (Dan 12:1-3). In this text "those who instruct others to justice" are particularly the teachers of the law, who probably suffered most under this persecution. They "will shine like stars for all eternity." This apparently means that bodily resurrection, for Daniel, also means bodily glorification. This is more than will be said by Second Maccabees, where resurrection is thought of more in terms of resuscitation. The Lord is the "Lord of spirits who holds all power" (2 Macc 3:24) or the "Lord of life and of spirits" (2 Macc 14:46), a text which associates spirit, probably in the sense of the life-breath, with resuscitation. In 2 Macc 7:23 this becomes clear: "He will give you back both breath (*pneuma*) and life (*zoe*)." Paralleled to life, *pneuma* (breath or spirit) is restored to those faithful to the covenant. Naturally, if man returns to life, his breath must return. "Spirit" is thus associated for the first time with resurrection, but only at the very primitive level of "life-breath" needed for resuscitation. The non-canonical Book of Jubilees (33:31), on the other hand, speaks of a resurrection of man's spirit, while his bones remain in the earth. We shall have to wait for the New Testament to develop the relationship of the spirit to the glorification of the body.

Concerning the general outpouring of the spirit in the present age, the later apocalyptic literature is totally silent. The spirit is given to certain inspired wise men, generally the authors of the apocalypses, who are heirs of the prophets (cf. Enoch 91:1; 4 Ezra 5:22; 14:22) but not to the people generally. The apocalypses have, however, introduced the concept of the two ages and above all the idea of resurrection as an essential element of the future salvation. The importance of this understanding will be seen in the New Testament.

9
The Spirit in the
Wisdom Tradition

As we have already mentioned, our interest in tracing the development of the wisdom tradition lies in the fact that it arrived at a notion of the spirit by starting from the level of everyday human experience. At the summit of its development, wisdom will be identified with the spirit. But let us start humbly with the oldest of our wisdom works, the Book of Proverbs.

The Book of Proverbs

The book of Proverbs itself contains several strata and shows us how the wisdom tradition developed. In what may be considered the oldest part, chs. 25-27, the advice that is given is largely secular and prudential. These sayings, it seems, were assembled by the schoolmen of King Hezekiah (circa 715-687 B.C.). They represent largely a humanistic, self-reliant wisdom based almost exclusively upon empirical phenomena. The politics suggested by such secular wisdom was one of immense pragmatism. When applied without reference to faith in Yahweh, such political pragmatism was denounced by the prophet Isaiah (Is 19:11-15; 28:14-29; 29:13-16; 30:1-2; 31:1-3).

The section with which we are first concerned (chs. 10-22:16), often called the "First Collection of Solomonic Proverbs," shows the growing influence of prophecy and the gradual assimilation of wisdom teaching to the religious life of Israel. Here we find the invocation of Yahweh's name and the recognition of his moral government of the world and men. This direction will be brought to its high point by the teacher who composed the long introduction in chs. 1-9. At any rate, the passages which we will first examine belong to a compilation of proverbs which is difficult to date in terms of particular proverbs. Some of it is pre-exilic, some of it belongs to ageless popular wisdom which Israel shared with surrounding peoples, and in its present form the section probably dates from the fifth or fourth century B.C.

A formal characteristic of these proverbs is their almost monotonous parallelism. The insistence on this form leads a number of scholars to assume that the first line was intended to be spoken by the teacher, calling forth the second line as an antiphonal response from the pupils.

Proverbs 16:1-3, 9: Can Man Be So Sure?

1. Man may make plans in his heart,
   but what the tongue utters is from the Lord.
2. All the ways of a man may be pure in his own eyes,
   but it is the Lord who proves the spirit.
3. Entrust your works to the Lord,
   and your plans will succeed.
9. In his mind a man plans his course,
   but the Lord directs his steps. (NAB)

Verses 1, 2 and 9 all treat the same subject—the basic difference between man and God is planning and executing life-decisions. This passage belongs to a later stratum of the wisdom tradition for it is a retort to the claims of the earlier wisdom based purely on human experience and secular pragmatism. In the end it is not man but God who has his way. "Man proposes, but God disposes." In vs. 9 the NAB properly translates the Hebrew "heart" by "mind" since it is a question of man's intellectual life. The word heart simply expresses the inwardness of man's plans in distinction to the outward realization of them, which depends on the Lord. Man does not have unlimited control of his destiny.

Vs. 2, which introduces the spirit into the discussion, concerns not only man's plans but the sincerity and the purity of his intentions. The Hebrew *zak* is used of pure, unadulterated oil. Though man may think his motives perfectly pure, the Lord's judgment is what really counts. Paul will later insist that even though his conscience does not reproach him, he leaves the judgment of himself to the Lord (1 Cor 4:4). In the Hebrew the word *ruoth* is the plural, "spirits." Though the NAB renders the sense correctly by the singular, this may lead us to overlook the fact that this is the earliest biblical appearance of the expression "testing the spirits."

The exact meaning of verse 1 is a bit more difficult to determine. It certainly does not mean that everything a man utters is inspired by God.

It can mean that after a man has thought out what he wants to say, he must count on the Lord for effective utterance, a kind of remote preparation for the saying of Jesus that one should rely on the Holy Spirit for proper defense before the court. Other authors think that the contrast is similar to vs. 9, that words, like actions, often produce results different from those which were planned—and consequently, as vs. 3 advises, one should entrust all projects to the Lord for a successful outcome.

We may retain from this brief section the awareness that man is not the sole master of his projects nor is he even an adequate judge of his own intentions. We are here at the dawning of a realization which will ultimately lead to a theology of inspired wisdom.

Proverbs 20:27: Man's Spirit and Self-Knowledge

A lamp from the Lord is the breath of man;
it searches through all his inmost being. (NAB)

This verse builds on the insight of the ones examined above and especially on 20:24, "Man's steps are from the Lord: how then can a man understand his way?" Man's ability to pick his way through life without going astray is limited. Even a rigorous educational discipline will not adequately assure the proper direction of life. Something more is needed. While it is not yet said that "The Lord is my light," vs. 27 points out that the *neshamah*, the "breath" which is God's direct gift at creation, is a lamp—that is, man has an inner light on which he can rely. Endowed with the power of introspection, he can examine the depths of his self and see clearly in the Lord's light what is there. Though not exactly the voice of conscience, it does enable man to avoid being a victim of self-deceit. This is certainly not yet the gift of the Lord's "holy spirit" but simply the gift every man receives at creation of reflection, of knowing right from wrong, and especially of self-knowledge. Paul may have been borrowing the language of this text when he wrote, in 1 Cor 2:11, that only a man's own spirit within him knows his own depths.

Proverbs 1:23: Wisdom Pours Out Her Spirit

20. Wisdom cries aloud in the street,
    in the open squares she raises her voice;
21. down the crowded ways she calls out,

at the city gates she utters her words:
22. "How long, you simple ones, will you love inanity,
23. how long will you turn away at my reproof?
Lo! I will pour out to you my spirit,
I will acquaint you with my words." (NAB)

This text marks an important development not only in the wisdom tradition but in the whole theology of the Old Testament. It belongs to the long introduction to Proverbs which extends through chapter nine, universally held to be the latest stratum of the book, the work of a wisdom teacher who has been strongly influenced by the prophetic understanding of Yahweh. One of the traits of this later view is the personification of wisdom, here depicted as a preacher who cries out in the street. The picture of those who love vanity and refuse to follow wisdom's invitation is sombre (1:20-23) but there are two words of encouragement—in vs. 33 the promise of security and peace, and in vs. 23, the promise that wisdom will pour out her own spirit and acquaint them with her words. Wisdom likens her "spirit" to a copious gushing spring, the effect of which is to seal a friendship, or at least a familiarity, between her listeners and her words. Such is the nuance of the Hebrew verb which the NAB translates "acquaint." In the context it means to make known, but not in the mere sense of telling or announcing, but rather of introducing as person to person, suggesting the creation a connaturality between knower and known.

Inasmuch as wisdom is here using prophetic terminology and motifs (spirit, word, appeal, denunciation, threat, promise) we might be led to suppose that wisdom is being personified as a prophetess. But there is something distinctly different here. For she is not presented as a messenger with an oracle beginning, "Thus says the Lord." Rather she speaks by herself, on her own authority, like a goddess. The wisdom author, therefore, while maintaining clearly his Yahwistic monotheism, has personified Yahweh's attribute of wisdom with motifs ultimately derived from ancient representations of a goddess of wisdom. Particularly the mocking laugh at man's self-imposed or at least deserved calamities, which we find elsewhere in the poetic literature of the Bible (Ps 2:4), makes one think of the laughter of the goddess Anath when she does battle with her enemies in the Ugaritic myth of Baal and Anath (cf. J. B. Pritchard, *Ancient Near Eastern Texts*, p. 136). The distinction from prophecy also appears in the way the spirit comes. In prophecy the spirit comes on the prophet so that he may speak. Here the spirit comes upon the listener and it is poured out by the speaker, lady wisdom, as her own spirit. No prophet could ever say that.

This leads us to pause at another new element, the fact that repeatedly in this section of Proverbs wisdom is personified as a woman (1:20-33; 4:5-9; 7:4; 9:1-6). The Hebrew word for wisdom, *hokmah*, is of course feminine to start with, so the feminine personification is etymologically natural. But the choice of this poetic form marks a significant shift in the understanding of the way God comes to man. The prophetic word through which God's will for men had been revealed, has a definite "masculine" ring to it: it is command, clearly enunciated with threat or promise, or both, and it comes most often as fire, or hammer shattering rock (Jer 23:29) or as a sword (Is 49:2; Heb 4:12), or as the roar of a lion (Amos 3:8). The earth trembles at the prophetic word as a house trembles at the footsteps of an angry father. Wisdom, on the other hand, comes as invitation, as to a banquet promising delight (9:1-6). She does not preach as if proclaiming a take-it-or-leave-it message, but *teaches*, suggesting a more "incarnational" approach. Showing how God's way concords with all that is humanly good and beautiful, she speaks to the heart. Hers is not the way of command but the way of holy seduction. Her words have not only clear intelligibility but sweetness and attraction, and—let us note it here for future reference—this is because she pours out her *spirit*.

Is it too much to say that Israel is discovering that in her experience of God she needs a mother as much as a father, a teacher's chair as much as a preacher's pulpit? We can at least say that she found that if secular wisdom needed to be redeemed by prophecy, prophecy in turn needed to be tamed by wisdom.

The Book of Job

The book of Job is classified with the books of wisdom because it is concerned primarily with a universal life-problem, the suffering of the just man. We will limit our considerations to the author's view of the spirit and the vocabulary he uses.

In Job *ruah* or *neshamah* for man's life-spirit is common. Sometimes it is translated breath, sometimes spirit. In 27:3 to still have "my *neshamah*" is the same as to have the "*ruah* of God." Both expressions mean *life*, so that the passage simply means, "I still have life in me." God can withdraw either: Job 34:14; 33:4. When Elihu says "The spirit of God made me, the breath of the Almighty keeps me alive" (33:4), he is recalling the Genesis tradition of man's creation by the inbreathing of God. For future reference let us note the terms used in 12:10: "In his hand is the soul of every living being, and the life-breath of all mankind." "Soul" here translates the Hebrew *nephesh* and the Greek *psyche*, while "life-breath" renders the Hebrew *ruah* and the Greek *pneuma*. Though the two concepts are very closely related, and the words may at times be used interchangeably, where there is a choice, *pneuma* more appropriately translates *ruah* and *psyche nephesh*. These distinctions may seem hopelessly academic at this point, but they will be helpful in discussing some of the texts of Paul.

Other usages in Job are poetic. In 37:10, the breath (*neshamah*) of God is a poetic way of expressing frost which congeals water (contrast "He lets his breeze blow and the waters run," Ps 147:18). In Job 4:9, the *ruah* of God is the judgmental and destructive wind or breath by which the wicked are destroyed, a usage we observed in Isaiah.

Let us now look at texts which concern other activities of the spirit in man. In 26:4 the *neshamah* is equivalent to the seat of understanding and inspiration: "With whose help have you uttered those words, and whose is the breath that comes from you?" In 32:8 an important distinction is made between experience and the spirit as sources of wisdom:

6. So Elihu, son of Barachel the Buzite,
   spoke out and said:
   "I am young and you are very old;
   therefore I held back and was afraid
   to declare to you my knowledge.
7. Days should speak, I thought,
   and many years teach wisdom!
8. But it is a spirit in man,
   the breath of the Almighty, that gives him understanding.
9. It is not those of many days who are wise,
   nor the aged who understand the right.
10. Therefore I say, hearken to me;
    let me too set forth my knowledge!" (NAB)

Elihu is a late-comer to the debate with Job; he held off while his elders tangled and only when they were flattened by Job did Elihu come forward. The youth naturally has to justify his speaking out. He insists that wisdom is not a matter of years but a spirit given by God: "It is a spirit (*ruah*) in man, the breath (*nishmath*) of the Almighty that gives him understanding." Although he does not mean infused wisdom as it would later be understood in the New Testament, there is clearly here the realization that experience of life is not an adequate assurance of wisdom.

Finally, in 32:18-20 the experience of the inner pressure by the spirit upon Elihu to speak out is beautifully described:

18. For I am full of matters to utter;
    the spirit within me compels me.
19. Like a new wineskin with wine under pressure,
    my bosom is ready to burst.
20. Let me speak and obtain relief;
    let me open my lips, and make reply. (NAB)

The spirit which compels Elihu is the spirit within him. It is not the inspiration of the Holy Spirit (a New Testament view), nor the overwhelming power of God's word (as in Jeremiah 20:9). For it is certainly by no means clear that Elihu's speech is divinely inspired, no matter how highly he himself regards it. God speaks *after* Elihu has finished his long discourse. However the spirit in Elihu is more than the intellectual faculty. The idea is a fullness that cannot be contained. It is the characteristic of the spirit to move by feeling or impulse. But since such compelling movement may come from either the good spirit (Acts 20:22) or the bad, Paul will call for discernment in identifying its origin (1 Cor 12:1-3).

Qoheleth (Ecclesiastes)

Qoheleth, like Job, belongs to that part of the wisdom literature that wrestles with a problem. Like Job, Qoheleth challenged the simple principle derived from Deuteronomy, that good is always rewarded and evil punished in this life. He is also opposed to the dreamers or idealists who expect to get too much out of life, and he urges his readers to enjoy the present for what it is worth but not to exaggerate the possibilities of present pleasure (or grief, for that matter) or future promise. "Spirit" for Qoheleth always means something in man. The Hebrew *ruah* is often used pejoratively as in the frequent expression "chasing the wind" (1:14; 2:11, 17, 26; 4:4, 6; 6:9). So too in 5:15 and 11:4 *ruah* means vanity or futility. But in the passage 11:4-5, the Greek translators caught a nuance not expressly contained in the Hebrew.

4. One who pays heed to the wind (Heb. *ruah*, Gk. *anemos*)
   will not sow,
   and one who watches the clouds will never reap.
5. Just as you know not how the breath of life (Heb. *ruah*, Gk. *pneuma*)
   fashions the human frame in the mother's womb,
   so you know not the work of God
   which he is accomplishing in the universe. (NAB)

Though the same Hebrew word means in the one case "wind" in the pejorative sense and in the second the "breath of life," the Greek translator had at hand the word *anemos* to translate wind in the first sense and *pneuma* to translate "breath" or "spirit" in the second. It is the Greek word *pneuma* rather than *anemos* that will provide the vocabulary for the spirit in the New Testament.

Sirach (Ecclesiasticus)

An interesting development (and in some aspects a conservative regression) appears in the Wisdom of Sirach. Though in wide use in Jewish and Greek-speaking synagogues prior to the first century, Sirach never made it into the Hebrew canon, in part because of its late date (around 180 B.C.) but mainly because its teachings were too close to those of the Sadducees and not close enough to those of the Pharisees, whose opinion prevailed in establishing the Jewish canon toward the end of the first century B.C. Since the Protestant canon follows the Jewish canon, and the Catholic the Greek, Sirach appears as part of canonical scripture in Catholic Bibles, and in Protestant Bibles is either omitted or printed separately as one of the Apocrypha. In either case, Sirach is helpful to read as a witness to one way in which the wisdom tradition developed.

The book came about in this way. Somewhere around 180 B.C. a cultured townsman, himself most probably a scribe and director of a wisdom school in Jerusalem (51:23) began to write down some of the teaching he had been accustomed to deliver orally. Though Aramaic was the common language of Jerusalem at this time, Ben Sira chose to write in Hebrew, the classical language of the Old Testament. A curator of the past, he has a special affection for the books of Proverbs and Deuteronomy. Often he will take a simple saying of Proverbs and develop it into a meditation. He has a high regard for wisdom, as his opening praise of wisdom shows (1:1-29). It is a gift from the Lord, but worldly wisdom and divine wisdom are of the same kind and differ only in degree. Thus wisdom covers a wide range of skills—craftsmanship, business, cleverness, cunning, caution in word and act, discernment, self-control, right-living—and, of course, the fear of the Lord which is the foundation of it all. He touches on every conceivable topic, from behavior at table to what a father should do with a headstrong daughter.

Ben Sira has no doctrine of resurrection and has nothing to say about a future life. It is here on earth that God rewards and punishes

(11:14—a strong revival of the lesson of Deuteronomy!). The wicked man, though he may enjoy prosperity all his life, in his last hours will experience such pain that all his former delights are wiped out (11:26-28). Add to this Ben Sira's great interest in the temple worship and his reverence for the priests (7:29-31) and we understand why many scholars hold that he was a Sadducee.

Most important for the development of the wisdom tradition is Sirach's identification of wisdom with the Torah and its observance (19:17-20; 24:22). Though Sirach is a strong believer in prayer (22:27-23:6), we get the impression that the great times of Israel are in the distant past. He devotes a long section to the praise of the fathers (42:15-50:24). Pneumatic activity or being filled with the spirit refers to past heroes, especially their marvelous deeds (48:12-13). The spirit of the ancient prophets like Isaiah consisted in working miracles and foretelling the future (48:22-25). There is respect for the visions of the prophets, as long as they are past (48:22; 49:8). But Sirach is critical of anyone who now looks to dreams as medium of revelation or self-understanding (34:1-8). True wisdom is the *"spirit of understanding,"* for which the profession of the scribe provides the best milieu. The scribe pours out teaching *like prophecy* (24:31). He will study the law, cultivate wisdom through experience and travel, and pray to the Lord, who, if it pleases him, will fill him with the spirit of understanding:

1. How different the man who devotes himself
   to the study of the law of the Most High!
   He explores the wisdom of the men of old
   and occupies himself with the prophecies;
2. he treasures the discourses of famous men,
   and goes to the heart of involved sayings;
3. he studies obscure parables,
   and is busied with the hidden meanings of the sages.
4. He is in attendance on the great,
   and has entrance to the ruler.
5. He travels among the peoples of foreign lands
   to learn what is good and evil among men.
6. His care is to seek the Lord, his Maker,
   to petition the Most High,
   to open his lips in prayer,
   to ask pardon for his sins.
   Then, if it pleases the Lord Almighty,
   he will be filled with the spirit of understanding;

> he will pour forth his words of wisdom
> and in prayer give thanks to the Lord,
> 7. who will direct his knowledge and his counsel,
>   as he meditates upon his mysteries.
> 8. He will show the wisdom of what he has learned
>   and glory in the law of the Lord's covenant.
> 9. Many will praise his understanding;
>   his fame can never be effaced;
>   unfading will be his memory,
>   through all generations his name will live;
> 10. peoples will speak of his wisdom,
>   and in assembly sing his praises.
> 11. While he lives he is one out of a thousand,
>   and when he dies his renown will not cease. (39:1-11 NAB)

Wisdom is not totally identified with meditation on the law, for the "spirit of understanding" is a gift of God to be sought in prayer. But the riverbed in which the spirit flows is the law—an encouragement to all later ages who find the prayerful reading of scripture, the *lectio divina*, a way to meet the Lord.

The Wisdom of Solomon

The understanding of the spirit in the wisdom tradition reaches its high point in the book known as the Wisdom of Solomon. Attributed to Solomon by a literary convention we meet in other wisdom books (Proverbs, the Canticle of Canticles, Qoheleth), the work was written in Greek around the middle of the first century B.C., probably in Alexandria. Its author was a Jew who was concerned to strengthen the faith of his fellow Jews at a time when the philosophic and religious ferment of the Hellenistic world was putting new and difficult questions to the faith of their fathers. The answers came from the heart and the mind of a man who not only knew the language and much of the thought of the Greek world but who had also spent years pondering the sacred books of Judaism. He depicts the whole of sacred history as the work of God's wisdom, and he does not hesitate to personify this attribute in most daring ways, one of which is to identify wisdom with the spirit of God.

Before examining the passages in which this identification is made, let us glance briefly at four passages which reflect the traditional doctrine of the *pneuma* as the life-principle in man.

Wisdom 15:11, 16: Man's Spirit on Loan

11. Because he knew not the one who fashioned him,
    and breathed into him a quickening soul,
    and infused a vital spirit.
16. For a man made them;
    one whose spirit has been lent him fashioned them. (NAB)

This passage belongs to the larger one of the satire upon the potter who fashions clay idols. The tragedy is that the potter who fashions such idols has not "known" the one who fashioned him. In the second part of the verse, the creator is said to have breathed into man a quickening soul (*psychēn energousan*). The text is obviously built, as many others we have seen, on Gen 2:7. The third part of the verse speaks of a "vital spirit" (*pnēuma zōtikon*) that is infused. The latter is parallel to the second part, and consequently *pneuma* ("spirit") here seems equivalent to *psychē* ("soul"). On the other hand, one may ask whether the author is not trying to distinguish the divine principle of life from actual life, or the *pneuma* as representing man's relationship to God, while the *psyche* represents the inward principle of activity.

In vs. 16 *pneuma* again appears as the life-principle in man, but the author insists that it is on loan to man by God. Unlike God, mortal man cannot breathe into an idol the breath of life and so make it live. The breath of life, then, is a gift which he receives directly from God and cannot communicate to the works of his own hands.

Wisdom 16:14: Man Cannot Restore the Spirit

Man, however, slays in his malice,
but when the spirit has come away,
it does not return,
nor can he bring back the soul once
it is confined. (NAB)

The point made in 15:11, 16 above is stressed in a new way in this passage, which shows that man can kill and thus expel the spirit or soul, but he cannot recall it. God, however, can, since he is Lord of life and death. In the verse immediately preceding we read, "For you have dominion over life and death; you lead down to the gates of the netherworld, *and lead back*." We would like to have our curiosity satisfied as to what the author means by "leading back" from the abode of the dead. There is no mention here of resurrection, but the text does lay a distant foundation for the ultimate Christian belief in the resurrection of Jesus and of all Christians, founded in the gift of the Spirit.

Wisdom 2:2-3: Man's Spirit Is Not Air

2. "For haphazard were we born,
   and hereafter we shall be as though we had not been;
   because the breath in our nostrils is a smoke
   and reason is a spark at the beating of our hearts,
3. And when this is quenched, our body will be ashes
   and our spirit will be poured abroad like unresisting air."
   (NAB)

This is a statement of the ungodly, possibly the reflection of an Epicurean idea, which of course the author wishes to reject. Certainly he wishes to say that it is a pagan idea that man's spirit at best retreats to become part of the universal spirit. For man's spirit, as we have seen, belongs to God; particularly is this true of the just whose "souls are in the hand of God" (3:1).

Wisdom 11:26-12:1: God's Spirit, Motive for His Love

26. But you spare all things, because they are yours,
    O Lord and lover of souls,
1. for your imperishable spirit is in all things. (NAB)

This short text belongs to the larger section 11:23-12:8, of which the theme is that God spares men because he loves them. Although the author describes God's love for all his creation, this verse obviously has to do with his dealings with men, as the sequence makes clear, and as we may also assume from the combined use of "souls" and "spirit" here. The expression "your imperishable spirit" is surprising, but it becomes less so if we realize that though man holds his life-breath precariously as a gift from God (Ps 104:29), in the view of this author at least, and probably in the view of the rest of the Bible, the breath of life really never ceases to be God's. On loan to man during his earthly life (Wis 15:16), it will return to its author at man's death, and thus from God's viewpoint it is imperishable. There may be a hint of personal immortality in this statement, although its intention is simply to show why God loves men so much—there is so much of himself in them!

Now let us turn to those texts in which the spirit is identified with the gift of wisdom.

Wisdom 1:1-15: Wisdom Is a Spirit

1. Love justice, you who judge the earth;
   think of the Lord in goodness,
   and seek him in integrity of heart;
2. Because he is found by those who test him not,
   and he manifests himself to those who do not disbelieve
   him.
3. For perverse counsels separate a man from God,
   and his power, put to the proof, rebukes the foolhardy;
4. Because into a soul that plots evil wisdom enters not,
   nor dwells she in a body under debt of sin.
5. For the holy spirit of discipline flees deceit
   and withdraws from senseless counsels;
   and when injustice occurs it is rebuked.
6. For wisdom is a kindly spirit,
   yet she acquits not the blasphemer of his guilty lips;
   because God is the witness of his inmost self
   and the sure observer of his heart
   and the listener to his tongue.
7. For the spirit of the Lord fills the world,
   is all-embracing and knows what man says.
8. Therefore no one who utters wicked things can go
   unnoticed,
   nor will chastising condemnation pass him by.
9. For the devices of the wicked man shall be scrutinized,
   and the sound of his words shall reach the Lord,
   for the chastisement of his transgressions;
10. Because a jealous ear hearkens to everything,
    and discordant grumblings are no secret.
11. Therefore guard against profitless grumbling,
    and from calumny withhold your tongues;
    for a stealthy utterance does not go unpunished,
    and a lying mouth slays the soul.
12. Court not death by your erring way of life,
    nor draw to yourselves destruction by the works of your
    hands.

13. Because God did not make death,
    nor does he rejoice in the destruction of the living.
14. For he fashioned all things that they might have being;
    and the creatures of the world are wholesome,
    And there is not a destructive drug among them
    nor any domain of the nether world on earth,
15. For justice is undying. (NAB)

The book of Wisdom opens with an exhortation to those who "judge the earth," that is, the earth's rulers and great men, urging them to love justice and seek the Lord in integrity of heart. This whole chapter is a kind of pre-catechesis or pre-kerygma for the gentiles and especially for those in power. Pagan man's secular wisdom needs the wisdom that only God can give.

What is merely suggested in the first two verses becomes progressively clearer as we read ahead. In vs. 4, wisdom appears not as a fruit of man's study nor of his wide experience of life but rather as a guest that enters (*eiseleusetai*) and comes to dwell (*katoikēsei*). Nor is she indifferent to the kind of dwelling she desires—one that is pure of evil and sin. Now in vs. 5 wisdom is described as the "holy spirit of discipline" (*hagion gar pneuma paideias*). Although *paideia* in the wisdom tradition refers primarily to the discipline of study of the law and bending one's own efforts to a regime of life that is not particularly easy in its beginnings, it is here described as a "holy spirit," and this suggests that there is more than simply learning or practice involved. The very fact that it is called "holy" suggests that its origins are transcendent, godly—although the author will only work up to this affirmation clearly in vs. 7. Furthermore, the spirit is personified as a person who is drawn to certain things and flees from others. In this case the holy spirit of discipline flees deceit, senseless counsels and injustice. Clearly the holy spirit of wisdom or discipline is related to the ethical life, without which it cannot dwell in man. We may compare the rebuking of the holy spirit here with Is 63:10, the "grieving" of the holy spirit.

Then in vs. 6 wisdom is described as "a kindly spirit." The Greek *philanthrōpon pneuma* means literally a spirit that loves man, hence a spirit that has his best interests at heart. Precisely for that reason it will not allow the evil in man to go unnoticed. Then in vs. 7 the reason for this is given in a text that would be obscure if we did not have the context: "For the spirit of the Lord fills the world, is all-embracing and knows what man says." This text, used in the Catholic liturgy of Pentecost and applied there to the person of the Holy Spirit, means in the context here God's omnipresence and knowledge, a spirit which becomes judgment for the sinner. Putting all of this together, then, we can see that the three expressions, "holy spirit of discipline," "wisdom, a kindly spirit," and "the spirit of the Lord (that) fills the whole world" are really identical. However, there is a gradual progression from the spirit in a more restricted sense, as related to discipline, to a broader understanding of it as a lover of men, and finally identifying it as the spirit of the Lord himself. As in the book of Proverbs, the spirit belongs to wisdom's invitation to those who have not yet experienced it, but it will demand a change in the life of him who would enter its holy presence.

Notice finally how in this passage the conclusion of the hymn of exhortation introduces the notion of immortality, accessible to him who lives in "justice," that is, a loyal covenant union with the Lord.

The introduction of the idea of the spirit as related to judgment upon sin reappears in Wis 11:20, where *pneuma* is used to describe the ease with which God extinguishes his enemies. The "mighty spirit" is the wind of judgment bearing off the chaff, a usage we first met in Is 4:4 and 32:28. It is possible too that this meaning underlies 5:23: "A mighty wind shall confront them and a tempest winnow them out." The Greek for "mighty wind" may also be rendered "spirit of power" and understood to be the judicial spirit of God, as in 11:20.

The point about the holy spirit in Wisdom 1 is that while man may reject the spirit of wisdom by his choice of an immoral life—which means that the spirit will withdraw from him as a guest—he cannot choose this path with utter impunity because the spirit of God is also a spirit of judgment, like the all-consuming fire which will ultimately burn up whatever is not worthy of the holiness of God.

So open is the author to the working of the spirit among the gentiles that we may wonder whether in his view every man, gentile included, has this holy spirit from birth and that all he need do is not lose it by sin. But this view is an over-simplification of the expansive optimism of the book of Wisdom. Wisdom and the spirit of wisdom are not possessed by man because of his birth but rather are a gift bestowed upon him who asks.

Thus in chapter 7, where the author sets out to tell where wisdom is found, he takes the mouth of Solomon, Israel's proverbial wise-man. This indicates the fact, confirmed throughout the book, that God's wisdom is revealed through the sacred history of Israel. But Solomon also protests that he is by birth exactly like every other man (7:1-6). If he attained to wisdom, it was because he prayed for it: "Therefore I prayed, and prudence was given me; I pleaded and the spirit of Wisdom came to me" (7:7). Further on in 9:17, it is expressly stated that God's wisdom is knowable only through the gift of his holy spirit: "Who ever knew your counsel, except you had given Wisdom and sent your holy spirit from on high?" And while the author depicts God as a lover of all men, he also says, "There is nought God loves, be it not one who dwells with Wisdom" (7:28).

We now turn to the final text, the summit at which the Old Testament theologies of wisdom and of the spirit meet and are identified.

Wisdom 7:22b-8:1: Traits of Wisdom's Spirit

22. For in her is a spirit
    intelligent, holy, unique,
    manifold, subtle, agile,
    clear, unstained, certain,
    not baneful, loving the good, keen,
    unhampered, beneficent,
23. kindly, firm, secure, tranquil,
    all-powerful, all-seeing,
    and pervading all spirits,
    though they be intelligent, pure and very subtle.
24. For Wisdom is mobile beyond all motion,
    and she penetrates and pervades all things by reason of her
        purity.
25. For she is an aura of the might of God
    and a pure effusion of the glory of the Almighty;
    therefore nought that is sullied enters into her.
26. For she is the refulgence of eternal light,
    the spotless mirror of the power of God,
    the image of his goodness.
27. And she, who is one, can do all things,
    and renews everything while herself perduring;
    and passing into holy souls from age to age,
    she produces friends of God and prophets.
28. For there is nought God loves,
    be it not one who dwells with Wisdom.
29. For she is fairer than the sun
    and surpasses every constellation of the stars.
    Compared to light, she takes precedence;
30. for that, indeed, night supplants,
    but wickedness prevails not over Wisdom.
 1. Indeed, she reaches from end to end mightily
    and governs all things well. (NAB)

This is part of a much longer section exalting the glories of wisdom and insisting that wisdom is a gift of God. In 7:22 we are told that in widsom is a spirit. How is this relationship conceived? Probably it is a continuation of the personification of wisdom: she breathes out a breath or spirit (as in Prov 1:20 she poured it out). For this spirit the author finds twenty-one attributes, or three times seven, a perfect multiple of a perfect number. This spirit is therefore the most perfect imaginable, such as only a divine gift could be. It is the very heart and essence of wisdom. One thinks immediately of the gifts of the spirit upon the Messiah in Is 11:2-3, or the nine fruits of the Spirit given by Paul in Gal 5:22, or the multiple activities of charity in 1 Cor 13:4-8.

We shall meditate briefly on each of these traits of the spirit of wisdom, though we may find some almost synonymous with others. The author was more interested in reaching twenty-one, the number of perfection, than in discovering a fine distinction between each characteristic. Nevertheless, those who seek to know how the spirit touches every facet of human life will find a meditation on these attributes rewarding. We shall simply follow the NAB list, giving the Greek word in parenthesis.

Intelligent (noeron): The word is drawn from Greek literature, where it was a highly prized trait. It was an epithet of Apollo. The spirit of wisdom first of all enlightens the mind.

Holy (hagion): The spirit is separated, set apart as belonging to the divine sphere. It is consecrated and consecrating. Thus it is basically different from man, coming from elsewhere. It is holy because of wisdom's origin from God (7:25-26), her avoidance of all evil (1:5) and the holiness which she produces (7:27).

Unique (monogenes): Literally "only-begotten." Another way of stressing its difference, standing in a unique relationship with God, to whom it properly belongs. Wisdom is thus like an only child, in whom God has put all his delight. We recognize at once the Old Testament word which accompanies the revelation at Jesus' baptism. It means both "only-begotten" and "beloved."

Manifold (polymeres): In slight contrast with the preceding traits, wisdom is complex, or better, mysterious. There are so many facets to the spirit of wisdom that it can never be exhausted.

Subtle (lepton): In its most literal sense, which appears rarely in classical Greek, it means peeled, husked. It is used (in the *Iliad*) for barley that is threshed out, or of dust that is very small and fine, or, in Homer frequently, for garments that are thin, fine and delicate. One thinks of those long and ample Indian dresses, so sheer that six yards of Sari can be folded into a match-box. Euripides used the word for breezes that are light and gentle. In the metaphorical sense, which is the most common, it means subtle or refined. Thus Euripides uses it in *Medea* for a refined mind. And a few rare times it is applied to the voice or to harmony that is fine and delicate. Characterizing the spirit of wisdom as *lepton* means that it is lightsome, not easily caught and held. It is the opposite of gross and clumsy. As a light breeze is perceived only by him who is perceptive, or a delicate sound only by someone who has a very sensitive ear, so is wisdom. It requires docility, listening and constant openness. It is quite the opposite of the "bull in the china shop" or the swash-buckling attitude of the man who "has got it made."

Agile (eukinēton): It moves quickly and gracefully, like a deer. In classical Greek the word is used of troops that are mobile, or the soul that is more easily moved than the body. The spirit of wisdom is not static nor is it contained by this or that time or space. This trait of mobility is developed in vs. 24.

Clear (tranon): It is used in 10:21 for a clear utterance which wisdom gives to children. The thought seems to be that there is no ambiguity as to the meaning which wisdom brings to human life.

Unstained (amolynton): A Greek inscription of Agrigentum uses the word of a virgin. Wisdom, despite her contact with all the beings she pervades, remains unstained and undefiled.

Certain (saphes): The meaning is not greatly different from "clear" (*tranon*) above. Used of persons it can refer to a messenger who is unmistakable or distinct, a friend who is reliable, a scribe who is accurate. It is especially used for seers, oracles and prophets who are "sure, unerring." The spirit of wisdom brings certitude.

Not *baneful (apēmanton):* The word can be taken either as a passive, "unharmed, unhurt," or in the active sense, "unharming." It is used of things which, because of their immense power, might seem dangerous or harmful but which in reality are not. So likewise wisdom (taking the adjective in the active sense) never harms, despite its exalted nature.

Loving the good (philagathon): The word was already used by Aristotle to describe the virtuous man who loves the good rather than his own interests. The word suggests that wisdom seeks and responds to the good wherever it appears. It is not narrow-minded but universal in its response to the good. In the New Testament it is one of the characteristics which a presbyter should possess (Titus 1:8).

Keen (oxy): Having as its primary meaning "sharp," it is a favorite biblical word for a sharp sword (Ex 5:1; Rev 1:16; 2:12; 19:15). In a secondary sense it means quick, swift. Wisdom is effective in penetrating men, like the word of God which is as keen as a two-edged sword (Heb 4:12).

Unhampered (akolyton): The meaning is similar to keen, in the sense that its penetrating power is great.

Beneficent (euergetikon): The word refers to the kind of goodness of which one in a superior position, such as a king or God himself, can exercise toward those who are beneath in power or dignity.

Kindly (philanthrōpon): Meaning literally "loving man" or "loving mankind," it is used in profane Greek especially for the benevolence of God or of a ruler towards his subjects. In Wis 1:6 we have already met this word applied to the wisdom of God. God's wisdom is offered to all men and it comes to them in kindly fashion.

Firm (bebaion): Having the literal sense of a root or an anchor that is strong or secure, it is used in the figurative sense for that which is reliable, dependable or certain. The spirit of wisdom can be relied on.

Secure (asphales): Often a companion word for "firm" (*bebaion*).

Tranquil (amerimnon): In classical Greek this word sometimes means "free from care," "unconcern." Paul will use it in 1 Cor 7:32 when he says that he wants his readers to be free from worldly cares or anxieties. The way of wisdom is one that relieves and frees man from useless anxieties. We may compare this with Jesus' teaching about trust in God and freedom from the cares of this world.

All-powerful (pantodynamon): Compare love's ability to do all in 1 Cor 13:7.

All-seeing (panepiskopon): Literally foreseeing or overseeing all. There is nothing that escapes wisdom's universality.

And pervading all spirits, though they be intelligent, pure and very subtle: In distinction from the breath of life, the spirit which is wisdom is not in all things. However, as we have seen, it permeates thinking men who are morally pure and who open themselves to wisdom in prayer. Because of their disposition for the spirit, these men are called "spirits" (*pneumata*) here in vs. 23. On the one hand, men (or spirits) who are intelligent, pure and very subtle are so because the spirit of wisdom pervades them. On the other hand, the spirit of wisdom is something that is quite beyond such spirits and greatly superior to them, for it remains unchanged in the sharing out of itself and yet permeates all other spirits. Is the author of this passage thinking of any persons in particular by the word "spirits"? Perhaps he was thinking of Solomon himself who has been named implicitly in 7:7 as one who, realizing wisdom is a spirit from God, opens himself up to it in prayer.

In conclusion to this litany of wisdom's traits, we can say that according to the author of this book, the spirit shares both God's transcendence over the world and also his participation in the events of the world —particularly in the events of sacred history—as is detailed in chs. 7-12 and in 15:18-19:22. Some have said that in this book wisdom or the spirit is completely dehistoricized. Such a position is misguided. Rather, the spirit and wisdom are universalized as touching all of sacred history.

The meaning of the litany is expanded in the remainder of the passage. We should note particularly the fact that wisdom makes men friends of God and prophets (vs. 27). Does the author apply this simply to the past and mean to say that it was wisdom that made Abraham and Moses and the other great heroes friends of God and raised up the prophets and moved them to speak? Or does he mean that such is the effect of wisdom in every age—and therefore in his own and ours? The expression "from age to age" and the fact that this is an appeal to the author's contemporaries would favor the second alternative. Certainly the New Testament understands the spirit of God to make the disciples of Jesus friends of God (John 15:15; Rom 5:5) and prophets (Acts 2).

The wisdom tradition of the Old Testament has brought us to the threshold of the New. Beginning like a tiny spring in the secular city of man's experience, far removed from the sanctuary of the priest or the cave of the prophet, it gradually came to confess its need for a wisdom from on high, even when it had a sacred text to read and follow. Enriched by the prophetic stream, wisdom brought to the theology of the spirit, long thought to be the peculiar gift of the prophet, an important relationship to the experiential, the daily living of God's revealed way, his wisdom. Paul, for example, would never have thought of praying that his readers be filled with the spirit of wisdom and discernment for daily living (Phil 1:9; Col 1:9-10; Eph 1:15) had the way not been prepared by the wisdom tradition. At the same time, by exalting wisdom and the spirit to the point of personification, dramatizing poetically their activities toward men with divine traits, the wisdom tradition laid the foundation for the New Testament understanding of God as revealed in the person of his Son, the Word or Wisdom of God, and made real and experiential by their mutual personal gift, the Holy Spirit.

But to set the stage for the New Testament even more clearly we must first turn to the rabbis and the Qumran community, sources of two parallel traditions which began prior to New Testament times.

10
The Spirit
and the Torah

The publication of the Pentateuch around 400 B.C. had greater consequences upon the future than were immediately perceived. While the apocalyptic tradition saw salvation as essentially future, belonging to the age when God himself would break in and begin his reign, and while the wisdom tradition sought to find God in present experience, another, not wholly isolated but still distinguishable, tradition was developing which focused on the Torah or Law as the means of finding God, salvation, and even the kingdom of God here and now. We can call this the rabbinical tradition, or the tradition of the Pharisees.

The Pharisees were not, of course, the first official proponents of the law. From the most ancient times the giving of Torah was the responsibility of the priests (cf. Jer 18:18), and during the exile the priestly tradition was solidified as the official teaching for the new Israel—as we see already in the book of the priest-prophet Ezekiel. After the exile, the priests were the major authorities in Jerusalem, and Ezra's reading of the Law to the people at the Water Gate (Neh 8:1-12) typifies their activity during the restoration—the Law of Moses, interpreted by the priests (Neh 8:8), was the blueprint for the nation. As the years went on, a priestly party developed, called the Sadducees (after the priest Sadok), and, largely because of their conflict with a new lay radical party, their teaching became more and more entrenched in the written law as opposed to oral tradition which applied and extended the law to many situations not foreseen by the letter.

The new party, first known as the *Hasidim* ("Loyalists"), owed its origin to the time when the Maccabees were resisting Greek tyranny. They were willing to die for the law of God—and many did. Later, under John Hyrcanus, when the storm had cleared, these *Hasidim* appeared primarily as teachers of the law, or "rabbis." The rabbis were "lay theologians" and the Pharisee party was basically a lay party committed to the most fervent and exact observance of the law. They were, in fact, the liberals of the day, but not in the sense that they promoted laxity. On the contrary, the very title "Pharisees" ("Separated Ones") was given them by the people because their strict ascetical practices and minute observances set them apart from the common lot. Their liberalism was rather an interpretative liberalism, in the sense that they believed that the Torah was meant to cover the whole of life and not simply those areas for which there was a written law. It was meant to be not a museum relic (as the Sadducees began to consider it) but a source of direction encompassing the pious Jew's ongoing experience. Though written in the past, it could provide sufficient guidelines for the resolution of any new problem, and thus the oral tradition came in practice to have an equal authority with the written Torah. What this meant was that the teaching of the rabbis, though handed on orally, was law.

Now this is a very interesting development, for what we see the Pharisees concerned with is a problem faced by any religious tradition— what is the *now* meaning of the *past* word? The Pharisees found the *now* meaning via the oral teaching of the rabbis. With the fall of Jerusalem and the temple in 70 A.D., all parties were wiped out with the exception of the Pharisees. Had it not been for them, the oral Jewish tradition would have been preserved in no other way than in Christianity, which accepted many of the beliefs of Pharisaism but rejected many of its practices and especially its method of finding the *now* meaning of the Torah via a genealogy of rabbinical interpretations.

The rabbinical tradition is interesting both for parallels and contrasts with the New Testament. But as soon as we begin to examine it we run aground of one gigantic difficulty. The oral traditions began to be written down only centuries after the Christian era. How then can we be sure about the date of a given teaching? And if both Christian and rabbinic teaching grew out of the Old Testament and, from the first century on, ran parallel to one another, how much influence did one tradition have on the other? These questions are notoriously difficult to answer, and in this study we shall not attempt to do so. We shall simply review briefly the rabbinical teachings for their comparative value with the New Testament and to see what role a heavily teaching-oriented tradition, interested in keeping that tradition alive, gives to the spirit.

First of all, concerning the constitution of man, we find in the rabbinic writings a development of the distinction between the spirit and the body, with a belief not only in the immortality of the soul but also in its pre-existence.[1] Man consists of a body derived from earth and a spirit

---

[1] For more detail than is possible here, the reader is referred to the long article by E. Sjöberg in Kittel's *Theological Dictionary of the New Testament* (trans. and ed., G. W. Bromiley, Grand Rapids: Eerdmans, 1968) VI, p. 377-388. We are indebted to this study for some of the material and references given in this chapter.

derived from heaven: "Man's soul (*nephesh*) derives from heaven, and his body from earth" (*Sifre Deut*. 306 on 32:2). Since this spirit comes from God, it is sometimes called "the spirit of God" or the "holy spirit of God" even when referring to a constituent part of man (Targum J. I Gen 6:3). Because the spirit in man is something different from the body, it can at times function independently of the body even after its union with it. According to Pirqe Rabbi Eliezer, during sleep the spirit (*ruah*) roams through the whole world and foretells future events in dreams, or, according to another text, the soul (*neshamah*) mounts to heaven and fetches new life for man (*Gen. R*. 14, 9 on 2:7).

After death, the spirit of man goes to the place appointed for it, where it lives on. This is clearly a development beyond the Old Testament texts we reviewed, where the most that was said was that at death the life-breath returned to God from whom it originally came. Theories differed as to what or where this place was—the seventh heaven, the heavenly store chamber, under the throne of God, or in paradise. The souls of the unjust are either banished to Gehenna or are condemned to wander about without rest. At the resurrection the spirit of the just is brought back into its sheath, the body, and thus "God sets his spirit in man"—but it is hard to determine whether this is the spirit of man returning or an effect of God's own spirit. At any rate the image of resurrection in Ezekiel which the prophet meant simply as a metaphor for the restoration of the nation is used now for the bodily resurrection of the just, which is an effect of the spirit of God: "God said of Israel, 'In this world my spirit has put wisdom in you, but in the future my spirit will make you live again, as it is said, I will put my spirit in you that you may live,' Ez 37:14" (*Exod. R*. 48 (102d); cf. also *Gen. R*. 96 (60d); 26, 6 on 6:30).

The expression "holy spirit," which we occasionally encountered in the Old Testament, becomes a commonplace among the rabbis to express the divine revelation which is found in the words of the Torah or on the lips of the prophets. A word of the Torah is a word of the holy spirit, since every word of scripture is divinely inspired. The holy spirit not only inspired the prophets; even the acts of the righteous, recorded in the Bible, are "done in the holy spirit." (*Gen. R*. 97 on 49:27). This does not mean the holy spirit inspired their ethical life but that their actions were indeed prophecies of what was to come.

This amounts to saying that the great work of the holy spirit, the spirit of prophecy, is past. It is expressly stated that the holy spirit departed from Israel after the last prophets Haggai, Zechariah and Malachi. It was even accepted by many that the holy spirit was one of the things which the first temple had and the second temple lacked.

As for the future, the spirit would be upon the messiah, as foretold by Isaiah. Rabbi Shimeon ben Laqish applies the text of Gen 1:2 about the spirit hovering over the waters to the spirit that will brood over the Messiah (*Gen. R.* 2, 4 on 1:2). The spirit would also renew the people, replacing their heart of stone with the spirit of the Lord; and, as Joel prophesied, in the final time all the people will be prophets. We have already discussed the role of the spirit in the resurrection of the just in the age to come.

But the present time for the rabbis is thought of as the age without the holy spirit. The closest man may come is the Torah, the supreme divine gift, which contains the words inspired by the holy spirit. Can we discover any more closely how the relationship between the Torah and the holy spirit is conceived?

To enter the kingdom of God certain conditions are necessary. One must belong to the holy people who are formed by the law and follow it. (*Aboth* 2:7; 2:11; *Sanh.* 10:1; *Ber* 28b). There are even some passages that suggest that man needs the divine gift to follow the law (*b. Ber* 16b). It is also said that in the future age men will be able to keep the command because of the gift of God's spirit. But there is no text anywhere to indicate that the justice or justification of men before God is the work of the holy spirit. The gift of the spirit is not (in the present age at least) the power by which one leads a righteous life but a reward for living it. Perhaps this is because the holy spirit is viewed more as the spirit of prophecy than as the ethical spirit. "He who undertakes a commandment in faith, is worthy that the holy spirit rest upon him" (Rabbi Nechemiah, *M. Ex.* 15, 1; Str-Bill. III, 135). "He who sacrifices himself for Israel will receive the wages of honor, greatness, and the holy spirit" (*Num. R.* 15, 20 on 11:16). Finally we may quote the so-called chain-saying of Rabbi Pinchas ben Yair: "Zeal (in obedience to the Law) leads to physical purity, this leads to cultic purity, this to abstemiousness, this to holiness, this to humility, this to abhorrence of sin, this to piety, this to the holy spirit, this to the resurrection . . ." (Sota 9, 15; cf. Str-Bill. I, 194). Though there are some rare exceptions in which this or that rabbi is said to have acted or spoken through the holy spirit, the general teaching is that the voice of prophecy is now past, there is no inspiration comparable to the written law, and what the spirit now wants must be sought humbly in study and in observance. One must thus merit the gift of the spirit; but it is unlikely that one would receive him in this life, for even when it is said that this or that rabbi merited the holy spirit, it is added that the spirit was not given him because the present generation is not worthy of the holy spirit (T. Sota 13, 3f. par. Str-Bill. I, 129).

There is a strange paradox in the rabbis' teaching. On the one hand, the oral law is authoritative, and no really pious Jew could claim to ob-serve only the written law without also observing the oral law which brought the written law more concretely into the circumstances of one's daily life. And yet, the age of inspiration is past, and even the teaching of the rabbis is not comparable to it. One now lives off the past age of inspiration through study, teaching, and observance. One is reminded of certain later ages of the church where the dominant mood was similar— the age of the Spirit is past and continuity with it is assured adequately through the documents of the past, through a teaching authority and obedient observance.

Much more could be said about the rabbinical view of the spirit, but the brief overview here given will suffice to show not only the simi-larities but above all the major differences we shall see in the New Tes-tament, where the Holy Spirit, both as charismatic and as sanctifying, is the present possession of all Christians and the first fruits of the life of the resurrection. Little wonder then that one of the major criticisms of Christians by the rabbis was the Christian claim that what was promised for the age to come had already burst upon the present age.

11
The Spirit in the
Community at Qumran

The leadership of the Jerusalem priesthood had not been sufficient to satisfy the spiritual needs of the Pharisees. Even in the priestly party itself there was a split, caused probably in 152 B.C. when Jonathan, brother of Judas Maccabaeus, accepted appointment as high priest of the Jews by the Syrian king. Jonathan was not a legitimate Zadokite, i.e., a member of the high priestly family. While many of the priestly party, soon to be known as the Sadducees, supported Jonathan for their own political advantage, this move was, in the eyes of the more religiously oriented priests, an unforgivable sin. A number of them, led by a mysterious figure known as the Teacher of Righteousness, fled Jerusalem to the Judean desert on the northwest bank of the Dead Sea and there formed a community which they considered to be the only true Israel. They sought to return heart and soul to the covenant and to observe the law in a purity which the secular world and especially the corrupt leadership in Jerusalem did not permit. This community, probably to be identified with the Essenes, lasted from around 140 B.C. until the Roman suppression of the Jewish revolt in 70 A.D. Possibly foreseeing the consequences of the latter event, the covenanters of Qumran seem to have hid their library—containing Old Testament scriptures and many of their other community documents—in caves in the countryside round about. Except for one or two possible disturbances over the years, there they lay until 1947, when a Bedouin looking for a stray goat tossed a pebble into one of those caves and struck a stone jar. It was the beginning of the discovery of what have been called the Dead Sea Scrolls.

These documents, still being published, have yielded precious information about the life and development of thought in a period immediately preceding and paralleling New Testament times. They will tell us what at least one fervent segment of Israel believed about the spirit at this time. We can distinguish three different ways in which *spirit* is used in the writings of this community.

116

1. The Two Spirits

In the "Community Rule" or the "Manual of Discipline," as it is also called (1 QS), there is a long section about the "two spirits" which contend for man's allegiance (1 QS 3:13-4:26). Sharpening the very old concept we already met in the books of Samuel and Kings, the document holds that not only the good spirit but also the bad spirit is a creature of God. These two spirits contend for the heart of man, that is, for his ethical life (1 QS 4:23). The functions of the good spirit are

> the enlightenment of the heart of man, and that all the paths of
> true righteousness may be made straight before him, and that
> fear of the laws of God may be instilled in his heart: a spirit of
> humility, patience, abundant charity, unending goodness, un-
> derstanding, and intelligence; (a spirit of) mighty wisdom
> which trusts in all the deeds of God and leans on His great
> lovingkindness; a spirit of discernment in every purpose, of
> zeal for just laws, of holy intent with steadfastness of heart, of
> great charity towards all the sons of truth, of admirable purity
> which detests all unclean idols, of humble conduct sprung from
> an understanding of all things, and of faithful concealment of
> the mysteries of God. (1 QS 4:2-6)[1]

A similar litany is given for functions of the wicked spirit (1 QS 4:9-13).

Read from a Christian perspective, these two spirits may too readily be identified as the "good impulse" or the "bad impulse" which Paul inherited from rabbinic Judaism and adapted to his purposes in the distinction between the flesh and the spirit as forces conflicting within man (Rom 7:13-25). But in a number of places in the scrolls, the two spirits seem to be personal beings, that is, angels. In fact, the above passages about the good and the evil spirit in man are introduced thus:

> [God] has appointed for [man] two spirits in which to walk
> until the time of His visitation: the spirits of truth and false-
> hood. Those born of truth spring from a fountain of light, but
> those born of falsehood spring from a source of darkness. All
> the children of righteousness are ruled by the Prince of Light

---

[1] All the English translations from the scrolls in this chapter are those of G. Vermes, *The Dead Sea Scrolls in English* (Baltimore: Penguin, 1962) with the exception of 1 QS 2:25b-3:12, from the same author's *Discovery in the Judean Desert* (New York: Desclee, 1956). Used with permission.

and walk in the ways of light; but all the children of falsehood are ruled by the Angel of Darkness and walk in the ways of darkness.

The Angel of Darkness leads all the children of righteousness astray, and until his end, all their sin, iniquities, wickedness, and all their unlawful deeds are caused by his dominion in accordance with the mysteries of God. Every one of their chastisements, and every one of the seasons of their distress, shall be brought about by the rule of his persecution; for all his allotted spirits seek the overthrow of the sons of light.

But the God of Israel and His Angel of Truth will succour all the sons of light. For it is He who created the spirits of Light and Darkness and founded every action upon them and established every deed [upon] their [ways]. (1 QS 3:13-26)

The two spirits seem therefore to be both outside man (as angels) and within him as forces. Each spirit leads to a consummation—the "spirit of truth" to healing, bliss and fruitfulness, the spirit of iniquity to destruction, damnation and disgrace.

But even the sons of justice who are guided by the spirit of truth cannot avoid all contamination by the evil spirit, and so in the final consummation God perfects their cleansing with his "truth," with the "spirit of truth" or with his "holy spirit":

Then truth, which has wallowed in the ways of wickedness during the dominion of falsehood until the appointed time of judgment, shall arise in the world forever. God will then purify every deed of Man with his truth; He will refine for Himself the human frame by rooting out all spirit of falsehood from the bounds of his flesh. He will cleanse him of all wicked deeds with the spirit of holiness; like purifying waters He will shed upon him the spirit of truth (to cleanse him) of all abomination and falsehood. And he shall be plunged into the spirit of purification that he may instruct the upright in the knowledge of the Most High and teach the wisdom of the sons of heaven to the perfect of way. (1 QS 4:20-22)

Note that through this cleansing the just receive a share in the wisdom of the angels, the paradisal lordship of Adam ("Man"), and a sealing in their election for an eternal covenant. The "spirit of truth" or "the holy spirit" here means God's revealing spirit, purifying the just at the final consummation.

2. The Spirit as the Creative Self of Each Man

The Qumran literature shares with the Old Testament the belief that man lives by God's breath, that is, his spirit. And thus sometimes the word *ruah* or spirit means simply the self. But its usage in this sense also reflects a kind of predestinationism. God by his creation predestined all spirits either to justice or injustice, with the result that man as flesh, that is, without the spirit of God, is capable of no justice, and he can live in the knowledge of God and in obedience only if God outfits him from birth with a spirit committed to justice. Thus the spirit of the just appears as a divine gift to which the same functions are ascribed as to the divine spirit. However, if the just possess the good spirit from birth onward, as long as they are outside the community the spirit is polluted and needs an act of cleansing upon entrance into the community: "Thou hast cleansed a perverse spirit of great sin that it may stand with the hosts of the holy ones, and that it may enter into community with the congregation of the sons of heaven" (1 QH 3:21; cf. also 11:12). Through this cleansing of his spirit the candidate shares in the revelation given to the community. The cleansing of the spirit takes place by the gift of the divine spirit, and this leads us to the third meaning of "spirit" in the scrolls.

3. The Holy Spirit Bestowed upon Entrance into the Community

2:25b. Whoever shall disdain to enter 26. [into the Covenant of Go]d that he may walk in the stubbornness of his heart, [let him not enter] into the Community of His Truth, for his soul 3:1. has rejected the intelligent instructions of righteous laws; he has not held fast to the Restorer of his life; may he not be reckoned with the upright. 2. Let him not bring his knowledge, his mind, and his property into the Council of the Community, for all his doings are wicked strife, and defilement 3. his quietness. Let him not be justified because of the plotting of his stubborn heart. Let him look upon darkness as though upon the ways of light; to the fount of perfection 4. let him not approach. Let him not be purified by atonement, nor washed by the waters of purification; may he not be sanctified in pools 5. and rivers; may he not be cleansed with any water for washing. Let him remain impure, impure for as long as he rejects the decrees 6. of God and does not correct his ways in the

Community of His Counsel. For it is through the spirit of God's true counsel concerning the ways of man that all his iniquities will be atoned 7. so that he may look upon the life-giving light; united through the holy spirit to His truth, man shall be cleansed of all 8. his iniquities; because of an upright and humble spirit his sin shall be atoned; through the submission of his soul to all God's ordinances his flesh shall be cleansed 9. when he shall be sprinkled with water for impurity and be sanctified by waters of purification. He shall direct his steps so as to walk perfectly 10. in all God's ways, as He has commanded to their solemn assemblies. Let him not swerve either to the right or to the left, nor 11. transgress a single one of God's words. Then shall he find grace before God because of the agreeable atonements and this will become for him a Covenant of 12. eternal Community. (1 QS 2:25b-3:12)

This passage is concerned with the requirements for entering the community, which is thought of as a holy place. He who does not enter it (hence everyone outside the community) is considered unclean in the light of the provisions of Lev 13:45-46. Righteousness, perfection, purity and holiness can be found only within the holy community and only through the spirit abiding in the community. The functions of the spirit expressly named are those of cleansing, expiation, justice and humility. Note that in vs. 6 the spirit is called "the spirit of God's true counsel" and paralleled to it in vs. 7 is the expression "united through the holy spirit to his truth." The Hebrew for truth here is *emeth*. It is the revelation given to the community, and that means concretely the Torah and the community's inspired interpretation of it. The holy spirit unites the neophyte to this revelation and gives him the possibility of observing all that it demands, as is indicated by the further description of the spirit as the spirit of justice and humility (3:8). This spirit obviously comes from God. Is it the good angel, the Prince of Light who presides over all just spirits? We cannot be sure. In any case, the spirit becomes so much the property of the faithful community member that it can be translated "disposition." The two meanings, divine (angelic?) spirit and human disposition, coalesce here.

Note further that the spirit also works expiation and cleansing. This is a remarkable spiritualization of the cultic teaching that sins were to be expiated by washings and sacrifice. The community certainly continued cultic washings, but according to the teaching here, these washings were useless without the holy spirit of revelation. We find this view expressed even more clearly in 1 QS 9:3-5:

> When these become members of the Community in Israel according to all these rules, they shall establish the spirit of holiness according to everlasting truth. They shall atone for guilty rebellion and for sins of unfaithfulness that they may obtain lovingkindness for the Land without the flesh of holocausts and the fat of sacrifice. And prayer rightly offered shall be as an acceptable fragrance of righteousness, and perfection of way as a delectable free-will offering.

The "spirit of holiness" is described here as the foundation or basis for the holy community. Because it is the spirit which reveals to the community God's true way, it is the source of expiation and perfect sacrifice, and this amounts to the right conduct and the inspired praise which in the community replaces the sacrifices of the Jerusalem temple.

The Qumran hymns (1 QH) confirm and complete this view. God is often praised for the knowledge he has bestowed on the community—that is, the grace of knowing his plan of salvation. This knowledge is attributed to the "spirit of knowledge" (14:25), to God's holy spirit (12:12; 14:12f.) or to the spirit of God which God has placed in the one who prays (12:11f; 13:18f). Most significantly, this knowledge given by the spirit is not an extraordinary charism given to special members but rather it is the endowment of each member simply because of his entry into the community. It is a saving knowledge, too, because it also means the power to act according to God's truth and justice. Thus it is said that God through his holy spirit "strengthens" or "rejoices" the petitioner so that he may stand in God's truth (9:32; 16:7).

The summit of the spiritual piety of Qumran is expressed in the last hymn we shall examine (16:1-12):

> Because I know all these things
>> my tongue shall utter a reply.
> Bowing down and [confessing all] my transgressions,
>> I will seek [Thy] spirit [of knowledge];
> cleaving to Thy spirit of [holiness],
>> I will hold fast to the truth of Thy Covenant,
> that [I may serve] Thee in truth and wholeness of heart,
>> and that I may love [Thy Name].
>
> Blessed art Thou, O Lord,
>> Maker [of all things and mighty in] deeds:
>> all things are Thy work!
> Behold, Thou art pleased to favour [Thy servant],

and hast graced me with Thy spirit of mercy
and [with the radiance] of Thy glory.
Thine, Thine is righteousness,
    for it is Thou who has done all [these things]!

.   .   .   .

And I know that man is not righteous
    except through Thee,
and therefore I implore Thee
    by the spirit which Thou has given [me]
    to perfect Thy [favours] to Thy servant [for ever].
purifying me by Thy holy spirit,
    and drawing me near to Thee by Thy grace
    according to the abundance of Thy mercies

.   .   .   .

[Grant me] the place [of Thy lovingkindness]
    which [Thou hast] chosen for them that love Thee
    and keep [Thy commandments,
that they may stand] in Thy presence [for] ever.

In this remarkable passage, the spirit appears both as already given and yet further sought. The petitioner praises God for the spirit of mercy already bestowed. He acknowledges that all righteousness or justice is God's alone and if the faithful covenanter stands in righteousness it is only by God's gift. But there is a further purification by the spirit desired, so that the faithful may draw near to God and stand eternally in his presence. Even more clearly than the texts of the community rule examined above (1 QS 3:6-12; 9:3-5), to the spirit here are attributed in a most remarkable and spiritualized way the cultic functions of purification, appeasement and entry into the divine presence.

Conclusion

Though the Qumran sect had peculiarities of its own, dedicating itself as it did full time and in a community setting to the life of contemplation, it attained a remarkable spiritual insight, which combined much of the best in the apocalyptic, wisdom and rabbinic traditions.

The community could be called an apocalyptic community in the sense that it believed the final times were near. These would be introduced by a gigantic battle between the "sons of light" and "the sons of darkness," an angelic warfare in which the community would be fighting on the side of the hosts of heaven. If the eschatology of Qumran did not give a clear place to the resurrection of the body, it did associate the holy spirit with a final purification of the just, who are, of course, the members of the community.

With the rabbinical tradition the Qumran theology coincided in the central place given to the law and its observance. But it is not the Pharisaic interpretation of the law but the community's interpretation which is authoritative. Scripture is fulfilled in the persons and events, past, present, and future, of the community. Moreover—and here the Qumran tradition departs even more from the rabbinic to join the wisdom tradition—the inspired understanding of scripture's meaning is the effect of the "spirit of truth" or the "holy spirit." While this certainly does not exclude the teaching of the masters in the monastery, a much greater stress is laid upon the fact that the covenanter's inner disposition and understanding is due to the gift of God's spirit. This holy spirit also effects cleansing and justification, making possible the perfect sacrifice of praise. Quite clearly, man's ability to stand in God's gracious approval is an effect of God's grace. If the "grace" aspect of Qumran is pushed to a predestinarian extreme, it at least provides a counter-balance to the kind of justification by works which viewed the holy spirit as something which very holy men might merit. For the Dead Sea covenanters the holy spirit is less the prophetic spirit than the spirit of inner revelation and understanding, and the purifying spirit. It is, in any case, a gift from without, though in individual passages it is not always easy to determine to what extent the gift is thought to be the breath or power of God himself, to what extent the holy angel, and to what extent a disposition put into the faithful. The notion of the championing angel will become helpful when we study the Paraclete in John. While in none of the senses we have examined does the term "holy spirit" attain the understanding the Christian community later came to, we cannot but marvel at the spiritual depth reached by the Qumran community, especially regarding the revelational and purifying character of the "holy spirit." The piety of Qumran reflects in this regard both the tradition of wisdom as God's gift and the deep spirituality of Psalm 51, confessing that righteousness before God can only be the effect of God's own gift, humbly sought in prayer.

This purification by the holy spirit takes place in a primary and radical way upon entry into the community. The "holy spirit" abides in the holy community, and is the possession of all. This anticipates to some degree the Pauline view of the church as the holy community, successor to the temple in which God's spirit dwells. But there is a rigid exclusivism and separation about the Qumran sect which we will not find in the New Testament, where the Holy Spirit impels to a mission of preaching the gospel to every creature and to embracing all men in love.

PART II
THE NEW TESTAMENT

Introduction

As we pause to catch our breath at this point in our ascent, looking backwards at the topography of the Old Testament and the intertestamental literature, we are rewarded with a truly impressive view. But it is dwarfed by the kind of Mount Everest that looms ahead of us, the New Testament. How are we to approach it? Method here is, in fact, as difficult as it is important. The complexity comes from the very obvious difference we must note in the New Testament between historical sequence and literary sequence. The historical sequence of the events of the first century, at least in general outline, is familiar to us—Jesus' birth, life, ministry, death; the resurrection event, its preaching by the church in Judea and then throughout the world, the fall of Jerusalem and the destruction of the temple in 70 A.D.—and so on. By literary sequence we mean the order in which the New Testament writings appeared. And here is a paradox. The letters of Paul, which are concerned with problems in his churches rather than with the events of Jesus' life, are the earliest documents in time of appearance. The gospels, on the other hand, which treat the ministry and message of Jesus, appear after Paul, one of them, that of John, at the end of the century. The later documents concern the earlier events. Which sequence, then, shall we follow —the historical or the literary? Since the early church considered the written gospels her "final word" about the Christian message even though they dealt with the earliest historical period, we shall follow her lead and accept the literary sequence as our method. This also corresponds to the sequence many Christians are accustomed to in their liturgy, where the worshipping community listens first to a reading from the epistles and then stands in reverence to hear the gospel of Jesus Christ as the final word.

12
The Spirit
in Paul's Early Letters:
Thessalonians and Philippians

1 Thes 1:4-6: The Spirit and Receiving the Word

> 4. For we know, brethren beloved by God, that he has chosen
> you; 5. for our gospel came to you not only in word, but also in
> power and in the Holy Spirit and with full conviction. You
> know what kind of men we proved to be among you for your
> sake. 6. And you became imitators of us and of the Lord, for
> you received the word in much affliction, with joy inspired by
> the Holy Spirit. (RSV)

In this earliest document of the New Testament, written around 51
A.D., the Spirit of the Lord is not only called "the Holy Spirit" but is
mentioned in such a fashion as to evoke a well known element of the
Christian experience. Paul recalls the first days of his evangelization of
the community at Thessalonica. He knows with certitude that their
response to the good news was the effect of a divine election, for it was
accompanied by signs "of power, the Holy Spirit and firm conviction."
At this point the Holy Spirit seems to be the charismatic Spirit promised to accompany the apostolic preaching (Acts 1:8) by signs of healing,
deliverance and miracles but also by utter conviction in the apostle's
manner of preaching. This power in Paul's evangelizing was matched by
a similar firmness on the part of the Thessalonians, manifested not only
by perseverance under persecution but by joy. Thus the first appearance
of the Holy Spirit in the New Testament literature shows that it is the
source of charismatic power and spiritual joy—an interesting combination of what Paul will later call the *gifts* and the *fruits* of the Spirit. In
the context, the meaning is that power and conviction in the preacher,
and joyful endurance in the believers, is a sign of the presence of the
Holy Spirit, which is, in turn, the sign and seal of authentic divine election.

1 Thes 4:1-8: The Ethic of the Holy Spirit

> 1. Finally, brethren, we beseech and exhort you in the Lord
> Jesus, that as you learned from us how you ought to live and to
> please God, just as you are doing, you do so more and more.
> 2. For you know what instructions we gave you through the
> Lord Jesus. 3. For this is the will of God, your sanctification:
> that you abstain from immorality; 4. that each one of you
> know how to control his own body in holiness and honor,
> 5. not in the passion of lust like heathen who do not know
> God; 6. that no man transgress, and wrong his brother in this
> matter, because the Lord is an avenger in all these things, as
> we solemnly forewarned you. 7. For God has not called us for
> uncleanness, but in holiness. 8. Therefore whoever disregards
> this, disregards not man but God, who gives his Holy Spirit to
> you. (RSV)

After recalling the beginnings of the church in Thessalonica (1:4-
3:5), expressing his desire to see them again (3:6-10) and offering a
prayer for their continued growth (3:11-13), Paul launches into the
moral exhortation of the letter with our passage. The principle is that
God wills their continuing sanctification. Here this implies a very specific expectation in the area of sexual morality. However, it is not clear
whether in vss. 4-6 Paul is referring to sexual control in general or to the
more specific case of forbidden marriages with close blood relatives. In
vs. 4 the expression is literally "to acquire his vessel." Many understand
this to mean "to take a wife." Others invoke a more common meaning
of the Greek word *skeuos* as a metaphor for the body in general (2 Cor
4:7; 2 Tim 2:20, 21; Rom 9:22, 23). Since the whole passage vss. 3-8 has
a general theme, the more likely meaning is that of sexual morality in its
broadest sense. The pagan society in which Paul's readers lived considered fornication a perfectly legitimate satisfaction of one's sexual needs.
The ethic of the Holy Spirit is different. Verse 6 has to do with cove-
tousness, whether in matters of sex or of material goods. Paul will one
day list self-control as one of the fruits of the Spirit (Gal 5:22).

Most interesting here, however, is the triple motivation for this self-
control: (1) The Lord—here meaning the Lord Jesus—avenges such conduct. (2) God—and by this term Paul habitually means the Father—
calls to holiness. (3) God gives his Holy Spirit. Paul is alluding to Ez
36:27, "I will put (Greek: *give*) my spirit within you and make you live
by my statutes, careful to observe my decrees." Paul is probably thinking too of Ez 37:14, "I will give my spirit within you . . ." In Ezekiel,

as we saw, the gift of the spirit results in right moral conduct. Paul reinforces this idea by adding the adjective "Holy" to "Spirit," thus placing his moral teaching in the Christian tradition about the Holy Spirit already given. Here, however, Paul uses the present tense of the verb: God "is giving" his Holy Spirit. The gift abides so really that it is being constantly given. The gift is therefore not a thing like a toy or a tool which contains only a remembrance of the giver. It is rather like the constant embrace of the Giver himself. But man's freedom is such that at any moment he may reject this gift, and he can do so when he turns from the ethical demands of the Lord Jesus.

This text is a precious one, for it shows not only that to be a Christian is to have an identifiable code of conduct, but it roots that conduct in an experiential Trinitarian life identified with the Holy Spirit received as a gift constantly being given by the Father.

1 Thes 5:19-22: Stifling the Spirit

19. Do not quench the Spirit, 20. do not despise prophesying, 21. but test everything; hold fast what is good, 22. abstain from every form of evil. (RSV)

This passage belongs to a series of short moral counsels with which Paul concludes his letter. In vss. 18-22 the counsels become rhythmic. Christians are to give thanks in everything, for this is what the Father wants them to do in Christ Jesus (vs. 18). Then, they should not "quench" the Spirit. The Greek verb is often used for putting out a fire, though the same word may be used for water that dries up. In the figurative sense it means to suppress, stifle, or, as in our translation, to "quench." The Spirit here is not qualified as the Holy Spirit, probably because what Paul has directly in view is not the individual or collective ethical life, as in the preceding passage, but the charismatic manifestation of the Spirit in the community. If Paul makes this a counsel, it can only be because the activity of the Spirit does depend to some extent on an encouraging atmosphere. The Spirit can be stifled if enough individuals in the community choose to do so. What is at issue here is particularly the Spirit of prophecy, as the next expression indicates: "Do not despise prophecies." Obviously charismatic, the Thessalonian community experienced the active use of the gift of prophecy. Paul's counsel is not to suppress these charismatic expressions but to discern them and to hold to what is good (a counsel reiterated in 1 Cor 14). In vs. 22, Paul's addition of the word *eidous*, "form" or "appearance" or "semblance" indicates he is still thinking of a manifestation of prophecy and the need for discernment.

1 Thes 5:23: Spirit, Soul and Body

> May the God of peace himself make you holy through and through. And may your whole being, spirit, soul and body, be kept sound and blameless at the coming of our Lord Jesus Christ. (Author's translation)

Paul draws his letter to a close with a liturgical blessing, asking that God, the author of all wholeness, make his readers holy "through and through." To further describe the total extent of God's sanctifying action he describes the Christian as "spirit, soul, and body." Spirit (*pneuma*) here, of course, is not the Holy Spirit but something in man. It has doubtless the meaning "life-breath" we encountered so often in the Old Testament. But placing it alongside "soul" (*psychē*), Paul seems to indicate a distinction of the two, for obviously they are not synonyms. It is highly likely he has in mind the elements in the creation of man in Gen 2:7—*spirit* as the life-breath (*ruah*) from God, *soul* as the animating principle (*nephesh*) and body as the material element relating man to the earth (*adamah*). It is not, of course, a philosophical trichotomy that Paul is implying here but simply man's relationship to material creation (*body*), over which he stands as the highest of living being (*soul*) because he has received his life from God and is therefore related to him (*spirit*). Man functions in wholeness when all three of these elements interact properly. In 1 Cor 2:13-15 Paul contrasts the man who lives by the spirit with the "natural man"—the man who lives only by the *psychē*, the "soul." The latter cannot perceive or appreciate the things of God, because his horizon is limited to what his senses and his human mind can see. This "psychic" man is incomplete. Paul prays that his readers will live the life of the spirit, source of life even for the soul and the body —and that they will be found in this state at Christ's final coming in glory.

2 Thes 2:1-3: A False Spirit

> 1. Now concerning the coming of our Lord Jesus Christ and our assembling to meet him, we beg you, brethren, 2. not to be quickly shaken in mind or excited, either by spirit or by word,

or by letter purporting to come from us, to the effect that the day of the Lord has come. 3. Let no one deceive you in any way . . . (RSV)

With most scholars, we consider the second letter to the Thessalonians to be an authentic letter of Paul's written about six months after the first. One of its purposes was to clarify Paul's earlier teaching and to clear up some confusion in the community about the second coming of the Lord Jesus. For our purposes here it suffices to note that "spirit" here refers to a false and misleading prophecy. The NAB translates "oracular utterance." Not only does this text confirm Paul's directive that all prophecy should be discerned (1 Thes 5:21) but it also shows that Paul's teaching authority prevails over any contrary prophecy.

2 Thes 2:11: A Misleading Tendency

11. Therefore God is sending upon them a perverse spirit which leads them to give credence to falsehood . . . (NAB)

This passage must be read in the light of what we said about God "sending an evil spirit" on occasion in the Old Testament (cf. 1 Sam 16:14-23). Paul does not use *pneuma* but *energeia* here, and we should note that the reason why these men are said to be under the evil influence is that they "refused to accept the love of the truth to be saved" (vs. 10).

2 Thes 2:13: Sanctification by the Spirit

13. But we are bound to give thanks to God always for you, brethren beloved by the Lord, because God chose you from the beginning to be saved, through sanctification by the Spirit and belief in the truth. (RSV)

There is first of all a textual problem here, because some manuscripts read "as firstfruits" instead of "from the beginning" (a difference of only one letter in the Greek). In either case, the salvation for which the Christian readers have been chosen is "through sanctification of Spirit and faith in the truth." Spirit here could conceivably refer to the spirit of the Christian which is sanctified. Such a usage is surely possible (see 1 Thes 5:23 above). But it is more likely that the spirit here is the

Holy Spirit, the title "holy" being dropped to avoid redundancy with "holiness" (or "sanctification") already mentioned. If salvation is generally in Paul the future consummation to which the Christian looks forward, this sanctification by the Spirit is clearly a presently experienced reality—in fact it is simultaneous with coming to "believe in the truth." This text makes clear what was already implied in 1 Thes 1:6, that the Holy Spirit does not belong to a "second moment" of the Christian life but is there from the very beginning. Texts such as this must be kept in mind when discussing the so-called "baptism in the Holy Spirit." If the Holy Spirit is described as coming on a later occasion to one or more Christians, it does not mean he was previously absent.

Philippians 1:19: The Holy Spirit as "Equipment"

> 19. Yes, and I shall rejoice. For I know that through your prayers and the help of the Spirit of Jesus Christ this will turn out for my deliverance. (RSV)

Paul, imprisoned, considers the possibility that his death may be imminent and thus he may not live to see "the day of the Lord." The "this" which will turn out for his deliverance probably refers to Paul's imprisonment and the fact that some preachers are preaching from impure motives. Paul now quotes from the Greek text of Job 13:16: "This will turn out for my deliverance." Does his deliverance refer to release from prison or to salvation in the final judgment before Christ? We cannot be sure, but in either case there are two instruments which Paul considers effective to change an otherwise bad and contrary situation into salvation: the prayers of his readers and the "support" or "help" of the Spirit of Jesus Christ. Notice that the Spirit is described here as the Spirit of Jesus Christ rather than the Holy Spirit or the Spirit of God or of the Lord. The suggestion is that the support Paul expects to receive from the Spirit is the very same that Jesus received in his own trial. The Greek *epichoregia* means "equipment," what soldiers would call "gear." It means all the protective uniform and weapons which, in this case, will enable Paul to stand in the struggle, whether the trial be human or divine. There may be an allusion here to the saying of Jesus that the Holy Spirit would give the disciples in the hour of trial whatever they need to say. This text is a distant preparation for Rom 8:28: "We know that for those who love God, he makes all things work together unto good." Here, it is the prayers of Christians and the support of the Holy Spirit that enable this transformation to happen.

Conclusion

These first New Testament documents introduce us to the Holy Spirit as a phenomenon so well known in the Pauline communities as to form the reference for further teaching. As the Spirit of sanctification, the Holy Spirit does not appear here as greatly different from the spirit of judgment and salvation that began with the ethical preaching of the prophets and reached its high point in Psalm 51 and in the Qumran pneumatology. But otherwise there are several important differences. The Holy Spirit plays an important role in confirming the apostolic preaching in the listeners, and prophecy springs up in the community in a way it certainly was not understood to have done in pre-Christian Judaism. That is to say, the Holy Spirit appears so much as the dynamic of the entire community that no easy analogue can be found in the Old Testament community, save perhaps in those prophetic groups where the spirit was given to all (Numbers 11 and the prophets presided over by Samuel) or in the democratization of prophecy promised by Joel. The fact that the word and the Spirit come simultaneously upon the community seems to be a democratization of the kind of individual prophetic experience described in Ezekiel. This same kind of prophetic understanding of the Spirit underlies Paul's assurance that the Spirit will help him to come through his trial successfully. That it is the Spirit of Jesus Christ tells us that the Spirit experienced by Paul and his first communities is the sharing out of the Spirit promised in the Old Testament to rest upon the Messiah, who is Jesus.

13
Spirit and Body
in 1 Corinthians

1 Cor 1:4-7: The Corinthians Favored with Gifts

> 4. I give thanks to God always for you because of the grace of God which was given you in Christ Jesus, 5. that in every way you were enriched in him with all speech and all knowledge— 6. even as the testimony to Christ was confirmed among you— 7. so that you are not lacking in any spiritual gift, as you wait for the revealing of our Lord Jesus Christ. (RSV)

Most of Paul's letters begin with a thanksgiving, and in nearly every case the thanksgiving bears on his reader's faith or hope or charity, or some combination of these. In the case of the Corinthians, however, Paul gently avoids mentioning these virtues, because if we may judge from the rest of the letter charity at least seems to be singularly absent in the community. This does not keep Paul from sharing the Corinthians' positive attitude toward the *charismata*. This is the first appearance of this term, which will come in for such ample discussion in chapters 12-14. Both the RSV and the NAB here translate it (in the singular), "spiritual gift." Though the word "spiritual" does not appear in the Greek, it is obviously the gifts of the Spirit Paul means. It is worth noting at this point that the word *charisma* itself means gift, so that the English expression "charismatic gifts" is really a redundancy.

The gifts Paul praises are those highly prized in the community—speech and knowledge. He will have much to say later about putting these gifts in proper perspective, but for the moment he thanks God for them—and for all the charisms manifested in the community, for they authenticate the gospel and are signs pointing to the total revelation of Jesus Christ at his coming. This latter point will reappear later in chapter 13 where the charisms are presented as anticipations, at once revealing and concealing, the day when all signs and figures will pass away.

134

1 Cor 2:4-16: The Spirit Knows and Reveals the Things of God

4. and my speech and my message were not in plausible words
of wisdom, but in demonstration of the Spirit and power,
5. that your faith might not rest in the wisdom of men but in
the power of God. 6. Yet among the mature we do impart wisdom, although it is not a wisdom of this age or of the rulers of
this age, who are doomed to pass away. 7. But we impart a
secret and hidden wisdom of God, which God decreed before
the ages for our glorification. 8. None of the rulers of this age
understood this; for if they had, they would not have crucified
the Lord of glory. 9. But, as it is written, "What no eye has
seen, nor ear heard, nor the heart of man conceived, what God
has prepared for those who love him," 10. God has revealed to
us through the Spirit. For the Spirit searches everything, even
the depths of God. 11. For what person knows a man's
thoughts except the spirit of the man which is in him? So also
no one comprehends the thoughts of God except the Spirit of
God. 12. Now we have received not the spirit of the world,
but the Spirit which is from God, that we might understand the
gifts bestowed on us by God. 13. And we impart this in words
not taught by human wisdom but taught by the Spirit, interpreting spiritual truths to those who possess the Spirit.
14. The unspiritual man does not receive the gifts of the Spirit
of God, for they are folly to him, and he is not able to understand them because they are spiritually discerned. 15. The spiritual man judges all things, but is himself to be judged by no
one. 16. "For who has known the mind of the Lord so as to instruct him?" But we have the mind of Christ. (RSV)

In vs. 4, the Greek word *apodeixis*, here translated "demonstration," means a convincing proof. Philo (*De vita Moysis* 1, 95) uses it
for proofs in signs and wonders in contrast to mere words. Such is
Paul's meaning here, where the idea is identical with 1 Thes 1:5. The
apostle's preaching, like that of Jesus, was not just something addressed
to the mind. It was accompanied by healings and other charismatic
manifestations. "Spirit" is practically equivalent to "power" here, and
both stand in contrast with the merely human word. Endowing the message with "power," the Spirit assures that man's assent is not merely to
an idea or to what is humanly attractive and beautiful but is a turning of
his whole being to God who comes first in his "otherness."

In vs. 6, after the long demonstration of the difference between the gospel and human wisdom and eloquence, Paul turns to a positive exposition on spiritual wisdom. We remember the identification of wisdom and the spirit in Wis 7:22. As there it was available to "holy souls," here it is available to the "mature." The Greek word *teleoi* means literally "perfect," but here it is properly translated "mature" because it describes those who are able to judge the gospel not by the standard of human wisdom or rhetoric but by God's standard, which is real power.

This wisdom Paul now describes in more detail beginning in vs. 9. He borrows freely from Is 64:3: "No ear has ever heard, no eye has ever seen, any God but you doing such deeds for those who wait for him." Paul has modified the text in two ways, so that the good things are those that God *has prepared*, and the faithful are described not as those who wait for the Lord but as those who *love* him.

Are these good things those of the heavenly kingdom yet to come, or those of the redemption already achieved? While not excluding the ultimate fulfillment to come, the context suggests that Paul has in mind primarily the death and resurrection of Jesus, for had "the rulers of this age" known the mystery, they would not have crucified the Lord of glory (vss. 6, 8). A number of translations, including the NAB, introduce vs. 10 with an adversative expression such as "yet" or "but": "Yet God has revealed this wisdom to us through the Spirit" (NAB). The meaning would then be a contrast between the humanly unknowable wisdom of God and the fact that through the Spirit this wisdom has actually been revealed to us. And "us" would stand in opposition to the "rulers of this age" who did not have the wisdom to recognize what was happening and who Jesus really was.

However, the meaning of the Greek word *gar* introducing vs. 10 is "for" or "since." And the sentence makes most sense if it is immediately tied with Paul's original twist in the quotation, his use of "who love him." Christians are those who *love* God *because* God has revealed to them what is humanly impossible to attain—so that the translation should be: " '. . . for those who love him' because God has revealed these things to us through the Spirit." God's revealing Spirit enables Christians to love him. This interpretation fits well Paul's constant doctrine that man of himself has nothing with which to barter or beg, it is all God's work. In this case, the revelation is not attributed to the message or the word but to the Holy Spirit, whose role it is to give understanding of the mystery of Christ (1 Cor 12:3; Jn 14:26; 15:26; 16:13). He can do so because he *fathoms all things*, as is said in vs. 10. The verb means to explore, examine, search out (Jn 7:52; 1 Peter 1:11). "Depths" is a word used in the Old Testament for the depths of the sea. It was easily transferred to mean the obscurity or, better, the limitless nature of an object surpassing man's power to encompass—above all God (Rom 11:23). Here it is less the depths of the divine nature than those of God's secret plan to save the world through Jesus Christ.

Paul now strengthens his point by an argument *a fortiori*. The intimate thoughts of a man are known only by man's own spirit (2:11). *Pneuma* is used here, for, although it is practically equivalent to *nous* (mind) or *psychē* (soul), the word "spirit" will make easy the transfer to the Spirit of God. As it is only a man's spirit that knows a man's thoughts, so it is only the Holy Spirit who knows "the things of God," God's intimate thoughts and plans. If it is not clear from this text that the Spirit is a person distinct from Father and Son, it is at least said that the Holy Spirit possesses the divine consciousness and the Spirit is clearly distinct from the human spirit, for it is a spirit "which we have received" (vs. 12). Its first effect is to awaken the consciousness of the believer to the grandeur of the gifts he has received. "If you only knew the gift of God!" (Jn 4:10).

Not only revelation and knowledge result from the Spirit, but inspired speech as well, given in language appropriate to the mystery (vs. 13). The spirit does not work a mystic incommunicability but inspires communication and the choice even of the proper words. But this communication cannot take place really unless both parties are moved by the Spirit. This is the point made in vs. 13 and developed in vss. 14-16. Conversation (such is the force of the Greek *laloumen* in vs. 13) about matters of the Spirit can be fruitful only if speaker and listener are under the influence of the Spirit. The "unspiritual" man is categorized by the Greek word *psychikos*, which doesn't mean "fleshly" precisely, but simply "soulish" or "natural" in the sense that he operates within the horizon seen by his natural faculties without the openness to the divine which his *pneuma* could give him. If his spirit were open to being touched by the Holy Spirit, he would be able to experience divine sonship and even converse meaningfully about it (Rom 8:15-16).

In saying that the spiritual person is above all judgment (vs. 15) Paul certainly does not mean that the movements of the spirit are exempt from discernment. He had established the need for discernment in 1 Thes 5:20-21 and will return to it in this very letter (1 Cor 12:1-3; 14:29). He means rather that the Christian who allows himself to be led by the Holy Spirit sees things in a light higher than that of the natural or "psychic" man and therefore stands beyond judgment by him, just as (to use an example of Thomas Aquinas), he who is awake judges properly about himself and about the one asleep, whereas the sleeper cannot judge rightly about either. Concretely, what Paul means in the case of the Corinthians is that if they are truly spiritual as they claim, they would appreciate the wisdom of the cross calling them to a kind of knowledge of God that would seek the common good and unity of the community. Their knowledge and wisdom is more of the inflating kind which does not really build up the community (8:1). It is not therefore as spiritual as they think; it makes them resemble more the "psychic" or natural man.

1 Cor 3:16-17: The Spirit and The Temple

> 16. Do you not know that you are God's temple, and that God's Spirit dwells in you? 17. If any one destroys God's temple, God will destroy him. For God's temple is holy, and that temple you are. (RSV)

"The temple" refers here not to the individual body of the Christian but to the Christian community as such. Its holiness, like that of the Jewish temple, derives from the indwelling of God's spirit. Note that this community-temple belongs to God but the Father's indwelling is effected by the Spirit. The sin of destroying the community, as factions and party interests tend to do, is really a sacrilege because the community is the successor to the temple of Jerusalem—it is God's holy dwelling place. The ethics of community relations are thus inserted into a liturgical framework as they had been in a similar way at Qumran. This ethical motif will recur in 1 Cor 6:19-20 and Rom 12:1.

1 Cor 5:3-5: Absent in Body, Present in Spirit

> 3. For though absent in body I am present in spirit, and as if present, I have already pronounced judgment 4. in the name of the Lord Jesus on the man who has done such a thing. When you are assembled, and my spirit is present, with the power of our Lord Jesus, 5. you are to deliver this man to Satan for the destruction of the flesh, that his spirit may be saved in the day of the Lord Jesus. (RSV)

This text is part of the passage in which Paul deals with a case of public incest that was tolerated in the Corinthian community. Though absent in body, Paul is present in spirit. The spirit, obviously Paul's rather than God's here, transcends bodily limitations. In vs. 4 the sense is the same, except that Paul's presence in spirit is sufficient to assure his authority too. The final verse refers to excommunication, which has a destructive influence only for man's "flesh." By depriving him temporarily of the support of the Christian community, Paul hopes that "his spirit" will be saved on the day of the Lord. Thus the intention of this excommunication is not vindictive but therapeutic.

1 Cor 6:9-11: Justified in the Spirit

> 9. Do you not know that the unrighteous will not inherit the kingdom of God? Do not be deceived; neither the immoral, nor idolaters, nor adulterers, nor homosexuals, 10. nor thieves, nor the greedy, nor drunkards, nor revilers, nor robbers will inherit the kingdom of God. 11. And such were some of you. But you were washed, you were sanctified, you were justified in the name of the Lord Jesus Christ and in the Spirit of our God. (RSV)

Paul has just been discussing the scandal of Christians suing one another before pagan courts. Now rising from the specific to the general, he introduces the question of the conditions for entrance into the kingdom of God. "Do you not know?" is a Pauline cliché by which he frequently recalls the fundamental Christian catechesis which preceded or accompanied baptism. And that is surely the case here. As Christian baptism was a rite by which one prepared for the coming of the kingdom, it was accompanied often by the memorization of vices to be avoided. Such lists were all the more important for pagan converts who had not been formed in the ethics of the Old Testament and had to learn that conversion to the Lord Jesus meant a radical break from the values of the pagan world. The lists varied considerably in the early Christian communities, but they were habitually presented as vices to be avoided if one wished to be admitted to the kingdom of God (cf. Rev 21:7-8, 27; 22:14-15).

While that kingdom is still thought of as future, and thus as something which might still conceivably be lost by infidelity, the radical break was understood to have taken place in baptism, and Paul concludes by referring specifically to the rite. "Washed, sanctified and justified" all refer to the moment of baptism. We will note however that these effects are ascribed equally to the name of Jesus and to the "Spirit of our God." The parallelism of the Spirit with the Name is probably Paul's own, but as far as the Spirit is concerned he is reflecting a tradition that the primitive Christian community already found in the Old

Testament (especially Psalm 51 and Ez 36:26) and perhaps knew from Qumran—that sanctification and justification were the work of God's spirit. "God" here of course for Paul stands for the Father—thus giving us a triadic reference. Both elements, the name of Jesus and the Spirit, belonged to the baptismal catechesis Paul inherited. To be baptized was to be ascribed to the name of Jesus, that is, to become his (Acts 2:38; 8:16; 10:48; 19:5), a point Paul makes emphatically with the Corinthians (1 Cor 1:13). But it also meant to possess the Holy Spirit, and entrance into the kingdom depends as much on the possession of the Spirit as upon belonging to the Name. In fact Paul will soon write the Romans that they cannot belong to Christ without possessing his Spirit (Rom 8:9). Though not as clearly tied to Christ here as to baptism, the Holy Spirit is nonetheless the ethical spirit of Christians, so that to resist the new way of life is to resist the Holy Spirit himself, as we already saw in 1 Thes 4:8.

We should retain for future reference this relationship of the Holy Spirit to the entrance requirements for the kingdom, for Paul will return to it in Gal 5:19-24.

1 Cor 6:19-20: Temple of the Holy Spirit

19. Do you not know that your body is a temple of the Holy Spirit within you, which you have from God? You are not your own; 20. you were bought with a price. So glorify God in your body. (RSV)

As with the preceding moral exhortation, Paul concludes this one concerning sexual morality with an appeal to the Holy Spirit, or more specifically with an appeal to the dignity of the Christian body which is now a temple of the Holy Spirit. "Do you not know?" is again the signpost of an allusion to earlier catechesis, but in this case it is very likely Paul's own. For while the Holy Spirit as the principle of Christian morality belonged to the pre-Pauline tradition, and probably too the idea of the Christian community as the successor of the temple, there is no indication in the preceding sources that the temple theology was applied to the body of the individual Christian before Paul. He was led to it apparently by the need to show how sexual morality derived from the Holy Spirit given in baptism. He individualized the corporate temple theology. The abiding presence of the Spirit within recalls Ezekiel's promise of the Spirit to be put within the people (Ez 36, 37) and the purchase price is an allusion to the cross of Jesus Christ. The final exhortation to "glorify God in your body" further transfers the temple imagery to the bodily morality of the Christian. As God was glorified by sacrifice and praise in his temple, so he is now glorified and praised by the very bodily life of the Christian.

We shall return to the earlier part of this text in connection with 1 Cor 15:35-50, which we must now examine.

1 Cor 15:42-50: The Second Adam, Life-Giving Spirit

42. What is sown in corruption, rises in incorruption.
43. What is sown in humiliation, rises in glory.
    What is sown in weakness, rises in power.
44. A natural body is sown, it rises a spiritual body.
    If there is a natural body, there is also a spiritual body.
45. Thus also it is written:
    "The first man, Adam, became a soul having life."
    The last Adam became a spirit imparting life.
46. But first came not the spiritual organism,
    but the natural and then the spiritual.
47. The first man was from the dust of earth,
    the second man from heaven.
48. As was the man of dust,
    so are they who are of the dust,
    and as is the Heavenly Man
    so are those who are heavenly.
49. And just as we have borne the likeness of the man of dust,
    so let us bear the likeness of the Heavenly One.
50. I tell you this, brothers:
    flesh and blood cannot inherit the kingdom of God,
    nor does the perishable inherit the imperishable.

(Author's translation)

Paul's first letter to the Corinthians begins with a theology of the cross and ends with a theology of the resurrection. In the process of trying to answer the question of how the resurrection of the just can take place, Paul is led to introduce the idea of the *spiritual body*, thus linking two concepts that seem contradictory. For to us "spiritual" ordinarily means "immaterial" and "body" means the opposite of "spirit." Not so for Paul. The opposite of "spirit" is not *body* but *flesh*. The body may be a body of flesh, a body that may be subject to sin, but it may also be the body of the redemption, the body of the resurrection, and for this

Paul finds the most apt term *soma pneumatikon*, the spiritual body. Verse 44, in which Paul first introduces the term, is a bridge between the comparisons preceding and the scriptural reasoning beginning in vs. 45. Paul pins his entire argument on a proper understanding of Genesis 2:7. We recall that there the Lord took the dust of the earth, breathed into it the breath of life and man became a living being—*psychēn zōsan*. This made Adam a "psychic body," i.e. an animated body—or, as we translate, "a natural body." Paul does not complicate his reasoning by trying to deal with the way Adam did or did not possess the life-breath or the spirit of God. If he transmitted life in any way to his descendants, it was only a life shadowed by the certainty of returning to the dust. Later in Romans Paul will call Adam the source of death. Here however Paul's view simply focuses on the superiority of the resurrection of Jesus Christ over its type, the creation of Adam. For while Adam came to *have life* as a result of God's inbreathing, Christ became a *life-giving spirit*. This apparently implies that Paul sees the Father's breathing into the body of Jesus in the tomb the power of the Holy Spirit (cf. Rom 1:4 discussed below) and the result was that the risen body of Jesus possessed the Spirit in a way to give it to whoever contacts the risen Lord through faith and sacrament. The fact that he is life-giving Spirit does not mean he ceases to be body. On the contrary, it is his body which becomes the seat and the source of the Spirit.

As Adam was made in the image and likeness of God, so Christ is now the image of God (2 Cor 3:18). We have borne a likeness to Adam by having a "natural body." But because of union with the spiritual body of the Lord Jesus we have been given the likeness of Jesus himself. This thought provides Paul with the occasion for an exhortation which picks up the catechetical traditions about conditions for entering the kingdom of God (vs. 50). He does not, however, focus on vices to be avoided or virtue to be practiced, but simply remarks that the natural man cannot of himself inherit the kingdom of God. Only a body joined to the risen body of the Lord by a living faith and transformed by the Holy Spirit derived from that union, can enter the kingdom.

We have struck here a vein of Paul's thought that is truly original with him. Paul sees the whole life of the Spirit as rooted in a "bodily" union with the risen Lord. We can truly speak of Paul's theology of the Spirit as a somatic pneumatology. How realistically Paul considers this "spirit-body" union with the Lord not only at the final resurrection but even here and now in the Christian life may be seen from 1 Cor 6:13-17:

13. . . . The body is not for fornication but for the Lord, and

the Lord for the body. 14. Now just as God raised the Lord, he will raise us up too by his power. 15. Do you not realize that your bodies are members of Christ? Shall I then take the members of Christ and make them the members of a prostitute? Never! 16. Do you not realize that whoever unites himself to a prostitute becomes one body with her? So says the Scripture: "The two shall become one flesh." 17. But he who unites himself to the Lord becomes one spirit with him. (Author's translation)

In dealing with the matter of fornication, which the pagan world considered a perfectly legitimate diversion, Paul does not appeal to any philosophical ethic but rather to the religious consecration by which, in baptism, the Christian was joined to Christ. This gives the Christian's body a destiny unknown to him otherwise: the body is for the Lord, that is, the risen Lord Jesus. And the Lord's sole purpose, so to speak, is to be the principle of resurrection for the body of each of his members. Sexual union with a prostitute violates the destiny and the consecration of the Christian's body. To drive the point home, Paul uses the Scripture of Gen 2:24 to show how intimate the sexual union is—the two become one body, one flesh. But he who unites himself to the Lord "becomes one spirit with him," At first glance, it would seem that Paul's contrast bears on the spiritual nature of the Christian's union with Christ over against the physical nature of union with the prostitute. But a closer look leads us to a very different conclusion. The word "unites himself to" (*ho kollōmenos*) is the same in both cases, the sexual union and the union with the Lord. Moreover, Paul has just said that the Christian's *body* is a member of Christ's (vs. 15). The union with Christ is therefore some kind of bodily union. To say that this union is purely spiritual is exactly what Paul is trying to condemn—the schizophrenia which the Corinthian libertines were promoting whereby the spirit could belong to the Lord while the body was given to the prostitute. No, Paul insists, Christ is Lord of the Christian's body as well, and union with Christ is a bodily union. But once that point is established Paul goes on to show that the effect of this bodily union with Christ is different from the effect of union with the prostitute. When one is bodily united with Christ, one becomes "one spirit with him." This is because, as we have seen in 1 Cor 15:44, the risen Lord is a *sōma pneumatikon*, a spiritual body.

The context of 1 Cor 6:13-19 tells us that this "body-spirit" union with Christ takes place in baptism, and the point reappears in 1 Cor 12:13: "In one Spirit were all baptized into one body, and we were all given to drink of the one Spirit." The "one body" here is not directly the Church but the spiritual body of the Lord Jesus Christ, which mediates the Spirit.

But there is another way that this body-spirit union is fostered—the eucharist. In 1 Cor 10:16 Paul asks, "Is not the bread we break a sharing in the body of Christ?" And in 10:1-5 there are allusions to both baptism and eucharist under the Old Testament figures of passing through the sea (baptism) and the "spiritual bread" of the manna and the "spiritual drink" of the water from the rock (the eucharist). "They drank from the spiritual rock that was following them, and the rock was Christ" (vs. 4). This curious statement is an allusion to a Jewish midrash in which the problem of having the water supply throughout the desert journey was solved by having the rock follow the Israelites as they moved on. But Paul sees the "spiritual rock following" as Jesus Christ, who did indeed "come after" the desert Israel. In calling Christ the spiritual rock, Paul seems to be saying, in a sacramental context, what he says in 1 Cor 15:44 in an eschatological context: spiritual body, spiritual rock—both images convey the same reality of a visible, tangible reality that is source of the Spirit. This imagery will reappear in John 7:37-38.

Conclusion

It would not be an exaggeration to say that in 1 Corinthians Paul is dealing with one basic problem: is the spirit related to or separate from the body? The Corinthians, at least many of them, had experienced the Spirit very powerfully. But their theorizing about it was much too influenced by eastern dualism to suit Paul—for it led to the kind of ethical dualism which severed body and spirit. Paul comes down hard on the unity of the two, rooted in the inseparable unity of body and Spirit in the risen Lord.

But *body* also means the Church. To see how this same theology is applied to the dynamics of the Christian community we now turn to the spirit-body ecclesiology of 1 Cor 12-14.

14
The Spirit and the
Service of the Body:
1 Corinthians 12-14

So far in the Pauline letters we have noticed that the Spirit is presented as: (1) the authentication of the first Christian preaching by signs and especially by conviction in the listeners' hearts; (2) the basic entrance-requirement for the kingdom, bringing with it a clearly discernible ethic; (3) the contemplative power by which the Christian is granted a penetration of the gifts and mysteries of God; (4) the principle of the divine indwelling both in the individual and in the community; (5) the principle of the resurrection of the Second Adam and of those joined to him through faith, baptism and eucharist; (6) the charismatic spirit of prophecy.

In this chapter we must follow the terrain of 1 Corinthians and look at the corporate or ecclesial role of the Holy Spirit, for the longest section of the letter deals with this topic. Already in the opening lines Paul had alluded to the spiritual gifts (1:4-7). Now he returns to them specifically in chapter 12 and 14, interrupting his exposition by the hymn to eternal charity, placed in the central position and illuminating the whole development. If we wish to savor fully Paul's teaching on the Spirit we must follow closely the entire text.

1 Cor 12:1-3: Impulse and the Spirit of Jesus

1. Now concerning spiritual gifts, brethren, I do not want you to be uninformed. 2. You know that when you were heathen, you were led astray to dumb idols, however you may have been moved. 3. Therefore I want you to understand that no one speaking by the Spirit of God ever says "Jesus be cursed!" and no one can say "Jesus is Lord" except by the Holy Spirit. (RSV)

12:1: Paul's way of introducing the topic of the gifts of the Spirit

("Now, brothers, concerning. . . .") indicates that he is responding either to a report about the state of affairs in the Corinthian community or to a series of questions that have been addressed to him. In either case the topic was the *pneumatika*, which the translations usually render "spiritual gifts," even though the word "gift" is not in the Greek. It is simply the neuter plural of the adjective "spiritual," and it has the most general sense of any kind of manifestation of the spirit. It was perhaps the term used by the Corinthians. Paul quickly drops it in favor of *charismata* which means "gifts" (12:4), the term he had used in the opening lines of his letter (1:7). He knows how powerful these gifts are for the community if they are properly used, for they manifest the very power and presence of the risen Lord in the midst of the community (14:25; Gal 3:2-5) and build it up (14:12). For that very reason it is crucial that the Corinthians know what the gifts are all about, for nothing is more dangerous than a powerful instrument misused.

12:2: One of the reasons why the spiritual gifts are so powerful is that they transcend the rational and are indeed an impulse from the Spirit going beyond the careful control of human logic and discernment. But Paul is also aware that there are other movements to which the human spirit is subject which lack both human and divine logic. Hence mere impulse of itself is no criterion of genuine religious experience, for even as pagans his readers, some of them at least, knew of the prophetic trance of the Pythia of Delphi and of the priestesses of Dodona. They knew too that in the celebration of the feast of Dionysos the human participant was often swept into an orgiastic frenzy, and the process of "incubation," that is, going to sleep in a temple in the hope of having a revelation or a cure in a dream, was commonly practiced in the religion of Asclepius. Paul is not downplaying man's non-rational side, for he knows that the "spirit" in man goes quite beyond the horizon of the rational. What he is saying is that the non-rational movement can lead to a subservience not to the living God but to "mute idols," with all the dehumanizing results which the Hellenistic Judaism of his day held in abhorrence. It is interesting to note that Paul describes the pagan idols precisely as "mute," that is, incapable of speaking. By way of implicit contrast, he is suggesting that the living God of the new Israel is a God who speaks to his people. His word is available in the scriptures and in the full manifestation of that word in Jesus Christ, brought to the Corinthians by the apostle's preaching.

12:3: As in the Old Testament, conformity with traditional doctrine is the touchstone of the true prophet (Deut 13:21-22). The confession "Jesus is Lord" is the earliest Christian creed (Rom 10:9; Phil 2:11).

Whatever utterance the Spirit gives the prophet, if it truly comes from the Spirit of God, it must be "according to the proportion of faith" (Rom 12:6), that is, within the parameters set by the basic Christian confession. Now it seems very unusual that anyone speaking "in the Spirit of God" could possibly say, "Cursed be Jesus," for it is abundantly clear elsewhere that the Spirit of the Father is also the Spirit of the Son (Gal 4:6). Since the word "anathema" ("cursed") is uniquely a Jewish usage, and since elsewhere in this letter Paul refers to and condemns gnostics who pretend a great spirituality but lack a solid rooting in the human, incarnated, cross-bearing Jesus, many scholars think that Paul is referring here to Jewish gnostics who may even be "Christian" in the sense that they believe in a spiritual Messiah or Christ, but reject his connection with the man Jesus. They would be similar to those referred to by 1 John 2:22; 4:1-2, who did not deny that the Messiah had already appeared but did deny Jesus, that is, that the Messiah had come "in the flesh." Perhaps they are the "Hebrews" of 2 Cor 11:22, who, though qualifying as Christians, deny that this Christ is born "from a woman" (Gal 4:4) and that he is Jesus. Much later, Origen speaks of gnostics who "admit no one to their fellowship who has not cursed Jesus" (*Contra Celsum* VI, xxvii). At any rate, a very important principle has been laid down here, that authentic Christian spirituality is rooted in the human Jesus. Therefore, whatever the activity of the Spirit, he leads the Christian to know Jesus of Nazareth. The Spirit comes from no other source than the risen humanity of that Jesus who was born of a woman, lived a very real human life, preached, healed, suffered and died on a cross. It is indeed conceivable (and Paul's rebuke here indicates that it may really have happened) that Christians claiming to be under the powerful influence of the Spirit would enter into a rarified and gnostic kind of spirituality that would lead them to cut all roots of the Spirit in the earthly Jesus, reject or at least despise the humble way of Nazareth and the cross, and pursue instead a very esoteric mysticism without any real historic memory of Jesus. The writing of the gospels, however, indicates that the mainstream of orthodoxy in the early Church wished to root its intense experience of the Spirit in the earthly Jesus, his words and his life. Paul's statement here clearly aligns him with that direction of the Spirit. Furthermore, he also indicates that whoever confesses that "Jesus is Lord" in a meaningful way can do so only under the influence of the Holy Spirit. The Holy Spirit is therefore already present in anyone who makes this confession, even if the charisms are not yet in great evidence. It is not the charisms in the first place that makes one an authentic Christian but the confession that "Jesus is Lord."

1 Cor 12:4-7: The Gifts Are One in Source and Aim

> 4. Now there are varieties of gifts, but the same Spirit; 5. and
> there are varieties of service, but the same Lord; 6. and there
> are varieties of working, but it is the same God who inspires
> them all in every one. 7. To each is given the manifestation of
> the Spirit for the common good. (RSV)

Paul now sets out to show that while there are many gifts, there is
but one giver. He abandons the term *pneumatika* and substitutes three
other parallel terms: gifts (*charismata*), services (*diakoniai*), and "workings" (*energēmata*). Since Paul feels free to interchange these terms, we
gather already that the spiritual gifts are services and gifts of interaction
in the body. Nevertheless, the three terms are attributed to different persons of the Trinity. The gifts are attributed to the Holy Spirit who is the
gift of God (Rom 5:5). Services or ministries are attributed to the Lord
Jesus both because being a Christian means to serve the Lord Jesus (cf.
Mt 8:15; 25:21, 23) and also to imitate Jesus the servant (Mark 10:45).
Indeed though Jesus had the divine titles to glory by right, he forsook
them in order to become a servant, and it was through this act of humble service unto death that he merited the Father's response instating
him as Lord (Phil 2:6-11). And the Christian's most brilliant witness to
the Lordship of Jesus is the fact that he now, by the power of Jesus'
Lordship, can become a servant in love to his brothers (Gal 5:13). Finally, the "workings" are attributed to God, that is the Father, who is the
worker par excellence (Eph 1:11; 4:6; John 5:17). In verse 7 we are
told that the gifts are a *manifestation* of the Spirit. The Greek word
for manifestation (*phanerosis*) suggests a kind of brilliant epiphany, like
the sparkling reflection of a crystal ball as it rotates in the light. The
gifts, which here are described less as stable offices than as passing
movements by the Spirit, manifest the presence of the Spirit of God in
the Christian community. They are given however, "for the common
good"—that is for the building up of the Church. Another way of saying
this is that the gifts, when properly used, make it obvious both to those
within the community and to those who are drawn to it from the outside
that God is truly present there (14:25).

1 Cor 12:8-11: Example of Gifts

> 8. To one is given through the Spirit the utterance of wisdom,
> and to another the utterance of knowledge according to the

same Spirit, 9. to another faith by the same Spirit, to another gifts of healing by the one Spirit, 10. to another the working of miracles, to another prophecy, to another the ability to distinguish between spirits, to another various kinds of tongues, to another the interpretation of tongues. 11. All these are inspired by one and the same Spirit, who apportions to each one individually as he wills. (RSV)

Paul now for the first time lists some of the gifts to illustrate the variety of ministries that come from the same Spirit. There are at least three other places in the Pauline epistles where gifts are listed. Later in this same chapter in vss. 27-28 he will line up the gifts according to their descending order of importance. Then in Rom 12:6-8 he gives another list to demonstrate how to use the gifts. Finally in Eph 4:11 there is a list of offices illustrating order, especially in doctrine. The order of appearance of the gifts in this present passage, however, is of no particular importance, since its purpose is simply to illustrate the variety of gifts on the one hand and the unity of the Spirit on the other.

The first of the gifts mentioned is the *word of wisdom*. What is meant by this? It is not mentioned anywhere else in the list of spiritual gifts, and Paul does not develop his description of it here. So we are left with the indirect method of inferring from the general background of the Bible and the particular background of the rest of Paul's writings what he means by it. One thing is certain, the wisdom which is in question here, if it has any Biblical roots at all, is not the speculative wisdom of the philosophers or of the rhetoricians. It is essentially a practical wisdom. In the very primitive text of the Old Testament, a man who is expert in his trade merits the name of a wise man (1 Chron 22:15; Jer 9:16; Is 40:20). But it applies supremely to the man who is an expert in the art of living well, an art that is learned primarily by reflection on human experience. That is why in the earlier stages of the wisdom literature, wisdom was equated with gray hair because only the man who had a lifetime of experience could have an adequate store of wisdom: "Wisdom is found in the old, and discretion comes with great age" (Job 12:12). But God has no need to live a long life in order to be wise, for his wisdom is infinite and inscrutable (Is 40:13-14; Rom 11:34), and this refers not so much to the abyss of God's inner nature but the mysterious wisdom of his dealing with man. While of itself inaccessible it can be bestowed on a man by pure gift if God so desires. Enriched by the influence of prophecy, as we saw, the wisdom tradition later spoke of it as a gift of God's spirit (Job 32:7-9): "The Lord himself is the giver of wisdom, from his mouth issue knowledge and discernment" (Prov 2:6). It is especially in the book of Daniel that the wisdom tradition blends with the prophetic, as Daniel is hailed both as a prophet and as a wise man whose surpassing insight is attributable only to the presence of the spirit of God in him (Dan 5:11-14). The book of Wisdom as we saw, gives the fullest development of wisdom as a gift of the spirit (Wis 1:6; 7:22-26; 9:13-18).

Paul is quite aware of this Old Testament background, especially of the chasm that separates the divine wisdom as a way of life from the sham wisdom of pagan polythesism and its consequent immorality (Rom 1:18-32). He is aware that the divine gift of wisdom in the Old Testament was identified in later Judaism with the law (Sir 15:1; 24:22), and he is painfully aware that in his own experience as a Pharisee he became so enamored of the law as a thing in itself that he was no longer able to see the graciousness of God coming to him in Jesus. Now, however, as a Christian, he identifies the wisdom from God with Jesus and him crucified (1 Cor 1:24). This means that Paul's understanding of wisdom, while still retaining its eminently practical side, is also transfused with an intense Christo-centric personalism. Jesus *is* the wisdom from God (1 Cor 1:30).

What, then, does all this have to offer toward understanding what Paul means here by the word of wisdom? It would seem to refer to a special insight given in a transient way by the Holy Spirit to an individual of the community by way of a directive or a counsel on how best to live the Christian life. It would be made, of course, in the light of the great and wonderful deeds of the Lord, particularly in Jesus Christ, but it would focus upon the practical aspect of the Christian life—how, in short, to live it. Paul's own letters give ample evidence of this kind of practical spiritual teaching or advice, and the letter to the Corinthians contains abundant examples. He resolves the problem of the factions in the community in the light of a theology of the church as the temple of God (1 Cor 3:16-17) and as the body of Christ (1 Cor 12:27). In Rom 12:1-3, after a long teaching on the mystery of God's plan of salvation for Jew and Gentile alike, he suggests that the Christian life is a liturgy offered to God, and all moral directives flow from that concern to offer one's whole being as a living sacrifice to the Lord. Inasmuch, however, as Paul speaks of a *word* of wisdom, it seems that he is not discussing a stable gift, even less a stable office—there was no office of "wise men" in the early Church—but rather simply a passing movement by the Holy Spirit whereby someone in the community is given a flash of insight into the living of the Christian life. The normal context, then, for the word of wisdom is the prayerful gathering of the community. However, it would seem likely that under this heading might easily be classified the "emergency" situations in which by a special gift of the Lord the disciples of

Jesus are endowed with "a mouth and wisdom" which could effectively reply to their adversaries (Lk 21:15), since these utterances are attributed to the Holy Spirit speaking within them (Lk 12:12). Jesus among the doctors of the temple won the amazement of all by his intelligence and his replies (Lk 2:47). And more than once during his public ministry, Jesus brilliantly answered his enemies seeking to ensnare him by their questioning (Mt 21:25; 22:21). It is perhaps the kind of answer attributed to Joan of Arc, who, when asked by her inquisitors whether she was in the state of grace or not, calmly replied, "If I am, I ask the Lord to keep me there; if I am not, I ask him to put me there."

What is meant by the *word of knowledge*? There is no other place in Paul where this gift is explained or referred to. In the history of the Christian interpretation of this gift two different meanings have been attached to it: one concerns an inspired knowledge of a fact, the other an inspired insight into the Christian mystery granted especially for the purpose of teaching. Examples abound, both from the Biblical and post-Biblical times of an unusual endowment of knowledge given to someone about a particular fact or event. The prophet Nathan, for example, knows of David's sin with Bathsheba, and he uses the clever parable about the poor man and the lamb to lead up to the accusation, "You are the man!" (2 Sam 12:1-12). Daniel, on the other hand, is given a charismatic awareness of the innocence of Susanna and calls for a test for her accusers which ends in proclaiming her innocence (Dan 13:44-49). Several instances reported of Jesus in the gospels show his amazing clairvoyance. He tells his disciples that they will find a donkey tied at a certain place (Mk 11:2) and that on entering the city they will meet a man carrying a pitcher of water (Mk 14:13). He tells Nathaniel, "I saw you under the fig tree" (Jn 1:48) and the Samaritan woman that she has had not one but five husbands (Jn 4:18). In these latter two cases, the effect of this "word of knowledge" is to lead the person toward conversion and faith. The lives of saints and missionaries in every age have been highlighted by occasional events of this type. When Jesus was blindfolded and struck by the soldier with the taunt, "Prophesy! Who hit you?", it meant that Jesus was being asked for this kind of "word of knowledge," which, under the circumstances, he refused.

Such an unusual gift is obviously a passing and brilliant manifestation of the Spirit meant to lead others to the faith or to confirm them in it. However, a less spectacular but no less important function of knowledge is that of simple insight into the Christian mystery. Paul lays great store, at least in his later letters, on a kind of knowledge for which he uses the special Greek word *epignōsis*. It means the kind of knowledge of the object of the Christian faith which leads to a firmer appreciation of all that God has given in Christ and a greater attachment and stability in the Christian life (Phil 1:9; Col 1:9, 10; 2:2; 3:10). It is one of the elements which bring about the unity of the Church through a common understanding of the faith (Eph 4:13) and thus contributes importantly to its upbuilding in love (Eph 4:16). In Eph 1:17 it is paired, as here, with wisdom, both of them a gift of the Spirit: "May the God of our Lord Jesus Christ, the Father of glory, give you a spirit of *wisdom* and revelation in the full *knowledge* of him." And this gift of insight is made more specific in what immediately follows: "May he enlighten the eyes of your mind so that you can see what hope his call holds for you, what rich glories he has promised the saints will inherit, and how infinitely great is the power that he has exercised for us believers" (Eph 1:19). Now, since the effect of the "word of knowledge" when properly used is exactly the same as this gift of knowledge, namely, the building up of the community (1 Cor 12:7; Eph 4:13-16), it would seem that the two are very closely related if not identical. Surely they are important gifts for teaching in the community. Paul's letters themselves are a brilliant illustration of the gift of knowledge given him of the mystery of Christ (cf. Eph 3:2-4). Experience confirms that there is a great difference between a teaching that is carried out in a pedestrian and functional way, and teaching that is truly anointed by the Spirit and lifts the listener to prayer, worship, and glorification of the Father. This, it would seem, is what makes the word of knowledge precisely a special, passing gift of the Spirit and distinguishes it from mere human learning and teaching.

The gift of *faith* does not refer here to the faith that is necessary for salvation (Mk 16:16; Heb 11:6) but rather to a special intensity of faith for a specific need. It was the kind of faith that Elijah manifested on Mount Carmel when he realized that the honor of Yahweh was at stake and was willing to expect the miracle of the most grandiose kind to win the victory over the prophets of Baal (1 Kgs 18:33-35). It is the kind of faith that Jesus is probably referring to in Mark 11:22, "Have the faith of God," the kind of faith which, though ever so small, could move a mountain (Mt 17:20). It was the kind of faith that Peter manifested when he suddenly felt the urge to tell the cripple at the temple gate to get up and walk in the name of Jesus Christ (Acts 3:1-10), a miracle which Peter immediately attributes to faith in the name of Jesus (Acts 3:16). Properly exercised, this gift builds up the faith not only of him who uses it and him who directly benefits from it, but the whole community that comes to know that the power of the Lord is alive and active now as much as in the distant past.

Some members of the community are endowed "by the same Spirit" with the gift of "*healings*." This does not refer to the science or the art of medicine, though the early church counted among its most illustrious members Luke, the physician (Col 4:14). The gift of medicine was surely not despised, and no doubt it was incorporated happily into the total ministry of the community. But what is at issue here is clearly a gift of the Spirit and not the result of mere human learning or experience. The miracles of Jesus and those of early evangelists (Acts 3:12; 8:6-7; 14:15; 28:8-10) were primarily works of healing, for of all the possible ways of changing the world and human life, healing is the most "sacramental"—that is, it is the best visible sign of God's purpose with man, namely to save him by bringing him to the fullness of life. Some members of the Christian community have a special anointing to engage in this ministry. The fact that they do, however, does not preclude the whole community of believers in the Lord from laying hands upon the sick for their recovery (Mk 16:18) or the elders in the church from anointing with oil for healing (James 5:14). The Lord guarantees his presence in these general or "official" ways in the church as well as through the charismatic endowment of certain individuals.

The next gift is literally "operations of works of power." In the translations this is often shortened to simply "miracles." This probably refers to rather outstanding examples of power, such as are reported in Peter's raising Dorcas to life (Acts 9:40) or Paul raising Eutychus (Acts 20:10) in contrast to healings which seem to be of a more common or ordinary occurrence.

The gift of *prophecy* is one on which Paul sets high store because of its ability to build up the community (1 Cor 14:1-2). Paul develops his thought on prophecy at some length in chapter 14. In its broadest sense, of course, prophecy can mean anything that builds up the faith life of the community. But that is also the function of all the gifts. What then distinguishes prophecy from the other gifts? It is first of all, in distinction to tongues, intelligible speech. But it is not quite the same, it seems, as inspired preaching or exhortation. The text of 14:30 suggests that the gift involves a sudden revelation at the moment—the Greek word is *apokalypsis*, revelation. It does not necessarily mean a prediction of the future, for even in the Old Testament the prophet was primarily the man who spoke the word of the Lord for the contemporary community—that is, what the community needed most to hear at this moment. Occasionally there were promises or threats about the future, but all these emerged out of a concern for hearing the word of God in the present moment and responding to it. The fact that someone in the community speaks in a prophetic form does not mean, of course, that his prophecy is infallible, for the community is told to "judge the truth" of what he says (14:29), a statement which obviously indicates that there are degrees of "anointing" in prophecies uttered for the benefit of the community. Furthermore, "directive" prophecy, occasionally sought for in the Old Testament system of prophecy, is conspicuously absent in the New Testament. There is no instance of anyone going to a "prophet" to ask for a decision. There was an instance in which Agabus foretold a forthcoming famine (Acts 11:28) or Paul's impending imprisonment in Jerusalem (Acts 21:11), but in neither case did the prophet himself direct the community or Paul concerning their course of action. It is also significant that in the dispute about circumcision which was discussed in the council at Jerusalem in Acts 15 and in Paul's decision in what to do next in his ministry (in Acts 16:6-10) there was no resorting to direction from a prophet, though on both occasions Silas, a recognized prophet (15:32) was present. However, with these reservations, it is clear that the gift of prophecy was very widespread in the early church and that it was highly esteemed. It is a way in which the word of God comes in a highly inspirational, even revelational way, and where it is absent it seems that teaching becomes stiff, routine and pedestrian, if not dead.

Next comes the gift of the *discernment of spirits*. The Greek word *diakrisis* means literally "a judgment through," hence an ability to "see through," to distinguish or discern. This gift seems to have been especially necessary in the community of Corinth for three reasons: (1) The community was made up largely of converts from paganism. On literally every page of this letter Paul is heavily at the task of showing his readers how the promptings of the Spirit of Jesus are really different from those of the demons (1 Cor 10:20) or the false freedom of self-indulgence (6:12; 10:23). It was simply not obvious to the Corinthians, for example, that Christianity really required a change of ethics in the matter of sexuality; the pagan mystery religions did not require any such "conversion" of their neophytes. And Paul himself would have to remind the Corinthians that simple impulse is no criterion for identifying the spirit of God (12:2). (2) The Corinthian community was a highly charismatic one, and Paul praises the community for yielding to the gifts of the Spirit (1:4). Even, therefore, among those who are using the gifts, there is need for discerning the degree of anointing—that is, how *much* of the statement comes from the Lord (14:29) as well as the need to discern *how* the gift is to be used in a community setting (all of chapter 14). (3) It is indeed surprising that there is no reference to any locally established elders or leaders of the Corinthian community anywhere in Paul's letter other than in the brief reference to "administration" in 12:28. It seems that this community was still very much under the direct authority of Paul or of his itinerant delegates, and if there were any locally established authorities, there is no evidence of them in the letter.

But there is evidence that a discernment of the Spirit was all the more essential since the community apparently did not look to the intervention of a recognized authority, other than Paul's, in the case of an abuse of the charisms. In 6:1-6, Paul chides the Corinthians for taking their disputes to judges outside the community rather than bringing them before someone within the community "wise enough to decide between members of the brotherhood." It is matters such as these and the increasing impossibility for Paul or his delegates to be in constant touch with the community that led ultimately to a more structured authority in the early Christian communities, and then discernment became a normal expectation of the function of their office. The Corinthian letter, however, indicates that discernment of spirits is a charismatic gift which certain members of the community have been given.

The New Testament itself provides guidelines for discerning the Spirit (Mt 7:15-23; 1 Cor 12:3; 1 Jn 4:1-6). An example of the use of this gift is given in Acts 13:9 in which Paul identifies the sorcerer. Still other examples might be Peter's dealing with Ananias and Sapphira (Acts 5) and his denunciation of Simon the magician (Acts 8:23). Finally, Paul's rebuke to the spirit possessing the slave girl at Philippi is still another example (Acts 16:16-18). The gift of discernment of spirits is not mere rationality, for it takes a special gift of the Spirit in order to discern the Spirit (1 Cor 2:14-16). This gift, like all the others, is aimed toward the upbuilding of the community, particularly in shielding those who are still weak in the ways of the Lord from misleading influences to which they are easily susceptible.

The next gift listed is, literally, *"kinds of tongues."* The use of the plural along with the word "kinds" is instructive to this extent at least, that the gift is not clearly defined or limited to any particular language or kind of language. In 14:2 we are told that the one who speaks in an unknown tongue speaks not to men but to God, and in 14:14, 16, 17 it is obvious that this is a gift of prayer, of praise, and thanksgiving. Its primary function is not, therefore, intelligible communication. It is precisely for this reason that interpretation of the meaning of such prayer is necessary if the community is to be built up (14:5). That individuals who listen might at times receive a special communication in their own language is not therefore inherent in the gift but would be due to some special arrangement of providence, as Luke apparently reports concerning the Pentecost phenomenon in Acts 2. The evidence in Paul, then, indicates that the gift of tongues is a kind of non-rational prayer of the heart—or more precisely of the spirit (14:14-16)—in which the individual praying, as well as anyone listening, has no intellectual "reading" of the contents. The value of this kind of prayer of praise seems to lie precisely in its non-rational character which somehow allows the Spirit to break the barrier of rational thought and to pray as depth speaking to depth (Rom 8:26-27). If this is so, then the final gift listed here is not precisely translation but rather interpretation, that is, a rendering of the general sense in approximative intelligent speech. Speaking or praying in tongues would, then, be analogous to one person being inspired with a melody and another who hears it being inspired with the appropriate words to fit the melody.

Paul concludes this list illustrating variety by returning to the principle that the variety of gifts is itself a gift of the Spirit and their distribution his determination.

1 Cor 12:12-13: One Spirit, One Body

12. For just as the body is one and has many members, and all the members of the body, though many, are one body, so it is with Christ. 13. For by one Spirit we were all baptized into one body—Jews or Greeks, slaves or free—and all were made to drink of one Spirit. (RSV)

12:12: From the thought of the one Spirit Paul's mind now swings immediately to the thought of the one body, and from here through the end of chapter 12 he will develop his thought on this matter. As the Spirit bears witness to the historical, earthly, incarnate Jesus (12:3) so it brings men into a body which is his community. And if the body of Jesus is not simply his own personal risen humanity but also all those who are united in faith and baptism to him, then no individual member of the body can pretend to a solipsism which not even the risen Lord claims—to be the *only* important member of the body. It is quite interesting that Paul's problem is not the philosophical one, "How can the many be one?" It is rather "How can the one be many?"—for "the body is not one member but many" (12:14). The word *body* was first used for the community of believers in 10:17. Here Paul will develop the theme announced there.

12:13: The Spirit is not to be had apart from the body. For if the Spirit was the initial gift that made them Christians, its immediate effect was to plunge them *into* one body. The expression "into one body" could be taken to mean, of course, "so that as a whole we make up one body" in the same way that persons who enroll in a university are said, in virtue of their several matriculations, to form the "student body." However, this interpretation falls far short of the meaning of Paul, which has a beautiful and stark realism here. The one body into which Christians have all been baptized is the risen body of Christ. They become members of that risen, glorified humanity by "clinging" to the Lord in faith and baptism (6:15, 17). This is precisely the strength in the point that Paul is making: not even the Lord Jesus himself wishes to be the only member of his body. By sharing his Spirit to all those who "cling" to him, he has diffused his own gifts of service throughout the community. The Christian must at least accept this diversity which he learns both from the example and the will of Jesus.

A wealth of teaching is concentrated in this brief line. For one thing, it is perfectly clear that the Holy Spirit is given in Christian baptism. Whether the Greek is translated "by one Spirit" or "in one Spirit" it is obvious that Paul is referring to the baptism by which his readers became Christians and members of the one body. It is clearly a "baptism in the Spirit" or a "baptism of the Spirit"—but there is no reason for thinking it is not identical with water baptism. When Pentecostals, then, use the term "baptism of the Holy Spirit" for the deep spiritual experience of the release of the Spirit, ordinarily accompanied by the laying on of hands, it would be wrong to imply that the Spirit is given only then, as if he were not already with the Christian from the moment of his initiation into the Christian life. In Titus 3:5 the sacrament of baptism is called "the bath of rebirth and renewal by the spirit." According to Luke, the conferring of the Spirit was ritualized, it seems, by the gesture of imposing hands on the newly baptized (Acts 8:17; 19:6), though other passages in the Pauline literature suggest that the rite of anointing signified this (2 Cor 1:22; Eph 1:13; 1 John 2:26-27). We are not certain exactly what was the full Christian ritual of baptism in the early decades, nor how the rites of water and anointing and laying on of hands were interrelated, nor even whether there was a generally uniform practice in the matter, nor how exactly they verbalized the relationship of the various elements of the ritual to the name of the Lord Jesus and to the gift of the Spirit. But for baptized, confirmed Christians today who are seeking a deeper experience of the Holy Spirit in their lives through the laying on of hands, it would seem preferable to speak of a re-awakening or a release or a yielding to the Spirit already given, after the fashion of the exhortation given in 2 Tim 1:6: "I remind you to stir into flame the gift of God bestowed when my hands were laid on you" (the next verse makes it obvious that the gift of God is the Holy Spirit).

The one Spirit and the one body into which Christians are baptized dissolves the distinction between Jew and Gentile, between slave and free citizen, and by implication all other distinctions that were previously experienced as barriers to real unity. The only distinctions that remain in the Christian community are the gifts of service, all of which are aimed at building up the same body.

In writing "and all of us have been given to drink of the same Spirit" Paul is obviously alluding to the Biblical image of water for the Spirit. The image of water was deeply graven in the memory of the desert people who had been saved through the Red Sea and who were given water to drink in the wilderness from the rock (Ex 17:1-7; Num 20:1-13; Ps 78:16, 20; 114:8; 48:21). The Lord is himself the fountain of living water for his people (Jer 2:13), but as they have abandoned him to dig for themselves leaky cisterns that hold no water, the coming restoration of the people is presented as the return of the gift of water in the desert (Is 43:20) or as a river of life that will flow from the New Temple (Ez 47:1-12), with waters in which the people will find purity (Zech 13:1), life (Joel 4:18; Zech 14:8) and holiness (Ps 46:5). In Is 44:3, we saw that this promised water is specifically identified with the spirit of the Lord: "I will pour out water upon the thirsty ground, and streams upon the dry land; I will pour out my spirit upon your offspring, and my blessing upon your descendants. They shall spring up amid the verdure like poplars beside the flowing waters." We have already seen how Paul identifies the desert rock from which the water flowed as Christ, source of the Spirit (1 Cor 10:4).

1 Cor 12:14-26: One Body, Many Members

14. For the body does not consist of one member but of many. 15. If the foot should say, "Because I am not a hand, I do not belong to the body," that would not make it any less a part of the body. 16. And if the ear should say, "Because I am not an eye, I do not belong to the body," that would not make it any less a part of the body. 17. If the whole body were an eye, where would be the hearing? If the whole body were an ear, where would be the sense of smell? 18. But as it is, God arranged the organs in the body, each one of them, as he chose. 19. If all were a single organ, where would the body be? 20. As it is, there are many parts, yet one body. 21. The eye cannot say to the hand, "I have no need of you," nor again the head to the feet, "I have no need of you." 22. On the contrary, the parts of the body which seem to be weaker are indispensable, 23. and those parts of the body which we think less honorable we invest with the greater honor, and our unpresentable parts are treated with greater modesty, 24. which our more presenta-

ble parts do not require. But God has so adjusted the body, giving the greater honor to the inferior part, 25. that there may be no discord in the body, but that the members may have the same care for one another. 26. If one member suffers, all suffer together; if one member is honored, all rejoice together. (RSV)

Paul here develops at length the imagery of the body to illustrate his principle that the body is not one member but many. In so doing he wishes to direct each individual member to a consciousness of his need for every other and to a sense of solidarity both in suffering and in joy. Many Corinthians have used the gifts for their personal glorification and thus for the dispersal of energies from the community rather than for the integration and harmonious interaction of them.

1 Cor 12:27-28: Order of Ministries

27. Now you are the body of Christ and individually members of it. 28. And God has appointed in the church first apostles, second prophets, third teachers, then workers of miracles, then healers, helpers, administrators, speakers in various kinds of tongues. (RSV)

Paul now summarizes the preceding section and then returns to the gifts by way of application of what he has just said, this time listing them according to a hierarchical order and insisting that it is God himself who has placed this order in the Church. The apostles are those especially commissioned to preach the gospel, a title applied especially to the Twelve (Mt 10:2; Mk 3:14; Lk 22:14; cf. 6:13; 9:10; 17:5; Acts 1:26; Rev 21:14). But the title is not limited to the Twelve. It is also applied to Paul (Rom 1:1; 11:13; 1 Cor 1:1) and Barnabas (Acts 14:14), Andronicus and Junias (Rom 16:7) and James, the Lord's brother (Gal 1:19). They possessed the most important spiritual gift and are the supreme authority in the church. In Acts they appear as a governing board with the elders (Acts 15:2, 4, 6, 22f; 16:4) and whenever listed with other offices, always come first. Though in the first chapters of Acts it seems that one of the necessary traits of an apostle was that he have been with the Lord Jesus "from the beginning" of his ministry, the story of the Acts itself and especially of Paul indicates that there was an evolution in the understanding of the office of apostle. Paul considers his vision of the risen Lord and his personal commission by him to equate him with the rest of the apostles (1 Cor 9:1).

The second office is that of prophet, consistently listed immediately after that of apostle (Eph 2:20; 4:11). It is instructive that in the dynamics of church-building, next to those who first bring the good news and found the communities stand those who animate it with inspired messages. The office of prophet continues to be an important one in the early church into the early second century. Only in the third place appear teachers, those whose method of communication is less "revelational" and more catechetical—the passing on of the shaped tradition according to accepted formulations, with amplification according to their own understanding as enlightened by the Spirit. The teacher is perhaps similar to the *hacham* or *sophos* ("Wise Man") of later Judaism. These "wise men" become respected teachers in the community because of their knowledge of the sacred tradition and their spiritual insight. It is perhaps here that we have the beginnings of "historical theology" and catechetics. As the gift and the office evolved, it came to be closely associated with that of the *shepherd*, for the two titles are listed under a single article in Eph 4:11, probably because in this case the shepherd also exercised the function of teaching. Such is also the case in the *Didache* 15:1, where the "episkopoi and deacons" discharge the "liturgy of the prophets and teachers." What is characteristic of the gift of teaching is, it seems, the combination of learning by human industry on the one hand and spiritual insight both in the learning process and especially in the communication to others. A truly charismatic teaching is one in which the special anointing of the Spirit becomes obvious. It is most remote from the kind of teaching which is simply the transfer of the notes of the teacher to the notes of the students without having passed through the mind or heart of either!

In the next place Paul lists miraculous powers and the gift of healing, inverting the order he had given above in vss. 9-10. A new title then follows: helpers (*antilēmpseis*). This little gift, because it lacks a miraculous character, is often paid little attention. It simply means services of love in dealing with the community. Whether it refers to an office officially recognized in the community or whether it simply refers to a passing movement of the Spirit inspiring a work of service, it seems to address itself to those humble tasks which one does not need a spectacular gift to perform, which are therefore considered the kind of menial things that "anyone can do"—and because apparently anyone can do them, they often don't get done! Paul sees the ability to undertake these humble tasks of love in the community as the expression of a special gift of the Spirit. If such persons are needed for the smooth functioning of the community, in terms of personal attitude, it certainly must make a difference whether such a person views this service as a functional job or whether he views it (as did Paul) as a special gift of the Spirit given to him to share gladly with the community.

The next gift, tucked away near the end of this list, is that of administrators (*kybernēseis*). The Greek word comes from a verb meaning "to steer a ship." In classical Greek the noun is used for a statesman who steers the ship of state. In the Greek Old Testament the noun appears three times; it is connected with wisdom (Prov 1:5; 11:14; 24:6) and means "wise or right direction." Here it means someone who gives direction to the community, as the helmsman gives direction to the ship. Hence, a director. The proclamation of the word probably was not one of his tasks originally. The office or the gift sounds very much like that described in Rom 12:8 as "those who preside" or "those who are in authority." The Greek word *proistamenos* used here has various nuances of meaning: "to preside, lead, conduct, direct, govern." It especially conveys the idea of standing before someone or going before someone as a protector, and hence the notion of *caring for* is also conveyed. It refers especially to those set aside by the Spirit to care for others, and this is confirmed in the Roman text by its placement between the gift of almsgiving and that of works of mercy. In the pastoral epistles the verb means to rule, to take care of a household or a community, but especially with a note of devoted concern. It appears then that from the earliest times the need for authority in the community was felt. While the fledgling communities were still under close direction by the apostles, the need for a strong local authority was not felt. As the communities developed and as contact with the original founders became more difficult and less frequent, the role of the local shepherds (Eph 4:11, which could be elders or the episkopoi) became more important (Acts 20:28). For those who today must bear the leadership and responsibility for the Christian community, it should come as a word of consolation that there is a special gift of administration given by the Holy Spirit. Used properly, it will help to build up the community. It is important to realize that not just any administration, even humanly wise, is at issue here, but rather the enlightened discernment and decision-making full of personal concern for the Lord's little ones, which can only come from the Holy Spirit.

The gift of *tongues* comes at the end of this list, obviously in the most humble position. It is not for that reason to be despised (14:39), but Paul does not want it to get out of focus.

Finally, we should note that Paul makes no distinction between office and charism here. The "gifts" of vs. 31 refer back to all those listed here. Though there was most probably a rite of installation associated with some functions, all are seen to be gifts of service given by the Lord for the building of his church. The distinction between a "charismatic" church and an "institutional" one is a modern invention not founded in the New Testament.

1 Cor 12:29-31a: Not All Have Every Gift

29. Are all apostles? Are all prophets? Are all teachers? Do all work miracles? 30. Do all possess gifts of healing? Do all speak with tongues? Do all interpret? 31. But earnestly desire the higher gifts. (RSV)

12:29-30: It is obvious from these verses that no one gift contains all the others nor is it expected that any one gift be had by all. Not all are expected, for example, to speak in tongues, any more than all are expected to be apostles. To say therefore that unless one speak in tongues he cannot be sure he has received the "Baptism of the Holy Spirit" goes counter to this text. There should be an openness to the gifts, certainly, and even a seeking of them more and more (12:31; 14:1) but the gifts are diverse and it is up to the Lord to judge how and when they are to be distributed (Eph 4:11; 1 Cor 12:28).

12:31a: Clearly the gifts are to be sought (14:1), but since the good of the community is uppermost in Paul's mind, he urges them to seek the "greater" gifts. How does he measure what is greater? By the degree to which such a gift is effective in building up the life of the community (14:12).

Logically at this point chapter 14 would follow immediately, for it develops the idea of the "greater gifts." However Paul interrupts his development on the "greater gifts" by a long praise of love which is above all gifts and in a class by itself. We think it important to meditate on this chapter in our ongoing study of the Holy Spirit not only because the love of which he speaks here is said in Rom 5:5 to be "poured into our hearts by the Holy Spirit" but also because Paul thought his treatment of the charisms needed the context of love to be properly understood, and it is precisely from the viewpoint of love's relation to the charisms that Paul writes here.

1 Cor 12:13b-13:3: Love Is Essential

31b. Now I will show you the way which surpasses all the others. 1. If I speak with human tongues and angelic as well, but do not have love, I am a noisy gong, a clanging cymbal. 2. If I have the gift of prophecy and, with full knowledge, comprehend all mysteries, if I have faith great enough to move mountains, but have not love, I am nothing. 3. If I give everything I have to feed the poor and hand over my body to be burned, but have not love, I gain nothing. (NAB)

12:31b: The last part of verse 31 is sometimes translated: "And I will show you a way which is *better still*" or "a more excellent way"—as if Paul were drawing a comparison between charity and the preceding gifts. But in fact he does not introduce charity as a gift here; he calls it "a way." And the Greek expression does not mean "better." It means rather "beyond measure." The NAB translates it: "the way which surpasses them all." The sense is: "I will show you a way which is utterly beyond comparison." Charity does not, therefore, fall into the categories of the gifts, which are "measured out according to Christ's bestowal" (Eph 4:7). With charity there is no measure—it surpasses understanding (Eph 3:19); and if it is something which is poured out (Rom 5:5) it tends to overflow the limits of any vessel (1 Thes 3:12; Phil 1:9).

Charity, then, would seem to be a value in itself, and yet it is described here as a "way." What does this mean? Literally the Greek word and its Hebrew equivalent mean a path or road. In Israel, as in other ancient cultures, it quickly became an image for "way of life." There is the good road that leads to life, the bad road that leads to perdition (Ps 1:6; Prov 4:18f; 12:28). The good road consists in practicing justice (Prov 8:20; 12:28), being faithful to the truth (Ps 119:30; Tob 1:3) and in seeking peace (Is 59:8; Lk 1:79). The Lord's dealing with his people in the Old Testament was not only a matter of revealing to them a way to live in his covenant instruction on Mount Sinai, but it was also acted out on the plane of history as a leading of his people—out of Egypt, in the Exodus, through the desert by the column of cloud and fire by night (Ex 13:21f). Though this period also had its difficulties and thus became a time of testing in which the people experienced God's road as long and winding (Deut 2:1f), it was a road that led to rest and blessing, so that Israel could sing: "The ways of the Lord are love and truth" (Ps 25:10) and "all his ways are right" (Deut 32:4).

To "walk in the ways of the Lord" (Ps 123:1) became associated more and more with the observance of his law (Bar 3:37; 4:1). Led off into exile because she had abandoned the path of justice, Israel was promised a glorious return. Second Isaiah heralded it with the words "prepare in the desert a *highway* for the Lord" (Is 40:3).

It was upon this text that the preaching of John the Baptist built:

"Prepare the way of the Lord" (Lk 3:4). It was probably in dependence upon this tradition that the earliest name given to the Christian community according to Luke was simply "the way" (Acts 9:2; 18:25; 24:22). Though this new way demanded a return to a sincere moral conscience of which the law was the external expression, the early Christian community differed from its Jewish contemporaries in that it considered the way of the Lord no longer to be the law but Jesus in person ("I am the way," John 14:6). Thus, while the psalmist of old urged his compatriots to "walk in the law of the Lord" (Ps 119:1), Paul says instead, "As therefore you received Christ Jesus the Lord, so walk in him" (Col 2:6). To walk in the Lord Jesus means in effect to walk in love (Eph 5:2), according to the teaching of Jesus and above all according to his example (Eph 5:2) and by the power of that same love poured into the heart by the Holy Spirit (Rom 5:5; Gal 5:22). Love, that is, the divine agape rooted in the teaching, the example and the spirit of Jesus, is the essence of the Christian life. Quite fittingly, therefore, does Paul call it the way that surpasses all charismatic manifestations of the Spirit, for if the gifts are useful for building up the church if they are used in love, love builds up of its very nature (1 Cor 8:1). In other words, the charismatic gifts are to be instruments and ministries of love. The charisms are slaves, love is the master.

13:1-3: In this first section of the hymn, Paul describes the hypothetical person who might have highly prized gifts yet would lack charity. He begins with tongues. There is no reason whatever to press the distinction between "tongues of men" and "tongues of angels" as if the former were used to communicate with men and the latter to be used to worship God, for the "tongues of men" used in the prayer meeting is primarily a language of worship (14:16). Paul simply wants to be as inclusive as possible. The tongue speaker who lacks love is like a hollow cymbal or gong. Cymbals were part of the ancient temple liturgy, and castanets, cymbals, tambourines, and other brass instruments are known to have been used in the various Greek religions of Paul's day. The use of tongues, just as the exercise of any of the other gifts, is no infallible sign of charity and if a man does not have love in his heart, all his tongues do is to manifest the emptiness within him.

Paul then progresses to higher gifts according to his own scale, the gift of knowledge, prophecy and working of miracles. These gifts, Paul himself has said, are of greater utility to the church—but if the user does not have love, he is simply nothing.

In the climactic position Paul considers the gifts of service (recall 12:28). He imagines the highest form of external charity, a case in which one distributes everything he has to the poor—the Greek verb suggests dividing what one has into small pieces or mouthfuls to give it away, thus not only giving up what one does not need, but reducing oneself to absolute indigence. Could anything more heroic be imagined? Paul adds one final, seemingly heroic self-sacrifice—giving one's body to be burned. Some Scripture scholars think that "to be burned" refers to the ancient practice of branding a slave, and that Paul would here be considering the magnificent act of selling oneself into slavery for someone else. This is indeed possible, but there is no parallel to such a usage anywhere else in the Bible. On the other hand, both in the Bible and outside it there are several instances recorded of persons who gave themselves to be burned as a sacrifice. Paul may have in mind the reference in Dan 3:95 to the three young man who "yielded their bodies rather than serve or worship any God except their own God." Ancient Greece knew of other philosophers or "holy men" who burned themselves alive—the Hindu philosopher Calanos and another Hindu Zarmanochegas who had himself burned in Athens in 20 A.D., the inscription on his tomb reading: "He made himself immortal." There was also the legend that at the time of an invasion by Dorians, Hellotis and one of her young sisters threw themselves into the flames of a burning temple in Athens, a myth commemorated by the funeral feast called the *Hellotia*. Paul may not have all of these instances before his mind as he writes, but may be simply thinking of some magnificent act of self-immolation which would not be motivated by love. He is not envisioning the Christian martyrs of the future—though even they need to be reminded that the human glory of martyrdom is not a sufficient reason for choosing it, as T. S. Eliot brilliantly underlines in Thomas' last temptation in *Murder in the Cathedral:* "The last temptation is the greatest treason, to do the right thing for the wrong reason."

1 Cor 13:4-7: Love Does Everything

> 4. Love is patient; love is kind. Love is not jealous, it does not put on airs, it is not snobbish. 5. Love is never rude, it is not self-seeking, it is not prone to anger; neither does it brood over injuries. 6. Love does not rejoice in what is wrong but rejoices with the truth. 7. There is no limit to love's forbearance, to its trust, its hope, its power to endure. (NAB)

13:4: In verse 4-7 Paul develops the second section of this hymn by personifying charity as a living, feeling, thinking guide of the Christian life. "Love is patient," says the NAB text. In our contemporary language "patience" covers a wide range of experiences, all the way from waiting in line at the supermarket checkout counter to refraining from honking the horn in a traffic jam. The Biblical term is more precise. It means to be slow to anger, and not to return injury for injury. The New Testament writers pointed to Jesus' example of it in his passion. It does not mean merely restraining an inner hatred under a pleasant exterior but refers even to the inner dispositions. Love is never bitter, and it does not desire to "get even."

"Love is kind." In modern language our word "kindness" has become worn so thin that it often suggests mere external gentility. Paul is so concerned to describe the uniqueness of love in this trait that he coins a word not found elsewhere in the Bible or even in non-Biblical Greek. It suggests the warm, benevolent welcome that the Christian gives his brothers. It suggests magnanimity, hospitality and generosity with time and service, an eagerness to make one's brother and sister in the Lord experience their preciousness.

After two positive characteristics, Paul gives eight negative ones. Love is not jealous or envious. Such a remark would be especially appropriate for the Corinthian community split by party spirit (chs. 1-3) and competitive pretensions in the matter of the spiritual gifts (8:1; 12).

Love "does not put on airs." Here is another word not found elsewhere in the Bible or even in profane Greek. Apparently it means to brag or boast. And probably Paul has in mind the kind of boastful ostentation he has already pointed out in the Corinthians. The same may be said of the next trait, "it is not snobbish." Webster's definition of the snob may be helpful here: "One who blatantly imitates, fawningly admires, or vulgarly seeks association with those whom he regards as his superiors," or "one who repels the advances of those whom he regards as his inferiors." Charity, on the other hand, seeks out the lowly (Rom 12:16). The love given by the Spirit is like water poured out which always seeks to fill the lowest level first and is comfortable with its own level only when the needs of those around it are filled.

13:5 "Love is never rude." It is not ill-mannered or lacking in propriety. It acts with respect, delicacy, with an instinct for what is most appropriate. This trait is singularly lacking in the Corinthian community, as Paul has pointed out in many ways. The Corinthians have been taking their disputes to pagan courts, there was a public scandal of incest, some had turned the Eucharist into an orgy, and some of the Corinthians who lived in a city in which ritual prostitution had been practiced at the temple of Aphrodite had apparently not come to see that the agape of the Spirit of Jesus excluded the *eros* promoted by Aphrodite.

"It is not self-seeking." Unlike *eros* and other forms of love, the love of agape is a purest seeking of the other's good and not a promotion of one's own self-interest. It is not a question here of merely refraining from excess or injustice in dealing with one's neighbor but even being inclined to give up one's own rights for the good of a neighbor. According to Mt 5:38-42, Jesus told his disciples that the kind of love he was offering them would lead them to give up their rights in certain cases. It was the kind of love, Paul says, that Jesus himself showed: "Christ did not please himself" (Rom 15:3). Though Paul himself had every right to monetary support from the communities he founded, he often renounced this right (1 Thes 2:9; 2 Thes 3:8; 1 Cor 9:15). After chiding the Corinthians for taking their law suits to pagan courts and asking them why they could not settle their disputes within the Christian community, Paul asks whether it might not even be better to allow themselves to be cheated than to rise up against a brother (6:7). In particular some of the "enlightened" gnostics of the Corinthian community had used their private knowledge to offend the consciences of their weaker brothers and thus lead them into sin (8:1ff.).

"Love is not prone to anger." The root verb in the Greek means "to make sharp or pointed, to make acid or sour." In the moral sense, it means to irritate or to provoke to anger, to exasperate. Under pressure, the highest human love is likely to collapse. Not so the divine love. It may suffer much, but, far from being easily piqued, its capacity to endure without responding in bitterness or collapsing under the attack, points to its origin in the Lord.

"Neither does it brood over injuries." Literally, the Greek says, "It does not think unto itself evil." The Greek verb can mean "to plot," as in Zech 8:17, and in this case it would mean that charity does not plot evil. However, this negative description of charity would seem to be so obvious and minimal that it would hardly fit the present position amid this litany of the heroic marks of charity. Among the several secondary meanings of the word, the one "to take note of" seems best, and this in turn can be interpreted in two ways: either that charity does not judge the evil that it notices in one's neighbor—it refuses to condemn (2 Cor 5:19) and would rather even not know about it (see Ps 144:3)—or it may mean that charity pays no attention to the evil done to oneself—that is, "it does not brood over injuries," or, as the *Good News* version renders it, "Love does not keep a record of wrongs." It means more than simply the absence of bitterness, more even than forgiveness. It means that the memory of the evil is healed so that the state of the person's feeling is more perfect than it was before the injury was sustained. Obviously, one cannot rewrite history in terms of suppression of facts, but one can rewrite it in terms of reinterpreting those facts in a way that is healing both for oneself and for the offender. Whether this has taken place can be judged by whether or not the Christian's reaction to the other is constrained or inhibited by the memory of past wrongs sustained or whether on the other hand, it has the freedom and the energy to be fresh in its response to the good in others. Charity, then, resists putting the other in a box and keeping him there. If the other insists on keeping himself in a box, it should only be because the box is of his own making and not because its walls are buttressed by the judgments and the memories of his fellow community members. For when the Lord forgives, biblically speaking, he casts man's sins behind his back, and that means he sees them no longer (Is 38:17).

"Love does not rejoice in what is wrong but rejoices with the truth." If up to this point charity seems to be a passive and even a blind kind of virtue, this impression is now balanced by a positive description of its reaction to moral evil and to moral goodness. That charity which is so non-violent and even forgetful of evil done to oneself is keenly sensitive to evil done to someone else. The prophetic nature of charity thus comes to the fore, for God's love finds no joy in evil or suffering—even when evil befalls one's enemies! More than that, "if your enemy is hungry, feed him; if he is thirsty, give him something to drink . . . do not be conquered by evil but conquer evil by good" (Rom 12:12-21).

Such is the way charity responds to evil. In the presence of the good and the true, charity rejoices—with a strong emphasis on rejoicing *with*. Truth here, of course, does not mean philosophical or scientific truth isolated from the total context of human living. It has essentially rather the very practical meaning which truth has in the Old Testament in terms of goodness and fidelity. It does mean, of course, that charity rejoices when it comes to know the Lord and his goodness better. The later Pauline epistles will develop the "knowing" or contemplative aspect of charity as the fire in whose light Christians contemplate the mystery of God. But here it seems to refer more to mutual relationships and means that, impelled by divine love, the Christian will actively applaud the good and the true wherever it is found. To speak out and even acclaim the good we find in others is just as important a function of charity as forgetting the evil that is done to oneself. To do this is not easy, for to praise someone's goodness is really to go out on a limb for him, to take a risk, without assurance that the person praised will continue to show himself worthy of the praise given, and should he fall short of it, the one who praises might blush in the embarrassment that his trust was mistaken. And thus only one who is rooted in the deep self-assurance that comes from experiencing God's love can really risk praising others. To praise the other is not only to respond to the good already there but also to believe in the unseen future which is now but a seed. But it is also, as an effect of the divine love, the most certain nourishment for that growth (Rom 8:14-39).

13:7: "There is no limit to love's forbearance . . ." Sometimes this expression is translated "Charity endures (or bears) all things." But as that would simply be a repetition of the first quality listed in vs. 4, it seems that the other meaning of "to cover, keep hidden" is meant here. Charity prefers to keep the faults of the neighbor hidden. It does not gossip, neither to spread scandal nor even to relate unfavorable news about a neighbor. The meaning is profound, and perhaps some of the categories of contemporary psychology might help us to understand what is at issue here. In embracing the neighbor, love not only embraces the bright side, the virtue of the person, which has a certain rational attraction about it, but it even extends to embrace his dark side, his weaknesses, and even those things which he does not like to face about himself. Like God himself, the arms of charity go all the way around the person loved. That is why charity is not eager to talk about the dark side of the other, because it knows that that side is mystery, that it is moreover not all there is to say about the person, and that moreover the mystery of the person is kept enshrined in the precious sanctuary of one's own heart where profane traffic is not allowed to pass.

"No limit to its trust . . ." Literally, "believes all things." Since it is not a question here of the faith that saves or directly of one's response to the Good News, the word "believe" must refer to interpersonal relations. It does not mean, of course, that charity is naively credulous but rather that it is by nature (that is, by gift of divine grace) inclined to believe the good about others and to trust them. It is not inclined to be suspicious.

"No limit to its hope." Literally, "hopes all things." The slight shade of difference between this and the preceding seems to be that charity not only is inclined to believe the good about the other's past or present, but that it believes also in the future of those it loves, and it communicates this belief, this hope. Even when there has been evil in the past and charity (which loves the truth) must admit it, it knows that "for those who love God, he makes all things work together unto good" (Rom 8:28), and, not willing to forego this hope, it communicates its confidence and trust to the other. This kind of trust is not the conclusion of a rational syllogism or mere good business sense based on the fact that the other has already proven his trustworthiness. It is rather the creative trust that comes from love and is willing to risk when the trustworthiness of the other has not been proved.

"No limit to its power to endure." Literally, "it endures all things."

In the context of what immediately precedes, the sense would seem to be that even when every hope is thwarted, love is never crushed nor defeated. The one who loves will continue to carry his neighbor in redemptive suffering and prayer even when it takes years. It is the kind of "bearing" that Monica did for Augustine—eighteen years of prayers, tears, and trust in the outcome.

Father Ceslaus Spicq, to whom the present author is indebted for many of these insights into Paul's hymn to charity, notes a progression in the last three traits of charity: "When charity sees no evidence of evil, it believes the most favorable thing possible of others. If its faith is contradicted by facts, it still hopes for the best. If its hope is disappointed, it is not discouraged." (*Agape in the New Testament*, II, St. Louis: B. Herder, 1965, p. 160).

These activities of charity described in verses 4-7 can be compared to the fruits of the Spirit or of love in Gal 5:22: "The fruit of the Spirit is love, joy, peace, patience, kindness, generosity, faith, mildness, and self-control." It can also be pointed out that Jesus himself is the supreme model of each of these traits of love and that one could reread the whole section substituting "Jesus" wherever the word "love" appears.

1 Cor 13:8-13: Love Lasts Forever

> 8. Love never fails. Prophecies will cease, tongues will be silent, knowledge will pass away. 9. Our knowledge is imperfect and our prophesying is imperfect. 10. When the perfect comes, the imperfect will pass away. 11. When I was a child I used to talk like a child, think like a child, reason like a child. When I became a man I put childish ways aside. 12. Now we see indistinctly, as in a mirror; then we shall see face to face. My knowledge is imperfect now; then I shall know even as I am known. 13. There are in the end three things that last: faith, hope, and love, and the greatest of these is love. (NAB)

13:8-11: After having shown that charity is essential (vss. 1-3) and that it is universal in effect (vss. 4-7), Paul now in this final strophe shows how charity outlasts everything else in the Christian life. "Love never fails." The Greek verb is used in its literal sense to describe something falling—an animal or a city or a person. In its transferred sense it is often used in the Bible to describe the faithful man who lives in righteousness for awhile and then gives in to temptation and falls (Prov 24:16; Sir 1:30). God's gifts and promises, however, do not fail (Jos

23:14; Ruth 3:18). The love of charity is not like *eros* which is fickle. The love of charity never ceases to act and, as will be evident in what follows, it will not be basically any different in eternity than it is here in time. In this sense it differs essentially from prophecy and tongues and the kind of partial knowledge which is characteristic of our present ways of knowing and of communicating (vs. 8-10). The difference between the now and the then can be likened to the difference between the state of childhood in which one thinks and talks and reasons like a child and that of adulthood in which the imperfections of childhood are put aside. Perhaps Paul has in mind childish babbling in the term "to talk like a child," and thus is making a veiled allusion to tongues. If so, he does not conceive of this kind of communicating passing away during this life, for it seems to be an inevitable characteristic of the partial expression of the mystery which is as much as Christians are capable of in the present life.

13:12: Mirrors today give a rather faithful reflection of the individual who looks at himself in one. Not so in ancient times, for the mirrors were not well polished and they were usually concave or convex, so that the image was both dim and distorted. Corinth was famous for the mirrors manufactured there. They were often used for divination. The person would look into the water or into the mirror and gaze intently until some kind of image appeared either there or in his imagination which could then be interpreted in terms of the future or of something hidden or unknown in the present. The story of Narcissus gazing at an image of himself, falling in love with himself and being transformed into the flower, was well-known. The world itself was thought to be a mirror through which one can arrive at some knowledge of God, as the Jew Philo taught. Paul himself will stress this in Rom 1:20, that God is knowable not directly but through his creation. But the use of the expression "indistinctly," which is the NAB's translation of the Greek *en ainigmati*, points us to the biblical roots of Paul's conception here. In Numbers 12:6-8, the Lord declares that he made himself known to prophets in visions and spoke to them in dreams, but to Moses he spoke mouth to mouth plainly and not in riddles (the same Greek word used here in Paul's text). Now the charismatic gifts of communication operative at Corinth resemble these imperfect revelations of the Old Testament. However marvelous they may be in their means of communication, they are essentially imperfect and obscure. However necessary they may be for the present life they cannot compare with the face to face encounter (the expression replaces *mouth to mouth* of Num 12:8 and alludes instead to Ex 33:20, which assures man that he cannot see God face to face in this present mortal life).

"Then I shall know even as I am known." It is obvious that our knowledge even of the world around us has an obscurity and an imperfection about it. But of no knowledge is this obscurity so characteristic as of our self-knowledge and self-understanding. We know how energizing it is to come to an insight into ourselves through a dream or by the reflection which a friend gives us upon ourselves. Even this, of course, is partial, since no other human being knows us perfectly either. Who then does? Only God—and one of the promised joys of the future life is to know ourselves as God knows us, that is, to see in him not only the mystery of his own nature but also everything else that he sees and knows, particularly the mysterious depths of our self. In the present life our depths are known only by God. But if we live in charity and love we have an assurance of being known by God as the special object of his elective love; "If anyone loves God he is known by God" (1 Cor 8:3). Thus the perfect knowledge into which we may enter in the future life is the sharing of God's own knowledge but in this life the sharing of God's life is done more by love than it is by clear knowledge.

13:13: This verse is quite difficult to interpret. The Greek literally says, "Now then there abide three things . . ." The question is whether the "now" is simply a way of introducing the summary of all that has gone before, or whether it is to be taken in a real temporal sense referring to the present life in which case the sense would be, "In this present life there are three things . . ." This seems to be the preferable meaning, for Paul himself elsewhere insists that faith and hope disappear in the state of glory when the soul is in possession of the object of its search (2 Cor 5:7; Rom 8:24). Paul seems, then, not only to put charity in a completely different category above the charisms but to join to it as well the virtues of faith and hope which are the necessary preambles to charity in this life. In the context of the charisms, perhaps it would be better to say that faith, hope, and charity belong to the foundation or the root (Col 1:23; 2:7; Eph 3:17) of the whole spiritual organism of which the charisms are the manifestations (1 Cor 12:7).

1 Cor 14:1-5: Prophecy, Tongues and Interpretation

1. Make love your aim, and earnestly desire the spiritual gifts, especially that you may prophesy. 2. For one who speaks in a tongue speaks not to men but to God; for no one understands him, but he utters mysteries in the Spirit. 3. On the other hand, he who prophesies speaks to men for their upbuilding and encouragement and consolation. 4. He who speaks in a tongue edifies himself, but he who prophesies edifies the church.

5. Now I want you all to speak in tongues, but even more to prophesy. He who prophesies is greater than he who speaks in tongues, unless some one interprets, so that the church may be edified. (RSV)

14:1: If love is a gift put in our hearts by the Holy Spirit (Rom 5:5), it is nevertheless something to be sought after and pursued constantly. This suggests that charity does not work automatically or blindly but that the Christian must prize it and seek to grow in it. However (and Paul's Greek is clearly adversative here), the pursuit of genuine charity is in no way opposed to desiring and earnestly seeking after the spiritual gifts. The Greek word *zēloute* comes from a root verb meaning to boil, bubble or glow (Rom 12:11), with the transferred sense of zeal or ardor. Suggesting a passionate desire and an active seeking of the gifts, it implies that the gifts would not come simply automatically, that they must be yearned for and prayed for. It is not a question of being passively open to receive them "if God wants to give them," but rather of making them the object of intense intercessory prayer in the name of Jesus (Mk 11:24; Lk 11:9-13; Mt 7:7-11; Jn 14:13-14). This surprising exhortation makes sense only if the gifts are understood to be modes by which the Christian life operates under the Holy Spirit. Thus if tongues is seen not as an esoteric language but as a gift of inspired praise, and prophecy seen to be a special gift for hearing the word of God for the community here and now, and healing a way in which the redeeming power is made real—then to have the gifts is not a matter of indifference but of growth. The charisms then would be the laboratory in which God is experienced as gift. The gift that should especially be sought is that of prophecy. Paul now develops his thoughts on this gift.

14:2: Paul develops the excellence of prophecy first by comparing it with tongues. He who speaks in a tongue speaks to God. Obviously, therefore, the gift of tongues is primarily a gift of prayer both of praise and of unconscious petition. "Tongues" has to do with the upward movement of prayer rather than to its downward or horizontal movement. He who speaks in a tongue "speaks mysteries in the Spirit." From this text it is abundantly clear that the gift of tongues is non-rational speech. What is meant by the "mysteries" which are uttered in the Spirit? Obviously the mysteries of God himself, particularly his unspeakable gifts to men:

"What we utter is God's wisdom in mystery, a hidden wisdom planned by God before all ages for our glory. None of the rulers of this age knew the mystery; if they had known it, they

would never have crucified the Lord of Glory. Of this wisdom
it is written: 'Eyes have not seen, ears have not heard, nor has
it so much as dawned on man what God has prepared for those
who love him.' Yet God has revealed this wisdom to us
through the Spirit. The Spirit scrutinizes all matters, even the
deep things of God. . . . No one knows what lies in the depths
of God but the Spirit of God. The Spirit we have received is
not the world's spirit but God's Spirit, helping us to recognize
the gifts he has given us. We speak of these, not in words of
human wisdom but in words taught by the Spirit, thus interpreting spiritual things in spiritual terms." (1 Cor 2:7-13—
NAB)

In our present passage, where spirit is contrasted with intelligible speech
(as it is later in 14:15) it obviously refers to a kind of prayer of the heart
(or "of the spirit") that moves from the mysterious depths or the inward
mystery of the self towards the depths of God in ways that cannot be put
into words (Rom 8:26). If Paul sees here the limitations of tongues as a
means of communicating with the community, in the text in Romans he
portrays the advantage of this kind of prayer precisely because it can
transcend the limits of human understanding and control (Rom 8:26-27).
It is perhaps what the author of the Epistle to the Ephesians is referring
to by "praying in the Spirit" (Eph 6:18). Others may indeed enter into
the spirit of this prayer, but the intelligible meaning of it is not readily
available to them.

   14:3: The prophet speaks to men. Hence this gift involves an intelligible message understandable by those who are around. The Greek
text says literally, "he who prophesies speaks to men edification and encouragement and consolation." The object of the message (and not just
its purpose) is described in three terms, the first of which is "edification." Paul chooses the word from the architectural language of the day.
It describes the process by which a house is built up to perfection and
completion. In Paul it means anything that contributes to the increase of
faith, hope, love, and unity in the community. It is interesting to compare this text with the prophetic function assigned to Jeremiah at the
time of his call: "See, I place my words in your mouth! This day I set
you over nations and over kingdoms to root up and to tear down, to destroy and to demolish, *to build* and to plant" (Jer 1:9-10). Old Testament prophecy had the negative function of destroying what was not
truly from the Lord. If that function remains in the New Testament, it
certainly does not receive much emphasis in connection with prophecy,
and it is completely ignored here in Paul, primarily, it seems, because
the Corinthian community needed the positive effects of unifying love,

encouragement and consolation. It had already been openly fragmented by an individualistic use of the charisms. Hence there seem to be very good reasons in the concrete circumstances of the Corinthian community why Paul would not stress the exorcizing and destructive function of prophecy. It was part of Jesus' prophetic role, of course, to identify and exorcize the demonic powers he encountered, whether these were cases of possession of individuals or of false teaching. And in the charismatic community at Corinth there was also the gift of the discerning of spirits (1 Cor 12:10). But perhaps Paul is aware that it is all too easy to canonize one's own personal hostilities and grievances under the guise of prophecy, and that, practically speaking, it is better to direct the prophet to exercise his gifts in terms of the positive goals he here describes. In addition to upbuilding, Paul adds the message of *encouragement.* The Greek word is *paraklēsis*, from which the word paraclete comes. The latter means literally someone like a lawyer, who stands by one's side and speaks in one's behalf. If the Holy Spirit will be described by John as the "other paraclete" *par excellence* (Jn 14:16, 26), it is, in Paul's view, primarily through the gift of prophecy that he ministers this word of encouragement to the church. Though not explicit here, it is obvious that prophecy can have a deeply healing effect. The word of Jesus was sufficient to heal (Mt 8:16), and the word of the Lord coming afresh to a community or to an individual who truly listens can have the same effect. The third content Paul lists is consolation. In this he joins the ancient tradition of the Old Testament that the prophet is to console the afflicted (Is 61:1). While true in some way of all Old Testament prophets, it was particularly the role of Second Isaiah to bring to the people in exile the good news of the return to their homeland (Is 40:9). The New Testament prophet continues heralding that "good news" in terms of its complete fulfillment in Jesus Christ and in the ongoing work of the Spirit in the community. The consolation of which there is question here, then, is not a mere expression of sympathy but a communication of the powerful message of hope rooted in the Christ event which can transform sorrow into joy (Jn 16:20).

14:4: It is precisely because Paul wishes these effects to reach the entire community that he sees the advantage of prophecy. With him who speaks in tongues, the effect reaches only the individual. Notice there is no condemnation whatever of the concern to "build up oneself." Obviously any time an individual himself grows in faith, hope or love the community is built up indirectly. The prophet, however, reaches the entire community directly: "He builds up the church."

14:5: Since the effect of tongues is likewise to build up, Paul cannot refrain from desiring that all speak in tongues in order to experience in themselves as individuals the effect of the up-building power of this gift.

His preference for prophecy, however, is evident because of its broader effect. In saying "He who prophesies is greater than he who speaks in tongues *unless* there is interpretation of the tongue," Paul equates interpreted tongues with prophecy. This gives us an insight into the relationship between the experience of tongues and that of interpretation or prophecy. The prophetic word to the community is prepared, it seems, by the gift of tongues, very much in the way in which pregnancy prepares for birth. The non-rational experience of the Spirit has a great advantage precisely because it temporarily at least puts the mind to rest and seeks a deeper union with God in faith and love without words. But just as pregnancy is frustrated without birth, so the activity of tongues is not an end in itself but should normally terminate in some clear message for the community. Precisely because this message is prepared for by a turning over of the self to the Spirit in a deep mood of listening, the word can come indeed as a gift with the freshness and the otherness which a "word of the Lord" can have. If tongues were of no advantage whatever in the overall upbuilding process, then Paul would surely have condemned them outright. As it is, he wants them to be sought and used, but he wants the activity to reach its intended fruit in the upbuilding of the community, which can happen only if the Spirit's meaning comes across to the community in prophecy or interpretation. This leads to a consideration on interpretation.

1 Cor 14:6-12: Communication of Meaning

6. Now, brethren, if I come to you speaking in tongues, how shall I benefit you unless I bring you some revelation or knowledge or prophecy or teaching? 7. If even lifeless instruments, such as the flute or the harp, do not give distinct notes, how will any one know what is played? 8. And if the bugle gives an indistinct sound, who will get ready for battle? 9. So with yourselves; if you in a tongue utter speech that is not intelligible, how will any one know what is said? For you will be speaking into the air. 10. There are doubtless many different languages in the world, and none is without meaning; 11. but if I do not know the meaning of the language, I shall be a foreigner to the speaker and the speaker a foreigner to me. 12. So with yourselves; since you are eager for manifestations of the Spirit, strive to excel in building up the church. (RSV)

14:6: To emphasize the point made above, Paul uses his own case as an example. The Corinthians have heard him many times preaching and teaching. If suddenly he should come to them using the gift of tongues simply to impress them without any kind of meaningful speech they would indeed be surprised.

14:7-11 Paul drives home his teaching with simple comparisons with musical instruments and languages.

14:12: Since it is obvious that the Corinthians have followed his recommendation to "seek the spiritual gifts" (14:1), it is necessary only to remind them not to be satisfied with the gifts they have but to think of the good of the church and to seek these gifts which most build it up.

1 Cor 14:13-19: Interpretation

13. Therefore, he who speaks in a tongue should pray for the power to interpret. 14. For if I pray in a tongue, my spirit prays but my mind is unfruitful. 15. What am I to do? I will pray with the spirit and I will pray with the mind also; I will sing with the spirit and I will sing with the mind also. 16. Otherwise, if you bless with the spirit, how can any one in the position of an outsider say the "Amen" to your thanksgiving when he does not know what you are saying? 17. For you may give thanks well enough, but the other man is not edified. 18. I thank God that I speak in tongues more than you all; 19. nevertheless, in church I would rather speak five words with my mind, in order to instruct others, than ten thousand words in a tongue. (RSV)

Interpretation, like the other gifts, is given in response to prayer, and therefore the gift of tongues, when it is a message addressed to the community, is incomplete without the gift of interpretation (vs. 13). In vs. 14 and following it seems obvious that "praying with my spirit" or "singing with my spirit" or "in the spirit" is a technical term for the gift of tongues especially. In the contrast which Paul draws between spirit and mind it is also obvious that the gift of tongues is non-rational prayer. While praying in tongues, the mind is "empty" or "fruitless." This is precisely the value of praying in the Spirit, namely to relieve the mind of its feverish cerebral activity so that it may rest and be refreshed ultimately by a new word of the Lord. But again the upward movement of non-rational praise of God is only half of the movement of prayer; it needs to be completed by the descending word which will address itself to "my mind as well" (vs. 15). This is especially true in the community context (vs. 16). It is also evident from vs. 16 that the prayer in tongues is primarily praise and thanksgiving, and that it was customary, after an individual offered a spontaneous prayer, for others in the community to respond "Amen." Some commentators think that the "thanksgiving" here refers to a specific part of the Eucharistic celebration. As a matter of fact, in the *Didache*, in the section concerning the Eucharist, there is a rubric reading, "But let the prophets give thanks as they wish" (*Didache* 10:7). Note in vs. 18 that Paul himself has the gift of tongues to a highly developed degree. The emphatic "but in the assembly (or church)" indicates again that tongues are helpful for building up the individual but that their function in the assembly is limited unless they bear fruit in interpretation.

1 Cor 14:20-22: Tongues a Sign

20. Brethren, do not be children in your thinking; be babes in evil, but in thinking be mature. 21. In the law it is written, "By men of strange tongues and by the lips of foreigners will I speak to this people, and even then they will not listen to me, says the Lord." 22. Thus, tongues are a sign not for believers but for unbelievers, while prophecy is not for unbelievers but for believers. (RSV)

After a chiding to "grow up" in their attitudes, and that means to take on a community concern, Paul quotes freely from Is 28:11-12. The whole section of Isaiah 28:1-13 is an oracle of doom uttered against Samaria before its fall to the Assyrians in 721. Isaiah sees the capital city seated on a hill wreathed with its walls like the head of a drunken king, unaware that an enormous storm is about to destroy him and his people. Even priest and prophet stagger from drunkenness and no longer have the power of discernment (28:7). In vss. 9-10 the complacent enemies of Isaiah mock him with the words, "To whom would he impart knowledge? To whom would he convey the message? To those just weaned from milk, those just taken from the breast? For he says, 'Command on command, command on command, rule on rule, rule on rule, here a little, there a little!' " They say that Isaiah is lecturing them as he would lecture children. The Hebrew of his message is *saw lasaw saw lasaw qaw laqaw qaw laqaw, ze'er sham, ze'er sham.* What is being mocked is not so much the message but its sing-song childish sound, a message too simple for adults to listen to. The text makes this interpretation clear as it continues: "Yes, with stammering lips and in a strange language he will speak to this people" (vs. 11). Isaiah has simply repeated again and again the word of the Lord, demanding indeed yet scandalously simple. The drunken mockers accuse him of acting like a school master trying to teach the people by rote, and the message, though crystal-clear to Isaiah, is nothing but a babbling to the mockers. The result, Isaiah says, will be that they will learn this lesson not from him but from the foreign-language Assyrians: "So for them the word of the Lord shall be (here Isaiah repeats verbatim the babbling message of vs. 10), so that when they walk, they stumble backward, broken, ensnared, and captured." Note that to the listeners, who, for all their religious titles are really unbelievers, the sing-song message is a stone of stumbling. What was in itself a sign that should lead to faith became, in the case of the mockers of Samaria, a sign of judgment because of their bad dispositions. Now speaking in tongues has this same kind of ambiguity, as every sign does. A sign is something that makes a person stop and think —and the gift of tongues at Pentecost did just that for the Jews of all languages living in Jerusalem, at least according to Acts 2. It got their attention. In this sense it was a sign for those who did not believe, of whom some would come to believe, some would not. For those who come to believe and receive the gift of the Spirit, tongues no longer have the "mysterious" attraction they did before; they are understood now and used as the language of the Spirit, as a personal way of praising God. It is no longer an ambivalent occasion of faith or disbelief but it becomes a language and an expression of the faith itself.

Prophecy, however, Paul says, is for those who believe. Although one might conclude that in virtue of the parallelism with the preceding part of vs 22, prophecy is implicitly a sign, Paul does *not repeat* the word *sign* when he describes prophecy. He simply says it is not for nonbelievers, but for believers. He does not therefore consider prophecy to be a sign, as tongues are. Its meaning is clear and unambiguous within the context of a believing community. It is not a missionary gift but a gift for building up the community.

1 Cor 14:23-25: Prophecy for Visitors

23. If, therefore, the whole church assembles and all speak in tongues, and outsiders or unbelievers enter, will they not say that you are mad? 24. But if all prophesy, and an unbeliever or outsider enters, he is convicted by all, he is called to account

by all, 25. the secrets of his heart are disclosed; and so, falling
on his face, he will worship God and declare that God is really
among you. (RSV)

At first sight these verses seem in exact contradiction with what
preceded, at least if "sign" is taken in a missionary sense as the occasion
for coming to faith, for Paul says that such a sign is likely to turn the
non-believer off (vs. 23), whereas prophecy will tend to convert him (vss.
24-25), which would obviously mean that prophecy has a missionary
function. How can we avoid the conclusion that Paul contradicted himself in these short verses? One solution might be that what Paul is really
objecting to is the disorderliness of all speaking in tongues at once. Vs.
24, though, is exactly parallel to verse 23, and there Paul finds it good
for the unbeliever that "all are uttering prophecy." Since he does not
approve of disorderliness in prophecy any more than in tongues (14:29-
30), it would seem rather that he is not concerned at this point with
disorderliness but rather with the nature of tongues and prophecy themselves.

A better solution may be found in understanding the meaning of
sign. Because of its natural ambiguity, a sign can be viewed in different
ways, like a glass that may be called half-full or half-empty. A sign is a
visible thing that points to and invites faith in a superior reality. Inasmuch as it is given as a means of faith, it is good and for many people
the occasion for their coming to the faith. However, inasmuch as a sign
is not the divine reality itself, it has its limitations, as is confirmed by
the fact that many people see the sign and still do not go on to experience the reality to which it is a sign. So, too, the ambiguous nature of
tongues as a sign seems to be in Paul's mind in the quotation from
Isaiah. Isaiah's message was indeed the word of the Lord, but it was not
understood as such by those who listened. It was just babbling. So likewise the babbling of tongues can be open to misinterpretation. As a sign
it has a pointing value, but that value is limited certainly for the unbeliever. (For the believer it is really no longer in the category of invita-
tional sign, which has ambiguity, but rather in the category of expres-
sional sign, in which the user is certain of its significance.) This being
the case, tongues should not normally be used as a missionary device,
certainly if they are used without interpretation. The danger, however,
of prophecy being confusing to non-believers who happen to be attend-
ing the Christian assembly is less, for prophecy speaks directly to the intelligence, and it has a convincing and converting power (vss. 24-25).

A final comment might clear up the ambiguity altogether. Since

Paul explicitly says further on that tongues are not to be suppressed, it seems that when he is speaking of tongues here, he means *uninterpreted* tongues. Uninterpreted tongues may not be an obstacle to the believing community (though Paul doubts their upbuilding value), but they can be a great obstacle for the unbeliever or the unlearned. They would seem sheer madness. Tongues, then, have a limited value, for they are preparational to hearing the word. Their limitation becomes greater if there is no clarification of meaning for the community or for those who are drawn to the phenomenon. So too in Acts 2, the crowds are drawn to the phenomenon of tongues, but Peter's explanatory sermon is an example of interpretation which was immediately given.

1 Cor 14:26-33a: Practical Directions for Order

> 26. What then, brethren? When you come together, each one has a hymn, a lesson, a revelation, a tongue, or an interpretation. Let all things be done for edification. 27. If any speak in a tongue, let there be only two or at most three, and each in turn; and let one interpret. 28. But if there is no one to interpret, let each of them keep silence in church and speak to himself and to God. 29. Let two or three prophets speak, and let the others weigh what is said. 30. If a revelation is made to another sitting by, let the first be silent. 31. For you can all prophesy one by one, so that all may learn and all be encouraged; 32. and the spirits of prophets are subject to prophets. 33. For God is not a God of confusion but of peace. (RSV)

14:26: Paul gets right to the point in this verse: use all the gifts and let everything be done for building up the community.

14:29: The number "two or three" is approximative and is directed toward putting some order in the Corinthian enthusiasm. Implicit in this statement is the fact that no prophet can claim absolute authority for what he says, and that there can be degrees of validity to prophetic speech. The "others" are to discern what the individual prophet says. Who are "the others"—the rest of the prophets or the entire community? We do not know. What is to be retained is not only the need for discernment of prophecy but Paul's trust that the community either as a whole or through certain offices has the ability to discern. If the prophecy is in line with the Christian profession of faith (1 Cor 12:3) and if it produces the fruits of the Spirit (Gal 5:22), the community will be able to say, by its mood if not in actual words, "Amen!" (cf. 14:16).

14:30-33a: Paul here provides simple rules of order and sequence, adding the important statement that "the spirits of the prophets are under the prophets' control." This is in contrast to the impulsive and chaotic manifestations in the pagan rites (12:2). The fundamental reason is, of course, that the author of all these gifts is God himself, whose gift and purpose is peace.

1 Cor 14:33b-40: Paul's Authority in the Matter

> 33. As in all the churches of the saints, 34. the women should keep silence in the churches. For they are not permitted to speak, but should be subordinate, as even the law says. 35. If there is anything they desire to know, let them ask their husbands at home. For it is shameful for a woman to speak in church. 36. What! Did the word of God originate with you, or are you the only ones it has reached?
>
> 37. If any one thinks that he is a prophet, or spiritual, he should acknowledge that what I am writing to you is a command of the Lord. 38. If any one does not recognize this, he is not recognized. 39. So, my brethren, earnestly desire to prophesy, and do not forbid speaking in tongues; 40. but all things should be done decently and in order. (RSV)

14:33b-35: Taken at its face value, this text bars women from any public utterance in the assembly, in flat contradiction of 11:5, 13, where it is assumed they pray and prophesy. These verses also disturb the flow of thought from vs. 33a to 37, which concerns, as does all of chapter 14, the regulation of prophetic and praying activity, not questioning by women. Some manuscripts of the Western tradition have verses 34-35 after vs. 40. For these reasons and others too detailed to discuss here, a number of contemporary scholars consider them, along with a similar passage in 1 Tim 2:11-15, to have been added by a later hand, possibly as an answer to the Montanists in the second century. These factors have to be considered when trying to weigh the authority of this text which the Church did receive into the canon of inspired scriptures. If it is original to Paul, to avoid a contradiction with 11:5, 13, the speaking must refer only to discussion, not to praying and prophesying.

14:36: Paul again skewers the self-righteousness of the Corinthians

The body of Christ is the universal Church, and it is utter stupidity for an individual community to become an island unto itself, cut off from the mainland of the Christian experience.

14:37-38: Here Paul emphasizes that prophecy and the spiritual gifts are to be subordinate to the teaching of Jesus and to the authority of the apostle. In precisely what sense "what I have written you is the Lord's commandment" is not clear, except that Jesus himself urged his disciples to be at peace with one another and not to be ambitious for the higher ranks (Mk 9:35-37, 50). Likewise, it is clear that the word of the Lord Jesus is to be the discerning touchstone for all charismatic activity in the Church. The Gospel of Matthew, as we shall see, was written for the purpose of providing to a community divided in its charismatic leadership a great store of the words of Jesus to which the community should return for discernment.

14:39-30: For the third time Paul urges his readers to seek the gifts, particularly prophecy. And he insists that tongues are not to be forbidden. His final point is that everything be done properly and in order.

Conclusion

If we have treated the charisms and charity with such detail in this long chapter, it is in the conviction that the church has suffered much from too rigid a separation of its treatment of charisms from its discussion of the spiritual life and the growth of charity. Though aimed at building up the body in charity, the spiritual gifts are also important elements for personal growth in charity. The major charismatic gifts reveal a structure of inspired prayer that is useful for both individual and community. The gift of tongues is simply a gift of inspired praise. If nothing else, it reminds us that prayer is primarily praise and thanksgiving, and that we need sufficient freedom and spontaneity to allow such praise to be expressed in non-conceptual ways. Prophecy is an inspired hearing of the word of God, and it alerts the community and the individual to the importance of listening in prayer. The gift of healing opens a dimension of the "coming" of God into human life that is intimate and deep, the God who "touches" us in our deepest selves, even physically. And the gifts of service remind us that service is not only a duty, it is a gift, and when it proceeds from a heart that praises, listens, and is healed, it can refresh in the service.

Obviously, this chapter confirms even more than the preceding ones, that the roots of the charismatic spirit are in the Old Testament phenomenon of prophecy, here experienced in a community dimension. But it is also clear that in such a community, authority and tradition also play a necessary role, and that the community prophetic spirit inspires order rather than individualistic chaos. The ultimate reason for this is that over the symphony of interacting gifts in the community presides one supreme inspiration and one supreme conductor—love.

15
The New Covenant
of the Spirit:
2 Corinthians

What is called the Second Letter to the Corinthians belongs to the same general period of Paul's ministry as the first, though it may actually be a collection of several letters of Paul to the community in Corinth. It contains several rich texts on the Holy Spirit.

2 Cor 1:21-22: The Spirit as "Down-Payment"

21. God is the one who firmly establishes us along with you in Christ; it is he who anointed us 22. and has sealed us, thereby depositing the first payment, the Spirit, in our hearts. (NAB)

In defending his ministry as sincere and not wishy-washy, Paul thinks of God's own sincerity in fulfilling his promises, and of Jesus Christ who was the "yes" to all those promises. For this reason when we worship together we address our Amen to God thru Jesus Christ (vs. 20). The idea of worship and especially the word *Amen*, coming from the Hebrew verb meaning "to strengthen, establish," leads directly to our verse. "God firmly establishes us with you unto Christ." The mention of Christ suggests to Paul that Christians, like Christ, are anointed. There is a word play here in Greek (*eis christon kai chrisas*) which we could catch in English only by translating: "God firmly establishes us in union with his Anointed One—he has anointed us too!" In the Greek the first verb, "establishes" or "strengthens," is in the present tense and the other three, "anointed," "sealed" and "depositing" are all in aorist tense—a past tense indirecting a single, once-done act. Clearly Paul is referring to the initial moment at which he and his readers became Christians. The question arises, though, whether there is any distinction to be seen in the different expressions—whether, for example, the "anointing" refers to a rite connected with baptism, or whether it refers

185

to the spiritual anointing by which the Lord first touched their hearts
and turned them to Christ, prior to baptism. This is a difficult question
to answer, but inasmuch as we have no New Testament evidence of a
ritual of anointing *prior* to baptism, it seems likely that the anointing
refers to the spiritual grace of conversion. It has, let us repeat, been suggested to Paul by the mention of Christ the Anointed One.

What is meant by the second expression, "he has sealed us"? Most
authorities take this to refer to baptism, the Christian successor to circumcision, which Jewish tradition considered the *seal* of Yahweh's covenant with his people (Rom 4:11). Baptism, like circumcision, was a visible sign of belonging to Christ and thus to God's new covenant people.

The third expression says literally in the Greek, "and he gave us the
pledge (or down payment) of the Spirit in our hearts." The "giving of
Spirit in our hearts" is Paul's appropriation of the language used in
Ezekiel's promise of the new covenant of the Spirit (Ez 36:26-27; 37:14),
on which Paul leans heavily in this letter and elsewhere. However, nowhere in the Old Testament is the Spirit called the *pledge* or *downpayment* (the Greek *arrabōn* which the NAB translates, "first payment"). The only place the term appears in the Old Testament is in Gen
38:17-20, where Jacob leaves his seal, cord and staff with Tamar as a
pledge that he will send the gift promised. In the Greek of the secular
world it most often means "earnest money," that is, a partial payment
which gives the buyer a legal claim to the item purchased and to the sell-
er the promise that the rest of the payment will soon be coming. It
always promises something greater yet to come.

Paul's meaning then is clear. The Holy Spirit already given is the
"first installment" of the fulness yet to come. In Eph 1:14 the same term
is used to describe the Spirit: "the pledge of our inheritance, the first
payment against the full redemption of a people God has made his
own." Further on in 2 Cor 5:5, in the midst of a passage in which Paul is
contemplating the future glory for which the Christian longs, he describes the Spirit in the same way: "God has fashioned us for this very
thing and has given us the Spirit as a pledge of it." In Rom 8:23, the
Spirit is called the "first fruits." This term makes clear that the Spirit is
not only a pledge but the very beginning, the "foretaste" (Heb 6:4-5) of
what is to come, the resurrection.

Where did Paul get the idea of calling the Holy Spirit the pledge or
the first-fruits? Not from the Old Testament, surely, for the Spirit is
never referred to under that image. We have seen already in 1 Corinthians that Paul considered the indwelling Spirit to be the effect of "bodily" union with the risen Lord. Now the risen Lord, in 1 Cor 15:20, is
called the "*first-fruits* of those who have fallen asleep." Since the Chris-

tian experience of the Holy Spirit is a participation here and now in the risen life of the Lord, it too could be called the "first fruits." In a context in which Paul wishes to emphasize God's fidelity to his promises, he may have been led to use "pledge" instead of "first-fruits" because it reflected better the idea of a guarantee of what is yet to come. At any rate, the newness of insight here is that the Spirit is the gift of the future in the present and here again we find Paul parting ways with the views of late Judaism and of the rabbis, who held that the gift of the Spirit was appropriate only for the age to come.

2 Cor 3:1-3: The Community, Work of the Spirit

> 1. Am I beginning to speak well of myself again? Or do I need letters of recommendation to you or from you as others might? 2. You are my letter, known and read by all men, written on your hearts. 3. Clearly you are a letter of Christ which I have delivered, a letter written not with ink but by the Spirit of the living God, not on tablets of stone but on tablets of flesh in the heart. (NAB)

This passage is found in the very heart of Paul's defense of his authenticity as an apostle. Certain Christian opponents who claim the title apostle profess that they belong to Christ (10:7; 11:23). Like Christ they claim Israelite descendence (11:22), and above all they appeal to their "spiritual" deeds to prove their authenticity (5:12ff.; 11:4ff.; 12:11ff.). One of the ways in which they demonstrated their apostolic authority was by displaying a letter of recommendation from the community in which their deeds were related (3:1 with 12:1ff.). Another way, strangely, was by allowing themselves to be supported financially by the community (12:13ff.).

In response to them, Paul says: "You are my letter, known and read by all men, written on your hearts" (vs. 2). But Paul was not really the author of the letter, only its deliverer: "Clearly you are a letter of Christ which I have delivered, a letter written not with ink but by the Spirit of the living God, not on tablets of stone but on tablets of flesh in the heart" (vs. 3). Paul needs no letter of recommendation from the community, for the community owes its very existence to Paul's ministry. In fact, Christ himself is the author of the community and he has fashioned it by the "Spirit of the living God" (note the triadic reference). The metaphor is sufficiently clear to show that Paul is thinking of the new covenant of the heart promised by Jeremiah and Ezekiel and that he sees this new covenant realized in the community itself. It is a document giving living proof to the reality of Christ and his Spirit.

2 Cor 3:4-6: The New Covenant of the Spirit

> 4. This great confidence in God is ours, through Christ. 5. It is not that we are entitled of ourselves to take credit for anything. Our sole credit is from God, 6. who has made us qualified ministers of a new covenant, a covenant not of a written law but of spirit. The written law kills, but the Spirit gives life. (NAB)

Here Paul defends his qualifications and explicitly uses the term *new covenant* for the new order of salvation. He sharpens the contrast between letter and spirit in a way not foreseen by Jeremiah or Ezekiel. Though these prophets spoke of an inward covenant, it is clear that this was not opposed to an outward formulation of the law—certainly not in Ezekiel, for whom the gift of the spirit was to result in better observance. Ezekiel could surely say with Paul "The spirit gives life," but he certainly could not say "The letter kills." But Paul's own life prior to his conversion showed him how a compulsive observance of the letter of the law could be deadening, and he would have to struggle to liberate the church of Galatia from the same tendency. Here he only briefly touches on the opposition, suggested by the obvious superiority of the community itself to the written document. We should retain from this that God's new covenant is first of all his Church, the community of believers in whose lives Christ and his Spirit are shown to be real. Even the written New Testament, like the rest of God's word, lives only in the living community which hears that word, lives it and manifests its power to the world.

2 Cor 3:7-18: The Lord Is the Spirit; The Spirit Is Freedom

> 7. If the ministry of death, carved in writing on stone, was inaugurated with such glory that the Israelites could not look on Moses' face because of the glory that shone on it (even though it was a fading glory), 8. how much greater will be the glory of the ministry of the Spirit? 9. If the ministry of the covenant that condemned had glory, greater by far is the glory of the ministry that justifies. 10. Indeed, when you compare that li-

mited glory with this surpassing glory, the former should be declared no glory at all. 11. If what was destined to pass away was given in glory, greater by far is the glory that endures.

12. Our hope being such, we act with full confidence. 13. We are not like Moses, who used to hide his face with a veil so that the Israelites could not see the final fading of that glory. 14. Their minds, of course, were dulled. To this very day, when the old covenant is read the veil remains unlifted; it is only in Christ that it is taken away. 15. Even now, when Moses is read a veil covers their understanding. 16. "But whenever he turns to the Lord, the veil will be removed." 17. The Lord is the Spirit, and where the Spirit of the Lord is, there is freedom. 18. All of us, gazing on the Lord's glory with unveiled faces, are being transformed from glory to glory into his very image by the Lord who is the Spirit. (NAB)

Here Paul enters into a Jewish way of reasoning with the help of an Old Testament text, Ex 34:29-35, the account of the radiance of Moses' face as he came down the mountain with the written tablets of the law. Paul contrasts the two covenants in terms of glory. The glory of Moses, though brilliant, was due to fade, that of the ministers of the new covenant is meant to last. And although the reason Moses veiled his face was apparently that the Israelites not be frightened by his radiance, Paul sees the reason as forestalling the disappointment they would have when eventually the glory faded. Then Paul's associative mind jumps to a symbolism he sees in the veil. The real veil is the mental block which the Jews had and which Paul says endures to this day. For when the law is read in the synagogue the veil remains over the writings as over the hearts of the Jews.

In vs. 16 Paul adapts to his purposes Ex 34:34. The text says that whenever Moses turned to face the Lord, he lifted the veil. Paul applies this now to Israel and more specifically to their hearts and says that when they turn to the Lord (Jesus) the veil will be lifted.

Verse 17, a celebrated one in Pauline exegesis, has been interpreted in various ways. Let us stick to the context and note that the Lord here is the risen Jesus, and he is the spirit first of all in contrast to the letter, that is, the old law. (see 3:6). But in the second part of the verse Paul's thought advances. Having mentioned the spirit, he speaks of the "Spirit of the Lord," that is, not just the Lord who is the spirit in contrast to the letter, but the Spirit given by the Lord as the initial gift to all the baptized. Since this Spirit transcends the letter of the old law both in objective revelation and subjective experience, it brings freedom from the limitations of the law. We shall see more about the relation of covenant and freedom in Gal 4:21-31, and inquire further what Paul means by so opposing the Spirit to the law.

For the moment, let us note the light the next verse casts on what Paul has just said. Freedom is not so much a freedom *from* something as it is entry into the full inheritance, the attainment once again of the divine image and paradisal glory. The verse is exceedingly rich. "All of us" is a further contrast of the new covenant with the old. Whereas Moses was necessarily separated from the Israelite community in order to experience the divine glory, such a separation between leader and followers, between teacher and taught, is abolished in the new covenant, as Jeremiah had foretold (Jer 31:34). There is no secrecy or concealment (all have their faces unveiled) because the glory now contemplated will never fade. Some versions translate the Greek participle here "*contemplating* as in a mirror," others "*reflecting* as in a mirror." Either translation is possible. The expression "we are being transformed" does not refer here to the initial justification but to the ongoing process "from glory to glory." And the image into which Christians are being transformed is Christ himself, who is the image of God (2 Cor 4:4). Here we pass beyond the imagery of the exodus to that of creation, for Adam was made to be the image of God. Christ then is the new Adam.

Translations of the last three words (*apo kyriou pneumatos*) vary. The expression can mean: (1) "by the Lord of the Spirit"; (2) "by the Spirit of the Lord"; (3) "by the Lord who is the Spirit" (NAB; RSV); or (4) "by the Lord who is spirit." In the light of the immediate context "the Lord" surely means the Lord Jesus, and he has already been called "the Spirit" in the preceding verse. However, "the Spirit" cannot mean merely, as in vs. 17, the spirit in opposition to the old Law, for we are in the imagery of the new creation. In 1 Cor 15:44-45, as we saw, Christ surpasses the old Adam in that he is life-giving Spirit. This means a dynamic identification (but not a personal identity) of the Lord Jesus with the Spirit, inasmuch as the Spirit proceeds from Jesus risen. The basic idea is the same, but whereas in 1 Cor 15 the stress was on the final new creation at the resurrection of the just, here it is a question of the ongoing transformation of the community here and now, from one degree of glory to another.

Finally, note that the recreation of the divine image here is not conceived as an individual matter but a community one—the whole Church regaining in Christ the divine image.

We can conclude that in Second Corinthians Paul not only renews his close association of the Spirit with the risen Lord as its source but sharpens the dynamic role of the Spirit in the Christian life here and now. The Spirit is the "downpayment," the beginning of the glory to come as well as its guarantee. More than that, the Holy Spirit has a central role in the progressive transformation of Christians "from glory to glory" into the divine image. In using the prophetic image of the new covenant, Paul not only sees it as a covenant of the Spirit but introduces an opposition between the Spirit and the law which we shall have to explore in the next chapter.

Before leaving Second Corinthians there are three minor texts to be noted. In 2 Cor 6:6, Paul lists the Holy Spirit in the midst of various marks of the true apostolate. Does he allude to miracles or prophetic gifts or to the fruits of the Spirit such as patience and love which frame the expression "Holy Spirit"? We do not know.

In 2 Cor 7:1 Paul urges his readers to purify themselves "from every defilement of flesh and spirit." The spirit here is obviously the spirit in man. Not only man's flesh but also his spirit may be defiled— by being misled by false spirits?—and therefore must be renewed and purified.

In 2 Cor 13:13 we have a triadic blessing familiar from its liturgical usage: "The grace of our Lord Jesus Christ, and the love of God, and the fellowship of the Holy Spirit be with you all." While *grace* is attributed to the Lord Jesus, and *love* to the Father, *koinōnia* is attributed to the Holy Spirit. This rich word means *communion*, *union with*, the *community* formed as a result of union, and *fellowship*. All these senses seem to underlie the usage here, which is as broad as possible. This unifying effect of grace and love is most fittingly attributed to the Holy Spirit, who creates community not only among the members of the church but also introduces the Christian to an experiential, familiar, even intimate union with the Father and the Son. Such a role is certainly without precedent in the Old Testament.

Second Corinthians has, then, given us a rich insight into Paul's understanding of the new covenant as the covenant of the Spirit. Ezekiel's prophecies have been fulfilled beyond expectations, for the glorious, risen Jesus is the spirit that makes the letter obsolete, but more than that, the Holy Spirit he gives to the church is transforming it into the image of God, who is the Lord Jesus himself.

16
The Spirit,
Proof of Sonship,
Gift of Freedom: Galatians

Authority, unity, order and morality—these had been the major problems of the Corinthians. Basically their raw enthusiasm, coming out of a largely pagan culture, had to be tamed and refined. They needed a little "law and order" and Paul provided it for them in his letters. About the same time that Paul was dealing with the Corinthians on the western front, he had to deal with what he considered an even greater threat arising in some of the communities he had evangelized to the east in central Asia Minor—the Galatians. Their problem was at the other extreme from the Corinthians. Largely Jewish converts, they had accepted the good news of Jesus Christ from Paul, and had received an outpouring of the Holy Spirit (Gal 3:2). Yet for some strange reason they did not seem to have fully appreciated how radically different this new life was from the regime of the old law under which they had previously lived. When, in Paul's absence, a number of Jews or Judaizing Christians sought to restore the primacy of the old law, with circumcision and other observances, the fledgling Christians were all too easily led back to their old ways. This development Paul considered most serious because it threatened the foundations of the gospel—is salvation through the gracious gift of God offered in Jesus Christ, or does it come through observance of the Law? In Paul's mind there was no question. If the Corinthians did not have enough "law and order," the Galatians had too much. If the Corinthians had too much freedom, in the sense of license, the Galatians had too little. And if out of the Corinthian crisis Paul developed the "bodily" implications of the Spirit (the humanity of Jesus, the Church, the "bodily" Christian ethic), out of the Galatian crisis he will develop the *spiritual* implications of those "bodily" observances (circumcision and the legal prescriptions) which had been his Jewish heritage from the Old Testament. And he will show how the fulfillment in Jesus Christ of all that those things promised now makes futile a return to them. If in the Corinthian letters Paul sought to "tame" the Spirit for the body, in Galatians he seeks to free the Spirit from the old law. Naturally, since Paul is dealing with Jewish converts, his argumentation often introduces Old Testament background which at times we shall have to explain.

Gal 3:1-5: The Spirit, Proof of Faith's Superiority to the Law

1. O foolish Galatians! Who has bewitched you, before whose eyes Jesus Christ was publicly portrayed as crucified? 2. Let me ask you only this: Did you receive the Spirit by works of the law, or by hearing with faith? 3. Are you so foolish? Having begun with the Spirit, are you now ending with the flesh? 4. Did you experience so many things in vain?—if it really is in vain. 5. Does he who supplies the Spirit to you and works miracles among you do so by works of the law, or by hearing with faith? (RSV)

This passage falls in the midst of Paul's teaching that justification of a man in God's eyes comes by faith in God's gifts, which is Jesus Christ. Nowhere better than in the cross does the gift-nature of God's redemptive act appear. "I still live my human life, but it is a life of faith in the Son of God, who loved me and gave himself up for me. I will not treat God's gracious gift as pointless. If justice is available through the law, then Christ died to no purpose!" (Gal 2:20-21). To buttress his argument Paul the Jew becomes extremely pragmatic with his Jewish brethren and asks them, in fact, "What gets more evident results—the law or faith?" Of course, since the end of time is neither upon Jew nor Christian, the question cannot yet be answered in terms of the kingdom. But it can be answered in terms of present visible effects, and here Paul points to the *fact* of the outpouring of the Spirit upon the new community as a sign of the effectiveness of faith on the one hand and the ineffectiveness of mere legal observance on the other. The experience of the community itself demonstrates that the Holy Spirit is not given as a reward for perfect observance of the law (as we saw taught in the rabbinic tradition). It is given in response to faith, faith in Jesus Christ, and it is pure gift.

When Paul says in vs. 3, "After beginning in the Spirit are you now to end in the flesh?" he does not mean a falling into sexual sins. Picking up the ancient antithesis of spirit-flesh we already met in Is 31:3, Paul means a return from faith to a regime of the old law as the norm for Christian life and as the security for justification and salvation.

"Flesh" is probably an allusion to circumcision. Since the Spirit is the power by which the Galatians began to live as Christians (5:18; Rom 8:14), they cannot abandon this gift now for any sign in the flesh.

Paul pursues this thought in vss. 4-5. God supplies the Spirit and works wonders (literally "powers," *dynameis*). The two parallel expressions here suggest that the Spirit is the charismatic Spirit, for elsewhere in Paul these "works of power" are attributed directly to the Spirit (Rom 15:13, 19; 1 Cor 12:11). For the apostle, authentic faith is manifested by an outpouring of the charisms and not merely by internal sanctification. He does not consider the charisms to be "thrills and frills" but rather essential to bring faith and God's power to visibility. It would perhaps not be too much to infer that Paul would see a waning of charismatic activity in the community as a waning of genuine faith. At any rate, this present text gives a positive theology of the "works of power" which did not come through as clearly in 1 Cor 12-14.

One question remains: If Paul elsewhere habitually shows the gift of the Spirit flowing from the risen Christ, why do we have it here connected instead with the preaching of the cross? Probably because the self-gift of Jesus upon the cross depicts even more poignantly than the resurrection the mystery of God's love as *gift* (Gal 2:20-21). Paul does not say, as John later will, that the Spirit came from the dying Christ (Jn 19:30, 34 with 7:38-39), but the way is opened for that development.

Gal 3:6-14: The Spirit, Fulfillment of the Promise Made to Abraham

6. Thus Abraham "believed God, and it was reckoned to him as righteousness." 7. So you see that it is men of faith who are the sons of Abraham. 8. And the scripture, foreseeing that God would justify the Gentiles by faith, preached the gospel beforehand to Abraham, saying, "In you shall all the nations be blessed." 9. So then, those who are men of faith are blessed with Abraham who had faith.

10. For all who rely on works of the law are under a curse; for it is written, "Cursed be every one who does not abide by all things written in the book of the law, and do them." 11. Now it is evident that no man is justified before God by the law; for "He who through faith is righteous shall live"; 12. but the law does not rest on faith, for "He who does them shall live by them." 13. Christ redeemed us from the curse of the law, having become a curse for us—for it is written, "Cursed be every one who hangs on a tree"— 14. that in Christ Jesus the

blessing of Abraham might come upon the Gentiles, that we
might receive the promise of the Spirit through faith. (RSV)

Having appealed to Christian experience Paul now pursues his
thesis in a kind of rabbinical, midrashic way, the logic of which we may
find difficult to follow. In this chain of Scriptural meditations the apostle heightens the contrast between the covenant with Abraham and the
covenant with Moses. The antithesis lies in the first place between blessing and curse. In Gen 12:3 (and 18:18), Abraham was promised that all
nations would find blessing in him. In Gen 15:6 Abraham's response of
faith was recorded as making him righteous in God's eyes. On the basis
of these texts Paul shows that only those are sons of Abraham and
therefore sharers of the promised blessing who live by faith. This is how
the promise becomes fulfilled that all the nations would be blessed in
Abraham. The Scripture "foresaw" that God would justify the gentiles
by faith. By sharing Abraham's faith they share Abraham's blessing. On
the other hand, turning to the Mosaic covenant and basing himself on
Deut 27; 26, Hab 2:4 and Lev 18:5, Paul shows that those who choose to
live under the law really inherit a curse, for the law demands action, and
whoever cannot totally fulfill the law is condemned by it. The paradox
of God's plan of redemption is that Christ took the curse of the law
upon himself and thus delivered us from it, now making it possible to receive by gift what could not be attained by works.

And what is the gift? It is the Spirit. This is an astonishing and
unexpected twist to Paul's thought. Christ is, of course, the one *in* or
through whom the blessing is received, but the *content* of the blessing
promised to Abraham and now fulfilled "in us" is here not the kingdom,
nor the inheritance, but "the Spirit."

Paul's thought has moved so fast, we must replay it in slow motion.
The Greek word *epangelia* (promise) is very close to *euangelion* (good
news). Paul sees the "promise" as simply the Old Testament form of the
"good news." Abraham believed in the good news when it was promise.
Christians believe in it as fulfilled. The promise is fulfilled in the good
news, and the good news is fulfilled in the Spirit who brings the good
news to visibility and experience. Therefore, the Spirit is really the substance of the promise made to Abraham. This brings us back to the role
of the Spirit in the previous text, 3:1-5. Why does not Paul say that the
promise is fulfilled in the kingdom yet to come, or in the resurrection of
Christians, or the second coming of Christ, or the inheritance of heavenly glory? The answer is simple. He wants to show that the promise has
already been fulfilled in present experience. There is, no doubt, still a
greater fulfillment to await. But for its essence, the Holy Spirit *is* the life

Jesus gives, the Holy Spirit *is* the future already now, the Holy Spirit *is* the blessing God promises to every believer beginning with Abraham. And—the point Paul wants to make again with the Galatians—the Holy Spirit is received not through the law but through Jesus Christ and faith in him.

Gal 4:6-7: God's Spirit, Proof of Sonship and Inheritance

> 6. And because you are sons, God has sent the Spirit of his Son into our hearts, crying, "Abba! Father!" 7. So through God you are no longer a slave but a son, and if a son then an heir. (RVS)

This text is the culmination of the section begun at 3:15 which introduces another antithesis between the new covenant and the old. Whereas the previous section had contrasted Abraham's covenant of faith with Moses' covenant of law, showing how blessing came through the former and a curse through the latter, here the contrast is between slavery and sonship. These themes too were associated in the Old Testament with election and covenant. When occasionally God is described as father and Israel as his son, it is not by natural creation but rather by God's free choice and intervention into Israel's history and the sealing of a covenant. Thus in the Old Testament already there is an analogy with the Greek notion of adoption. If Israel lives in obedient recognition of this relationship, sonship means freedom and the promised inheritance: "How I should like to treat you as sons, and give you a pleasant land, a heritage most beautiful among the nations! You would call me, 'My Father' . . . and never cease following me" (Jer 3:19). But Israel's infidelity to the relationship has meant a loss of both freedom and inheritance: "Is Israel a slave, a bondman from birth? Why then has he become booty? . . . They have made his land a waste . . ." (Jer 2:14-15; 3:19-25; cf. Sib 3:702ff.; 3 Mac 6:28). Restoration would be marked by the renewal of the sonship relation as it was in the primordial age when Israel was first called (Hos 11:1-4; 2:1; Deut 8:1-5; Jub 1:25). Now if the early Church understood itself to be God's restored community of the final times, a relation of sonship to God was surely part of it. And the relationship was inaugurated by faith in Jesus Christ and baptism into him: "Each one of you is a *son* of God because of your faith in Christ Jesus. All of you who have been baptized into Christ have clothed yourselves with him. There does not exist among you Jew or Greek, *slave* or *freeman*, male or female. All are one in Christ Jesus" (Gal 3:26-28).

And then Paul immediately adds that this means also the inheritance: "Furthermore, if you belong to Christ, you are the descendants of Abraham, which means you inherit all that was promised" (3:29).

Before giving any clue as to what the content of the promise is, Paul plays on the notion of slavery and freedom, noting that the freedom of sonship means freedom from the law. Then comes our text, in which for the third time Paul points to the Holy Spirit presently experienced in the community as authentication. As the Spirit proved the authenticity of the gospel (3:1-5) and the fulfillment of the blessing of Abraham (3:4), so he "proves" that Christians are sons. How so? The Christian "knows" his sonship by the experience of Christian prayer. For Paul more than for any other New Testament writer, authentic Christian prayer is inspired and thus has the same status as prophecy (1 Thes 5:18-20; 1 Cor 11:4-5; 1 Cor 14:13-17; Rom 8:26-27; Eph 6:18). In this sense all genuine Christian prayer is "charismatic," that is, spirit-inspired. For the Spirit manifests himself not only in prophecy, in healing or in miracles but in the first place by enabling the Christian to say, "Abba!" This Aramaic word goes back to the prayer of Jesus himself, so treasured that it was handed down in Aramaic even in the Greek-speaking communities. It is not the common word for "father," and although the Old Testament speaks of God as Father 14 or 15 times, it never calls him "Abba!" For the word *Abba* is, like the English "Daddy!", a title of great intimacy and familiarity. Along with *imma* ("mommy") it is the first name a child learns. Though part of the Christian's earliest baptismal instruction, "Abba" here is seen as prompted not by an external teacher but by the Holy Spirit himself, given in baptism (the Greek aorist tense "sent" refers to a significant past moment of time). And he makes the Christian *cry out* as in a liturgical shout or acclamation. (Note that Paul did not say, "He sent the Spirit . . . whereby we mumble"!)

The Spirit given "in our hearts" recalls Ezekiel's prophecy of the new covenant (Ez 36:26). But here it is the "Spirit of his Son." This no doubt picks up the tradition of Jesus' own baptism which was a manifestation of the Spirit and of Jesus' divine sonship. That tradition itself, as we shall see, combined several Old Testament texts, especially those which associated the Spirit with the Messiah (Is 11:2; 42:1). But as far as sonship is concerned, nowhere in the Old Testament nor in Judaism do we find the gift of the Spirit as the basis for sonship. Where then did Paul get the idea? From the tradition of Jesus' baptism, probably. But there is another possibility. According to the Old Testament, righteousness was a presupposition for prayer (Deut 4:7-8; Is 58:2, 8-9; Job 16:17). As the Holy Spirit is the author of righteousness (Ps 51, Qumran and Paul above) he is also the author of Christian prayer. Sharing with Christians the holiness of Jesus, the Spirit also gives them the prayer of Jesus.

As the Spirit proves the sonship, the sonship guarantees the inheritance. Paul is faithful here to the Old Testament association of the two ideas as seen above, where "sonship" expressed the perfection of the covenant relationship and "inheritance" meant the holy land. But what, concretely, is the inheritance for the Christian? Whatever else it contains, the context here and in the parallel passage in Rom 8:15-17 indicates that the inheritance is nothing else than God himself now known as Father. And it is the Spirit of God's own Son who already now introduces the Christian to that treasure.

Gal 5:5-6: The Spirit and Hope, Faith and Love

> 5. For through the Spirit, by faith, we wait for the hope of righteousness. 6. For in Christ Jesus neither circumcision nor uncircumcision is of any avail, but faith working through love. (RSV)

In two ways this passage goes beyond the perspectives of chapters 3 and 4. First, and surprisingly, Paul describes justification as a future good of salvation. This balances, without denying, the earlier view that justification has already happened through faith. There is a sense in which justification is the final acquittal to which Christians still look forward. In the meantime the present life is led by the Spirit in faith. Paul is preparing for the concluding part of the letter which has to do with the way the Christian is to live in this world.

Secondly, and also in preparation for his ethic of the Spirit in 5:13-26, Paul introduces the idea of love. If faith is the new regime of salvation, it is not a lifeless existence and certainly not one that countermands the intention of the law, for faith manifests its energy through love. This leads to the next passage.

Gal 5:13-26: How the Spirit Frees Us from the Law

> 13. For you were called to freedom, brethren; only do not use your freedom as an opportunity for the flesh, but through love be servants of one another. 14. For the whole law is fulfilled in one word, "You shall love your neighbor as yourself." 15. But

if you bite and devour one another take heed that you are not consumed by one another.

16. But I say, walk by the Spirit, and do not gratify the desires of the flesh. 17. For the desires of the flesh are against the Spirit, and the desires of the Spirit are against the flesh; for these are opposed to each other, to prevent you from doing what you would. 18. But if you are led by the Spirit you are not under the law. 19. Now the works of the flesh are plain: immorality, impurity, licentiousness, 20. idolatry, sorcery, enmity, strife, jealousy, anger, selfishness, dissension, party spirit, 21. envy, drunkenness, carousing, and the like. I warn you, as I warned you before, that those who do such things shall not inherit the kingdom of God. 22. But the fruit of the Spirit is love, joy, peace, patience, kindness, goodness, faithfulness, 23. gentleness, self-control; against such there is no law. 24. And those who belong to Christ Jesus have crucified the flesh with its passions and desires.

25. If we live by the Spirit, let us also walk by the Spirit. 26. Let us have no self-conceit, no provoking of one another, no envy of one another. (RSV)

Paul's ethic of the Spirit is so radical and so condemnatory of the Old Law that even a conscientious Christian may wince as he reads. Paul's opponents did more than wince. They accused him of flinging open the door to moral chaos (Rom 3:8). It would not suffice then, in attempting to show how faith in Jesus Christ has replaced the law, to adduce the evidence of the Spirit in charismatic signs and in the new kind of intimate prayer to the Father. It was necessary also to answer the objection that abandoning the Law was licence. His letter to the Galatians concludes with a magnificent exposition on the Holy Spirit as the moral life of the Christian.

He begins by repeating the principle stated in 5:1, that all Christians have been called to live in freedom. But this freedom is not only freedom from the law but also freedom from the flesh—that is, from man's innate tendency to selfishness and evil. The Christian is liberated from this evil tendency in order, precisely, to have the freedom to indenture himself out of love to the service of his brothers and sisters. Because love sums up all that the law requires, he who loves fulfills the law (vs. 14) and thus escapes the law's condemnation (vs. 23b; Rom 8:1).

But how can this be done without falling again into a legalism which would really cater to the flesh even in the name of love? One must walk by the Spirit (vs. 16) or let oneself be led by the Spirit (vs. 18).

This little statement is theological dynamite. The Christian life is not a list of things to do and things to avoid. It is not virtue acquired by practice. It is a gift of being moved by the Spirit of God, and the key to life is to allow the Spirit to lead. Paul clearly speaks here of an inspired ethic and of inspired action—and it is not reserved for the holy few but is the birth-right of all who believe in Jesus. And it is readily available. A crucial point: When confronted with any moral decision, great or small, the Christian's first question should be "Where does the Spirit lead me in this?" Other norms, as we shall see, may be consulted, but they are only secondary and ancillary to this supreme one.

The contrast between the flesh and the spirit appears again here. Both Paul and Qumran have an ethical dualism, but Paul's is not the good spirit versus the bad in man but the spirit versus the flesh. Paul then lists the works of the flesh—a catalogue of vices which probably belonged to the instructions given to converts concerning the entrance requirements for the kingdom. Paul here is heir to the Christian tradition preceding him, but his attributing these vices to the flesh and implicitly to the condemning power of the law is Paul's own stress. These vices are called works because they are man's own doing—and the use of the plural suggests that there is no order or unifying principle to them. Like the man possessed, their name is legion (Mk 5:9). In contrast, the effect of the Spirit is called the fruit—gift of life and single in its source though multiple in its manifestations. Charity is mentioned as the first fruit not merely because of its pre-eminence but because it really contains all the rest. Joy comes second. It is not so much a virtue as it is the blush of love. Peace is the great Easter *shalom* of the risen Lord. It connotes not just the "tranquility of order" but the overflowing abundance of all good things—and here in the spiritual sense it means wholeness and, in the light of the community situation reflected in vs. 15, it means the warmth of healthy fraternal relationships. The two fruits of joy and peace recur in Rom 14:17: "The kingdom of God is not a matter of eating or drinking (this or that), but of justice, peace and the joy that is given by the Holy Spirit." The list of traits Paul gives here recalls the way in which he described the activity of love in 1 Cor 13:4-7.

"Against such there is no law!" (vs. 23b). Here Paul reveals finally why the regime of the Spirit is superior to that of the law. It does all the law requires and more. And the reason why this is possible is that "Those who belong to Christ Jesus have crucified their flesh with its passions and desires" (vs. 24). The baptismal union of the Christian with Christ has brought him into the new covenant of the Spirit. But just as this covenant was established at the price of Christ's death on the cross, so it is experienced only on condition that one be crucified with Christ (Gal 2:19) by faith and baptism. And this means, in effect, the crucifixion and death of one's selfishness (the flesh) in order to live for God (Gal 2:19).

But how can Paul make such a claim of perfection through the Spirit when he knows that not only among the Corinthians who boasted of the Spirit but even among the Galatians, those who possessed the Spirit often fell victim to the flesh and thus manifested they were still sinners? Paul was aware of the objection: "If, in seeking to be justified in Christ, we are shown to be sinners, does that mean Christ is encouraging sin?" (Gal 2:17). And his answer is quite simple: If God has given me righteousness as a free gift and not as a reward for my observance of the law, to return to the old law for justification would be to reject his gift, and that would be the greatest sin of all:

> 18. But if I build up again those things which I tore down, then I prove myself a transgressor. 19. For I through the law died to the law, that I might live to God. 20. I have been crucified with Christ; it is no longer I who live, but Christ who lives in me; and the life I now live in the flesh I live by faith in the Son of God, who loved me and gave himself for me. 21. I do not nullify the grace of God; for if justification were through the law, then Christ died to no purpose. (Gal 2:18-21, RSV)

That is why Paul considers the Spirit rather than the law to be the *director* of the Christian life: "If we live by the Spirit, let us follow the Spirit's lead" (vs. 25).

At certain high points in the development of the Old Testament pneumatology, we saw that the gift of the spirit was seen to be needed in order to fulfill the law (Ps 51; Ez 36:26-27; and Qumran). But nowhere was the gift of the spirit ever thought of as doing away with the law. At best the spirit enabled the faithful Israelite to keep the law. But Paul has clearly gone beyond this. "The law of the spirit, the spirit of life in Christ Jesus, has freed you from the law of sin and death" (Rom 8:2). The Spirit does away with law as the norm of Christian living.

Or does it? Obviously the Spirit does away with the Old Law to the extent that clinging to its observances means a rejection of the gift of God in Christ Jesus (Gal 2:17-21). And yet, side by side with Paul's insistence on the Spirit doing away with the law we find him setting down norms of Christian behavior for his communities, sometimes basing them on a "word of the Lord," sometimes on his own authority (see, for example, 1 Cor 5-11, especially 7:10, 12, 25). And not only does he attribute these authoritative decisions to the Holy Spirit (1 Cor 7:40; 14:37), but he says that anyone who refuses to accept them is rejecting the Holy Spirit (1 Thes 4:8). Clearly then there emerges, even in this herald of freedom in the Spirit, an informal body of "law," that is, principles laid down by apostolic authority and binding on the communities, and a constant insistence upon obedience to the apostolic authority. Freedom in the Spirit is not therefore license for individualism, for "doing your own thing." And certainly it is not moral subjectivism. It is obviously meant to be compatible with authority and identifiable norms in the church.

There is, then, a "new law" emerging in the Christian church of the first century. Its supreme monument will be the gospels, where Jesus' words and example are the ultimate norm for Christian living. But does this mean that, in the last analysis, Paul's view is really no different from those Old Testament writers who said that the Spirit was needed in order to observe the law? Is the only difference that he believed the Spirit was needed to observe the new law? No. That way of putting it makes the law above the Spirit and sees the Spirit only as the promoter of willing obedience. In Paul's moral theology, the Spirit is the "prime mover" of the Christian. He is the *life* of the Christian. Concrete norms of behavior, such as those published by Paul in his letters, belong rather to the process of *discerning* the Spirit. The Spirit's action is never limited to fulfilling those norms. It is a constantly inventive and creative agent. "Law," if we must use the term for published authoritative norms, is not that to which the Spirit enables Christians to measure up, and certainly it does not create life. Rather it is a norm for discerning the movement of the Spirit. Paul certainly considers the normal activity of the Spirit to be so pure and noble that it transcends any of the negative prescriptions of the law, old or new. Thus, "The fruit of the Spirit is love, joy, peace, patience. . . . Against such the law has nothing to say" (Gal 5:22-23). On the other hand, he is also aware that not every impulse is from the Holy Spirit and that every movement must be tested (1 Thes 5:19-21). Norms, such as Paul's teaching, and the virtue-and-vice lists we find in Gal 5:19-22, were one of the tools for such discernment.

Conclusion

We may conclude our study of Galatians by saying that Paul pursues and elaborates here the opposition between the Holy Spirit and the letter of the old law, tying it in very closely with the themes of sonship and freedom. The Holy Spirit continues to be the charismatic spirit, but he also demonstrates to the Christian that he is a son and therefore free from the law and assured the inheritance. But the Spirit delivers from the law precisely because the ethical life he gives is superior to the perfection available under the law.

17
The Spirit and the
Christian Journey: Romans

Paul's letter to the Romans is generally understood to have followed rather closely that to the Galatians. The principal reason for this judgment is that many of the ideas first sketched out in a polemic way to the Galatians are, in Romans, worked out in a more systematic presentation. This being the case even in the matter of Paul's teaching on the Spirit, we may expect to find only greater elaboration of what we have already encountered in his previous letters.

Early in the letter Paul reflects probably an early Christian catechesis when he says, in 1:4, that Jesus "was made Son of God in power according to the Spirit of holiness, by his resurrection from the dead." "Spirit of holiness" is probably a primitive Jewish way of saying "the Holy Spirit." In any case, the reference here is to the enthronement as Son of God in power at the resurrection. The curious expression "Son of God according to the Spirit of holiness" is probably due to the parallelism Paul wishes to draw with the preceding expression "Son . . . of David according to the flesh" (1:3). The contrast is therefore between the lowliness and humiliation of Jesus' human life in contrast to the power and glory shown in his resurrection, the latter being the work of the Spirit which also made the new Adam life-giving spirit (1 Cor 15:45).

In 1:9 Paul says that his preaching of the gospel is the way he now worships God "in the spirit." The gospel preaching is the spiritual replacement for the sacrifices of the old law. In 7:6 the contrast between the letter of the old law and the Spirit of the new covenant reappears. These are minor texts that add little to what we have already seen. Let us now turn to the major texts of Romans to see what further insight Paul may have to offer on the Spirit.

Rom 5:1-5: The Love of God Poured Out

Therefore, since we are justified by faith, we have peace with

God through our Lord Jesus Christ. 2. Through him we have obtained access to this grace in which we stand, and we rejoice in our hope of sharing the glory of God. 3. More than that, we rejoice in our sufferings, knowing that suffering produces endurance, 4. and endurance produces character, and character produces hope, 5. and hope does not disappoint us, because God's love has been poured into our hearts through the Holy Spirit who has been given to us. (RSV)

In the first four chapters of Romans Paul has dealt with the problem of justification or "righteousness," showing that without the gospel of grace both Jew and gentile are alienated from God (that is, they are under his wrath) and that through the gift of God in Christ God's saving justice is revealed and available to all. For his readers the act of justification has already happened through faith and baptism. But the consummation of this mystery is yet to come, as "we rejoice in our hope of sharing the glory of God" (vs. 2). Only in chapter 8 will Paul develop the thought of the future fulfillment introduced here. For the moment he goes on to say what this means for the present life of Christians. So powerful is the hope and the assurance of glory that they can boast even of present afflictions because these strengthen endurance and test virtue and this in turn "works out hope," that is, gives hope an even firmer assurance of its fulfillment. But the principal reason for the Christian's assurance that this hope of glory will be fulfilled is that "God's own love has been poured into our hearts through the Holy Spirit who has been given to us" (vs. 5). Once again we notice familiar language. The new covenant in the heart had been promised by Jeremiah (31:33) and Ezekiel had added that the spirit would be given within (Ez 36:26-27; 11:19-20). The pouring out of the spirit from on high is language used by Isaiah (Is 32:15). However, what is new here is the central place given to love. The divine *agape* is neither *eros* (love in emotional or physical sense) nor *philia* (the love of friendship). It is rather the lucid love of benevolence which seeks the good of the beloved and acts with freedom and magnificence on the beloved's behalf. It is a disinterested love rooted in the high esteem of the other as precious and dear (a sense which the Latin equivalent, *caritas*, captures beautifully). In our present text the question naturally arises whether "The love of God poured into our hearts" means "God's love for us" or "our love for God." Paul does occasionally speak of *agape* as a love ascending from Christians to God (1 Cor 2:9; 16:22; Rom 8:28) but the major focus of his contemplation is God's descending love for his people manifested in the great act of redemption in Jesus Christ. And that sense would seem to fit the context better here, for what Paul is concerned with in this text is not so much the ethical life of Christians as their assurance of reaching the goal of salvation. There is no reason to doubt that God will complete what he has begun, for if he has gifted us already with his righteousness, he has also poured his own love into us. And so the focus is upon the fact that Christians are the object of God's love—not only in the sense of having it "depicted before their eyes" (Gal 3:1) but in the sense that God's love has touched them with the intimate awareness of how much they are loved. And this love is the power which will carry them through the storms of this life to the haven of salvation. And this gift of God's love is attributed to the Holy Spirit given. The gift of the Spirit is the gift of God's love.

Nowhere in Paul up to this point has this relationship of the Spirit and charity been stated so clearly and succinctly. In 1 Cor 13 Paul had interrupted his treatment of the gifts of the Spirit to talk about charity —but he did not explicitly connect charity with the Holy Spirit. In Gal 5:22 he listed charity as the first fruit of the Spirit. But in both those cases charity had to do primarily with charity towards one's neighbor. Paul had already spoken of Christians as the "beloved of God" (1 Thes 1:4), and in 2 Cor 13:13 he had joined "the love of God" and "the fellowship of the Holy Spirit" but the relation between the two was not clearly stated. Here the love of God touches the Christian's heart giving the assurance that, being loved by the Father, he will surely be led home.

After a long digression Paul returns to this theme in 8:14-39 which we shall see below.

Rom 8:1-13: The Way of the Spirit and the Way of the Flesh

There is therefore now no condemnation for those who are in Christ Jesus. 2. For the law of the Spirit of life in Christ Jesus has set me free from the law of sin and death. 3. For God has done what the law, weakened by the flesh, could not do: sending his own Son in the likeness of sinful flesh and for sin, he condemned sin in the flesh, 4. in order that the just requirement of the law might be fulfilled in us, who walk not according to the flesh but according to the Spirit. 5. For those who live according to the flesh set their minds on the things of the flesh, but those who live according to the Spirit set their minds on the things of the Spirit. 6. To set the mind on the flesh is death, but to set the mind on the Spirit is life and peace. 7. For the mind that is set on the flesh is hostile to God; it does not submit to God's law, indeed it cannot; 8. and those who are in the flesh cannot please God.

9. But you are not in the flesh, you are in the Spirit, if the Spirit of God really dwells in you. Any one who does not have the Spirit of Christ does not belong to him. 10. But if Christ is in you, although your bodies are dead because of sin, your spirits are alive because of righteousness. 11. If the Spirit of him who raised Jesus from the dead dwells in you, he who raised Christ Jesus from the dead will give life to your mortal bodies also through his Spirit who dwells in you.

12. So then, brethren, we are debtors, not to the flesh, to live according to the flesh— 13. for if you live according to the flesh you will die, but if by the Spirit you put to death the deeds of the body you will live. (RSV)

Many of the elements of Paul's thought here we have already met in Galatians. We shall not therefore repeat what we saw there but focus only on what is unique about this passage. Having just described the lot of unredeemed man whose mind is attracted by the law of God but whose flesh serves the law of sin (7:7-25), Paul shows what a difference belonging to Christ makes. For this division, and the condemnation it brings, is radically healed by the "law of the spirit of life in Christ Jesus" (vs. 2). Normally, Paul opposes the spirit, as he does faith, to the law (2 Cor 3:6). But occasionally he uses the concept of law in a positive sense to show that the old law is replaced by the superior law of Christ (Gal 6:2) or of faith (Rom 3:27) or "of the spirit of life in Christ Jesus" (here). The law of sin and death, which got its foothold in man's flesh, that is, in his moral weakness, no longer binds Christians, for they have been delivered by Christ whose death on the cross as a sin offering "condemned sin in the flesh." The result was that by his gift all the just demands of the law might be fulfilled "in us who walk according to the spirit" (vs. 4). What does this mean? It means that the Christian in living according to the Spirit does so by God's gift which was made available through the sacrificial death of Jesus Christ. This delivers from the accusing power of the law (vs. 1) because the law's just demands are fulfilled. The law has "nothing to say" against those who live by the Spirit (Gal 5:23). Notice again that the Spirit is not given to fulfill the law, but one of its effects is to fulfill all the law expects and thus to give freedom from its accusing power.

In vss. 5-13, Paul develops the antithesis between flesh and spirit which we already met in Gal 5:13-26. Here the reason why Christians are "in the spirit" is specified as the indwelling in them of the Spirit of

God (vs. 9). This same Spirit is also the Spirit of Christ, and that means therefore that Christ himself "is in you" (vs. 10). This is a crucial text. On the one hand, it shows that the Spirit of Christ is possessed by all Christians from the moment of their baptism, and, on the other, it shows that what is attributed to the Holy Spirit's action in the Christian and in the church can also be attributed to Christ, because the Spirit is the Spirit of Christ. The critical importance of this principle will be seen when we look at the pneumatology of the gospels.

As the text continues we notice in vs. 10 that Paul has gently substituted "body" for "flesh" because he is preparing to show that while the body is "dead" as flesh, it will be brought to life as spirit through the Spirit of the risen Christ "dwelling in you." This shows us how Paul thinks of the Holy Spirit. It is, of course, God's spirit, because it was the Spirit of "him who raised Jesus from the dead" (vs. 11; cf. Rom 1:4), but it was also Christ's Spirit inasmuch as it made him life-giving Spirit (1 Cor 14:45). The Holy Spirit is therefore the Spirit of the risen Lord now dwelling in his members as the principle and assurance of their own resurrection.

Finally, let us note in vs. 13 that the gift of the Spirit does not mean an abdication of the spiritual combat. The Spirit is a gift that must be used. And however much Paul has said that the flesh and sin have already been put to death, he nonetheless says that the deeds of the flesh must still, even in baptized and Spirit-filled Christians, be put to death —and they must use the power of the Spirit to do so (vs. 13).

Rom 8:14-17: The Spirit of Sons

14. For all who are led by the Spirit of God are sons of God. 15. For you did not receive the spirit of slavery to fall back into fear, but you have received the spirit of sonship. When we cry, "Abba! Father!" 16. it is the Spirit himself bearing witness with our spirit that we are children of God, 17. and if children, then heirs, heirs of God and fellow heirs with Christ, provided we suffer with him in order that we may also be glorified with him. (RSV)

This text is similar to the one we analyzed in Galatians (4:5-7). Here the idea is set in the slightly different context of the "two ways" which precede and the eschatological longing which follows. Verse 14 supplies the link with the preceding. After showing that the Spirit is the guiding principle of Christians' life, Paul says that such a way of life also makes them sons. It is not a question here of the title of sonship but of the experience of sonship. For obviously everyone who has received God's spirit, which is also the Spirit of his Son, may be called God's son. But Paul says rather all who are *led* by the Spirit are sons. That is, the activity of the Spirit confirms the sonship. This was already said in Gal 4:6, but here we have added the word *adoption*, which evokes the fact that the sonship is the effect of a free and loving election on God's part, and the "co-witnessing" of the Spirit "with our spirit." In Jewish law, where there was any doubt in evidence, no judge's decision could be considered valid and definitive without the testimony of two witnesses (Deut 19:15). In any contest of man with God, there never could be equality, as Job already said, and there could be no umpire who might put his hand on the head of each and decide between them (Job 9:33). But Job did believe he had a witness in heaven (Job 16:19)—though it is not clear whether this witness is an angel or Job's own prayer. Here, however, it is God's own spirit who testifies in behalf of the Christian and joins his witness to the witness "of our spirit." Here the divine and the human spirit meet in one common testimony. The human spirit knows, as God's spirit knows, that the Christian is God's son. And the joint outward testimony, as indicated by the context, is the liturgical cry "Abba!"

And since the son is also the heir, and Christians are sons because they have become one with God's firstborn Son, Jesus, they too are "heirs of God." This may mean that they inherit all God has promised. But it may also mean that God, as Father, is the inheritance himself.

The last part of vs. 17 modulates into a minor chord—"provided we suffer with him"—in order to do justice to the real paradox of the Christian present and to answer the obvious question, "If we are sons, why do we suffer?"

Rom 8:18-27: The Groaning of the Spirit

18. I consider that the sufferings of this present time are not worth comparing with the glory that is to be revealed to us. 19. For the creation waits with eager longing for the revealing of the sons of God; 20. for the creation was subjected to futility, not of its own will but by the will of him who subjected it in hope; 21. because the creation itself will be set free from its bondage to decay and obtain the glorious liberty of the children of God. 22. We know that the whole creation has been groaning in travail together until now; 23. and not only the cre-

ation, but we ourselves, who have the first fruits of the Spirit, groan inwardly as we wait for adoption as sons, the redemption of our bodies. 24. For in this hope we were saved. Now hope that is seen is not hope. For who hopes for what he sees? 25. But if we hope for what we do not see, we wait for it with patience.

26. Likewise the Spirit helps us in our weakness; for we do not know how to pray as we ought, but the Spirit himself intercedes for us with sighs too deep for words. 27. And he who searches the hearts of men knows what is the mind of the Spirit, because the Spirit intercedes for the saints according to the will of God. (RSV)

Paul is still thinking of sonship in terms of liberation from slavery. His view now becomes cosmic as he thinks of all creation yearning to share in the deliverance promised to God's sons. This "eager awaiting" is described as a groaning, attributed first of all to the entire creation, and then to Christians themselves. The NAB translation, unlike the RSV, takes the Greek "having the first-fruits of the Spirit" as slightly adversative—*although* we have the Spirit, we groan. This interpretation takes the sense to be that although the Spirit is already the beginning of the end, it is only the beginning, and we groan for the consummation which is the resurrection (vs. 23). We groan *in spite* of possessing the Spirit. However, in vs. 26, the groaning is attributed to the Spirit himself—so that probably the better sense is that *since* we have the Spirit as a foretaste, we can only long for the fulfillment, as the sip of wine invites us to drink deeply of the cup.

In vss. 26-27 a further important role is given to the Spirit. Intimately connected with the preceding by the word *hōsautōs*, meaning "in the same way," "similarly," "likewise" (RSV), the help of the Spirit "in our weakness" parallels the awaiting with patient endurance of vs. 25. Both are seen to be traits of the Christian interim. "Weakness" here does not refer to suffering or to moral weakness as it often does elsewhere but simply to inadequacy to pray "as is appropriate," that is, as God would have it. It is an inability to know *what* to pray. Though the RSV, NAB and other versions translate "how" to pray, the Greek has to do with the content of prayer, suggesting that we do not know what words to choose or even what to talk about when we address God. Some scholars have proposed that Paul here is borrowing a Gnostic idea: man does not know the secret words with which to win access to the divinity but once initiated the divine spirit speaks through him the correct formula which may never be communicated to the public. But that is far from Paul's thought here. True, the words "Abba" and "Jesus is Lord" are Spirit-inspired (Gal 4:6; Rom 8:15; 1 Cor 12:3), but the meaning here is that neither man nor God needs words to communicate. The Spirit intercedes nonetheless.

The Spirit as intercessor for man is new. The *ruah* of the Lord in the Old Testament was never sufficiently personalized or personified to be a separately operating entity, and certainly not toward God as in the case here. Intercession was the function of the prophet (Ex 32:11; Am 7:2; Jer 15:1; 18:20 etc.) or, in later Judaism, of angels, either by presenting the prayers of the faithful before the throne of God (Tob 12:12) or by themselves personally interceding (Zech 1:12). Here in Romans the heavenly intercession is attributed equally to Christ (8:34) and to the Spirit (here). So here again we encounter the same theological dynamic as above in 8:10-11, where identical functions are applied in one case to Christ and in another to the Spirit. The shade of difference here is that Christ apparently intercedes in heaven and the Spirit here on earth. But the close association of the two and the apparently "separable" character of the Spirit as an interlocutor with God like Jesus himself, points to an understanding of the Spirit akin to the Johannine paraclete, which we shall encounter later.

The Spirit is said to intercede with "sighs too deep for words" (RSV) or "groanings that cannot be expressed in speech" (NAB). We must first ask whether the Greek word *alalētois* used here means unspoken in the sense of being incapable of any kind of human articulation, thus bypassing any outward manifestation, or whether it means "incapable of being put into words"—which would allow at least some non-verbal outward expression. In favor of the former is the passage in 2 Cor 12:4 which refers to the language of heavenly revelation as "things" or "words" that cannot be told. Some authors so press the role of the Spirit as advocate here that they leave virtually no room whatever for any kind of human participation in the divine activity. But this goes quite counter to the role of the Spirit described elsewhere as the author of *koinōnia,* divine fellowship (2 Cor 13:13), as communicating an understanding of the gifts of God (1 Cor 2:9-10), and as bearing witness "with our spirit" to the divine sonship (Rom 8:16). Consequently the second alternative seems preferable. The groanings are such that they cannot be put into human words, but this does not exclude other forms of expression on the human side.

But why is this intercession of the Spirit described as manifested in "groanings" (or "sighs") rather than some other word? The only other New Testament context in which we find groaning mentioned is in Mark's account of Jesus' cure of the deaf-mute: "and looking up to heaven, he (Jesus) groaned and said to him, Ephphatha, that is, Be opened" (Mk 7:34). Though the word "groan" is not explicitly used in the raising of Lazarus, John notes twice that Jesus was "troubled in spirit" (11:33, 38) and cried out with a loud voice (11:43). The "groaning" then seems to be the moment of prayer during which the power of the Spirit is built up prior to its release in a redemptive act. Thus, at the climactic moment of the passion, Jesus emitted a loud cry and gave up his life-breath (Mk 15:34; Mt 27:46; Lk 32:46), releasing cosmic signs, the rending of the temple veil (Mark, Matthew), an apocalyptic earthquake and opening of the tombs (Matthew) and conversion in the gentile centurion (all three synoptics). The sequence in each case is the same— the groaning or the being troubled in spirit or the loud cry belongs to and is a sign of the preparatory stage for a mighty redemptive act.

Now in Paul this "groaning" has already been used to describe the entire Christian life in this world as a longing for the glory to come (2 Cor 5:2, 4; Rom 8:23). What appears in the gospels as a passing preparatory moment appears here as a life-long activity until the final consummation of the redemption. But there is probably an even more specific biblical reference in Paul's mind. The context here of groaning for deliverance from slavery into sonship may well reflect the groaning of Israel in Egypt in Ex 3:7, to which Stephen refers in his long speech before the Sanhedrin: "I have witnessed the affliction of my people in Egypt and have heard their groaning, and I have come down to rescue them" (Acts 7:34). In Jewish tradition the Exodus was understood to be God's deliverance of his son, Israel, from slavery unto the freedom of the promised land (Ex 3:7-10; Hos 11:1). If this motif has influenced Paul's thought here—as it certainly did in Galatians—then the groaning here is the prayer of God's sons voiced by the Spirit and winning the assurance that God *knows* their plight (explicitly mentioned in the Exodus text 3:7 cf. also 2:25 and in vs. 27 of our text of Romans) and will soon bring about the consummation of their deliverance.

Is there any empirical activity of Christian prayer with which these "groanings of the Spirit" can be identified? One thinks immediately of the prayer in tongues, which, as we saw, belongs to the pre-rational or pre-verbal stage of prayer. This is possible. But there is one significant difference between Paul's description of that kind of prayer in 1 Cor 12-14 and the groaning of the Spirit here. There Paul insisted that tongues not only could be interpreted into intelligible words but *should* be, for the edification of the community. Here it does not even occur to him to speak of interpretation—in fact, such "verbalization" seems impossible. Either, then, it is a different kind of prayer Paul is describing here or, no longer faced with the Corinthian abuse, he admits that the non-rational prayer of the Spirit is beyond words and need not, in fact cannot be interpreted. Perhaps some light might be shed on the question by Paul's assumption that prayer in tongues for private use is for addressing God and for one's own spiritual growth and need not, apparently, be interpreted (1 Cor 14:2) whereas the case is different in a community context (1 Cor 14:5-6). But we are not sure that he is speaking of tongues at all here. What is certain is that he is speaking of non-verbal prayer— and, we believe, not simply the Spirit speaking soundlessly in place of the Christian who remains silent but rather in and through some kind of non-rational expression which outwardly reveals the groaning of the Spirit just as the cry "Abba" outwardly reveals the inner witness of the Spirit (8:15).

At any rate, the Christian is aware that he is not alone in his prayer and that God knows what is being communicated from within the one praying even when the one praying cannot say what it is (vs. 27). But perhaps, in focusing on the verbal or non-verbal expression, we lose the view of the woods for the trees. If the Exodus motif lies behind this passage, then the major idea Paul wishes to communicate is that the Christian and cosmic groaning for the fullness of sonship, the resurrection, is a prayer inspired by the very same Spirit of adoption that inspired the cry "Abba" (vs. 15), and God, who knew what the groaning of his sons in Egypt meant, certainly with all the more reason knows what his own Spirit is pleading in his sons in the Egypt of this present age. And if he heard and acted in the first exodus, we can be all the more certain that he hears and will act in the New.

Rom 12:6-8: How To Use the Gifts

6. We have gifts that differ according to the favor bestowed on each of us. One's gift may be prophecy; its use should be in proportion to faith. 7. It may be the gift of ministry; it should be used for service. One who is a teacher should use his gift for teaching; 8. one with the power of exhortation should exhort. He who gives alms should do so generously; he who rules should exercise his authority with care; he who performs works of mercy should do so cheerfully. (NAB)

Though this passage does not explicitly mention the Spirit, it does contain an interesting complement to Paul's treatment of the spiritual gifts in 1 Cor 12-14 in three ways. First, some charisms are mentioned here which do not appear there. "Ministry" (*diakonia*) is not a general classification for all the gifts as in 1 Cor 12:4 but is a specific gift. It might be waiting on tables or providing for the community meals (as in Acts 6:1 and Lk 10:40), or it might be any other discharge of service in love such as the household of Stephanas showed (1 Cor 16:15). One with the *power of exhortation* (*ho parakalōn*) is one like the prophet who speaks in an inspired way to the community for its encouragement and strengthening (cf. 1 Cor 14:3). The giving of alms (*ho metadidous*) was probably one whose function it was to distribute the community goods to the needy. "He who rules (or presides)" (*ho proistamenos*) is one on whom the pastoral case of the community especially devolves. Although there is certainly authority involved, the emphasis is rather upon the responsibility to care for the community. It is of the same persons that Paul wrote in 1 Thes 5:12, "We beg you, brothers, respect those among you whose task it is to exercise authority in the Lord and admonish you." From this last text we can see that one of their functions was to correct without provoking or embittering. Finally "he who performs works of mercy" (*ho eleōn*) may be anyone who does this in a passing way, or he may be one acknowledged by the community to act in its name. In any case, with all these gifts no distinction is made between "office" and "gift." The recognized and appointed functions are just as much gifts as are the seemingly more direct inspirational gifts.

The second interesting point about this text is that Paul urges his readers to use the gifts, and in some cases suggests an attitude with which they should be exercised. Particularly interesting—and this is the third point—is the directive as to how prophecy should be used. "Its use should be in proportion to his faith" is the NAB translation (12:6). The Greek says literally, "If prophecy, according to the proportion of (the) faith." The Greek word *analogia* can mean "proportion" or "measure" or "rule." Does Paul mean that the prophet in speaking should be guided by his own conscience or his own faith? The NAB translation suggests this by inserting "his" before faith. But there is no "his" in the Greek. It is just "the faith," and the use of the definite article suggests something objective. As a matter of fact, "faith" in Paul can stand for the entire content of the gospel teaching, and, if we compare what Paul says about the use and discernment of prophecy in 1 Thes 5:19-21 and 1 Cor 12-14, the sense here seems to be that the prophet should exercise his gift within the parameters set by the Christian faith and sound teaching and not pretend that the Spirit could be truly inspiring anything that went counter to that deposit of faith. Thus the sense would be: "If your gift is prophecy, use it according to the norms set by the faith."

Rom 15:13: The Holy Spirit and Hope

13. May the God of hope fill you with all joy and peace in believing, so that by the power of the Holy Spirit you may abound in hope. (RSV)

Fittingly our final text on the Spirit in Romans is a prayer of Paul for his readers. The thought is that as Christians exercise their faith, by God's grace, they will experience joy and peace, and these fruits of the Spirit (Gal 5:22) will in turn increase their certitude concerning the "more yet to come."

Conclusion

In Romans Paul develops many of the aspects of his pneumatology we have seen previously, particularly the opposition of the Spirit to the law and the flesh, and the relationship of the Spirit to the experience of divine sonship. The central thrust of the pneumatology of Romans is, however, the role of the Holy Spirit as the effective presence of the love of God accompanying the Christian on his journey and sustaining him even in the face of death with the invincible assurance of God's love for him in Christ Jesus.

18
Eclipse and Return
of the Spirit:
Colossians and Ephesians

The Puzzle of Colossians

Between the writing of the letter to the Romans and that to the Colossians considerable time has elapsed. Luke's reconstruction of the events during that period (Acts 23:3 to the end) tells of Paul's return for the last time to Palestine, his imprisonment there, his appeal to Caesar and his journey to Rome. It was from there, apparently, that he sent the letter to the Colossians.

Colossae, some one hundred miles inland east of Ephesus, was evangelized by one of Paul's disciples, Epaphras (Col 1:7). Difficulties have arisen in the community. Judaizing elements have been at work undermining the gospel Paul preached. They promote circumcision (2:11-13), dietary practices (2:16, 21), the observance of feasts and sabbaths (2:16). This raises for Paul the old issue about the Law (2:14) and its provisional and preparatory character (2:17). But there is something quite different here from the clashes Paul had with judaizers. A philosophical element has been introduced (2:8). Exactly what this was is hard to say. Some scholars think it was a gnostic or pre-gnostic ferment, others that it was a form of neo-pythagorean speculation of which we get a hint in Paul's allusion to "cosmic powers" in 2:20. In any case, there is no need to think that these ideas came from any other source than the Jewish element, for Asia Minor at the time was a seedbed of religious syncretism. The "movement" is marked by an excessive asceticism (2:23) and a special affection for the hierarchies of angels (2:18). In both these points Paul sees a threat to the authentic gospel, in which Christ is Lord over all, even the angels. He responds by stressing the centrality of Christ in the Church and in the cosmos of matter and spirit, and the importance of clear and precise knowledge of the mystery (1:27).

What place does the Spirit have in this letter? In 1:8 Paul says he has heard of the Colossians' "love in the spirit." The expression echoes

216

Rom 15:30 where Paul had spoken of the love the Spirit inspires. Here, however, there is no development of the idea, except that it is immediately followed by Paul's prayer that his readers grow in knowledge of God's will "in perfect wisdom and spiritual insight." It is characteristic of the epistle that growth in love is presented as a growth in understanding ("taught by love" is a better way of rendering the Greek in Col 2:2, which the NAB translates "united in love"). And here, to the pair of words, "wisdom and insight" which he borrows from Is 29:14 as he had done in 1 Cor 1:19, Paul adds the adjective "spiritual." For us who recall the great discourse on the wisdom of the Spirit in 1 Cor 1:18-3:3, this little adjective may be very meaningful. However, Paul does not here exploit it. Quite possibly he has mentioned it simply to recall the baptismal catechesis on the need for the Spirit to lead a life worthy of the kingdom (vs. 10).

The adjective "spiritual" appears again in 3:16 where Paul urges his readers to "sing gratefully to God from your hearts in psalms, hymns and inspired ("spiritual") songs." By the last of these three expressions Paul probably means songs of a more spontaneous variety, perhaps even singing in tongues (as in 1 Cor 14:15), but the use of the adjective instead of the expression "singing in the Spirit" indicates the expression and the practice had become commonplace.

In only one other place does the word "spirit" appear and that is in Col 2:5, where Paul speaks of being present "in spirit" when bodily absent (as in 1 Cor 5:3).

Our tally sheet in Colossians thus gives us only four places where "spirit" or "spiritual" appears, and none of them reaches the heights we have previously seen in Galatians and Romans. How explain this? A first response might be to say that Paul's subject matter did not lend itself to discussing the Spirit. But a rapid review of the subject matter indicates that the topics are precisely those which elsewhere in Paul evoke his most-developed theology of the Spirit. The tendency to return to the Law evoked from Paul in Gal, 2 Cor and Rom an insistence on the Spirit as the characteristic of the new covenant, the Spirit in contrast to the letter, and an ethic of walking in or according to the Spirit. The same problem in Colossians leaves Paul silent about the Spirit.

Above all in 2:11-15 where baptism is treated there is no mention of the Spirit. Paul does not exploit the contrast with circumcision (vs. 11) as one between flesh and spirit, as he did in Phil 3:3. He says only that Christian circumcision is not done by hand but that the body of flesh is put off by Christ's circumcision. The omission of the Spirit here when it would have been so natural and "Pauline" in the context is indeed surprising. Even more surprising is the absence of any reference to the Spirit in 2:12-13, which concerns the mystical aspect of baptism. When we recall the formula of 1 Cor 12:13, "In one Spirit we were all baptized into one body and we were all given to drink of the same Spirit," we find it unusual to omit the Spirit altogether from a baptismal text. Or again we may compare our text with 1 Cor 6:11.

1 Cor 6:11

> 11. And such were some of you. But you were washed, you were sanctified, you were justified in the name of the Lord Jesus Christ and in the Spirit of our God. (RSV)

Col 2:12-13

> 12. And you were buried with him in baptism, in which you were also raised with him through faith in the working of God, who raised him from the dead. 13. And you, who were dead in trespasses and the uncircumcision of your flesh, God made alive together with him, having forgiven us all our trespasses. (RSV)

In the moral exhortation of 3:1-5, we likewise miss any word about walking in the spirit or the fruit of the spirit (as in Gal 5:22-25). We find instead the exhortation to walk in Christ (2:6) or in wisdom (4:25). In terms of the gospel itself, we see it defined as "the message of truth" (1:5), and though it is said to bear fruit, there is no mention of the Spirit in any kind of charismatic confirmation as was the case in 1 Thes 1:5, Gal 3:5, 1 Cor 1:4-7.

What has happened? Some authors wonder whether the difference is not so great as to indicate that Colossians was written by someone other than Paul, at least by a secretary who was less enthusiastic about the Spirit. But this way to resolve the inconsistency is not necessary. The best clue to what has happened is given in 2:15, which follows immediately upon the baptismal text analyzed above. By nailing the curse to the cross, God thus "disarmed the principalities and powers. He made a public show of them, and leading them off captive, triumphed in the person of Christ." What is endangered by the Colossian crisis is not so much the doctrine of the Spirit as the doctrine of Christ. Excessive worship of the angels is a kind of separation of the world of the "spirits" from the headship of Christ. It is even plausible to think that rash talk about the Spirit, mixed in with talk about the angels and the cosmic powers, has led to this diminution of interest in Christ. Paul does not withdraw his doctrine of the Spirit—there are enough traces of it, if only four, to show that he is faithful to his own previous teaching. However, it cannot be denied that some stress on the Spirit has been sacrificed in the interest of the person and the primacy of Christ. Of course it is the role of the Spirit precisely to foster this awareness (1 Cor 12:3); and we have seen too how the person of Christ can be used interchangeably for his Spirit (Rom 8:10-11). But for the moment, in the Colossian situation, the urgency of the Spirit's role as such seems to have yielded to the more pressing urgency of Christology—which also lends itself more easily to doctrinal clarification than does the more elusive notion of the Spirit.

Does a similar preoccupation underlie the gospels? We shall see.

Ephesians: Retrieval of the Spirit in Liturgical Piety

If emphasis on the Spirit waned in favor of other interests in Colossians, a resurgence appears in the so-called letter to the Ephesians, where the Spirit is referred to at least a dozen times. This frequency is, for the length of the letter, a higher percentage of occurrence than in any of the Pauline letters except possibly for Romans with its concentration of references in chapter 8.

Two preliminary questions are important here: what occasioned the writing of Ephesians, and who in fact wrote it? In answer to the first, one thing is certain. The absence of any polemic in the letter shows that it was not written, as most of Paul's letters were, in response to a problem or a crisis. Nor is it a personal letter like Philippians or Philemon. There are no personal references or greetings by name; and the author does not seem to know his readers or they him (1:15; 3:2-4; 4:21). In some ways the letter could be compared with Romans in that it is a comprehensive theological treatise beyond and above *ad hoc* responses to problems. But Romans is a brilliant theological exercise of a Christian rabbi, Ephesians is rather a lyrical praise of a poet-preacher.

The author is certainly interested in doctrine, especially the mystery of the Church and its call to unity. But even this is not polemical but contemplative and exhortatory. As a matter of fact the first part of the letter is composed mainly of a long hymn of praise and thanksgiving; and the epistolary parts, especially the exhortation from 4:1 to the end, draw heavily on the ideas already expressed in the letter to the Colossians, so that the dependence on this letter, at least on its ideas, is easily demonstrated.

Obviously the author intended the work to be a letter, but most of it is a prayer and an exhortation, an illustration probably of the kind of activity which prophets and exhorters fulfilled in the early Christian communities (1 Cor 14:3; Rom 12:6-8). If we have difficulty in determining what might have occasioned the casting of these elements in the form of a letter, we have little difficulty in discovering the occasion for thanksgiving prayer and exhortation—it was the community assembly for worship. To this we shall return in examining the two major parts of the letter.

Who authored such a letter? Tradition as well as the opening address attribute the letter to Paul. But if so, how could he imply unfamiliarity with his readers (1:15; 3:2-4; 4:21), since he spent at least three years in Ephesus? This problem is easily resolved by noting that the words "at Ephesus" in the opening lines are missing from some major Greek manuscripts, making it highly probable that the association of the letter with Ephesus was due not to its being originally addressed to the Ephesians but to its being especially treasured by them. At any rate *this* item does not impugn Pauline authorship of the letter.

The author of this brilliant work surely was a Jewish rather than a gentile Christian, for he knows the rabbinic exegetical methods (see his use of Is 57:19 in 2:12-19 and Ps 68:18 in 4:8-9), applies Jewish ideas on proselyte baptism to Christian baptism, is familiar with Jewish cultic traditions, and is convinced of the importance of Israel in the plan of salvation (2:12-14). Who better than Paul would fit this category?

And yet, it must be admitted that there are significant differences of style in the letter, a great dependence on Colossians, the accumulation in this one letter of many of Paul's expressions from his earlier letters, the introduction of some ideas that show possible Qumranian influence. We think it most likely, then, that the actual composition of the letter was done by a disciple thoroughly imbued with his master's thoughts, a disciple in whose memory the letter to the Colossians was still very fresh, a disciple who nonetheless could publish a letter in Paul's name without anyone questioning his authority to do so. The most likely candidate for this role would be Tychicus, Paul's "dear brother, faithful minister and fellow slave in the Lord" (Col 4:7; Eph 6:21-22). Bearing Paul's full power to speak in his name, and intimately familiar with Paul's thought and letters from long association with him (cf. Acts 20:4) Tychicus could easily have reworked Colossians into a circular letter of exhortation for the other churches of Asia Minor, omitting from the Colossian letter whatever might have been too particular to be of value to a more general audience and using as his overall framework a liturgical hymn (chs. 1-3) and a sermon of exhortation (chs. 4-6). This mission of exhortation is specifically given to Tychicus by Paul for this journey ("I am sending him . . . to put fresh heart unto you," Col 4:8).

At any rate, enough has been said to show on the one hand that Ephesians is quite properly included in the body of Paul's letters as a legitimate development giving us a precious reflection of early Christian worship. Let us now look at the letter in detail to discover what role the Spirit is given in each of the two major parts of the letter.

We have said that the first part is largely a hymn of thanksgiving. Actually, if we bracket the epistolary parts (1:1-2, 15-23; 3:1-13), what remains is a perfectly integral Christian *berakah*, a prayer form common in the Jewish synagogue worship and recognizable by the opening words "Blessed [or praised] be God. . ." or "Blessed art Thou. . ." After the opening praise of God, the *berakah* would list blessings received, sometimes add a prayer, and always conclude with a doxology and an Amen. Paul was accustomed to begin his letters with a prayer of thanksgiving, and on one occasion, 2 Cor 1:3-5, he uses the *berakah* form. Here we have the *berakah* extended to greater lengths than anywhere else in Paul, and to it is joined the more usual Pauline thanksgiving form in 1:15-16. Some authors are so convinced of the liturgical origin of this *berakah* that they suggest it may have been used for the eucharist. They point out that in form it represents a stage between the old Jewish *berakah* and the eucharistic prayer form we find in Hippolytus' *Apostolic Tradition.* At any rate, it has an opening praise (1:3), a listing of blessings received in general (1:4-9), then more specifically in the divine plan for the world and the destiny of the "called" (1:10-14), involving bringing of the dead to life (2:1-10) and the enfranchising of the alien (2:11-22), then a prayer for deeper understanding of the mystery (3:14-19) and finally a doxology with an Amen (3:20-21).

With this understanding of the context we are now able to appreciate the references to the Spirit. In the opening line God is praised for bestowing in Christ "every spiritual blessing in the heavens" (1:3). "Spiritual" here is hardly different from "heavenly." Both indicate the divine origin and destiny of the blessings which will be detailed in the sequence: election (1:4), sonship (1:5), redemption, forgiveness (1:7), knowledge (1:9), the Spirit (1:13) and the inheritance (1:14). In the last two of these verses, the verbs "heard, believed, and were sealed" are all in the aorist tense in the Greek, thus referring to a definite past moment when all these events happened. This is obviously the moment of conversion and baptism, the latter being the sealing with the Spirit (2 Cor 1:21), Christian successor to the seal of circumcision (Rom 4:11). Paul had used identical terms in 2 Cor 1:20-21, which we examined in detail above. Here, as there, the Spirit is the beginning, the down payment of the complete inheritance to come.

In the prayer begun in vs. 17, the author prays for "a spirit of wisdom and revelation" that they might know better the Father of glory. In form the prayer echoes that of Col 1:9, with "insight" being changed to "revelation" and the adjective "spiritual" being strengthened to "the spirit." Again the primitive Pauline idea of the Spirit as revealer of the gifts of God (1 Cor 2:10) is recalled here in a way slightly stronger than in Colossians.

In 2:11-22 the author expands on what the Christian call means in

terms of the old categories of Jew and Gentile. The section has two references to the Spirit (vss. 18, 22) but to situate them properly we need to
observe that they are part of an extended chiasmus, that is, a symmetri-
cal arrangement of ideas like stones in an arch leading up to and away
from a central idea. How chiastic the form is can be seen in the following printing of the passage (in which we have stuck more literally to the
Greek word order than the NAB permits):

READ DOWN (By Sections)	READ UP (By Sections)
Therefore remember that once you gentiles *in the flesh*—	22. in him you are being built into a dwelling place for God *in the Spirit.*
who are called the uncircumcision by what is called the circumcision *made in the flesh by hands*—	21. in whom the whole structure is fitted together and takes shape as a *holy temple in the Lord;*
12. that in former times you had *no part in Christ*	20. You form a building which rises on the foundation of the apostles and prophets, with *Christ Jesus himself* as the *capstone,*
and were *excluded from the community of Israel.*	You are *fellow-citizens of the saints* and *members of the household of God.*
You were *strangers* to the covenants of promise;	19. This means that you are *strangers and aliens no longer.*
You were without hope and *without God* in the world.	18. Through *him* we both have access in one *Spirit* to the *Father.*
13. But now in Christ Jesus you who once were *far off*	and peace to *those* who were *near.*
have been *brought near* through the blood of Christ.	17. He came and announced the good news of peace to you who were *far off*
14. It is *he who is our peace,* and who made the *two of us* one by breaking down the barrier of *hostility* that kept us apart	and *to make peace,* 16. reconciling *both of us* to God in one body through his cross, which put that *hostility* to death.
15. *In his own flesh he destroyed* the law of commandments and ordinances	*to create in himself* one new man from us who had been two

We notice that vs. 18 is a "Trinitarian" formula contrasting with the expression "without God" of vs. 12. Naturally the more generic term "God" is used to describe the gentile situation where God was really unknown, while now both gentile and Jew are granted access to the Father in one Spirit. Three points should be made about the pneumatology of this passage. (1) The biblical background is that of the conditions for entering the divine presence in the temple. We saw how, as the Jewish tradition developed, the thought of the Spirit as purifying and enabling one to enter the divine presence (especially at Qumran) was particularly stressed in the early baptismal catechesis of the Christian Church. (2) Here, the access is to "the Father," the God now known as "Abba" of Gal 4:6 and Rom 8:15; (3) the one Spirit demolishes the old distinction between Jew and Gentile (nowhere more pronounced than at the temple entrance) for all are admitted on equal footing to the Father.

The imagery is slightly shifted when we reach vs. 22, for instead of being pilgrims into the temple, purified by the Spirit, Christians are in the process of becoming a very part of the temple itself. We note at once that they are being built both "in the Lord" and "in the Spirit." The interchangeability of the two, already chartered by Rom 8:9-10, permitted Paul to speak only of Christ and not of the Spirit in important passages in Colossians. Here however not only does the "Spirit" return but it occupies the emphatic position at the climax of the whole passage. Aware of the symmetry, we note the contrast with the flesh in vs. 11. But Spirit here surely means more than simply the opposite of "flesh." In the context in which "the Lord" and "God" are mentioned, it highlights the personal and even trinitarian character of the Spirit's role here. The Church has replaced the temple as the place for God's dwelling. It has a visibility in the person of Jesus Christ, the apostles and prophets and finally in the members themselves. But the life of the community, its unifying and upbuilding power, is the Holy Spirit.

Beginning in 3:1 an epistolary digression interrupts the *berakah*. In 3:5 we read of the mystery of Christ "unknown to men in former ages but now revealed by the Spirit to the holy apostles and prophets." At one time in biblical studies it was held by a large number of scholars that Paul had borrowed the word "mystery" from the pagan mystery religions of his day to describe that into which Christians were initiated. Today few still hold this position, for it has been shown that the roots of this word are biblical. It means God's plan for history and for the world, especially the secret of his coming rule. A similar use of "mystery" is found in the Dead Sea scrolls. Here it means not merely God's plan to sum up everything under Christ's headship (1:10) through the Church (1:18, 22-23) but that the gentiles share in it equally with the Jews (3:6). The mystery is revealed by the Spirit, as in 1 Cor 2:10.

But the expression "to the holy apostles and prophets" is quite unlike Paul. It is one of those expressions which make it likely the letter was that of a disciple of Paul. "Holy apostles" indicates that the apostles are beginning to be revered as heroes of a past age. We have nevertheless here perhaps an authentic souvenir of the fact that Jesus limited his earthly mission to the Jews and that the mission to the gentiles was the work of the Spirit after the resurrection. Luke will take great care to show how the Spirit led, through surprising turns of events, to win the apostle Peter to an effective gentile mission (Acts 10:28). In Acts 13:1-3, the commissioning of Barnabas and Saul to their first journey of evangelism was done because of the leading of the Spirit of prophecy. In fact, Barnabas and Saul are then called "prophets and teachers." Here too we see prophecy as an office rather than as a passing movement. If this letter is written by Tychicus in the spirit of Paul as part of his mission of exhortation (Col 4:8), it is tempting to think that "holy apostles" is a reference to Paul and "prophets" a reference to Tychicus who shares Paul's understanding of the mystery as a Christian prophet. By the time the Didache was written, prophets were highly revered. Not every community had one, and when a visiting prophet presided at eucharist he was not bound by a fixed formula in the eucharistic prayer ("Let the prophets give thanks however they wish," *Did.* 10:7). If the long *berakah* here is Tychicus' composition, we can get an idea of what kind of thanksgiving prayer might have been composed by a Christian prophet.

In the final prayer of this long hymn, (3:14-19) the Spirit is again mentioned: "May he grant you from the riches of his glory to be strengthened with power through his Spirit for the progress of the inward man" (vs. 16). This "inward man" is the one who in Rom 7:22 sides with "mind" and "spirit" against "sin" working through "the flesh." As man of himself does not know how to approach God unless strengthened by the Spirit (Rom 8:26) so here the strengthening by the Spirit is the first of a chain of graces—Christ's indwelling through faith, growth in love, a knowledge of the mystery of Christ's love—culminating in the very "fullness of God." The first effect of the Spirit's strengthening is a new coming of Christ to dwell in the hearts of the faithful. Usually the indwelling in the spiritual temple is attributed to the Father (2:22) or to the Spirit (1 Cor 6:19; Rom 8:11) while Christ has the more physical role of being the chief element of the temple, the foundation (Col 2:7) or the chief stone (Eph 2:20). Of course Paul had equated the Spirit's indwelling with Christ being "in you" (Rom 8:10-11). But here, where it is not a question of the initial indwelling begun at baptism nor simply the abiding indwelling of the divine friendship but a new departure in the already existing relationship (as is obvious from the context of the prayer and from the use of the aorist *katoikēsai* in the Greek), the Spirit's role is to prepare the individual and the community for this new inhabitation of Christ. On the one hand it is remarkable how the Spirit here is not thought of as an independent power and certainly not as the goal of his activity. It is the Father who acts *through* his Spirit, and the Spirit's strengthening brings Christ to indwell more deeply. On the other hand, the role of the Spirit is quite real. In terms of Old Testament pneumatology, it is less the spiritualization of the entrance ritual where the Spirit purifies for entrance to the holy, than the transfer of prophetic categories to a significant moment of growth in the Christian life. As the Spirit came upon the prophet, already God's friend and servant, to prepare him for the word, which "comes" (e.g. Ez 11:5), so the spirit readies the Christian for a new coming of Christ in his heart. This involves a significant growth in divine love which in turn makes possible a contemplative experience of Christ's measureless love and then the perfection of God (vs. 19). The whole process is initiated in the strengthening "by his Spirit." Note, however, that the Holy Spirit is not thought of here as preparing Christians for the Second Coming of Christ. Whereas in 1 Cor 1:7-8, the present spiritual gifts prepare for the revelation of Jesus Christ on the last day and Paul says the Father will *strengthen* them to the end, the "day of our Lord Jesus Christ" (1 Cor 1:8), here the coming of Christ is now and the Father prepares it, even brings it about by the strengthening of his Spirit. And the ultimate goal is not the parousia but "all the perfection God has to give"—hence a growth without limits.

This marks a significant development not only in the greater emphasis it places on the present growth of Christians but on the role of the Spirit in the dynamics of that growth.

We now turn to the second part of the letter, the exhortation (4:1 to the end). If the Father has brought his new people into the mystery of unity, the first consequence of this gift should be to seek the unity of the Church above all (4:1-16) and then to live in the truth and in the light 4:17-6:24. The Spirit plays a key role in the living out of these consequences. Since there is only one Spirit, just as there is one body (vs. 4, a point already made by Paul in 1 Cor 12:13), they must "Spare no effort to make fast with bonds of peace the unity which the Spirit gives" (vs. 3). This is G.H.P. Thompson's translation of the Greek, which reads literally, "Striving to preserve the unity of the Spirit in the bond of peace." The best way to understand the meaning seems to be this: The mystery into which Christians have been called is a mystery of unity— the reconciling of heaven and earth, of Jew and gentile through the cross of Christ which established all in peace (2:15-16). The inner essence of this new state is the one Spirit who gives access to the Father (2:18). In the Christian community peace is the outward sign—the bond—which shows the reality of the one Spirit. Already given by Christ (2:15-17), peace must be clung to as his precious gift and the visible fruit of his Spirit (Gal 5:22).

In 4:7-16 Paul shows how the diversity of ministries in the Church, far from threatening its unity, are rather builders of it. The gifts listed are primarily the offices of authority and teaching, because the unity of the body cannot be preserved without them. While in 1 Cor 12:4-11 the gifts are attributed primarily to the Spirit, here they are attributed to the risen Lord—or better, the ascended Lord. Using a recasting of Ps 68:19 known to the rabbis, the author sees the gifts of ministry as obtained by Christ upon his "ascending on high" and then poured out by him upon the Church. Though the Spirit is not mentioned in this process, we should note that Ps 68 was prescribed in the liturgy of the synagogue to be recited on the feast of Pentecost, which Luke tells us was the occasion for the outpouring of the Holy Spirit (Acts 2). Nevertheless we must respect the fact that nowhere in the New Testament is the Spirit thought of as detached from the Father or the Lord Jesus who give it, and hence at times the gifts can be attributed to the Spirit, as in 1 Cor 12:4-11, at other times to the Father (1 Cor 12:28) and at other times to Christ, as here.

We now turn to the more specific ethical exhortations in the concluding part of the letter. "Be renewed in the spirit of your mind" (4:23) simply means to accept the new way of thinking which is given in the new creation (4:24). In 4:30, the readers are exhorted, "Do nothing to sadden the Holy Spirit, with whom you were sealed against the day of redemption." We recognize at once, in the first part of the verse, the language of Is 63:10, where the Israelites' infidelities to the covenant "grieved his holy spirit" and thus restricted the Lord's saving power and even changed the relationship into enmity. As the desert rebellion was in great part a sin of the lips, so the context here indicates that the saddening of the Holy Spirit happens primarily by sins of speech against fraternal unity. The Qumran community had especially severe punishments for slander and murmuring (1 QS 7:4-9) and they considered these sins the effect of yielding to the evil spirit (1 QS 5:25-26).

The second part of Eph 4:30 refers to the sealing by the Holy Spirit which we have already discussed at length in 2 Cor 1:20-21 and Eph 1:13.

In 5:18, Christians are urged to be "filled with the Spirit" instead of getting drunk on wine. Here the letter joins the same tradition we find in Luke concerning the gift of the Spirit on Pentecost, where the accusation of drunkenness was met by Peter's explanation of the coming of the Spirit (Acts 2:15). Though we have no incontrovertible proof that Ephesians was written as a liturgy for the celebration of Christian Pentecost (a theory advanced by J. C. Kirby), it might not be irrelevant to note that Pentecost was originally a harvest festival at which, naturally, wine-drinking would prevail. The infilling with the Spirit should overflow in "psalms, hymns and inspired songs" (the same expression as in Col 3:16) and in praise and thanksgiving (4:19-20). We should note that the "liturgy of the Spirit" incorporates the Old Testament psalms as well as Christian compositions, whether of fixed or spontaneous variety.

Toward the end of the letter the Christian life is described as a combat against the evil one. Divine armor and weapons are needed, for "our battle is not against human forces but against the principalities and powers, the rulers of this world of darkness, the evil spirits in region above" (6:12). The language evokes Is 59:17 and Wis 5:17-20, where God is depicted as a warrior against evil in the world, taking up the armor and the weapons of righteousness. But the conflict with the spirits of darkness evokes the belief of the Qumran community that in the final day they would be leagued with the angels in a cosmic battle with the "sons of darkness." Here in Ephesians the armor and weaponry of Roman soldiers is used to describe the Christian's resources in combat. The "sword of the Spirit" is the word of God (5:17). In Heb 4:12 the word of God is "living and effective and sharper than any two-edged sword. It penetrates and divides soul and spirit. . ." What does this word of God include here? Surely the Old Testament, but also the preaching of the gospel and the oral tradition about Jesus Christ. The close association of Spirit and Word here recalls the long development of this relationship which we traced through the Old Testament. Here the two are most intimately united in the climactic position of the passage. God's word is a sword because it bears the power of his Spirit.

Finally, the faithful are urged: "At every opportunity pray in the Spirit, using prayers and petitions of every sort" (6:18). It does not seem likely that "praying in the Spirit" refers to tongues here as it did in 1 Cor 14:15-16, since the expression is set in the midst of all kinds of prayers. It rather seems that the Spirit here is seen to be the universal atmosphere in which all Christian prayer is to be conducted.

Conclusion

Whether we suppose that Ephesians was written by Paul's own

hand or think it more likely the work of a disciple writing under his authority, this letter makes an important contribution to New Testament
pneumatology. Its mark will not be so much in anything new about the
Spirit, for nearly every passage we examined reflects an earlier idea or
phrase of Paul's. We do notice less charismatic interest (except for 4:7-
16, where, in the interests of unity the offices of authority and teaching
predominate) but this is compensated for by the ubiquitous reference to
the Spirit in Christian worship and life. For Ephesians is primarily a liturgical document, containing a long *berakah* which may have been used
to celebrate baptism or the eucharist, and a homiletical exhortation in
which traces of the Jewish liturgy of Pentecost can be found. The Spirit
is intensely present in word, sacrament, and life. We are pointed in the
direction of John's gospel and later liturgical developments.

In this, Ephesians provides a balance to the pneumatological bar-
renness of Colossians. Whatever reasons Paul had for diminishing his
references to the Spirit in that letter, it is important to note that he or
his disciple did not do so in the nonpolemical masterpiece called the letter to the Ephesians. This contrast is instructive on the centrality of the
Spirit in the Christian life. For the Church is most herself not when she
is defending or clarifying doctrine against attack, nor when she is cor-
recting ethical abuses—but when she prays. Her prayer language is her
language "at home." And here she can never forget that she could not
even say "Abba" or "Lord Jesus" were it not for the Spirit pulsing
within.

19
The Spirit in Sacrament, Scripture and Ministry: The Pastoral Epistles

A final stage in the development of Pauline pneumatology is represented by the letters to Timothy and Titus. This can be said without prejudice to the question of whether they are Paul's own writing or the work of a disciple. They were in any case accepted as part of the apostolic writings at an early hour and as God's inspired word for his church. Called "pastoral" because they deal with the practical questions faced by the pastors to whom they were addressed, the letters are not doctrinal treatises nor are they a public liturgical manifesto like Ephesians. They are rather *ad hoc* responses and advice to important church leaders in the developing Christian communities of the first century. Now while these letters show a proportionately large concern about doctrinal purity and appropriate Christian behavior, in a tone that might be called conservative, there are nonetheless important passages in which the Spirit appears.

We may begin with a text which speaks, in somewhat mysterious language, of the relationship of the spirit to Christ:

1 Tim 3:16: Vindicated in the Spirit

16. Great indeed, we confess, is the mystery of our religion:
    He was manifested in the flesh,
    vindicated in the Spirit,
    seen by angels,
    preached among the nations,
    believed on in the world,
    taken up in glory. (RSV)

Virtually all biblical scholars hold that we have here a quotation from an early faith-profession formula or, more likely, from an early li-

229

turgical hymn. It is introduced by the exclamation, "Great indeed is the mystery of our religion (*eusebeia*)" which the NAB translates as "mystery of our faith," thus considering it equivalent to the latter expression in 3:9. If we try to understand the fragment as a list of the steps of Christian salvation history (from the birth of Christ to the ascension) we run into several difficulties, not the least of which is that the ascension follows rather than precedes the preaching to the gentiles. It is better simply to take the various phrases as a poetic play on contrasts—flesh, spirit; angels, gentiles; world, glory. Our interest here is in the first contrast. "Manifested in the flesh" apparently refers to the stage in which Christ passed through human birth, life and suffering upon the cross unto death. "Vindicated in the Spirit" refers to his risen state which manifested him to be God's son "by the Spirit of holiness." Spirit here then simply contrasts Christ's state of glory with his previous humiliation (as in Phil 2:6-11). What then does "vindicated" mean? Though some versions translate it "justified," the term surely does not mean that Christ entered into the state of justification after his death. For Paul, Christ *is* the justice of God (1 Cor 1:30) and justification is what man, not Christ, needs. The meaning here is rather exaltation after humiliation—a theme dear to the Palestinian communities who incorporated the theology of the Fourth Servant Song of Isaiah into their preaching and liturgy (of which Phil 2:6-11 is an example). "Spirit" here, then, simply means "the realm of glory."

Titus 3:4-7: Bath of Regeneration and Renewal by the Holy Spirit

> 4. But when the goodness and loving kindness of God our Savior appeared, 5. he saved us, not because of deeds done by us in righteousness, but in virtue of his own mercy, by the washing of regeneration and renewal in the Holy Spirit, 6. which he poured out upon us richly through Jesus Christ our Savior, 7. so that we might be justified by his grace and become heirs in hope of eternal life. (RSV)

This passage is so dense that it makes analysis difficult, especially at the point that interests us most, vs. 5, which reads literally in the Greek: "through the bath of regeneration and of renewal of the Holy Spirit." Let us begin with what is most certain. When we were lost in our own sinful selfishness (3:3), God manifested his goodness and loving-kindness (vs. 4). He saved us not because of any righteous deeds we had done (a strong Pauline thought) but because of his own mercy (vs.

5). At this point we would expect a mention of Jesus Christ, but this is delayed until vs. 6 in order to give prominence to the moment and the rite of Christian initiation. The bath of regeneration is clearly baptism in which we are reborn. The idea of "rebirth" is not a Pauline way of referring to baptism. It sounds more Johannine ("born again of water and the Spirit," Jn 3:5). In Matthew the word "rebirth" or "regeneration" is used for the final inbreaking of the new age when the Son of Man shall be enthroned in glory (Mt 19:28), a usage that is probably more primitive than the one here. As the tradition developed it was seen that, for all that really mattered, the regeneration took place in each Christian at his baptism when he became a son of God. (It certainly did not happen at some advanced stage, as in Gnostic doctrine, where the rebirth was thought to take place through the mystic and magic formula of the "regenerating word.")

The word "renewal" is however, a key word in Paul's pneumatology. The Psalmist had said that when God sends forth his breath (*ruah* or *pneuma*) all nature is renewed (Ps 104:30). The noun "renewal" (*anakainōsis*), however, appears nowhere in the Greek language before Paul and is apparently a word of Paul's own coining. This part of Titus 3:5 is therefore echoing a strong Pauline tradition.

How is the "renewal by the Holy Spirit" linked with the preceding? Is it a separate and subsequent moment or is it identical with the "bath of regeneration"? The word "renewal," unlike "regeneration," is a favorite one of Paul's. The verb and the noun always occur in contexts in which Paul speaks of the development of the Christian life subsequent to baptism. The inward man is being renewed day by day (2 Cor 4:16); he must walk in newness of life (Rom 6:4) and be renewed in the spirit of his mind and put on the new man (Rom 12:2; cf. Eph 4:23f); who, according to Col 3:10, is being renewed unto knowledge. Here, in Titus 3:5, however, there is every reason to believe that the renewal is linked to the bath as much as regeneration is, for not only is the Spirit constantly presented in Paul as the Christian's birthright in baptism (1 Cor 12:13; Rom 8:10) but here the verb "poured out" refers equally well to the waters of the bath as to the Holy Spirit which is the closer antecedent.

Is there then no difference between "rebirth" and "renewal"? There is a difference; for while rebirth corresponds to the once-done instatement as God's sons, the work of renewal is a process which, while beginning at baptism, continues in the Christian until the divine image, Christ himself, is perfectly achieved (2 Cor 4:16; 3:18). "Rebirth" is a word taken from the realm of nature; "renewal" is taken from the realm of art. Like an artist carefully restoring a faded or damaged mas-

terpiece, the Holy Spirit works upon the Christian until the divine image
is restored (2 Cor 3:18).

2 Tim 3:14-17: Inspired Scripture

14. You, for your part, must remain faithful to what you have
learned and believed, because you know who your teachers
were. 15. Likewise, from your infancy you have known the
sacred Scriptures, the source of the wisdom which through
faith in Jesus Christ leads to salvation. 16. All Scripture is
inspired of God and is useful for teaching—for reproof, correction and training in holiness 17. so that the man of God may
be fully competent and equipped for every good work. (NAB)

Our interest in this passage originates in the expression "inspired of
God" in vs. 16. The Greek means literally "breathed by God"—or
"inspirited by God." The "Scripture" here refers to the Old Testament,
either individual passages or books. For him who has faith in Jesus
Christ these books, viewed in the light of that faith, contain a saving
wisdom (vs. 15). And they are to be a guide for the "man of God." In
the Old Testament this was a title for prophets (2 Kgs 5:8) or Moses
(Deut 33:1). Though theoretically applicable to all Christians the title is
used in the pastorals for chief ministers like Timothy (cf. 1 Tim 6:11).
The proper understanding of the Old Testament writings will help the
leader of the church combat false doctrine and foster fruitful Christian
living. Here again we see the closest connection between the Spirit and
the word. And here the word is not the preached word but the written
word of the Scriptures.

Prophecy, Ministry and the Spirit

There are five short texts remaining to be examined, and they are
so closely interrelated that we will consider them together:

1 Tim 1:18-19:

18. This charge I commit to you, Timothy, my son, in accordance with the prophetic utterances which pointed to you, that
inspired by them you may wage the good warfare, 19. holding
faith and a good conscience. By rejecting conscience, certain
persons have made shipwreck of their faith. (RSV)

1 Tim 4:1:

1. The Spirit distinctly says that in later times some will turn away from the faith and will heed deceitful spirits and things taught by demons. (NAB)

1 Tim 4:14:

14. Do not neglect the gift you received when, as a result of prophecy, the presbyters laid their hands on you. (NAB)

2 Tim 1:6-7:

6. Hence, I remind you to rekindle the gift of God that is within you through the laying on of my hands; 7. for God did not give us a spirit of timidity but a spirit of power and love and self-control. (NAB)

2 Tim 1:13-14:

13. Take as a model of sound teaching what you have heard me say, in faith and love in Christ Jesus. 14. Guard the rich deposit of faith with the help of the Holy Spirit who dwells within us. (NAB)

Let us note the major role played by prophecy in the community which this letter reflects. Three of the above texts are concerned with it. In the first, the writer alludes to prophecies (plural) that "went before on you." This curious turn of phrase could refer to prophecies which pointed Timothy out to Paul and led Paul to select him for the ministry. But as we have no indication in Acts or in Paul's letters that his choice was indicated by prophecy, probably the second meaning is to be preferred, namely, prophecies which preceded or accompanied Paul's ordination of Timothy. This is the meaning of 1 Tim 4:14 in any case, though the exact correlation between the prophecy and the ordination is not clear. Did the prophecy direct that Timothy be ordained? Or did the prophecy provide confirmation and encouragement to the selection already made by Paul? The only thing that the text says is that Timothy's grace came (literally) "through prophecy with the laying on of hands."

The prestigious role of prophecy can also be seen from 1 Tim 4:1. Where does the Spirit say expressly that in future times people will fall away from faith? Various New Testament texts might illustrate this, such as Mk 13:21-23 or Acts 20:29-30. If the writer knew of an explicit word of the Lord Jesus, it would certainly have strengthened his case but apparently he does not have in mind a "word of the Lord."

The most plausible explanation is that he is referring to some explicit teaching of Christian prophecy. But if that is so, it means that prophecy was taken seriously in this community—so seriously that its general shape could be remembered and its specific statements referred to. From all this we can gather how important the role and function of prophecy had become. We are not far from the time and the view of the Didache, where prophets are held in very high honor and the Christian congregations have to be reminded that bishops and deacons are as important as prophets.

But the even more impressive novelty of 1 Tim 4:14 and 2 Tim 1:6 is that Timothy's ministerial gift, twice called *charisma*, is attributed, in the one case to prophecy and in the other to the laying on of Paul's hands. *Charisma* had previously been used by Paul of the various gifts, passing or stable, which built up the community (1 Cor 12-14; Rom 12:6-8; Eph 4:7-16). And we saw that he did not distinguish between "charismatic" and "official" gifts. All were the work of the one Spirit. We never saw in Paul a charism being generated in one member by a prophecy coming from another or by the laying on of hands—though the argument from silence should not be pressed, especially in view of Acts 13ᵗ1-3 where as a result of prophecy Barnabas and Saul were designated for the gentile mission and hands were laid on them. In any case, Timothy's charism is expressly attributed to prophecy on the one hand and ordination on the other.

The laying on of hands is a Christian gesture that can have different meanings according to the context. It can be a gesture of blessing (Mt 19:15), of healing (Mk 6:5), of conferring the Holy Spirit (Acts 8:17) and of conferring an ecclesiastical office (Acts 6:6). Here, of course, it is this last sense that is meant, though obviously the Holy Spirit is also given.

Scholars discuss how the laying on of hands by the presbyterate (i.e. the council of elders, 1 Tim 4:14) can be squared with the statement of 2 Tim 1:6 that it was Paul's hands that conveyed the grace. The solution is not as difficult as it seems. In 2 Tim 1:6 the preposition *dia* indicates that it was through Paul's hands that the charism was conveyed. In 1 Tim 4:14 the Greek preposition is *meta* meaning "with" or "accompanied by" the laying on of the elders' hands. The role of the presbyterate seems therefore only supplementary. The *charism* is conveyed by *prophecy* (1 Tim 4:14) and by *apostolic ordination* (2 Tim 1:6). Note that it is not by one in isolation from the other. Inasmuch as the texts sharpen the focus on one of the ways in which a charism emerges in the Christian community, they represent an advance over the previous undifferentiated panoply of gifts listed by Paul.

But we have not exhausted the pneumatology of 2 Tim 1:6. In it Paul urges Timothy to "rekindle" (RSV) or "fan to flame" (NAB) the gift that is in him. We are probably justified in extending the principle given here to all the gifts of the Spirit and of concluding that they are capable of waning or waxing in fervor, and that the one who is gifted has the responsibility of keeping the gift alive, using it and making it fruitful (compare the talents, Mt 25:14-30; Lk 19:12-27). It also means that periodically a gift that has remained largely latent may be reawakened, as embers may be fanned to flame. Here there is a scriptural foundation for the later development of the theology of the "grace of state"—that is, the grace connected with a public call or ordination to an office. At any rate the charism is a way in which God himself communicates his Spirit, as vs. 7 makes clear.

Three traits characterize this Spirit. It is first a Spirit of power (*dynamis*). The association of power with the Spirit of God goes back at least to Micah 3:8 (which we discussed) and is found throughout the New Testament, especially in Paul and Luke (1 Thes 1:5; Rom 15:19; Lk 1:35; 4:14; Acts 1:8; 10:38). Here it refers not to the outward manifestation of confirming wonders but to the inward strengthening Timothy needs (cf. Eph 3:16) to fulfill his ministry courageously. Young (1 Tim 4:2) and somewhat timid (2 Tim 1:8) he needs the conviction that it is not by his own power that he functions but by the power of the Holy Spirit, which is not a spirit of slavery and fear but of sonship (Rom 8:15).

This spirit is also one of love, as any disciple of Paul should know (Gal 5:22; Rom 5:5). Finally, it is a spirit of "self-control." A better translation of the Greek *sōphronismos* is "prudence." The word "prudent" and its cognates appear nine times in the Pastorals and only six in the rest of the New Testament. It is often related to moderation in the use and enjoyment of material goods. Rejecting the excessive asceticism of the gnostics, the author says that food is good and should be taken with thanksgiving (1 Tim 4:3-5). The Christian should avoid excess in wine (1 Tim 3:3, 8; Titus 1:7; 2:3) but moderate use is recommended (1 Tim 5:23). Youthful passions should be shunned (2 Tim 2:22) but young women should marry (1 Tim 5:14). Riches are dangerous, and one should be content with a sufficiency of food and clothing (1 Tim 6:7-10). But a certain amount of ownership of property in the congregation is taken for granted (1 Tim 6:17-19). Here in 2 Tim 1:7, it is the idea of prudence and moderation that should prevail in the pastor (cf. 1 Tim 3:2; Titus 1:6).

Is the introduction of "moderation" a settling for a contented mediocrity? What has happened to the ethic of absolute self-denial (1 Cor 9:24-27; Phil 3:8), the limitless voyage of love, the totality of self-gift that characterized Paul's earlier ethic of the Spirit under the expectation of Christ's imminent return? The answer lies in the new historical situation in which the pastorals were written. The church is buffeted by severe storms, not so much of persecution as of false teaching. Particularly an incipient gnosticism has reinterpreted the gospel as a myth of individual enlightenment like other myths. It is encouraging a withdrawing from the world, despising much of it as evil, and the asceticism it promotes, having the appearance of something very holy, is appealing to man's passion for the simple and the absolute. Is this not really the most spiritual of all ways? No. In this context, according to the author of the Pastorals, what is most extreme is not what is holiest. The Spirit God gives is indeed a spirit of *power*, but because its power comes from *love*, it is also the spirit of order and measure (2 Tim 1:7). It is linked to the sound and sober teaching about Jesus, and it is a spirit that guides Christian living in this age without seeking an escape from it. In the historical context of the times, the alternative to this understanding of the Spirit was gnostic dualism, which, for all its appearance of spirituality, really cut away the gospel's roots in the historical Jesus and the historical church.

That is why, for the author of the Pastorals, the Holy Spirit is the guardian of the sound tradition about Jesus (2 Tim 1:13-14). And this explains why the publishing of the gospels was not simply a pious project but an absolute necessity. To this major development we now turn.

20
The Spirit and
the Cross: Mark

Method in Studying the Synoptics

At this point of embarking on a study of pneumatology in the gospels, a word about the nature of these writings is necessary to guide our method. In the introduction to Part II we noted the difference between historical chronology and literary chronology—that is, the level of *events* recorded and the level of the *writing* about those events. We must now become more specific and observe that there are three levels or strata to our present gospels. The first and most accessible layer is that of the finished gospels as they lie before us. This level will yield not only a report of the deeds and words of Jesus but also the theological interests of the particular evangelist who is interpreting the message for the church of his day.

The second level is that of the traditions the evangelists used to compose their work. Obviously they did not write out of thin air. Putting their work into writing decades after the events, they were working with traditions that had been shaped by long use and re-use in the Christian communities—for liturgy, apologetics, instruction of converts, moral direction, and so on. Naturally the needs of the churches dictated to a great extent what was important to remember, and the underlining of certain aspects in the tradition obviously left its stamp. Since Matthew and Luke (according to the consensus of scholars) both used some form of Mark, we can at least observe where they differ from him, and since they also used another common sayings source not found in Mark (sometimes called 'Q' after the German *Quelle* meaning source) we have a second base of comparison. Beyond this level is that of the historic events which gave rise to the traditions—namely, what Jesus himself actually did and taught.

Obviously the top layer is easier to get to and identify. But we need not be overly skeptical about reaching the other two levels with a reasonable degree of certitude. We should simply note one thing—that scholars admit today that the methods evolved in the past by brilliant exegetes to discover the "Jesus of history" behind the "Christ of faith" —as if the former were more "real" than the latter—have proven inadequate to the task. To take one simple example, they evoked the principle of "discontinuity" by which they said that the only things about Jesus of which we can be historically certain are those in which he shows himself to be different from contemporary Judaism and also different from the later Christian preaching of those events. The hardly identifiable residue of this refining was a Jesus who resembled nothing Jewish or Christian!

For our purposes here we are most interested in the teaching of each evangelist about the Spirit. To determine that we shall have to discuss the preceding tradition, but hopefully without straining out the gnat at the expense of swallowing the camel. Although we are reserving a chapter for each of the evangelists, it will be less repetitive if, in treating Markan passages that are paralled in Luke and Matthew, we also discuss the parallel passages, so that we will not have to retrace our steps over the same terrain when we get to Luke and Matthew and may instead focus on what is proper to them.

Mark 1:7-8: John's Messianic Preaching

7. And he preached, saying, "After me comes he who is mightier than I, the thong of whose sandals I am not worthy to stoop down and untie. 8. I have baptized you with water; but he will baptize you with the Holy Spirit." (RSV)

In the preaching schema of the early church, the good news began with the appearance of John the Baptist preaching and baptizing at the Jordan river (Acts 1:22; 10:37-38). This is also what Mark means by opening his gospel with the words: "This is how the good news about Jesus Christ, the Son of God, began." (1:1). Luke and Matthew give us a sample of John's preaching about the imminent judgment to come (Lk 3:7-14; Mt 3:7-10), but Mark capsulizes it with the words, "preaching a baptism of repentance for the forgiveness of sins" (Mk 1:4) in order to give prominence to what distinguished John from the prophets before him—he announced the coming after him of the "mightier one." This title without a name sets a tone of mystery and suspense. It also sets the stage for the deeds of power which Jesus, in contrast to John, will perform. But more immediately the reason for the superiority of the coming one is the superior baptism he will give: He will baptize with the Holy Spirit (vs. 8).

Mark can get away with such brevity because his every phrase would evoke for his Christian audience a wealth of explanatory detail which either their memory or an inspired preacher would supply. For us at our distance there are many gaps about which we should like to have more information. For example, does Mark understand Jesus' baptism to be a plunging into the Holy Spirit in metaphorical contrast to John's plunging his disciples into water? After all "to be baptized" is used by Mark in a metaphorical sense in 10:38. Or is John's meaning, "I baptize with water only, but his (water) baptism will confer the Holy Spirit"? We cannot answer this question merely on the basis of this text, and at this point of our inquiry the question even distracts from the central point: the coming one will give the Holy Spirit.

Matthew and Luke both have John's words as: "He will baptize you with the Holy Spirit *and with fire.*" Where did this additional expression come from? The best solution is that it belonged to 'Q,' Matthew's and Luke's common source, which also provided an explanation: "His winnowing fork is in his hand, to clear his threshing floor, and to gather the wheat into his granary; but the chaff he will burn with unquenchable fire" (Lk 3:17; cf. Mt 3:12). This austere threat of judgment fits well the primitive view we encountered in Is 4:4 where the prophet announces the coming judgment in terms of the Lord's *ruah* (breath, wind, "spirit") and *fire.* We saw there, with the help of Is 30:28 and 27:4, 8, that the image is of winnowing in which the wind blows the chaff away to be burned. In trying to prepare a repentant people, John preaches the coming of a powerful judge who will mete out justice without respect of persons. John uses the language and the imagery of Isaiah, the wind and fire of the threshing floor. Whether or not the Baptist used the word "holy" in his preaching (it is omitted in some Greek manuscripts and in some of the Fathers) the idea would not be far from his thought, for the spirit would, like the "holy spirit" of nearby Qumran, be a spirit of purification, and thus holy in that sense. As the early gospel preachers retold the preaching of John, they were also aware of the way in which his preaching about this "holy spirit" was fulfilled beyond expectations in the charismatic ministry of Jesus and in the church. Luke and Matthew retained the more primitive expression of fire with the picture of judgment. Mark does not see the spirit as the spirit of judgment. He is much more interested in directing his audience to Jesus Messiah on whom this Holy Spirit rests.

Mark 1:9-11: The Baptism of Jesus

9. In those days Jesus came from Nazareth of Galilee and was baptized by John in the Jordan. 10. And when he came up out of the water, immediately he saw the heavens opened and the

Spirit descending upon him like a dove: 11. and a voice came
from heaven, "Thou art my beloved Son; with thee I am well
pleased." (RSV)

Jesus' baptism by John is related in all three synoptics, with only
negligible differences as far as pneumatology is concerned. As the gospel
tradition develops there is a growing concern to deal with the embarrassment raised by Jesus' submission to John's baptism of repentance. Thus
while Mark simply narrates the baptism and pictures the Spirit descending upon Jesus as he comes up from the water, Luke places the coming
of the Spirit more clearly after the baptism while Jesus is at prayer, and
Matthew introduces a dialogue between John and Jesus which deals with
the problem more directly—Jesus submits to John's baptism "to fulfill
all righteousness" (Lk 3:21-22; Mt 3:13-17).

For Mark, however, it is precisely the humble surrender of Jesus to
this rite that is so remarkable. We are not really prepared to have the
"mightier one" who will himself baptize with the Holy Spirit appear in
line with the other penitents to be immersed in the waters of the Jordan.
But this is important to Mark's overall theology, for Jesus is the hidden
Messiah, he emerges out of and not down upon the human context of
life. The secret of who he is will be revealed only little by little as the
gospel unfolds. It is perhaps for this reason that Mark says nothing
about the crowds or John perceiving the theophany. Jesus himself witnesses it—as does the Christian reader—and for the moment that is
enough.

All three evangelists agree in describing the descent of the Spirit in
the form of a dove (Luke adds "in bodily form"). What is the meaning
of this phenomenon? In the Jewish sacrificial system doves were used as
the sacrifice of the poor, but there is no other indication of sacrifice in
the text unless it is in the words "beloved son" which might evoke
Abraham's sacrifice of Isaac (Gen 22:2)—but this is much too far
fetched. Closer to the situation is the Canticle of Solomon 2:12, "the
song of the dove is heard in our land," which the Jewish Targum identified as "the voice of the Holy Spirit of salvation." As the dove is the
sign of a new spring in the Canticle, it was herald of the new world after.
The flood (Gen 8:8-12) and its association here with the waters of baptism may indeed suggest the opening of the new age. But how would this
be a suitable image for the Spirit? We recall from Genesis 1:2 that the
Hebrew verb used to describe the spirit of God over the waters was that
of a bird hovering over its nest and inciting its nestlings to fly. In later
rabbinic tradition the bird was expressly said to be a dove: "The spirit of
God was brooding on the face of the waters like a dove which broods

over her young but does not touch them" (Ben Zoma, *Bab. hag.* 15a). Surely, then, the descent of the Holy Spirit as a dove over the waters is meant to suggest that a new creation and a new age is being introduced. For such was the meaning of the Spirit of God hovering over the primeval waters; and the waters of the flood indeed closed the old age and opened the new—and the dove was the herald of the new age begun. So too in Jesus emerging from the waters a new age and a new creation has begun.

But the creation motifs are simply a projection onto a cosmic screen of the drama of salvation history, as the rest of the text now shows. What is the meaning of the "voice from heaven"? In rabbinic literature it was taught that since the days of the last prophets the holy spirit had not spoken directly to men. The best man can do is to hear the "*bath qol*," literally, "the daughter of the voice," or what we would call the echo, of the heavenly voice (cf. Strack-Billerbeck I, 125-128). If the heavens are now open and a voice is heard from heaven, if only by Jesus, it means that he is brought out of the realm of the rabbis and into that of the prophets. The Spirit of God and the word of God are now active anew.

But Jesus is more than a prophet. The heavenly message is a fusion of several Old Testament texts. The most obvious is Is 42:1: "Here is my servant whom I uphold, my chosen one with whom I am pleased, upon whom I have put my spirit." In Is 44:2-3 Jacob is called "my servant, the darling whom I have chosen," and after a mention of water there is a new promise of the outpouring of the Spirit. There is probably also an allusion to the messianic prophecy of Is 11:2, "The spirit of the Lord shall rest upon him," and Is 61:1, "The spirit of the Lord is upon me." This last text adds "because he has anointed me." The title "Messiah" simply means "Anointed One." We recall how the anointing of Saul and David was followed by the spirit coming upon them (1 Sam 10:1, 6, 10; 16:13). In Acts 10:38, a direct allusion to Jesus' baptism, it is said that God anointed Jesus with the Holy Spirit.

But the text has the word *Son* instead of *servant* or *Anointed One*. In the Old Testament Israel was called God's son (Hos 11:1), the meaning being the adoptive relationship begun in the exodus from Egypt and sealed by the covenant. In Matthew especially does the theme of Jesus as the New Israel appear. But the title 'Son' was also associated with the ceremony of enthroning the new king, where the words were chanted: "You are my son; this day have I begotten you" (Ps 2:7). In later times, when Israel looked forward to the Messiah-King, these words were especially applied, though they were always understood to mean adoption-upon-enthronement and not any kind of divine generation.

For Mark, of course, more than adoptive sonship is implied. The sequence of the gospel shows Jesus acting with divine power, so that each of his mighty works, and even some of his other actions such as the call of the disciples, are like theophanies. Consequently, in this scene of Jesus' baptism we have a fusion of many scripture-based teachings about Jesus: At his appearance on the stage of history the New Age has begun. He is prophet, Messiah and Son of God. The Holy Spirit, manifested in the form of a dove, functions in relationship to each of these motifs. He who will baptize with the Holy Spirit is shown to be the one on whom the Spirit rests. The age promised by the prophets has begun.

Does this passage have anything to say about Christian baptism? Though Mark's central interest here is on Jesus, we cannot forget that the tradition recorded here had been alive for decades previously in the church and even the telling of the story was probably shaped by its church use. Consequently it is likely that Jesus' baptism here is understood as a prototype for Christian baptism—where water, the Holy Spirit and divine sonship all play a part.

Mark 1:12-13: The Holy Spirit and the Temptation of Jesus

> 12. The Spirit immediately drove him out into the wilderness.
> 13. And he was in the wilderness forty days, tempted by Satan; and he was with the wild beasts; and the angels ministered to him. (RSV)

After the glorious identification of Jesus through the dove and the heavenly voice, we are now told what this consecration-manifestation means on the plane of human history. It is a plunging into the wilderness, into chaos, into temptation—not an immediate exaltation to glory. Thus the beginning of Jesus' ministry parallels the beginnings of Old Israel which came through the waters of the exodus into the desert for a period of forty years' trial. The mention of forty days in the synoptic story is surely meant to evoke this parallel, and the three temptations detailed by Matthew and Luke correspond to the temptations (and the falls!) of Israel in the desert. But for Mark, the background may even be more primitive. This whole section began with the word "beginning" (1:1). Could this be an evoking of the "beginning" in Gen 1:1? In Genesis there are two accounts of creation—the "wet" cosmogony which describes creation as a process from chaotic waters to the order of the dry land, and the "dry" or "desert" cosmogony which begins with dry land and then describes the fashioning of man out of the dust with the help of water and the inbreathing of God's *ruah*. The latter account goes on to describe the temptation and the fall, and in it the wild beasts have an important role.

Now the similarities and the differences with Mark become apparent. The Spirit *drives* Jesus out into the desert. We may be surprised at Mark's presentation of the Spirit almost as an overpowering force, like those occasions in the Old Testament when certain men were seized by the spirit and driven to various places (1 Kgs 18:12; 2 Kgs 2:16; Ez 3:12, 14f.; 8:3; 11:24; Acts 8:39f.). But the choice of words is less surprising if Mark is intending to carry out a diptych with Genesis. As the Lord drove Adam from the garden into the hard land of struggle (Gen 3:23), so the Spirit drives Jesus into the place where he shares totally the lot of unredeemed and struggling man. The Spirit upon Jesus does not mean exemption from struggle (an important theme in Mark's whole gospel) but confrontation and victory within it.

What do the wild beasts represent? Only Mark is interested in this detail. Some scholars think they simply illustrate the horrors of desert life. Others suggest that Mark has been influenced by the actual life-situation of his community, where Christians, baptized and Spirit-filled, have had to actually confront the wild beasts of the Roman arena. In the light of Mark's whole gospel, this allusion is certainly possible. But there is no hint of conflict with the beasts here. More likely then is the theme of paradise restored. Biblically speaking, the animal kingdom is alien to man only because of the fall of Adam. If God's angels protect the just man of Ps 91:11-13 so that the wild animals cannot harm him (as Job 5:22-23 also says), what is to be said of him with whom the new creation begins? He is the new Adam-Messiah who reverses the work of the first Adam. By resisting temptation he restores paradise and establishes peace with the wild beasts as Isaiah promised the Messiah would (Is 11:6-9; cf. 43:19-20).

The note that "the angels ministered to him" is taken by some to mean that the angels fed Jesus in the desert. But Mark says nothing about Jesus fasting, and the more likely meaning is that in his war with Satan Jesus as King-Messiah is attended by angels (cf. Mt 26:53). The desert-folk at Qumran believed they were leagued with the angels for a final war with Satan and his minions.

Let us now sum up Mark's pneumatology as it appears in this grandiose prologue to the public ministry of Jesus. The three items—John's preaching, the baptism of Jesus and the temptation—are linked together by the word *Spirit* which occurs in each unit (vss. 8, 10, 12). The promised baptizer with the Spirit is shown to himself possess the fulness of the Spirit as foretold in prophecy. A new age, indeed a new creation has begun, reversing the falls of Adam and Israel and their consequences. The Spirit does not spare Jesus from conflict but thrusts him into the heart of it. The final battle with Satan has begun on earth—but so has the peace of God.

Jesus' Charismatic Activity

We may now read Mark's gospel to discover how the prelude we have studied appears in Jesus' public ministry. Mark's pneumatology from here on does not appear so much in major texts as it does in the overall fabric of the entire gospel. Immediately beginning to proclaim the good news (1:14-15), Jesus calls his first disciples (1:16-20). There is no psychological preparation for this call in Mark's account as there is in Luke's (Lk 4:16-5:11). Jesus simply "passes by" and calls, and this call suffices for them to leave boat, net and father and follow him. From that moment onward, Jesus is surrounded by a community of intimates who foreshadow the church and tell us that all we see Jesus doing also concerns his disciples.

Then Jesus enters the synagogue on a Sabbath and begins to teach (1:21). The people are spellbound "because he taught with authority, not like the scribes" (1:22). What this teaching with authority means Mark immediately tells us, for Jesus at once delivers a demoniac, leading the people to say: "What is this? A new teaching! With authority he commands even unclean spirits, and they obey him" (1:27). Then Jesus cures Peter's mother-in-law (1:29-31).

These first two wonders that Jesus works stand at the beginning of the ministry as types of the two major charismatic activities which will be his—exorcism and healing. That this is so is confirmed by Mark's summary statement immediately attached: "They brought to him all who were ill, and those possessed by demons. . . . Those whom he cured were many, and so were the demons he expelled" (1:32-34). Let us look at these two types of wonders in Mark.

Exorcisms and the Holy Spirit

For Mark more than for any of the other evangelists, Jesus is the man anointed by the Spirit to challenge Satan. The first way in which this challenge is met in the ministry is through the exorcisms. Mark relates four specific cases: the demoniac in the synagogue (1:22-28), the "legion" in the possessed man of Gerasa (5:1-20), the Canaanite woman's daughter (7:24-30), and the "epileptic" boy (9:14-29). In addition he has the general statement: "Unclean spirits would catch sight of him, fling themselves down at his feet, and shout, 'You are the Son of God!' " (3:11).

In the light of the Old Testament literature we examined, the exorcisms appear as a surprise, for, aside from David using the harp to chase the evil Spirit from Saul, we did not note any account of deliverance from demonic possession or obsession. Yet in later Judaism the just man's struggle is occasionally described as a bout with a spiritual adversary. The prologue to Job speaks of "Satan," the Adversary, who precipitates calamities to test Job (Job 1:6-12; 2:1-7) and Tobit 6:7-18; 8:1-18 tells of the expulsion of a demon whom the angel Raphael pursued into Upper Egypt where he "bound him hand and foot" (Tob 8:3). Neither of these is properly possession, but the idea of the binding of Satan is an important detail of the background for the New Testament. The *War Rule* of the Qumran Community and *The Testament of the Twelve Patriarchs* speak in various places of a final victory over Satan and in one place in the *Testament of Levi* we read, concerning the Messiah: "And he shall give to the saints to eat of the tree of life, and the spirit of holiness shall be on them. And Beliar shall be bound by him, and he shall give power to his children to tread on evil spirits." (18:11-12). One of the problems with the *Testaments* is the uncertainty as to how much Christian influence there is in the texts as they have come down to us, but the background from the other literature of the period confirms the widespread belief that the coming of the Messiah would be an encounter with Satan and a victory over his power.

Mark's view of what the exorcisms mean is given in 3:19b-30:

Then he went home; 20. and the crowd came together again, so that they could not even eat. 21. And when his friends heard it, they went out to seize him, for they said, "He is beside himself." 22. And the scribes who came down from Jerusalem said, "He is possessed by Beelzebul, and by the prince of demons he casts out the demons." 23. And he called them to him, and said to them in parables, "How can Satan cast out Satan? 24. If a kingdom is divided against itself, that kingdom cannot stand. 25. And if a house is divided against itself, that house will not be able to stand. 26. And if Satan has risen up against himself and is divided, he cannot stand, but is coming to an end. 27. But no one can enter a strong man's house and plunder his goods, unless he first binds the strong man; then indeed he may plunder his house. 28. Truly, I say to you, all sins will be forgiven the sons of men, and whatever blasphemies they utter; 29. but whoever blasphemes against the Holy Spirit never has forgiveness, but is guilty of an eternal sin"— 30. for they had said, "He has an unclean spirit." (RSV)

This passage follows Mark's summary statement in 3:10-12 about Jesus' healing and exorcising activity and the call and commission of the twelve "to be with him, and to be sent out to preach and have authority to cast out demons" (3:15). Ending the list of the twelve with "Judas Iscariot, who betrayed him" (3:19), Mark has sounded once again the somber note first struck in 3:6 foreshadowing Jesus' death which results from the mounting opposition of certain influential groups in contrast to the approval of the crowds. This opposition is now described in terms of what actually is at work behind the exorcisms, which are interpreted negatively by both "his own people" and by the scribes. His own townsfolk think that he is "beside himself." In the context of the times this diagnosis of insanity probably implied some kind of demonic possession. But the actual identification is left to the scribes who go further and accuse Jesus of exorcising by the power of the prince of demons, Beelzebul. This provides the occasion not only for Jesus' retort that if such were the case, Satan's kingdom would be in a state of civil war and on the verge of imminent collapse. The collapse of Satan's kingdom has indeed begun, but only because its "strong man" Satan has been bound by the "Stronger One" announced by the Baptist (Mk 1:7). (For the biblical background of this title see Is 49:25; 53:12; Rev 6:15; 19:18; 10:1; 18:8, 21; 1 Cor 10:22.) Some scholars think that the binding of Satan was understood to have taken place in the temptation and the exorcisms are therefore the "plundering," but this subtlety is difficult to justify from the text. In any case Mark surely means that the exorcisms, done by the power of the Holy Spirit (vs. 29), are a sign that God has begun his victorious reign. Matthew and Luke are therefore simply expanding on Mark when they add the saying: "If it is by the Spirit of God (Mt; "finger of God," Lk) that I cast out demons, then the kingdom of God has come upon you" (Mt 12:28; Lk 8:20). In passing, let us note how surprising it is to find that the term "Spirit of God" here comes from Matthew and "finger of God" from Luke, for the latter would hardly have passed up an opportunity to mention the Spirit. Of course, both images are used in the Old Testament for the mighty power of God (cf. Ez 3:14; Ex 8:15; Ps 8:4). Luke's phrase contains a direct allusion to Ex 8:15, where, according to the rabbinical interpretation (*Exodus Rabba*, 10), Moses is contrasted with the Egyptian magicians and the finger of God with the power of demons.

Mark then adds the saying of Jesus about the sin against the Holy Spirit. It is probably a detached saying which each of the evangelists has put in his own particular context. It is quite broad in Mark and is related directly to the accusation against Jesus. To call the Spirit of Jesus unclean is to sin against the Holy Spirit. And this response could only come from a sin against the light, calling evil what is good, ugly what is beautiful, falsehood what is truth. Since this saying of Jesus must be balanced against his constant call and offer of repentance, it is understandable how Christian tradition interpreted the "sin against the Holy Spirit" to be that of final impenitence.

We should also note that Jesus does not claim to be the only exorcist of his day. In fact, he uses the practice of exorcism by others as part of his argumentation in Matthew and Luke (Mt 12:27; Lk 8:19). Jesus' uniqueness must lie elsewhere, in the significance he sees in these events as a sign of the inbreaking of God's kingdom and of his own unique role therein. Thus Jesus casts out demons by no magic ritual but by immediate personal command (1:25; 5:8; 9:25) or simply by the finger or Spirit of God (Mt 12:28; Lk 8:20). The disciples on the other hand cast them out only in Jesus' name (Mk 9:38; cf. Acts 16:18). The fact that no account of an exorcism by a disciple is attributed to an invocation of the Holy Spirit or to the "finger of God" but only to Jesus' name shows how the person and the name of Jesus become in the gospel the center of all charismatic activity. The Spirit (or the "finger of God") is replaced by the name of Jesus because in no other name is the Spirit or the power of God to be invoked (cf. Acts 4:12).

But Jesus encounters the demon not only in the exorcisms proper but in other ways as well, as Mark's terminology shows. Thus the attempts of his enemies to trip him up are throughout called "temptations" (8:11; 10:2; 12:15). And even his struggle with the ignorance and resistance of his own disciples is presented as a struggle with Satan (8:33). The debates with Jesus' enemies and even with his disciples are modeled on the exorcism stories to show that throughout his ministry the same powers are at work.

There is one difference, however. The spirits recognize Jesus at once for who he is, the Son of God (1:24; 5:7). This confession is not reached by men until the moment of Jesus' death (15:39). We shall return to the significance of this difference later. For the moment let it suffice to note that the supernatural world confesses Jesus as the stronger one and the Son of God from the very beginning, thus confirming the identity shown in the baptism: Jesus is God's Son on whom the Spirit rests.

Healings

Besides those healings connected with the exorcisms, there are others in which the demonic does not play an express role: Peter's mother-in-law (1:29-31), a leper (1:40-45), the paralytic (2:1-11), the daughter of Jairus and the woman with the flow of blood (5:21-43), the deaf-mute (7:31-37), the blind man at Bethsaida (8:22-26), the blind Bartimaeus (10:46-52). For Mark, these healings not only proclaim that the time of salvation promised by the prophets has arrived (cf. Is 35:4-6); they also reveal the beginnings of a tendency which will become predominant in John, namely, to see these mighty works as symbols of the post-resurrectional life offered to those who turn to the Lord. The healing of the paralytic is a manifestation of Jesus' power to forgive sins. The raising of the daughter of Jairus, like the raising up of the seemingly dead epileptic boy, is told in terms that evoke resurrection. Healed by Jesus, Peter's mother-in-law can now serve him and the community of his disciples. The blind Bartimaeus, once cured by Jesus, now follows him as a disciple. And the curious cure of the blind man in stages (8:22-26) is placed by Mark between Jesus' distress at his own disciples' blindness (8:14-21) and Peter's lucid confession of Jesus as Messiah (8:27-30), thus suggesting that what Jesus did gradually in a physical way for the blind man he does in a spiritual way for his disciples. In the cures, of course, it is the person of Jesus which is central rather than the Spirit. However implicit the Spirit may be in the light of the baptism-temptation prologue, it is Jesus who heals either by his touch alone (1:31; 5:28) sometimes accompanied by an anointing (8:23, 25), or by his word alone (2:11; 3:5; 10:52) or, by word and touch together (1:41; 5:41; 7:33).

When we consider the large amount of material in Mark devoted to exorcisms and healing, in relationship to the relatively small amount of teaching material, we can only conclude that for Mark the healings and the exorcisms are not simply confirmations of Jesus' teaching authority. They are rather the very ministry of Jesus itself. Mark 6:1-6 even shows that Jesus' normal ministry involved charismatic deeds and healing as well as teaching and that he was amazed when the disbelief of the townsfolk limited his action to mere teaching.

Beyond the Signs: Who Jesus Really Is

Parallel to Mark's concern to present Jesus as a highly charismatic person, there is also a concern to keep the pneumatic element quiet (1:44; 3:11, 12). This puzzling attitude of Jesus is part of the larger theme of the secret of Jesus' identity which, though known from the first to the world of the spirits, is revealed only progressively to the disciples and to the world. Jesus is not just a charismatic wonderworker like others of his day. He is more than an Elijah or an Elisha come back. He is the Messiah and the Son of God. And while the Messiah-Son of God is pneumatic, not every pneumatic is the Messiah-Son of God.

It is in 8:27-31 that the path of Jesus parts from the pneumatics of his day and even from the keenest spiritual insight to which the disciples themselves have arrived. Having been with Jesus from the first, the disciples have witnessed his wonders. They probably shared the crowds' identification of Jesus as a prophet (8:28). But Peter goes on and identifies Jesus as the Messiah (8:29). That this is a true identification appears from the fact that Jesus imposes silence upon his disciples about this matter as he did upon the spirits confessing him to be God's Son. But that even the role of Messiah, at least as understood by Peter on the basis of signs, was still not the total mystery of Jesus can be seen from 8:31, the turning point of Mark's gospel: "He began to teach them that the Son of Man had to suffer much. . ." The glorious, pneumatic element does not disappear but it is now accompanied by the shadow of the cross, and Mark's putting these two elements together like a constant see-saw is surely intentional. The saying about the coming of the kingdom in glory and the story of the transfiguration (9:1-8) is followed, four verses later, with another saying about the suffering (9:12). Then there is the marvelous cure of the epileptic boy (9:14-29), followed immediately with the teaching about the cross (9:30-32). Then comes a long series of the teachings of Jesus, particularly on the conditions of discipleship, culminating in the promise that those who have followed Jesus will reap a hundredfold (10:29-31). This, in its turn, is followed by the third prediction of the passion (10:32-34). As the first prediction of the passion (8:31-33) was followed by the assurance that the same lot is in store for the disciple (8:34-38), so the third prediction is followed by the story of the ambition of James and John who express their desire for glory, only to hear Jesus ask them whether they can share his passion (10:35-40). The language of this last text is significant, for Jesus calls his sufferings a *baptism*. Though the meaning here is metaphorical, Mark surely intends a flash backwards to Jesus' baptism as well as forward to his death on the cross. For now the true meaning of the baptism is beginning to emerge: Jesus is the suffering Servant whose greatest act is no miracle at all—it is the service of the giving of his life. This appears from the instruction on true greatness which immediately follows the prediction of his "baptism" of suffering: "The Son of Man has not come to be served but to serve and to give his life as a ransom for many" (10:45). There is no mention of the Spirit here, perhaps because Mark knows that the moment of the Spirit belongs *after* the descent into the waters and *after* the death on the cross. But at this point the crisis which the disciple, even charismatically endowed (3:13-19), must face is whether he will stop short at the pneumatic signs and wonders or whether he will follow the charismatic Jesus to the cross. That this is exactly Mark's point appears in the very next passage, the cure of the blind Bartimaeus (10:46-52). Note that Bartimaeus addresses Jesus as Messiah, Son of David—a correct Christian confession, even if incomplete as Peter's was (8:29). After the cure, Bartimaeus follows Jesus up the road (vs. 52). Where is Jesus going? To Jerusalem!

And what does Jerusalem mean? The Christian reader already knows it is the cross. But even the ministry of those last days in Jerusalem is different. There is a glorious approach, yes (11:1-11) but beyond that no miracle or exorcism. Jesus can only teach—probably for the same reason that he could do little more than teach at Nazareth—the city did not have the faith to be healed or delivered by the power available in Jesus. It would have to come about another way. Brought before the Jewish court and questioned about his identity, Jesus answered that he was Messiah and Son of God (14:61-62), adding that the Son of Man would be seen in glory (vs. 62). Strangely, however, Mark's gospel ends without any resurrection appearance of Jesus. (The longer ending in our present text 16:9-20, though dating from the first century and accepted as canonical and inspired, is generally held to be from a hand other than Mark's because of its vocabulary and style and also because it only summarizes the traditions found in the other gospels.) The women see only the young man dressed in a white robe who explains why the tomb is empty—Jesus is risen. But him they do not see. If we discount the possibility that a Markan tradition of resurrection appearances was simply lost, and accept at the same time that Mark believed as much as the other evangelists in the resurrection of the Lord (promised, after all, in Mk 8:31; 9:31; 10:34), then we must conclude that Mark is more interested theologically in the passion and death of Jesus than he is in the resurrection. A closer look at Mark's overall plan confirms this surprising discovery. Jesus' baptism and transfiguration are clearly meant to be parallel. But so are the baptism and the passion, as we have seen in Mk

10:38. And all three are connected by the theme of Jesus' identity, which runs throughout the gospel. In the baptism, the Father attests to Jesus' identity but not in the presence of the disciples, the demons or the crowds. And the dove is the sign of the presence of the Spirit. It is a glorious theophany, even if only Jesus is the witness. The exorcisms are theophanies in their own way; they are signs evoking from the spirit-world the confession that Jesus is the Son of God. But for the world of men the exorcisms, the healings and the teaching evoke the confession from the crowds that Jesus is a prophet and from the disciples that he is the Messiah (8:27-29). These signs are, on the plane of historical phenomena, what the dove was in the baptismal vision—the epiphany of the divine spirit upon Jesus. But they evoke at most the confession only of Jesus' messiahship. There is much more to learn. If Jesus is the Messiah, he will be a suffering Messiah (8:31-33). However "scandalous" such a turn may seem, Jesus is nevertheless God's Son—and this further revelation, already known to Jesus and the spirits, is made at the Transfiguration when the disciples are allowed to hear the Father's voice identifying Jesus as his unique Son (9:2-8). Here the overshadowing cloud performs the same function as the dove in the baptism—it is a visionary affirmation of the divine presence (Ex 40:34-38), and implicitly perhaps of the spirit.

But the inadequacy even of this theophany to convey a real understanding to the disciples is seen by the fact that Jesus' immediate allusion to his own death is incomprehensible (9:9, 10); he must repeat his prediction of the passion twice (9:31-32; 10:32-34), each prediction being followed by an obtuse dispute about greatness in the kingdom (9:33-37; 10:35-45). Where, then, and when, does the effective revelation of Jesus' divine sonship to men take place? Only at the moment of Jesus' death on the cross. What wins from the Roman centurion the confession, "Truly this was the Son of God" is the *way in which Jesus died* (15:39). What was known only to the Father and to the spirit-world, what was revealed ineffectually to the disciples at the transfiguration and to the Jewish authorities at the trial, is now successfully communicated to the gentiles and especially to Mark's Roman church in the person of the centurion. Jesus is the Son of God. What reveals this is the way Jesus died. To move from the Father's confession at the beginning of the gospel to the gentile's confession at the end, the death of Jesus is a necessary step for men, though it was obvious to the spirits in the exorcisms. Thus for Mark, men, even Jesus' disciples, do not understand the language of the miracles (cf. Mk 8:17-21). The taunting Jews are even more "put off" by the absence of signs on the cross (15:29-32). But the centurion who makes the full Christian confession, has understood the language of Jesus' death. In the baptism, only the Father knows who Jesus is; now the Roman world does.

And here we have the ultimate manifesto of Mark's pneumatology. What distinguishes the Son of God from other pneumatics is that he, unlike them, has come to serve to the extent of giving his life for the ransom of the many (10:45). Martyrdom, not miracles, is the ultimate testing of the Spirit.

Discipleship for Mark is, then, following Jesus beyond his signs and epiphanies to the cross (8:31-38), where alone the divine sonship is revealed. The Holy Spirit is guaranteed to the disciple as much as to the Master, but his function in discipleship is shown in the ability to witness fearlessly in the face of martyrdom: "When they bring you to trial and deliver you up (the same word used by Jesus for his passion, 9:31; 10:32), do not be anxious beforehand what you are to say; but say whatever is given you in that hour, for it is not you who speak, but the Holy Spirit" (13:11). Mark is strangely silent about the work of the Spirit in the charismatic activity of the disciples, though surely he is aware of it. He is much more interested in the power of the Spirit enabling the Christian to witness unto death. And if we wish to know why we have not far to look.

Mark wrote his gospel for the Roman church being persecuted, probably under Nero. Christians right and left were called to testify and to die for their faith. For a long time the Markan church had known the presence of the Spirit in praise, deliverance, healings and miracles. But now something more than these "success stories" was being asked of them. Could they prove by their *death* what they experienced in their life? We may surmise that some could not, and among their number were probably some great self-styled charismatics. The ultimate test of the Spirit, as of discipleship, was the wisdom of knowing how to die. The Spirit was not an escape from physical death, and the disciple should not expect deliverance in the hour of trial any more than Jesus did—but only the power to witness faithfully. In all of this, Jesus' own death was the great model. The resurrection may indeed have followed his death, and the inspired editor of the non-Markan conclusion (16:9-20) may indeed have been correct in adding how signs like new tongues and miraculous deliverance would accompany the gentile mission. But for Mark, the disciple of Jesus, who, like his master, is anointed by the Spirit from his baptism, will win the faith of the very Roman world that is his executioner, not by signs and wonders, even less by the last-minute intervention of a heavenly deliverer, but rather by the way he dies.

21
The Evangelist of the
Holy Spirit: Luke

Luke's two-volume work, his gospel and the Acts of the Apostles, is the longest attributed to any one author in the New Testament, including Paul. And surely if we had to single out any one evangelist as the "Theologian of the Holy Spirit," it would be Luke. While the word "spirit" occurs four times in Mark and five times in Matthew, the expression "Holy Spirit" occurs thirteen times in Luke's gospel and forty-one times in Acts. Because Luke intended the greatest unity between his two works, we are certainly justified in using one to illuminate the other.

There is every reason to believe that Luke knew of Mark's gospel and had some form of it before him as he wrote. But why did Luke consider Mark's work inadequate? Mainly because it was incomplete and tended to present Jesus from a Romanized Jewish point of view, which was not exactly that of the Hellenistic Christians. Aside from certain barbarisms of style which Luke sought to correct, there were many other things missing from Mark but available to Luke, traditions which had special appeal to him and the largely gentile community to which he belonged. Mark's picture of Jesus needed to be completed with these traditions. But more than that, Luke found the need to write an "orderly account" (Lk 1:3). This does not necessarily mean that his order is chronologically better than Mark's. It means rather that he has tried to put together all his material in such a way that it will have meaning for his gentile readers. Thus he uses time and place often for their catechetical significance. During his ministry only Jesus and not the disciples enjoy the Spirit—in order to highlight the period of the Church in Acts as the period of the Spirit. Jesus never departs from Jewish territory—in order to leave the gentile mission completely to the disciples after his resurrection. Thus Luke focuses on what is characteristic and memorable about a given time or place. If he is a historian, it is more after the fashion of Arnold Toynbee who tries to discern and portray a universal impression of a period using a few highly significant, sometimes symbolic, data. At

the same time Luke is capable of dramatizing certain key events with
the kind of "double exposure" technique by which Old Testament texts
and themes interpret the New Testament events. We have already seen
this at work in Mark's account of Jesus' baptism and transfiguration.
Luke carries it further.

Exorcisms

But let us begin by noting that in the area of pneumatology Luke
takes over all of Mark. If among the exorcisms he omits the story of the
Canaanite woman's daughter (Mk 7:24-30), it is because he wants to
keep a clear picture of Jesus' limitation of himself to Palestine during
his public ministry. Otherwise we see him using the exorcism material,
frequently substituting "demon" for "unclean spirit" either for variety
in style or perhaps because he wishes to reserve "spirit" as much as possible for its positive use as the Holy Spirit (4:33, 35; 8:27, 30, 33; 9:42).
In fact, the Beelzebul controversy in Luke is introduced immediately
after a teaching of Jesus on the Holy Spirit (11:13). Luke, unlike Mark,
describes the occasion for the controversy as the moment when Jesus
was exorcising a "demon that was dumb" (11:14). And the ensuing
controversy which we already discussed in Mark, provides Luke with the
occasion for adding the teaching about the return of the evil spirit
(11:24-26)—a warning to Christians who have received the Holy Spirit
(11:13) of the dangers of falling away (cf. Heb 6:4-6; 10:26-31).

In 10:17-20, an account found only in Luke, relating the return of
the seventy-two disciples from their mission, Jesus says that he saw
Satan falling like lightning from heaven. Earlier in 9:1 Jesus had given
to the twelve the commission to exorcise, to heal, and to announce the
kingdom. In commissioning the seventy-two others there is mention only
of healing and of announcing the kingdom (10:9). Nevertheless on their
return the disciples exclaim: "Even the demons are subject to us in your
name!" (10:17). In vs. 19 Jesus says he has given them a truly charismatic power "to tread on snakes and scorpions and all the forces of the
enemy, and nothing shall even injure you." The text sounds very much
like the Markan conclusion, Mk 16:17-18, where the setting is after the
resurrection. In the Acts, preaching and the exercise of the powers of
healing and exorcism are an effect of the coming of the Spirit. Here,
they are the effect of Jesus giving them *authority* (10:19). What there
comes from the Spirit of Jesus comes here from his word. That this
scene is only an "experiment in mission" is clear from the fact that
Jesus does not send his disciples out again. Moreover, the Holy Spirit is

associated expressly with the rejoicing of Jesus (10:21) and not with that of the disciples (10:17). While, therefore, charismatic authority may come directly from Jesus without mention of the Spirit, the fullness of the power (*dynamis*) will come upon them at Pentecost (Acts 1:8).

Finally, in vs. 20, there is a reminder to these charismatically endowed disciples that their own salvation is something more important to glory in than the supernatural powers given to them. The text thus lays a distant foundation for the later distinction between saving grace and the grace of the charisms.

Healings

But it is particularly in the healing narratives that Luke's interest is revealed. He uses all the healing narratives of Mark, with the exception of the deaf-mute (Mk 7:31-37) and the blind man of Bethsaida (Mk 8:22-26), which belong to Luke's "great omission" from Mark. Luke relates instead the casting out of a "dumb demon" in 11:14, and the cure of the blind man near Jericho (18:35-43) which along with such summary statements as 7:21, suffice to illustrate Jesus' power to restore sight (18:35-43). Luke amply compensates for these omissions. In the programmatic description of Jesus' ministry (4:16-30) which we shall examine later, Jesus implies that he is a physician (4:23). And Luke adds at least three cures not elsewhere in the gospel tradition: those of a woman with a "spirit of infirmity" (13:10-17), of a man with dropsy (14:1-6), and of the ten lepers (17:11-19). The first two of these, done on a Sabbath, act as an irritant to the Pharisees, who consider healing a "work," and they are for Jesus an occasion to illustrate the true meaning of his cures. If the Sabbath was the day God had given Israel as a release from the bondage of labor, far from being the wrong day, it was the most appropriate day to release the sick from the bondage of their infirmities. Healing, for Luke, is essentially liberation (4:18).

The cure of the ten lepers provides a further important insight into Luke's theology. All ten are cured as, in obedience to Jesus' command and the law, they journey to show themselves to the priests, as the law prescribed. But one of them, a Samaritan, delays his going to the authorities and "turned back, praising God with a loud voice; and he fell on his face at Jesus' feet, giving him thanks" (17:15-16). Jesus appears disappointed that the other nine did not do the same, and he says to the Samaritan: "Your faith has made you well" (17:19). It is characteristic of Luke's healing stories that the healed person responds by glorifying God or joyously proclaiming what the Lord has done for him (5:25;

8:39; 13:13; 18:43 and here). That this is more than a liturgical refrain common in Luke appears from the crucial significance of this response in our story for the Samaritan's healing. He, like the nine, was physically cured, but his cure was not complete—or shall we say, it was not Christian—until he burst out in thanks. And this thanksgiving in the text is called *faith*. Faith, for Luke, then, is essentially the act of gratitude by which the believer, receiving the healing power of God, praises and thanks him for it. It is grateful faith that gives total healing, that is, salvation. Such an attitude is more fundamental even than the legalistic fulfilling of the law. The Samaritan thus forecasts the enthusiastic joy of those gentile Christians who have come to understand that in the order of priorities, praise and thanksgiving precede even obedience. It is true that the cure began as an act of obedience to Jesus' word. But the Samaritan was praised and in Jesus' eyes healed for interrupting his obedience even to Jesus' word in order to give him thanks and praise.

Luke not only adds these stories to the healing traditions of Mark. He also heightens the aspect of healing in the common tradition as he passes it on. In the description of the sick healed at evening (Mk 1:32-34), Luke adds the very personalistic detail that "Jesus laid his hands on every one of them and healed them" (4:40). In the summary which follows the healing of the leper, Mark relates how the good news spread all over the country, but Luke adds that it resulted in great multitudes gathering "to hear and to be healed of their infirmities" (5:15). In the passage which immediately follows, Mark describes the crowds jamming Peter's house and Jesus preaching the word to them (Mk 2:2), but Luke notes that Jesus was teaching in the presence of the Pharisees and teachers of the law, and adds: "the power of the Lord was with him to heal" (Lk 5:17). Luke highlights the contrast of Jesus' teaching with that of the Pharisees and Scribes in terms of healing. As a matter of fact, what needs to be explained in the dialogue is not a text but Jesus' unusual pronouncement of forgiveness. And the proof of the validity of the forgiveness is the fact that the paralytic gets up and walks.

Likewise, Luke's way of describing the crowds who surround Jesus before the sermon on the plain stresses Jesus' healing power: "and he came down with them and stood on a level place, with a great crowd of his disciples and a great multitude of people from all Judea and Jerusalem and the seacoast of Tyre and Sidon, who came to hear him and to be healed of their diseases; and all who were troubled with unclean spirits were cured. And all the crowd sought to touch him, for power came forth from him and healed them all" (Lk 6:17-19). The "all" of course may be lyrical but the three-fold mention of healing shows even more clearly than Mark 3:7-12 the central importance Luke gives to this aspect of the ministry of Jesus. Luke, along with Matthew, adds that the day of the multiplication of loaves was not only one of preaching but one of healing (Lk 9:11; Mt 14:14; Mk 6:34). Finally, in 7:18-23, the story of the Baptist's committee sent to investigate Jesus, not only do we have Jesus' reply that they should go and tell John of the healings they have witnessed, but we are also given the Lukan introduction: "At that hour he was curing many of their diseases, afflictions and evil spirits; he also restored sight to many who were blind" (7:21).

The Holy Spirit and the Prayer of Jesus

Most significant about Luke's presentation of the Holy Spirit during the ministry is its close relation to the prayer of Jesus. This relationship had been heralded from the very beginning when the descent of the Holy Spirit occurred "while Jesus was praying" (Lk 4:21). But the relationship appears again when Luke introduces Jesus' prayer of praise to the Father (also related in Mt 11:25-27) with the words: "At that moment Jesus rejoiced in the Holy Spirit and said: 'I praise you, O Father, Lord of heaven and earth. . .' " (Lk 10:21). For Luke the gospel is essentially a message of joy (1:14, 28, 41, 44, 47; 2:10, 13-14; 19:6, 37-40; Acts 3:8-9; 8:39), and nowhere does this joy appear more Spirit-inspired than in praise (1:41, 46, 67; Acts 2:4, 11, 13-17). In all of these passages Luke joins the great *berakah* tradition of the Old Testament and of Judaism. He is unique in that he considers praise to be Spirit-inspired. Though this may have been implicit in the Old Testament descriptions of prophetic rapture, or in Joel 3:1, nowhere is praise explicitly attributed to the effect of the Spirit of God coming upon anyone. It is true that the psalmist expects to be able to praise the Lord in a new way after he has received the clean heart and a renewal of God's "holy spirit" (Ps 51:12-17), but praise is not there linked specifically to an inspired gift. In short, Luke shows here a dependence on the Pauline tradition of charismatic praise (1 Cor 12-14; Col 3:16; Eph 5:19). If in the Gospel this praise does not appear in tongues, it is probably because Luke, with his sense of historical epochs, sees tongues as the sign of the Church's mission to the gentiles after Pentecost (as we shall see later). Nevertheless, he does have an act of pre-rational praise in the leaping of John the Baptist (Lk 1:44)—mentioned immediately after his mother's being filled with the Holy Spirit—and evoking David's joyful dancing before the Ark (2 Sam 6:14-16).

But Luke wants to make it clear that if the Church knows how to pray, she has learned it from Jesus. A comparison of Luke's section on prayer (11:1-13) with Matthew's is instructive in this regard. Matthew simply includes the teaching on prayer as part of the sermon on the Mount (6:5-15). In Luke, however, the teaching on prayer is introduced by the note that Jesus was praying and when he had finished one of his disciples asked, "Lord, teach us to pray. . ." (11:1). The answer to this request is not only the Lord's prayer but, at the level of Luke's redaction at least, also the parable of the friend at midnight (11:5-8) and the exhortation about petitioning prayer, as follows:

> 9. "And I tell you, ask, and it will be given you; seek, and you will find; knock, and it will be opened to you. 10. For everyone who asks, receives, and he who seeks finds, and to him who knocks it will be opened. 11. What father among you, if his son asks for a fish, will instead of a fish give him a serpent; 12. or if he asks for an egg, will give him a scorpion? 13. If you, then, who are evil, know how to give good gifts to your children, how much more will the heavenly Father give the Holy Spirit to those who ask him!" (RSV)

All the commentators on this text note how strikingly the last line of this passage differs from Matthew who has "good things" where Luke has "the Holy Spirit." And they point out that for Luke the Holy Spirit is the sum of all good things and the only really necessary object to be prayed for. Doubtless there is a wealth of truth and beauty in this observation which comes from the "horizontal" comparison of the text with Matthew. Less frequently is attention paid to the vertical position this text plays in the immediate context of Luke's gospel and his overall theology. Let us note, first, that the passage itself, which in Matthew is separated by other material and placed at great distance from the Lord's prayer and therefore not intended to be a commentary on it, is brought by Luke into the discourse on prayer as the conclusion of Jesus' answer to the disciples' request that he teach them how to pray. It is therefore much more closely related to the Lord's prayer than in Matthew. Secondly, while the whole discourse concerns how the disciples should pray, we should not forget that the disciples' request had been occasioned by witnessing Jesus pray. Now it is already clear from the Baptism (to the Christian reader at least) that Jesus is not alone in his prayer but that the Spirit rests upon him in all that he does, above all in prayer. Consequently, it is not sufficient for Luke to have Jesus supply the words his disciples are to use without at the same time suggesting the essential role the Spirit is to play if their prayer is to be a real participation in Jesus' prayer. In fact, the most likely reason why Luke substitutes "the Holy Spirit" for "good things" is that he uses the saying not as a teaching about prayer requests in general but as the final response to the disciples' request to learn how to pray. It is as if Jesus were saying: Here are the words you are to use, but you must receive the Holy Spirit if you are to know what they mean—and the Holy Spirit will certainly be given if you ask the Father in prayer. Luke here then would be intending to reflect the Pauline tradition that the Holy Spirit enables the Christian to pray (Rom 8:26-27) and to cry out, "Abba! Father!" (Gal 4:6; Rom 8:15). In Paul, too, sonship entitles the Christian to the gift of the Spirit. "Because you are sons, God has sent the Spirit of his Son into our hearts. . ." (Gal 4:6). And here in Luke the gift of the Spirit supposes and responds to the relation of sonship.

It seems, however, that the gift of the Spirit here is not so much the initial gift as it is the ongoing gift for Christian living. We know that the eschatological meaning of the Spirit as the sign of the end-time gives way in Luke to its meaning for the period of the Church which may be of some duration. In keeping with this view we find Luke speaking of taking up one's cross *daily* (Lk 9:23) and, here in the Lord's prayer, "Give us *each day* our daily bread" (11:3). The parable of the friend at midnight, who comes, incidentally, to request bread, encourages perseverance in prayer when the answer is delayed. Did Luke intend the connection of this story with the preceding request for bread in the Lord's prayer? We cannot be sure; we are even less certain that he wrote, in vs. 11, "What father among you, if his son asks for *bread, will give him a stone . . .?"* The words appear in Matthew and in some major Greek manuscripts of Luke, but they are missing from other important manuscripts, and so textual critics generally conclude that they were not in Luke originally but were introduced by later scribes to make the text conform to Matthew. Hence they are omitted in the RSV and NAB. If they were in Luke's original, then the three teachings of Jesus on prayer would be linked by the common word *bread.* However, even if we cannot be certain of that link, we can see the common thread of ongoing, persevering, daily prayer. The prayer for the Holy Spirit is no different. The context assumes that the petitioner is already God's child. What is requested, then, is a new outpouring of the Spirit, the daily Spirit corresponding to the daily bread. Luke knew from the tradition about the Lord's prayer that there was no explicit mention of the Holy Spirit. As Jesus taught it, the prayer was for the coming of the kingdom. But Luke also knows of the Pentecost tradition in which the Holy Spirit was poured out upon the community assembled in prayer not only initially

(Acts 1:14; 2:1-4) but also in the course of the developing Church (4:31). He thus brings this new dimension of the Church's post-pentecostal prayer as close as possible to the Lord's Prayer without intruding upon it. By Luke's time, and for his community, the prayer of petition for the coming of the kingdom was understood in the daily living of the Church to be in a special way a prayer for the outpouring of the Holy Spirit.

There is an interesting variant reading of Luke's text of the Lord's Prayer which indicates that Luke's tendency to reinterpret the kingdom in terms of the Holy Spirit did not go unnoticed. Instead of "thy kingdom come," two late manuscripts have "thy Holy Spirit come upon us and cleanse us." Gregory of Nyssa in the fourth century, in one of his homilies on the Lord's Prayer, says expressly that instead of the petition for the coming of the kingdom Luke has "thy Holy Spirit come upon us and cleanse us." And Maximus of Turin in the fifth century says that what Matthew calls kingdom another evangelist has called "Holy Spirit," and he quotes the same reading. Luke's variant reading is taken by textual specialists to be a liturgical adaptation of the original petition for the kingdom, used perhaps when celebrating baptism or the laying on of hands. It is highly doubtful that Luke's original gospel had it, for it is such an obvious Christian and ecclesiastical formula that, were it original, we could not understand why it would later have been replaced by an expression originally much more Jewish in its piety. Suffice it to say, in the light of what we have seen here and will see in other ways further on, that it was not completely out of line with Luke's theology, for he saw the Holy Spirit to be as important an object of petition as the kingdom.

The Holy Spirit and Fearless Confession

One reason why the Holy Spirit was felt to be a daily need for Luke's community was that his was a community called daily to pay the price of discipleship, even under persecution. This appears now in the section which immediately follows the one studied above. The Beelzebul controversy is introduced by the Lukan note that Jesus "was casting out a demon that was dumb; when the demon had gone out, the dumb man spoke. . ." (11:14). Luke is not interested in the fact, related by Matthew, that the man was also blind. But he is very interested in the fact that the cured man can now speak out. After discussing by what spirit Jesus exorcises, Luke, like Matthew, adds the saying: "He who is not with me is against me, and he who does not gather with me scatters"

(11:23). The saying is an exhortation to fearless discipleship, and it tells us that the warning about the return of the evil spirit, immediately attached (Lk 11:24-26), is aimed at Christian disciples in danger of falling into apostasy. The Christian is one who has been delivered from the spirit of dumbness in order to speak openly. He should not cease to speak out, lest he show that the evil spirit has returned and worsened his state.

The saying about the blasphemy against the Holy Spirit, which Mark loosely attaches to the Beelzebul controversy (Mk 3:28) Luke places in the context of fearless confession.

> And I tell you, everyone who acknowledges me before men, the Son of Man will acknowledge before the angels of God; but he who denies me before men will be denied before the angels of God. And everyone who speaks a word against the Son of Man will be forgiven; but he who blasphemes against the Holy Spirit will not be forgiven. (Lk 12:8-10 RSV)

The only way we can avoid a contradiction in this text is by understanding the crucial difference for Luke between the period of Jesus, in which only he enjoys the Holy Spirit, and the period of the Church when the promised Spirit is given to the disciples. The martyrdom of the "Son of Man" was brought about by the betrayal by one of his own disciples (Lk 22:21, 48). The other disciples succumbed at the eschatological trial of Jesus (22:40, 46) and the chief of them, Peter, denied knowing him (22:54-62) in fulfillment of Jesus' own prediction (22:31-34). But this sin was forgivable and actually forgiven (Luke implies Peter's conversion in 22:32), because the Holy Spirit had not yet been given. Now, however, in the post-pentecostal Church, things are different. The Holy Spirit has been given, and with that gift the power to witness (Acts 1:8). To deny Jesus now is to reject the gift of the Holy Spirit. That this is what Luke means is confirmed by his immediate addition of the saying about the role of the Holy Spirit in assisting the Christian to speak fearlessly before "synagogues and rulers and authorities": "The Holy Spirit will teach you in that very hour what you are to say" (12:12).

In Mark this saying had appeared in the apocalyptic discourse (13:11). Luke also has the tradition in his apocalypse, but in a different form: "I will give you a mouth and a wisdom which none of your adversaries will be able to withstand or contradict" (Lk 21:15). The omission of the Holy Spirit here should not surprise us, for its appearance would simply repeat the saying of 12:11, and Luke generally avoids repetitions.

Instead, the saying shows Luke's awareness that the effects of redeeming grace can be attributed equally to the Holy Spirit or to the risen Lord, just as in Rom 8:10-11.

The Person and Program of the Spirit-Filled Messiah

Having examined Luke's use of the basic gospel tradition, let us turn to those passages which are more programmatic—that is, those in which the theology, and thus the pneumatology, of Luke become more apparent. This leads us to consider the baptism, the temptation and the opening scene of the ministry.

As we have already observed, Luke places the descent of the Holy Spirit after the baptism while Jesus was praying (3:21-22). Immediately after the account, Luke gives the genealogy of Jesus, tracing it all the way back to "Adam, the son of God" (3:38). Not only does this fact universalize the meaning of Jesus in a way that would be more meaningful for the gentile Christians than the Jewish genealogy of Matthew beginning with Abraham. It also picks up the Genesis creation motifs implicit in the baptism (as we saw when discussing the baptism in Mark) and carries them further by presenting Jesus as the Second Adam, son of God in a way that Adam was called to be but failed to maintain because of his disobedience (cf. Rom 5:19).

The temptation story, which immediately follows, benefits from the universalization of the genealogy. It is not the temptation of the New Israel (as in Matthew) but of the New Mankind begun in Jesus: "Jesus, full of the Holy Spirit, returned from the Jordan and was led by the Spirit for forty days in the wilderness, tempted by the devil" (4:1-2). Luke goes out of his way to insert the phrase "full of the Holy Spirit," replacing Mark's violent "the Spirit drove him." Luke avoids the suggestion that the Spirit is an agent over Jesus or independent of him. The Spirit does not "seize" or "drive" Jesus as he did certain men in the Old Testament. The words "full of the Holy Spirit" suggest that whatever subsequent action takes place is one of spontaneous freedom flowing from a plenitude. It is a favorite of Luke's to describe the Holy Spirit coming upon believers (1:15, 41, 67; Acts 2:4; 4:8, 31; 6:5; 11:24; 13:9, 52). Here, however, Luke's use of *plērēs*, as opposed to *plēstheis*, indicates that Jesus' fullness with the Spirit is continual and abiding. That this is so is confirmed by the importance of the temptation story for the whole ministry of Jesus in the eschatological conflict with Satan. Luke's description of the second temptation heightens its character of confrontation with political power manipulated by Satan: "To you I will give all this authority (*exousia*) and their glory, for it has been delivered to me, and I give it to whom I will" (4:6). Then, after the third temptation, the devil departs from Jesus "until an opportune time" (4:13). What is this opportune time? It is the hour of the passion, identified by Jesus as "*your* hour and the power of darkness" (22:53), and begun by Satan entering Judas (22:3). The time between the temptation and the passion is one free from the hindrance of Satan, one in which the "power of the Spirit" upon Jesus (4:14) triumphs effortlessly over the demons.

The program for the ministry is set by the sequel to the temptation, Luke 4:14-21:

14. And Jesus returned in the power of the Spirit into Galilee, and a report concerning him went out through all the surrounding country. 15. And he taught in their synagogues, being glorified by all. 16. And he came to Nazareth, where he had been brought up; and he went to the synagogue, as his custom was, on the sabbath day. And he stood up to read; 17. and there was given to him the book of the prophet Isaiah. He opened the book and found the place where it was written,

18. 'The Spirit of the Lord is upon me,
   because he has anointed me
   to preach good news to the poor.
   He has sent me to proclaim release to the captives
   and recovering of sight to the blind,
   to set at liberty those who are oppressed,
19. to proclaim the acceptable year of the Lord.'

20. And he closed the book, and gave it back to the attendant, and sat down; and the eyes of all in the synagogue were fixed on him. 21. And he began to say to them, 'Today this scripture has been fulfilled in your hearing.' (RSV)

Luke has done considerable editing here. First of all, he describes Jesus coming into Galilee "in the power of the Spirit" (vs. 14), recalling to the Christian reader the baptism and temptation and preparing for the mention of the Spirit in vs. 18. Secondly, Luke omits Jesus' initial preaching of repentance because "the kingdom of heaven is at hand" (Mk 1:15; Mt 4:17). In Luke this apocalyptic message is left to the Baptist, and the view of the imminent rule of God gives way to the proclamation of present salvation. The Spirit of God on Jesus means that the time of salvation has actually begun. The kingdom "is in your midst"

(Lk 17:21). *"Today* this scripture has been fulfilled in your hearing" (4:21). The Scripture verse which most admirably suits this situation is Is 61:1-2, which we examined in chapter four. The Spirit of the Lord upon Jesus replaces the theme of the imminent coming of the kingdom. This theological innovation of Luke's shows his concern to deal with the question of the delay of the Parousia which vexed second-generation Christians. Acts 1:6-8 will make clear that speculation about the time of the "restoration of the kingdom of Israel" is irrelevant. The answer to the delayed consummation is the Holy Spirit and the world-mission he inspires. Here in the Gospel, the presence of the Spirit on Jesus answers the same question for the period of his own ministry.

It is significant that, in the Scripture quotation, the saving activity is viewed primarily as liberation. The speaker proclaims a jubilee year. Likewise, the mention of the anointing connects this scene with the baptism, described as an anointing with the Holy Spirit in Acts 10:38.

But the programmatic scene continues in 4:23, where Jesus' allusion to the gentiles stirs up opposition and even an attempt to throw him over the cliff. Jesus, we are told in this scene, is not only anointed by the Spirit of God to bring salvation; he will be, in the end, rejected by his own. Thus we are given another forewarning that the period of Jesus' charismatic activity will be followed by the period of the "powers of darkness" (22:51) in the passion.

The Holy Spirit in the Infancy Narrative

We have reserved this for final consideration because, while Luke theologizes and interprets as he reports the tradition about Jesus' public ministry and teaching, he is limited by his materials from giving all the theological interpretation he might have liked. With the infancy narrative he had greater freedom. Not that he was free to create the tradition in this matter. He received the basic tradition here too. But this tradition was already well on the road to a profound theological interpretation which Luke made his own and pushed even farther. It was the nature of Old Testament infancy narratives to underline events which forecast the future of the child. The early Christian community, reflecting on the meager tradition about the birth and infancy of Jesus, came to see it already on a reduced scale in the intimacy of a Jewish family, as the "good news"—fulfillment of the Scriptures and foreshadowing of the public gospel that began with the preaching by John the Baptist and ended with the passion, death and resurrection of Jesus. But for Luke, author of Acts, there is also a foreshadowing of the life of the Church, and we will notice many intentional parallels between Luke 1-2 and the early chapters of Acts. This is why the infancy narratives, for Luke, occupy a place of importance similar to that of the prologue in John. In them the Spirit is related in the first place to Jesus but secondarily to the Church foreshadowed in the humble poor who receive the good news.

Lk 1:35: The Holy Spirit and Christology

35. And the angel said to her,
"The Holy Spirit will come upon you,
and the power of the Most High will overshadow you;
therefore the child to be born will be called holy,
the Son of God. (RSV)

Mary's dialogue with the angel consists of three parts. In the first the angel announces the coming of Messianic joy to Mary. The greeting is not the usual "Peace" but the unusual "Rejoice!" used in Old Testament texts to proclaim the dawn of salvation or the coming of the savior-king to "Daughter Zion," which is the whole people represented in their capital city, Jerusalem (Zeph 3:14-20; Zech 9:9), depicted already in the Old Testament as a virgin (Lam 2:13). The additional proclamation of Mary's blessedness in terms drawn from the blessing of great women in the Old Testament (Ruth 2:4; Judith 13:18) causes Mary to wonder what this greeting means (1:29). This leads to the second part of the angel's message, the reassurance, "Do not fear" (also drawn from Old Testament annunciations of salvation to the city, Zeph 3:16; Is 54:4), and the declaration that the prophecy made long ago to David (2 Sam 7:12-16) and repeated to his heirs (Is 9:6; cf. Mi 4:7; Dan 2:44; 7:14) will be fulfilled in the child to be born of Mary. This leads to our text, which is the third part of the dialogue.

A discussion of the virginity of Mary in the conception of Jesus would lead us too far afield. The interested reader is referred to other recent studies of the question. Suffice it here to point out that Luke 3:23 makes it clear Luke did not think that Joseph begot Jesus after the angel's annunciation to Mary. What is important to Luke at this point is that Jesus' divine sonship was not merely an adoptive one, as the baptism story alone might lead one to believe, but it begins with his very conception in the womb of Mary. In fact, the best way to understand the annunciation to Mary is to study it alongside its most obvious parallels in the gospel, the baptism and the transfiguration. In each scene, there is a heavenly voice identifying Jesus as God's son (1:35; 3:22; 9:35). In the

baptism the identification inaugurates the ministry; in the transfiguration it clarifies the nature of the ministry—Jesus will suffer in Jerusalem but all this is part of being God's son; in the annunciation the word
identifies Jesus in himself, prior to any mention of the ministry. The
Holy Spirit functions in a similar way. In inserting the statement at the
baptism that the Holy Spirit descended "in bodily form" as a dove,
Luke apparently intends to indicate that this was simply the visible
manifestation of what had already taken place in the unseen mystery of
Jesus' conception. Luke's choice of the word "overshadow" in the annunciation evokes Ex 40:34-38, the cloud which overshadowed the
Dwelling in the desert and assured the Israelites of the divine presence
and guidance. The very same word is used of the cloud at the transfiguration (9:34), and while the Holy Spirit is not mentioned there, the interpretative function is similar to the dove at the baptism and the Holy
Spirit's "invisible" overshadowing at the conception—it points to the
divine character of Jesus and his mission. But the annunciation makes it
clear how the work of the Spirit in Jesus differs radically from the
Spirit's coming on the Old Testament prophets and even from the Messianic king on whom the Spirit was to rest (Is 11:2). In a way totally unforeseen by the Old Testament, the very conception of the child will be
the work of God's spirit, bypassing the physical conception by Joseph,
and thus relating the child directly to God as his father. This is not a
gross presentation of the Spirit as the divine male principle or seed—in
the Hebrew, *ruah* is feminine. It is rather the supreme manifestation of
the principle that God uses the weak to confound the strong (1 Cor
1:27), the lowly to dethrone the mighty (Lk 1:52), the poor to despoil the
rich (Lk 1:53), the virgin to show that the divine sonship is not the work
of the flesh but the gift of the spirit (cf. Jn 1:12-13; 3:5-6). Jesus' conception by the Holy Spirit of the Virgin Mary is narrated by Luke less to
stress Jesus' exceptional character than to stress his supreme embodi-
ment of the universal principle of salvation—God's salvation is not the
work of man but the gift of God. Already in Is 7:14 the prophet had
bypassed Ahaz from consideration in the transmission of the Messianic
promise and focused on the Queen-Mother as the channel through which
the Lord would work his saving plan: "The virgin (maiden) will be with
child and bear a son and *she* shall name him Immanuel." Isaiah was
probably thinking of Hezekiah, to be born of Abijah, Ahaz's bride. He
did not envisage a virginal conception or birth. (The Hebrew *almah* simply means a young woman of marriageable age. Through the Septuagint
translation of the word as *parthenos* Matthew was provided with the
text which explained Mary's conception of Jesus as virginal.) Although

the Messianic prophecies of Isaiah spoke of the Spirit upon the Messiah, they did not imagine a conception of the Messiah by the Spirit. Nevertheless, the principle that salvation is not a matter of man's power but of God's spirit was, as we have seen, often asserted in the Old Testament (Is 31:4; Ez 36.26; Hag 2:5; Zech 4:6). In Paul, the relation of the humanity of Jesus to the Holy Spirit was presented first in terms of the resurrection: the Father breathes his Holy Spirit into the body of Jesus as the new Adam and raises him from the dead to constitute him God's son in power (Rom 1:4) and to make him, moreover, "life-giving spirit" (1 Cor 15:44 45). The early synoptic tradition sees this relationship foreshadowed in the transfiguration and the baptism. Luke sees it already in the mystery of the incarnation, where the humanity of Jesus is formed in the womb of Mary by the Holy Spirit, as it will be awakened from the tomb by the same Holy Spirit on Easter morning (cf. Acts 2:32-33 and compare Lk 1:32-33). Neither wonder is within the power of man's flesh to produce.

Forecast of the Passion

The infancy narratives in Luke also foreshadow the passion in a discreet way. They lead up to Jerusalem, where Jesus is presented in the Temple and Mary is told that the child is destined for "the downfall and the rise of many in Israel, a sign that will be opposed—and your own soul a sword shall pierce. . ." (2:34-35). Luke is aware that the period of the passion is one in which the Spirit, so active in Jesus' ministry, is momentarily eclipsed by the powers of darkness (22:53). But he compensates for this eclipse by making the passion itself a prior revelation by the Holy Spirit. Simeon, whose prophecy climaxes his role in the infancy story, is thrice presented as inspired by the Holy Spirit (2:25, 26, 27). The passion and death, for all its incomprehensible mystery to the disciples (24:21) was understandable to him who was Spirit-inspired (2:25-35), just as it was obvious to him who knew how to interpret the Old Testament prophecies (24:25-27). The spirit was not therefore "ousted" by the victory of violence in the passion. His word was rather fulfilled.

The Holy Spirit and Ecclesiology

We could be satisfied with the high Christology of the infancy narratives, but there are indications Luke intends to convey a proto-ecclesiology here as well. First, there are some factors in the infancy stories which elsewhere in Luke apply only to the post-Pentecostal church. During Jesus' ministry only he is "full of the Spirit" (4:1). Only at Pentecost and thereafter are the disciples and church leaders said to be "filled with the Holy Spirit" (Acts 2:4; 4:8, 31; 6:5; 11:24; 13:9, 52). Yet what Luke withholds from the disciples till Pentecost he does not hesitate to grant with carefree abandon to those in the infancy gospel. Zechariah is "filled with the Holy Spirit" (1:67); so is Elizabeth (1:35) and John from his mother's womb (1:15). The Holy Spirit is upon Simeon, reveals to him he will see the Messiah, and inspires him to come into the temple (2:25-27). Anna's inspiration by the Holy Spirit is implicit in the note that she was a prophetess (2:36). Mary, of course, is overshadowed by the Holy Spirit at the conception of Jesus (1:35). Moreover, the disciples understand nothing about the coming passion of Jesus, and Luke seems to excuse their ignorance as part of the divine necessity (9:45; 18:34), yet Simeon clearly prophesies it (2:34).

Beyond these plus-values there is the flood of rejoicing and praise unmatched by those cured in the ministry and by the disciples rejoicing at their triumph over Satan (10:17). The angels praise (2:13-14), the shepherds praise (2:20), John the Baptist leaps (1:44). Anna gives thanks (2:38), Mary, Zechariah and Simeon praise in hymns (1:46-55, 67-79; 2:29-32). Often there is explicit mention of the Holy Spirit inspiring such praise (1:41, 67; 2:25-27). We are really faced with a liturgical drama in which Luke is clearly up to something quite different from what he portrays during the rest of his gospel. It sounds as if the small circle around Mary have already experienced Pentecost! How explain this? Clearly, the infancy narrative which originated out of post-pentecostal meditation on the earliest beginnings, is meant to be in some way both the Gospel and the Acts in foreshadowing and anticipation. The result is not only a prologue to the Christology of the gospel but a prologue to the ecclesiology of Acts.

Other parallels between Luke 1-2 and Acts confirm this view. Mary is explicitly mentioned in the upper room with the disciples devoting themselves to constant prayer (as did Anna, 2:37), and she is obviously present at the descent of the Holy Spirit at Pentecost. The parallel between the Annunciation and Pentecost seems to be intentional, as would also be Mary's role as prototype for the community of believers who receive the Spirit (cf. 1:42-45; 2:19, 51; 11:28). But the other *dramatis personae* of the infancy gospel also form a proto-typical community of praise and prophecy, and their compositions, while thoroughly Jewish, give us some indication of the kind of cultic activity which went on in the Spirit-filled community so dear to Luke.

Luke 24:49: "The Promise of My Father"

> 49. And behold, I send the promise of my Father upon you; but stay in the city, until you are clothed with power from on high." (RSV)

This passage is the main bridge to the Acts, for there the "promise of my Father" is picked up again in the opening lines (Acts 1:4). There the promise clearly appears to be the Holy Spirit, mentioned immediately (Acts 1:5), and we could assume here that the Holy Spirit is likewise meant, especially in view of the expression "I send down upon you." Since in Acts 1:4 Jesus says the disciples have heard of the Father's promise from Jesus' mouth, we would expect to find it stated somewhere in Luke. But where? Is this promise an allusion to Lk 11:13, "How much more will the heavenly Father give the Holy Spirit to those who ask him"? The context there is a teaching on the importance of intercessory prayer, whereas the promise here and in Acts 1:4 does not seem to depend on petition for the Spirit but simply on God's free gift. We are thus driven back to other texts which have to do not with the Holy Spirit but with the kingdom: "Fear not, little flock, for it has pleased your Father to give you the kingdom" (Lk 12:32), and "I assign to you, as my Father has assigned to me, a kingdom, that you may eat and drink in my kingdom, and sit on thrones judging the twelve tribes of Israel" (22:29). That the promise is the kingdom seems implied by the disciples' response to Jesus' mention of the promise with the question, "Lord, will you at this time restore the kingdom to Israel?" (Acts 1:6). The disciples are clearly expecting the kingdom on the basis of Jesus' own words, and with reason, for we have also just been told that the teachings of Jesus during the forty days concerned the kingdom of God (Acts 1:3). But in vs. 8 Jesus reinterprets the kingdom in terms of the Holy Spirit and the universal mission of the church. This reinterpretation for the disciples is reserved for the Acts, but it is already prepared for in Lk 24:49 by the expression "promise of my Father" which Jesus will "send upon" them. The Christian reader familiar with the Acts (1:4; 2:33) has no trouble identifying the promise with the Holy Spirit, but for the disciples it is not that clear before Acts 1:8. In fact, the promise of Lk 24:49 that the twelve will be "clothed with power from on high" sounds very much like a renewal of the promise that they will be enthroned to judge the twelve tribes in the kingdom. Luke's concern in Acts 1:15-26 to bring the number of the Apostles back to twelve before the coming of the Holy Spirit shows, however, that he is fully sympathetic with the expectation about sitting on the twelve thrones. It is simply that Pentecost is the fulfillment, or the beginning of the fulfillment, of that promise. As the resurrection-ascension of Jesus is his enthronement as Messiah (Acts 2:33), so the outpouring of the Spirit on Pentecost is the clothing of the twelve with power from on high, and hence a sharing in Jesus' messianic reign.

Before leaving Luke's gospel, however, we should recall that for Luke Jesus possesses the Spirit from the beginning. How does he who is full of the Spirit become donor of the Spirit? Here the command to stay in the city gives us a clue. Jerusalem ties the gift of the Spirit to the ministry of Jesus. According to Luke, Jesus had to die not only in, but by the hands of Jerusalem (9:51; 13:22; 18:31; 19:28). "Today and tomorrow I cast out devils and perform cures, and on the third day my purpose is accomplished. For all that I must proceed on course today, tomorrow and the day after, since no prophet can be allowed to die anywhere except in Jerusalem" (13:32-33; cf. vs. 34, "O Jerusalem, Jerusalem, you *slay* the prophets. . ."). This saying views Jesus' ministry as comprising two significant stages: that of exorcisms and cures prior to Jerusalem, and that of martyrdom in Jerusalem. Jesus teaches in both periods, but the more "charismatic" activity is not for Jerusalem. He only teaches there (21:32-38), and the charismatic activity is replaced by sacrifice. Thus Luke modifies Mark's report of the Jewish leaders' concern not to kill Jesus on the feast (Mk 14:1-2) to suggest that Jesus had come to Jerusalem precisely to be sacrificed on the feast (Lk 22:1-2). Jesus himself could not pour out the Spirit upon Jerusalem in his ministry there. Is it a matter of chance that he describes what he would like to have done in the image of the bird hovering over her little ones, and Jerusalem's sin as the rejection of the spirit of prophecy (13:34)? Instead, his "third day" will be his own sacrifice, the necessary passageway not only to his own glory (9:31; 24:26) but to the release of the Holy Spirit, with signs and wonders, upon the disciples in the upper room (Acts 2:1-19). That is why they must stay in Jerusalem, to show the continuity not with the charismatic pre-Jerusalem ministry of Jesus (which would need no demonstration) but to show the continuity of the outpouring of the Spirit with the Jerusalem sacrifice, in which the manifestation of the Spirit had seemingly been eclipsed. The first day of the Church on Pentecost supposes and springs from Jesus' "third day" in Jerusalem.

22

The Gift of the Spirit
on Pentecost: Acts 1-2

For the reader studying Luke's theology of the Spirit, his second work, the Acts of the Apostles, presents a challenge precisely because of the wealth of material. The Holy Spirit appears everywhere. Nevertheless, closer examination shows that the core of Luke's pneumatology is found in the first two chapters. For that reason in this chapter we shall follow the text of these chapters closely, leaving the remainder of the Acts for a comprehensive thematic treatment in our next chapter.

Acts 1:1-8: Jesus Promises the Holy Spirit

> In the first book, O Theophilus, I have dealt with all that Jesus began to do and teach, 2. until the day when he was taken up, after he had given commandment through the Holy Spirit to the apostles whom he had chosen. 3. To them he presented himself alive after his passion by many proofs, appearing to them during forty days, and speaking of the kingdom of God. 4. And while staying with them he charged them not to depart from Jerusalem, but to wait for the promise of the Father, which, he said, "you heard from me, 5. for John baptized with water, but before many days you shall be baptized with the Holy Spirit."
>
> 6. So when they had come together, they asked him, "Lord, will you at this time restore the kingdom to Israel?" 7. He said to them, "It is not for you to know times or seasons which the Father has fixed by his own authority. 8. But you shall receive power when the Holy Spirit has come upon you; and you shall be my witnesses in Jerusalem and in all Judea and Samaria and to the end of the earth." (RSV)

The Holy Spirit appears in this passage three times explicitly (vss. 2, 5, 8) and once implicitly where he is identified as "the promise of my Father" (vs. 4), a phrase that provides one of the many links of the Acts with the Gospel (cf. Lk 24:49). In the first reference (vs. 2), it is not clear grammatically whether "through the Holy Spirit" is to be taken with "commanded" (RSV) or with "chosen" (NAB). In favor of the former we remember the command Jesus gave the apostles to remain in Jerusalem until they were clothed with power from on high (Lk 24:49). But that was a command *about*, not *through*, the Holy Spirit, though we might assume that such a command, like everything else Jesus did, would have been considered by Luke as Spirit-inspired. Though Luke in his gospel does not explicitly say that Jesus' choice of the twelve was Spirit-inspired, he alone mentions that preceding that choice Jesus spent the entire night in prayer (Lk 6:12-16), and we have already seen how Luke relates the Holy Spirit to the prayer of Jesus (cf. Lk 3:21-22; 11:1, 13). The likelihood, then, is that "through the Holy Spirit" refers to Jesus' *choice* of the twelve. They represent for Luke the authentic church, and here, at the very beginning of his second book, Luke wants to underline their authority by relating it both to Jesus and to the Holy Spirit. Though the twelve have not yet been endowed with the Spirit, they have been chosen by Jesus himself in an act that was Spirit-inspired. The authority of the twelve is thus implicitly related to the Holy Spirit, a point that is very important for understanding the pneumatology in Acts.

In the second reference (vs. 5), the coming of the Holy Spirit is described as a baptism—though it is the verb, not the noun, that is used. At this point in the text we do not yet know what being baptized with the Holy Spirit means, except that it is contrasted with the water baptism by John. But, like John's rite, it will be an immersion, for such is the meaning of *baptize*. However, with the exception of Acts 11:16, where Peter recalls this promise, the imagery of baptism is nowhere pursued further in Acts relative to the Holy Spirit. The disciples will be "filled" with the Holy Spirit (2:4; 4:31), those who are baptized in the name of Jesus will receive the gift of the Holy Spirit (2:38). Hence, the term "baptized with (or in) the Holy Spirit" seems to be used here to connect and contrast the beginning of the church with the beginning of the gospel and to parallel the coming of the Spirit upon the church with that of the coming of the Spirit upon Jesus. In both cases it happens after the baptism by John and while the recipient (Jesus or community) is praying (Lk 3:21; Acts 1:14; 2:1-4). The idea of being "immersed" in the Spirit does not appear to be Lukan, because it does not lend itself well to conveying the transcendent origin of the Holy Spirit. Thus, while Luke is sometimes said to be responsible for the term "baptism in the Holy Spirit," he never uses the noun, and he uses the verb only here and at 11:16. Hence, his use of it reflects his loyalty to the synoptic tradition (Mk 1:8; Mt 3:11; Lk 3:16) but not his preferred image for the pentecostal experience.

The third reference to the Holy Spirit, in vs. 8, is a key one for understanding Luke's view of the history of salvation. Every pious Jew hoped for the "restoration of the kingdom (i.e., the rule) to Israel," described in Sir 48:10 as the "restoration of the twelve tribes of Jacob." It was a legitimate question, and Jesus does not deny that the promise will be fulfilled. He only denies the revelation of when. Instead of this precise knowledge of the time of the restoration, however, there is an important substitute—or better, a beginning fulfillment to happen shortly, the gift of power, given by the Holy Spirit, to become witnesses throughout Judea and Samaria and to the ends of the earth.

If we recall the important place Psalm 68 had in the Jewish celebration of Pentecost, we can understand better perhaps why Luke describes the coming gift as a gift of power from on high: "Show forth, O God, your *power*, the *power*, O God, with which you took our part. . . Behold his voice resounds, the voice of *power*: 'Confess the *power* of God!' Over Israel is his majesty, his *power* is in the skies. . . He gives *power* to his people" (Ps 68:29-36). In each of the six occurrences of the word *power* in the short space of these verses, the word *dynamis* is used in the Septuagint, and it is this same word Luke uses in 24:49 and 1:8 for the coming of the Holy Spirit.

Jesus' response in this vs. 8 is in part Luke's answer to the second-generation church's question concerning the delay of the parousia: speculation on the time of the Lord's second coming is irrelevant. What is important is the present world mission of the church impelled by the Holy Spirit (cf. Acts 3:26 below). But it is also an important re-interpretation of the meaning of the kingdom, as we saw above in discussing Lk 24:49. We should not miss, either, the echo of the very language of the annunciation to Mary: "The Lord will give him the throne of David his father. He will rule over the house of Jacob forever, and his reign will be without end" (Lk 1:32-33). And to Mary's question as to how all this was to come about: "The Holy Spirit will come upon you and the power of the Most High will overshadow you" (Lk 1:35). Although the fulfillment of the promised reign takes place only when Jesus ascends to his heavenly throne in the resurrection (Acts 2:34), the Holy Spirit by coming upon Mary initiates the event which issues in the kingdom. In Acts the fact that the kingdom has begun is manifested on earth by the activity of the Spirit.

Acts 2:1-13: The First Christian Pentecost

1. When the day of Pentecost came it found them gathered in one place. 2. Suddenly from up in the sky there came a noise like a strong, driving wind which was heard all through the house where they were seated. 3. Tongues as of fire appeared, which parted and came to rest on each of them. 4. All were filled with the Holy Spirit. They began to express themselves in foreign tongues and make bold proclamations as the Spirit prompted them.

5. Staying in Jerusalem at the time were devout Jews of every nation under heaven. 6. These heard the sound, and assembled in a large crowd. They were much confused because each one heard these men speaking his own language. 7. The whole occurrence astonished them. They asked in utter amazement, "Are not all of these men who are speaking Galileans? 8. How is it that each of us hears them in his native tongue? 9. We are Parthians, Medes, and Elamites. We live in Mesopotamia, Judea and Cappadocia, Pontus, the province of Asia, 10. Phrygia, and Pamphylia, Egypt, and the regions of Libya around Cyrene. There are even visitors from Rome— 11. all Jews, or those who have come over to Judaism; Cretans and Arabs too. Yet each of us hears them speaking in his own tongue about the marvels God has accomplished." 12. They were dumbfounded, and could make nothing at all of what had happened.

"What does this mean?" they asked one another, while a few remarked with a sneer, 13. "They have had too much new wine!" (NAB)

This capital text falls into three parts: (1) A description of the phenomenon; (2) the assembling of the Jewish crowds from the world; (3) the divided reaction of amazement on the one hand and of an accusation of drunkenness on the other.

It is Luke alone who tells us that the Holy Spirit was given on the feast of Pentecost. In the earliest Israelite tradition Pentecost, or "the Feast of Weeks," was one of the three harvest festivals marked by pilgrimage to the sanctuary (Deut 16:16). The first of these was the feast of the Unleavened Bread, at which time the first sheaf of the barley harvest was offered (Lev 23:10). The last was the autumn festival at which the fruit harvest was celebrated, likewise with offerings (Lev 23:39; Deut 16:16-17). The "Feast of Weeks," which fell between these two, was observed by offering the first fruits of the wheat harvest (Lev 23:16). It was called the feast of Weeks (*Pentēcostēs* or "fifty days" in the Greek) because it was celebrated seven weeks after the feast of the Unleavened Bread, with which it always kept the closest association. For, as the tradition developed, the feast of the Unleavened Bread came to be considered the primary feast of the first fruits, and the feast of Weeks, at which a "new offering" (Lev 23:16) was to be made, came to be considered the closing of the fifty days (or seven weeks) after the offering of the first fruits. The fact that the loaves offered at the feast of Weeks were to be cooked with leaven indicated the return to normal living after the season of "Unleavened Bread."

In later Judaism the feast was given a historical meaning by attaching it to the events of Sinai, either by calling it the "feast of covenant renewal," as was done by the Essene and priestly tradition, or the "feast of the giving of the Law," as was done by the rabbis.

At the Essene monastery of Qumran, the feast of Weeks was the major feast of the year, on which the community celebrated the entry of new members and the renewal of the covenant. The Book of Jubilees, of which fragments have been found at Qumran, gives us an idea of how the Essenes viewed this feast. It summed up the great events of Israel's history, particularly those sealed by covenant. Noah celebrated this feast and so did the patriarchs. Forgotten by men, it was revealed again by an angel to Moses (*Jub.* 6:17). On this day occurred the great events of Israel's history: the covenant with Abraham, the promise and the actual birth of Isaac, the covenant with Jacob, and the Sinai covenant. Thus while continuing to be a feast of weeks (*shabu'oth*), it was celebrated as a feast of oaths (*shebu'oth*). This interpretation of the feast of Pentecost may very well be a development of the practice of covenant renewal described by the priestly author of 2 Chronicles (third century B.C.) and situated in the month when Pentecost was celebrated (2 Chron 15:10-14).

For the rabbis, Pentecost never became the greatest feast of the year. It never lost its close connection with Passover (a relation ignored by the Book of Jubilees), of which it was simply the conclusion. Pentecost, for the rabbis, celebrated the gift of the Law. For this reason, the rabbis gave more importance to the theophany of Sinai than did the sectarians of Qumran, because the theophany emphasized the gift of the Law itself (Ex 19-20) to which the ratification of the covenant (Ex 24) was merely the response. Nevertheless, the liturgical readings prescribed in the Mishnah and Talmud for the feast of Pentecost, while difficult to date, probably reflect a common tradition going back at least to the first century. For when the Pharisees after 70 A.D. sought to fill the void left by the loss of the temple and the priesthood, they must have prescribed liturgical readings which fit the long-standing and revered tradition of the pilgrimage feast of Pentecost. Consequently, these texts give important clues as to how a first century Jew would understand the meaning of Pentecost.

What are these texts? In the triennial cycle of Torah readings, the lessons for Pentecost were Genesis 11 (the tower of Babel) or 14 (Abraham's victory over the kings), Exodus 19-20 (the Sinai theophany and covenant) and Numbers 18 (concerning priests and levites). The Psalms read on the Sabbath afternoons in a triennial cycle were 9, 58 and 110. The Megilla prescribes a different series: the Law lessons were Deut 16:9-12 and Ex 19, the prophetic lessons Ez 1 and Hab 3, while the psalms for the day were 29 and 68. In these prophetic and psalm texts the common theme is the majesty and grandeur of God in theophany. While the use of some of these texts may be later than the New Testament period, the combination of them is a helpful indicator of the traditional meaning seen in the feast.

We may now return to the text of Acts. Although the NAB reading, "When the day of Pentecost came," is probably the most primitive, an ancient ecclesiastical reading (reflected in the Vulgate, the Old Latin, the Peshitto and the Armenian version) has "When the days of Pentecost were completed." The plural is used because, for the first three centuries of the church, the fifty day season was celebrated, after the Jewish pattern, as one continuous festival reliving the common mystery of the resurrection and the outpouring of the Spirit. However, the primitive Christian community knew the Jewish tradition of celebrating the theophany at Sinai on the fiftieth day, and wanting to establish the closest connection between Sinai and the gift of the Spirit, the Christian tradition which Luke reflects situated the event on the day of Pentecost itself. Hence "the day of Pentecost" in the singular seems the better reading.

Who are the "they" gathered in one place? Does Luke mean the twelve or the 120 disciples mentioned in 1:15? The fact that the number twelve must be completed before the Spirit is given (by the election of Matthias) and that this immediately precedes the descent of the Holy Spirit leads many exegetes to think Luke has in mind the twelve as the beneficiaries of the phenomenon. But if Luke is deliberately vague, perhaps this should warn us against attempting to distinguish too much between the twelve and the 120 here. If the twelve represent the twelve tribes of Israel assembled at Sinai, the 120 are necessary to show the immediate expansion into a larger multitude. The Greek has "they were *all* gathered," and the Joel prophecy that follows suggests an outpouring on a multitude.

Though translated "in one place," the Greek expression means more than local unity. It is frequently used in the Septuagint to render the Hebrew *yahad*, meaning unity of mind and heart, with essentially the same meaning as we find in Acts 1:14, where unity in prayer is meant. The Targum speaks of the Jewish community constantly occupied in prayer during the week prior to the reception of the Law and "united in heart" at the foot of Mount Sinai (*PsJon. Ex* 19:2b). Though Luke gives no explicit reason for all being in one place, we may assume that they have gathered to celebrate the feast of Pentecost.

Luke then gives the elements of the theophany, with remarkable economy. From the sky comes a sound "as of a mighty wind coming." The word *ēchos* (noise, sound) as a noun or in its verb forms belongs to the descriptions of theophanies in the Septuagint (Ex 19:16; 1 Sam 4:5; Ps 45:3), in Philo (*de Dec.* 33), in the epistle to the Hebrews referring to Sinai (12:19) and in Luke 21:25 describing the end-time. The wind is also a traditional element of theophanies, especially those of Sinai (1 Sam 19:11; Targums, 4 Esdras, Josephus). "It filled the whole house" is probably intended to evoke Ex 19:18, "The whole mountain trembled violently."

In vs. 3, the theophany becomes properly pentecostal. The Greek says, literally, "There appeared to them tongues as of fire, dividing [as from a single source] and they settled on each of them." Wind and fire appear frequently in the Old Testament as signs of theophany, especially of God's coming judgment (Is 4:4; 2 Sam 22:16; Ps 50:3; Jer 30:23; Is 66:15; cf. 4 Esdras 13:10). Here the image of tongues of fire evokes Is 5:24, "as the tongue of fire licks up stubble." The Book of Henoch speaks of "tongues of fire" in an apocalyptic vision (14:8-13; cf. 71:5) and a Qumran fragment speaks of the three tongues of fire (Milik-Barthélemy I, text no. 29, pp. 130-132). In every case, as also in the eschatological preaching of John the Baptist, the fire is the purifying fire of judgment. But for Luke these tongues of fire mean something else. They symbolize the gift of the Holy Spirit and the different languages the apostles will speak (vs. 4). Luke thus adroitly uses the word "tongue" as a bridge from fire in vs. 3 to language in vs. 4.

This marvelous communication was already prepared for in the Jewish traditions about Sinai. Deuteronomy had referred to the Sinai revelation as a voice "out of the heavens" seen on earth as "his great fire" and "you heard him speaking out of the fire" (Deut 4:36; cf. 5:4). Beginning with the Targum on Deut 33:2 a tradition developed according to which the Lord first offered his law to neighboring peoples (later in the tradition, to all the nations of the world), and only when they refused did he offer it to Israel. But obviously there was a problem—in what language was the Law offered to the nations? Rabbi Johanan said that the voice went out and divided into seventy voices, in seventy tongues, so that all the nations could understand (*Midrash Ex Rab* 5:9; 28:6). Although Rabbi Johanan lived after Luke's time, the tradition about a miraculous communication at Sinai, amid signs of fire and spirit, becoming intelligible to all the listeners is already found in Philo, a contemporary of Luke:

> The ten words . . . were delivered by the Father of All when the nation . . . were assembled together. Did he do so by his own utterance in the form of a voice? Surely not: . . . God is not as a man needing mouth and tongue and windpipe. I should suppose that God wrought on this occasion a miracle of a truly holy kind by bidding an invisible sound to be created in the air more marvelous than all instruments and fitted with perfect harmonies . . . which giving shape and tension to the air and changing it to a *flaming fire*, sounded forth like the *breath (pneuma)* through a trumpet an articulate voice so loud that it appeared to be equally audible to the farthest as well as the nearest. . . . The new miraculous voice was set in action and *kept in flame* by the power of God which breathed upon it *(epipneousa)* and spread it abroad on every side and made it more illuminating in its ending than in its beginning by creating in the souls of each and all another kind of hearing far superior to the hearing of the ears. (*De Decalogo*, 33-35; cf. also *Spec. Leg.* II, 189)

Although Luke qualifies the tongues by saying "*as of* fire," thus restraining an excessively physical understanding of the phenomenon, it is clear that he means something really visible. The Sinai tradition, as a matter of fact, already spoke of Israel "*seeing* the voice" (Ex 20:18 LXX; "voices" in the Hebrew), and Philo felt the need to explain how one could see a voice:

> Then from the midst of the fire that streamed from heaven there sounded forth to their utter amazement a voice, for the flame became articulate speech in the language familiar to the audience, and so clearly and distinctly were the words formed by it that they seemed to see rather than hear them. What I

say is vouched for by the law in which it is written, "All the people saw the voice," a phrase fraught with much meaning, for it is the case that the voice of men is audible, but the voice of God truly visible. Why so? Because whatever God says is not words but deeds, which are judged by the eyes rather than the ears. (*De Decalogo*, 46-47)

Visibility is thus essential to the gift of the Spirit. The single visible Spirit, like the single visible word, will be conveyed by the apostles into all the languages of men. But it is the essence of the communication of the Spirit that it be a *manifestation*, as Paul already said of the work of the Spirit in 1 Cor 12:7.

In vs. 4 the meaning of the theophany is at length given: "They were all filled with the Holy Spirit." In the Greek the article "the" is missing, as it is in most of the other Lukan passages which speak of infilling (Lk 1:15, 41, 67; 4:1; Acts 4:8; 6:5; 7:55; 9:17; 11:24; 13:9). Exegetes occasionally point out that this indicates that what is in the forefront in these passages is not the person of the Holy Spirit but the Spirit's activity. For our passage it would be more precise to call upon the practice of Greek grammar, in which a person or thing not yet known or experienced is first introduced without the article (Bl-Deb., #252), then is later referred back to by use of the article. Thus, since the apostles have not previously experienced the Holy Spirit but now experience the mysterious power for the first time, the article is not used, but when "the Spirit" is mentioned the second time in the verse the article is used. In Acts 4:31, an exact parallel with our passage, the article is used, to identify the Holy Spirit there as the same Spirit that came on Pentecost. Similarly when the Spirit falls on the household of Cornelius (10:44) the article is used for the same purpose but also bordering on personification (Bl-Deb., #257).

The first effect of this infilling with the Holy Spirit is that they "began to speak in other tongues as the Spirit gave them to proclaim." What is meant by "other tongues"? The expression can have a general meaning of "strange or unfamiliar speech," the kind of "tongues" we have described in 1 Cor 12-14 as non-conceptual or pre-conceptual speech. Or it can mean, in a stricter sense, "foreign languages" (as in the Prologue to Sirach 22 or Is 28:11). The NAB takes it in the latter sense. In favor of the former interpretation is the fact that the speakers are accused of being drunk (vs. 13)—an accusation that would have little basis if the speakers were manifesting a brilliance in foreign languages. Also, if the speakers were communicating so brilliantly with their audience, why would Peter have to preach at all? When he does preach, he addresses himself not to a phenomenon of speaking foreign languages but to the accusation of drunkenness. On the other hand, there is no doubt that Luke intends to highlight a marvelous communication to the different groups of Jews and the transmission of the single event into different actual human languages, however this occurred. The word "to proclaim" (*apophthengesthai*) is used in vs. 14 to introduce Peter's discourse and in 26:25 of Paul's proclamation before Agrippa. In both these cases it refers to a clearly conceptualized presentation. In both cases, however, we should note that there is a prior accusation of irrational conduct, drunkenness in 2:13, madness in 26:24.

There seems to be no way out of this impasse except by considering the nature of prophecy, the term Peter uses precisely to describe the phenomenon (2:17, 18). We saw repeatedly in the Old Testament that the coming of the prophetic spirit can at times have the effect of putting the recipient in a state of ecstasy (Num 11:25, 26-29; 1 Sam 10:10-11; 19:20-21), at other times inspire him with a clear message (Mi 3:8; Ez 36:1, etc.). In distinguishing prophecy from tongues, its pre-conceptual manifestation in 1 Cor 12-14, Paul separates what the Old Testament kept together in a single concept of prophecy. Luke, who knows the Pauline distinction and observes it in Acts 19:16 ("they spoke in tongues and prophesied"), considers the two together in Acts 2, and for reasons that are not difficult to find. Acts 2 is the primordial experience of the Holy Spirit but also the primordial missioning. The relevance of this experience for the nations and the rapid spread of the gospel is important here. Consequently, it seems that Luke has combined the earlier Pauline tradition of tongues as non-rational speech with the tradition of prophetic proclamation to the nations in various languages, and this accounts for the apparent inconsistencies in the text, some elements indicating ecstatic speech, others bold preaching in languages.

Another reason is that he wanted to tie the primordial manifestation of the Spirit to the Sinai tradition, and this tradition involved a transmission of the one word into many languages. Now, according to Rabbi Johanan's interpretation of Ps 68:12 (a Psalm, we remember, that was used for the Jewish celebration of Pentecost), the words, "those who publish the good news are a vast army" refer to the different languages spoken from Sinai by God himself. Much later, all the prophets were said to have been at Sinai, and these tongues were said to be the messages received by the prophets. For Luke, it is through the apostles that the one revelation reaches the many nations. And—an even more important difference—the whole theophany and the communication of its meaning is the work of the Holy Spirit. Nowhere in the Jewish Sinai traditions is the Spirit mentioned. The people gathered at the mount are at most a people of priests, not prophets (although the much later rabbinical tradition put the prophets back there too). The reason is that the universal gift of the Spirit was reserved for the final age (Joel 3:1-2; cf. *S-B II*, p. 612, "In this age some prophesy; in the age to come all Israelites will prophesy"). But that, according to Luke, is precisely what has begun. The upper room has become the Sinai of the final times, for the New Covenant of the Spirit has been given.

The rest of the text may be handled rapidly. The location of the event in Jerusalem (vs. 6) is crucial not only to assuring the continuity of the Acts with the gospel, and the gift of the Spirit with the death-resurrection of Jesus, but it is also important for the Sinai symbolism. The Jewish liturgy stresses that the Mount Zion of Jerusalem was really the successor to Mount Sinai, for while the Lord had revealed himself in an unspeakable moment on Sinai, he had come from Sinai to Mount Zion to make his perpetual dwelling there, and this equation of Zion with Sinai was expressly chanted in Ps 68:16-19, prescribed in the readings for the feast of Pentecost.

The composition of the crowd that gathers is as close a description of the entire gentile world as Luke is allowed by the tradition and by the plan of his own narrative. He knows that the actual coming of the Spirit to the gentiles occurs only much later in the apostolic mission. He knows too that the gospel is first to be preached to the Jews. So the crowd that gathers is a Jewish crowd yet one that represents the nations. It really does not matter whether they were diaspora Jews who had immigrated to Palestine or whether they had just come as pilgrims for the feast of Pentecost to join the "inhabitants of Jerusalem" (vs. 14). They represent the whole world. The list of nations does not seem to have been made at random. It corresponds quite closely to an ancient listing of the nations according to the twelve signs of the zodiac. Luke's list would thus not be illustrative but comprehensive.

Verse 6 raises the question: Was the phenomenon a miracle of hearing? The text says, "Each one heard them speaking in his own language." If the apostles were speaking foreign languages in the strict sense, then it would take no miracle for an Egyptian Jew, for example, to hear whoever among the Spirit-filled community was speaking his Egyptian dialect. Yet the Greek text says, "each one heard *them*." The idea is re-stated in vss. 8 and 11. The more normal meaning is that the whole explosive language phenomenon of the group was understood by each hearer in his own language. It would seem, then, that there was a miracle of hearing, or perhaps of interpretation of the tongues, as in

Paul. If this is so, then the "other tongues" of vs. 4 need not have been foreign languages at all but the phenomenon may have been exactly what it is described to be in Paul.

It may never be possible to sort out whether on the historical level Luke intended to describe a miracle of speaking or of hearing. It was in any case a marvel, and there can be no doubt as to how he interpreted the event on a literary and theological level: the first Christian Pentecost was the eschatological Sinai event where the promised covenant of the Spirit was given. But this event was also symbolic for all the nations of the earth, for it is a reversal of the curse of Babel. (We remember that the Babel story in Genesis 11 was one of the prescribed readings in the triennial cycle for the Jewish feast of Pentecost.) The divisive nature of languages, Genesis' climactic symbol of man's social disintegration due to his hubris, is now overcome by the one Spirit. When mankind, who could once communicate in the same language, decided to build a city with a tower that reached the sky, so as to make a name for themselves, their speech was confused and they were scattered over the earth. Now, by God's gift from the sky (vs. 2) the alienations of language are bridged, so amazingly that the scattered "nations" assemble at the sound and are confused at hearing this one event speak to them each personally (vs. 6). Luke chooses the same verb for this confusion as was used in Gen 11:9 for the confusion of tongues, but obviously he means to suggest the reversal of that confusion in amazement that the one event is understood by all the different languages. The final touch of the Babel reversal will occur when the hearers abandon the folly of making a name for themselves (Gen 11:4) and call on the name of the Lord (Acts 2:21).

The tongue-speaking is a sign. Like every other sign it is an invitation to faith but it does not compel faith. While some are amazed at the wonder, others think it nonsense (a frequent reaction in Luke-Acts to the news of the resurrection, Lk 24:11; Acts 17:32; 26:24) and accuse the apostles of being drunk with new wine. The accusation must at least have had some foundation in the state of exaltation in which the apostles found themselves. New wine was proverbially held to induce rapid drunkenness. One may be permitted to wonder whether Luke has not introduced his image here because of the synoptic tradition of the new wine brought by Jesus (Mk 2:22) which in Luke's version has the added saying that people used to drinking old wine do not like the taste of new (Lk 5:37-39). The context is the newness of Jesus' teaching over the categories of the Old Law and the practices of the Pharisees. In Acts 2:1-13, it is the new covenant of the Spirit that is given, and those Jews attached to their traditional ways may not find it to their taste, hence the accusation. The double reaction also forecasts similar reactions throughout the apostolic mission related in the Acts. At any rate, Jesus is the bringer of new wine (cf. also Jn 2:10), and in Eph 5:18 being filled with the Spirit is the Christian counterpart of being drunk on wine.

Peter takes the accusation at its literal face value and responds that physical drunkenness is excluded because it is only nine o'clock in the morning (vs. 15). Homilists generally exploit the humor in this response, but for Luke, the morning here is important, for it is a further identification with Sinai, where the theophany occurred in the morning (Ex 19:16).

Acts 2:14-39: Peter's Pentecost Address

14. Peter stood up with the Eleven, raised his voice, and addressed them: "You who are Jews, indeed all of you staying in Jerusalem! Listen to what I have to say. 15. You must realize that these men are not drunk, as you seem to think. It is only nine in the morning! 16. No, it is what Joel the prophet spoke of:

17. 'It shall come to pass *in the last days, says God,*
    that I will pour out a portion of my spirit on all mankind:
    Your sons and daughters shall prophesy,
    your young men shall see visions
    and your old men shall dream dreams.
18. Yes, even on my servants and handmaids
    I will pour out a portion of my spirit in those days,
    and they shall prophesy.
19. I will work wonders in the heavens *above*
    and *signs* on the earth *below*:
    blood, fire, and a cloud of smoke.
20. The sun shall be turned to darkness and the moon to blood
       before the coming of that great and glorious day of the
       Lord.
21. Then shall everyone be saved who calls on the name of the
       Lord.'

22. Men of Israel, listen to me! Jesus the Nazorean was a man whom God sent to you with miracles, wonders, and signs as his credentials. These God worked through him in your midst, as you well know. 23. He was delivered up by the set purpose and plan of God; you even made use of pagans to crucify and kill

him. 24. God freed him from death's bitter pangs, however, and raised him up again, for it was impossible that death should keep its hold on him. 25. David says of him:

> 'I have set the Lord ever before me,
> with him at my right hand I shall not be disturbed.
> 26. My heart has been glad and my tongue has rejoiced,
> my body will live on in hope,
> 27. for you will not abandon my soul to the nether world,
> nor will you suffer your faithful one to undergo corruption.
> 28. You have shown me the paths of life;
> you fill me with joy in your presence.'

29. Brothers, I can speak confidently to you about our father David. He died and was buried, and his grave is in our midst to this day. 30. He was a prophet and knew that God had sworn to him that one of his descendants would sit upon his throne. 31. He said that he was not abandoned to the nether world, nor did his body undergo corruption, thus proclaiming beforehand the resurrection of the Messiah. 32. This is the Jesus God has raised up, and we are his witnesses. 33. Exalted at God's right hand, he first received the promised Holy Spirit from the Father, then poured this Spirit out on us. This is what you now see and hear. 34. David did not go up to heaven, yet David says,

> 'The Lord said to my Lord,
> Sit at my right hand
> 35. until I make your enemies your footstool.'

36. Therefore let the whole house of Israel know beyond any doubt that God has made both Lord and Messiah this Jesus whom you crucified."
    37. When they heard this, they were deeply shaken. They asked Peter and the other apostles, "What are we to do, brothers?" 38. Peter answered: "You must reform and be baptized, each of you, in the name of Jesus Christ, that your sins may be forgiven; then you will receive the gift of the Holy Spirit. 39. It was to you and your children that the promise was made, and to all those still far off whom the Lord our God calls." (NAB)

This discourse is very carefully constructed. The first part looks back to and explains the Pentecost phenomenon as the fulfillment of Joel's prophecy (vss. 15-21). With vs. 22 the central theme of the sermon is introduced, the resurrection of Jesus (vs. 22-36), and this is related to the Pentecost event in vs. 33. The sermon concludes (vs. 38-39) with the call to repentance, to baptism and to the gift of the Holy Spirit—which ties in with the prophecy of Joel and relates the whole sermon once again to the Pentecost event.

The quotation from Joel is familiar to us from our Old Testament study. However, the way Luke reproduces it shows a few slight variants from the original Greek text of Joel. In the opening line the words "in the last days" are an addition to Joel, with the effect of strengthening the meaning of the Pentecost event as a sign of the end-time. Likewise, in vs. 18 we read the additional words, "they shall prophesy." Luke (through Peter) thus identifies the whole Pentecost event as a manifestation of prophecy, very much like the coming of the spirit upon the seventy elders in Num 11:27. As examples of prophecy, Joel, writing at the beginning of the apocalyptic period, had given visions and dreams. Though there are many of these related in the Acts (6:56; 9:10-16; 10:3-6, 9-20; 16:9; 18:9; 22:17-21; 23:11), Luke's preferred manifestation of the infilling by the Holy Spirit is tongues as praise and prophetic speech as proclamation (10:46; 19:6; 21:9).

Then in vs. 19 we find Joel's "I will work wonders in the heavens and on the earth" expanded to read, "I will work wonders in the heavens *above* and *signs* on the earth *below*." Is this simply a rhetorical heightening of the cosmic wonders given by Joel? Luke certainly knows apocalyptic language, for he uses imagery similar to Joel's in Jesus' words concerning the final times (Lk 21:10-11, 25). Such phenomena will precede and announce the coming of the Son of Man (Lk 21:25). However, this hardly explains why Luke, or his source before him, wanted to distinguish between activity in heaven and activity on earth, and above all why the combination "wonders and signs" results from the addition, for this expression is reserved exclusively in Luke-Acts for charismatic activity. The result of the change is that an apocalyptic statement about the end-time is changed into a prophetic Mosaic-exodus statement. The expression "signs and wonders" (*sēmeia kai terata*) is a stereotyped Septuagint expression for the marvelous deeds worked by God through Moses in bringing the people out of Egypt (Ex 7:3, etc.). The order here, of course, is reversed to "wonders and signs," but this is even more significant, for it points us to the one place in the Septuagint where the order is also reversed in the same way: "[Wisdom] entered the soul of the Lord's servant and withstood mighty kings with wonders and signs (*en terasi kai sēmeiois*)" and "made the tongues of those who could not speak eloquent . . . and prospered their works by the hand of the holy prophet" (Wis 10:16-11:1). The evidence then appears conclusive that the modification of Joel here was intended to point back to the Pentecost event as a wonder from heaven (Acts 2:2) manifested in the sign on earth of tongues (2:4-12), indicating the imminence of the day of the Lord and calling for conversion to him. At the same time it points forward to the "wonders and signs" (same order) performed by Jesus (vs. 22) and to those further signs and wonders done by the apostles in Jesus' name (2:43; 4:30; 5:12; 6:8; 7:36; 14:3; 15:12).

The last line of Joel's prophecy, "For on Mount Zion there shall be a remnant . . . and in Jerusalem survivors whom the Lord shall call," is omitted from the citation but it will reappear implicitly at the conclusion of the address, 2:39, in the expression, "those whom the Lord calls."

The second part of the address roots the Pentecost event and the gift of the Spirit in the ministry, death, resurrection and exaltation of Jesus. There are some ancient preaching formulas in this part of Peter's speech, for example, the view of the resurrection-ascension as the enthronement of Jesus as Messiah and Lord (2:36). But the most interesting passage is 2:33: "Exalted at God's right hand, he first received the promised Spirit from the Father, then poured this Spirit out on us. This is what you now see and hear." Obviously these last words mean that Peter is still explaining the Pentecost phenomenon. He links it to the exaltation of Jesus to God's right hand, at which moment he received the Spirit to give to men. This could be a relic of a very primitive idea from the earliest preaching that Jesus received the Spirit at his glorification (Rom 1:4), but in Luke's overall theology it would not deny Jesus' possession of the Spirit during his earthly life, and consequently if Jesus receives the Spirit when he returns to the Father, it means he receives it for the church.

But where did this model of transmission come from? We find a very close parallel in Eph 4:8, where Psalm 68:19 is quoted according to a rabbinic midrash: "When he ascended on high he took a host of captives and gave gifts to men." And this is applied to Jesus' ascension and the gifts of the Spirit to the church. That the same Psalm text lies behind our verse is further confirmed by vs. 34, where it is said that "David did not *ascend* to heaven." Now we know that Psalm 68 was part of the Pentecost liturgy, and we know too that as the rabbinic tradition developed, the "going up" was applied to Moses who went up the mountain to receive the Law, God's gift, and then to give it to the people. Now we have already seen how the Moses typology has influenced the Acts, and a brief examination of other texts will show that Luke identifies Jesus as the prophet-like-Moses of Deut 18:15. Twice this text is explicitly cited in Acts. In 3:22 Peter identifies Jesus as this prophet-like-Moses, and in Stephen's speech we are told just how Luke wants his readers to understand Moses as a type of Jesus. Moses was sent by God to be Israel's leader and savior (*archonta kai lytrotēn*, 7:35), leading them forth with "wonders and signs" (7:36), but they would not obey him (7:39). Similarly, Jesus is the "author (or leader) of life (*archēgos*, 3:15), the "leader and savior" (*archegos kai sōtēra*, 5:31), who has done wonders and signs (2:22) but was rejected and put to death (3:14). But God "raised him up" (the resurrection was the fulfillment beyond expectations of the promise to "raise up" a prophet like Moses, 2:33; 3:26; 5:31), and not only are the apostles witnesses of this raising up (1:8, 22; 2:32; 5:32) but they are the instruments of his prophetic authority, for through them the prophet-like-Moses is being sent to Israel today (3:26). And as the prophecy had said, "Him you shall obey" (Deut 18:15), so those who now obey him receive the gift of his prophetic spirit, the Holy Spirit (5:32).

It is clear, then, that Luke is continuing here in 2:33 the Moses-Sinai imagery we have already seen at work earlier. As Moses went up the mountain into the cloud and received from God the law, and, returning, gave this gift to the people (Ex 19-24), so Jesus goes up, hidden by a cloud (1:9) and receives from the Father the gift of the Spirit, and the first Christian Pentecost is the outpouring of the Spirit "which you see and hear" (2:33).

When asked what they should do, Peter indicates: "Reform and be baptized, each of you, in the name of Jesus Christ, that your sins may be forgiven, and you will receive the gift of the Holy Spirit" (2:38). The formula indicates that the Holy Spirit is given as a gift upon repentance and baptism in the name of Jesus Christ. (In Mt 28:19, the formula is given as "in the name of the Father, and of the Son, and of the Holy Spirit.") There is no indication in this text of any delay of the Spirit for a later moment. Baptism thus mediates the gift of the Spirit. (We shall discuss the exceptional cases of Cornelius and the Samaritans further on.) What is significant is that from here on the gift of the Holy Spirit is always mediated to men through the church, either apostles (8:14-24; 19:1-7) or disciples (Acts 9:17-19). And the deepest reason for this is given in 3:26: the ministry of the Spirit-filled community *is* God's sending of the prophet-like-Moses whom he has raised up.

In vs. 39, the "promise" probably again refers to the Spirit as the

promise of the Father (1:4; 2:33). Though offered first to the Jews represented by Peter's Jerusalem audience, the promise is also destined for
those "far off," not only the diaspora Jews but (in Luke's redaction at
least) the gentiles.

23

The Holy Spirit and the Development of the Church: Acts 3-28

We begin a new chapter here not simply as a convenient way to divide the copious material, but also because Acts 1-2 is a kind of once-for-all event, a paradigm for the rest of Acts. It was important there to follow the text carefully. In this chapter we shall approach the matter more thematically, for Luke, having made the gift of the Spirit the major focus of these first two chapters, now simply allows this bright thread to weave in and out of the rest of his tapestry, thus showing the all-pervasiveness of the Spirit's presence and direction in the life of the early church.

Charismatic Activity

After the summary description of the life of the primitive community in 2.42-27, Luke's first recorded event is the cure of the cripple at the beautiful gate of the temple (3:1-10). This cure is important not only in that it gives Peter another opportunity to preach Jesus Christ (3:11-26) but also because it is a sign typical of the messianic age (Is 35:3, 6) and moreover typical of the new life of the resurrection already experienced here and now (4:2). Significantly, though the Holy Spirit is not expressly mentioned in the speech, Jesus is portrayed as the prophet raised up and acting through the apostles (3:22, 26). The man is healed *in the name of Jesus Christ* (3:6, 16). It seems to be a consistent pattern for the Acts that while the charismatic gifts of tongues and prophecy are attributed to the Holy Spirit (Acts 2; 10:46; 19:6), cures and exorcisms are attributed to the name of Jesus (3:6, 16; 4:7, 10, 12, 30; 16:18; 19:13, 17). Why this difference? Is it that tongues and prophecy as a rule belong within the Christian community, that is, to those who already profess the name of Jesus and know that the Spirit comes from him (cf. 1 Cor 12:3), while cures and exorcisms, like preaching, belong primarily to the "signs and wonders" performed outside for those who have yet to learn to call on the name of the Lord? That this is so is suggested by the fact that the disciples preach expressly, just as they heal and exorcise, in the name of Jesus (Lk 2:47; Acts 5:28, 40; 8:12). The relationship between the Holy Spirit and the name of Jesus in the life experience of the church is illustrated by the "little Pentecost" of Acts 4:23-31, which follows the cure of the cripple and the consequent furor about the "name of Jesus" (3:1-4:22). Returning within the community, Peter and John join the rest in a common prayer for boldness in preaching and for "cures and signs and wonders to be worked in the name of Jesus, your holy Servant" (4:30). Then we are told, "The place where they were gathered shook as they prayed. They were filled with the Holy Spirit and continued to speak God's word with confidence" (4:31). The Holy Spirit here appears as the inward consoler and strengthener (cf. 9:31), the name of Jesus as the outward shape of the message and power. Similarly, in the Pentecost event, when, by way of exception, the powerful experience of tongues and prophecy is witnessed by the Jewish crowd without understanding, Peter must explain the event in terms of Jesus, concluding that his listeners must be baptized in Jesus' name if they wish to receive the Holy Spirit (2:38). So too, one can invoke the name of Jesus without having the Holy Spirit (Acts 19:13; Lk 9:49-50), but one cannot have the Holy Spirit without confessing Jesus. The Cornelius event is no exception to this but rather a confirmation. True, Cornelius and his household are baptized in the name of Jesus Christ after the Holy Spirit comes upon them (10:48), but we have already been told of their eagerness to receive the word and to do whatever Peter suggests (10:25-33), and it is immediately after Peter says, "Everyone who believes in him has forgiveness of sins through his name" (10:43) that the Holy Spirit falls upon them (10:44). It is this that convinces Peter that God has admitted the gentiles to the church on an equal footing because he has given them the full Christian experience he "gave to us at the beginning," i.e., on Pentecost (15:8). If then, the Holy Spirit belongs to the inward experience of the community, it would be understandable that those gifts intended primarily for the building up of the community within, namely tongues and prophecy, would be attributed to the Holy Spirit, and those that belong more properly to the outward mission be attributed to the name of Jesus. Thus, in the centrifugal unfolding of the church's life, tongues and prophecy precede healing, exorcism and other signs, while in the centripetal movement, healings, exorcisms and other signs precede as attractions to the name of Jesus and through that door to the Holy Spirit and the "domestic" gifts of tongues and prophecy.

To complete our review of the charismatic activity in the Acts, we should list the major references. Peter heals another paralytic in Lydda (9:32) and raises Tabitha from death (9:36-42). Philip heals, exorcises and works miracles in Samaria (8:7). Paul strikes the magician Elymas in Paphos with temporary blindness (13:9), cures a lame man at Lystra (14:8-13), exorcises a clairvoyant spirit in Philippi (16:16-18), restores Eutychus to life in Troas (20:7-12), heals a man of fever and dysentery on the isle of Malta (28:8-9), and is unharmed by a poisonous snake (28:3-6). There is a summary statement in 19:11-12 concerning Paul's cures and exorcisms in Ephesus. Finally we should note the major summary statement in Acts 5:12-16 concerning the many signs and wonders done by the apostles. This, like the cure of the cripple at the temple, provokes bitter opposition and imprisonment (5:17-18). The pattern of the early church in its charismatic activity will not be greatly different from that of Jesus. In his speeches Peter recalls Jesus' charismatic activity only to follow it immediately with the recalling of his being put to death: "God anointed him with the Holy Spirit and power. He went about doing good works and healing all who were in the grip of the devil. . . They killed him. . ." (10:38-40; cf. 3:22-23).

The Inner Life of the Church

We have already discussed the role of the Holy Spirit in tongues and prophecy, the more "domestic gifts" of the Spirit. We might add that the Old Testament, which was the only "book" that nourished the church in those early years, is habitually referred to by Luke as the utterance of the Holy Spirit (1:16; 4:25; 28:25; cf. 2:30). The rabbis, as we saw, frequently referred to the Scriptures in this way. But the expression in Luke does not mean simply that the words were inspired by the Holy Spirit in the past but also that they continue to speak prophetically to the present community. Luke also gives an important place to prophets as an accepted office in the life of the church (11:27-30; 13:1-3; 15:32; 21:9-10). The normal context for prophecy was the celebration of the liturgy, and prophecy seemed to be particularly active during a church fast (13:2).

But of the various offices we see emerging in the church, that of the apostle remains unparalleled in its primacy as the channel of the Holy Spirit. We already discussed how Luke grounded the choice of the twelve in an act of Jesus himself anointed by the Spirit (Acts 1:2), preceded by a whole night of prayer (Lk 6:12-16). The number twelve must be completed (Acts 1:15-26) because the twelve are the judges of the twelve tribes of Israel (Lk 22:9). The "signs and wonders" are done principally by the apostles (2:43; 5:12-16; 14:3; 15:12). Of the four things in which the young community "perseveres," the teaching of the apostles is listed first (2:42). In its early fervor of sharing, some members of the community sold their goods and property and laid them at the feet of the apostles (4:34-37). When Ananias and Saphira did the same but concealed the fact that they had held back some of the money, Peter, with inspired knowledge, reveals that they have "lied to the Holy Spirit" (5:3, 9) and both of them die. The only other place in the Greek bible where the word *nophizō* ("hold back") occurs is in Joshua 7:1, the story of Achan's sin and punishment. Luke, or his source, perhaps sees a parallel with the Achan story here.

With time, the authority of the apostles is shared with presbyters. The two combined can say, in their decision, "the Holy Spirit and we have decided" (15:28). And in his parting words to the presbyters of Ephesus, Paul says, "Keep watch . . . over the whole flock the Holy Spirit has given you to guard" (20:28). Though Luke would be the first to deny that he limits the Spirit's activity to the apostles or their representatives, he certainly considers it crucial that the development of the church be under their blessing and supervision. This explains the whole purpose for calling the "council of Jerusalem" (Acts 15). And it also sheds some light on the puzzling case of the Samaritans evangelized by Philip (8:4-25). After describing the amazing success of Philip's preaching accompanied by miracles, exorcisms and cures (8:4-13), Luke adds:

> 14. Now when the apostles at Jerusalem heard that Samaria had received the word of God, they sent to them Peter and John, 15. who came down and prayed for them that they might receive the Holy Spirit; 16. for it had not yet fallen on any of them, but they had only been baptized in the name of the Lord Jesus. (RSV)

The puzzling vs. 16 apparently makes a distinction between baptism in the name of the Lord Jesus and the gift of the Spirit, in this case received later when the apostles laid hands on them. This celebrated passage has been used often by Catholics as a proof-text for the sacrament of confirmation and by Pentecostals as a proof-text for the "baptism in the Holy Spirit" separable, often by years, from water baptism.

The problem, of course, rises mainly from the fact that Luke never intended to write a treatise on baptism or on the laying on of hands. Since we are asking our question of texts that are always speaking about something else, we need to be careful about drawing conclusions. The apostles themselves, in Luke's view, apparently received the baptism by

John (1:22). They later became disciples of Jesus (apparently without another baptism) but did not receive the Holy Spirit until Pentecost. Some Pentecostals have pointed to this fact as typical of the two moments of the Christian life: becoming a disciple of Jesus (through water baptism) and later receiving the Holy Spirit through the laying on of hands ("baptism in the Holy Spirit"). But does this really correspond to Luke's intention for the relation of discipleship to the Spirit? Luke makes it clear that the disciples experienced authentic faith in Jesus only at Pentecost, when their faith-act was accompanied by the gift of the Spirit. Peter's explanation of the Cornelius incident makes this clear: "The Holy Spirit fell on them as on us *at the beginning*. . . . God gave the same gift to them as he gave to us *when we believed* in the Lord Jesus Christ" (Acts 11:15, 17). The aorist *pisteusai (epi)*, used here, always in Acts means the decisive act of faith by which one becomes a Christian. Furthermore, it should be noted that while many instances of cures and conversions are related in Luke's gospel, there is no description of the faith-act in one or more of the intimate disciples (as there is in John 2:11, for instance). Luke thus seems consistent in withholding the meaningful faith-act till Pentecost. Whatever the case for the primitive disciples, Peter's Pentecost sermon sees no delay in the gift of the Spirit upon baptism (Acts 2:38).

In the Cornelius event the Holy Spirit was given without either laying on of hands or baptism, but Peter judged that Cornelius should be subsequently baptized (10:44-48). Baptism here makes sense only if it is seen, as Peter indeed sees it, as the visible sign of belonging to the new Israel to whom the Spirit is given. If God took the initiative to give the pagans the Spirit that normally comes by baptism into the community of believers, then this important sign of their belonging is not to be denied them. The Cornelius incident complements Acts 2:38 by showing that while the gift of the Spirit normally accompanies or immediately follows baptism, it may in exceptional cases precede.

Now the case of the Samaritans appears to be a second exception to this rule, in the opposite direction, namely, the giving of the Spirit some time after baptism. There are two possible explanations for this exception. The first is that something was missing in the dispositions of the Samaritans which impeded the full normal effect of baptism. Does the text give any evidence of this? The Samaritan audience differs from others in Acts in that they are described as having been previously under the spell of Simon the Magician. The reaction to Philip is closely joined to the reaction to Simon, who is baptized along with the Samaritans but tags along with Philip more for the signs and miracles than out of genuine faith. The Samaritans, Luke says, "believed Philip" (8:12). The expression is unique in the Acts. It is not said that they believed God or the Lord (Acts 5:14; 16:34) or *in* or *on* the Lord (with *eis*: 10:42; 14:23; 19:4; with *epi*: 9:42; 11:17; 16:31; 22:19), Luke's normal expression for authentic faith. Thus there is some evidence in the text that Luke had reservations about the Samaritans' dispositions, that he felt their faith perhaps too mixed with personal infatuation with Philip and still too undifferentiated from magic to benefit from their baptism by receiving the Holy Spirit at that moment. Hence the mission of James and John was, without rebaptizing, to remove their imperfect dispositions which prevented the normal initiation rite from having its anticipated essential effect, the gift of the Spirit.

The other explanation is that Philip's mission to Samaria was not officially commissioned by the Jerusalem church and the apostles in the first place (Philip simply left Jerusalem because of persecution) and that this event was a sign that the Samaritan mission was to be "regularized" by a sign of unity with the apostles in Jerusalem. The Samaritan mission was, in fact, a significant departure from the parameters within which the Jerusalem community had worked till then. The Samaritans were not gentiles of the kind we shall meet in Cornelius. But they were not Jews either. They were a kind of "half-breed" people sharing some Jewish tradition and blood but of mixed parentage going back to the Assyrian colonization. Jews certainly did not consider them an authentic part of the chosen people. The turn of events resulting from Philip's mission presented a new question to the apostles in Jerusalem, and to Luke the reporter, for it was to the twelve that Jesus had said, "You are to be my witnesses in Jerusalem, throughout Judea and Samaria. . ." (1:8). The delay of the Spirit in Samaria, and its coming through the apostles Peter and John, permits that word of Jesus to be fulfilled.

Perhaps the combination of both these explanations is best. Luke, aware of the Samaritans' fascination with magic and magicians, used the story at one level to distinguish authentic faith and the Holy Spirit from any possible confusion with the occult or with personalities. At another level he found the story an excellent example of how the order of the mission given by the risen Lord was in fact confirmed by the events. At any rate, as far as the relation of the Holy Spirit to baptism is concerned Luke narrates the Samaritan episode as an exception, and one cannot draw from it any kind of doctrine about an essential separation of the gift of the Spirit from baptism. On the other hand we cannot say that the laying on of apostolic hands is a universal requirement for receiving the Spirit, since Cornelius receives the Spirit without the laying on of hands, and Paul received the Spirit at the hands of Ananias, a disciple (9:17-18).

This passage, like the others, illustrates the fluidity of the initiation rites at this early period. Ananias lays his hands on the yet unbaptized Saul, saying, " 'Saul, my brother, I have been sent by the Lord Jesus . . . to help you recover your sight and be filled with the Holy Spirit.' Immediately something like scales fell from his eyes and he regained his sight. He got up and was baptized" (9:17-18). On the other hand, the Ephesian disciples of John the Baptist, who had received John's baptism but had not so much as heard that there was a Holy Spirit (19:3-4) are baptized in the name of the Lord Jesus and receive the Holy Spirit when Paul lays his hands on them (19:5-6). All that we can conclude from this confusing evidence about the relationship of the Holy Spirit to baptism in the Acts is this: To become a Christian means to be baptized in the name of Jesus Christ and to receive the Holy Spirit (2:38). Normally these two moments coincide as a moral unity (2:38; 9:17-18; 19:5-6). When, by exception they are separated, either in experience or in rite, what is missing should be completed. It seems that baptism was accompanied by the laying on of hands for the gift of the Holy Spirit, but the evidence is not compelling that this was always the case. As far as the outpouring of the Spirit is concerned, it is certainly not presented as a once-but-never again event, for in Acts 4:31 the "little Pentecost" is modeled on the first, the house shakes and, just as in 2:4, it is of the same community that it is said, "they were all filled with the Holy Spirit."

The Outward Mission

It goes without saying that each new step in the church's mission is led by the Holy Spirit. The expansion of the mission to the gentiles in the Cornelius event is perhaps the most striking example. Despite Peter's resistance (10:14), he is instructed by the Spirit to cooperate in this new direction (10:19; 11:12), and the Holy Spirit falls upon the gentile audience before Peter finishes preaching (10:44). But the decision of the Antioch community to undertake the evangelization of Asia Minor was clearly the Spirit's initiative too, as Luke relates it:

Now in the church at Antioch there were prophets and teachers, Barnabas, Symeon who was called Niger, Lucius of Cyrene, Manaen a member of the court of Herod the tetrarch, and Saul. 2. While they were worshiping the Lord and fasting, the Holy Spirit said, "Set apart for me Barnabas and Saul for the work to which I have called them." 3. Then after fasting

and praying they laid their hands on them and sent them off.
    4. So, being sent out by the Holy Spirit, they went down
to Seleucia; and from there they sailed to Cyprus. (13:1-4
RSV)

On the other hand, on Paul's second journey the missionaries are twice
prevented by the Spirit from preaching in certain areas:

> 6. And they went through the region of Phrygia and Galatia,
> having been forbidden by the Holy Spirit to speak the word in
> Asia. 7. And when they had come opposite Mysia, they at-
> tempted to go into Bithynia, but the Spirit of Jesus did not
> allow them. (16:6-7 RSV)

We are given no clue here as to how the Spirit indicated the directions.
Since elsewhere in Acts the Spirit speaks through prophecy, the most
likely origin is from a prophecy either given by a Christian prophet in
the communities through which Paul and Silas passed, or received directly by one of them. The Holy Spirit of vs. 6 is called "the Spirit of
Jesus" in vs. 7, perhaps for simple variety but again underlining the real
presence of the Lord Jesus himself through the activity of his Spirit.

Apostolic Witness

    The role of witness was first understood in the sense of testifying to
the facts of the life and teaching of Jesus (10:39) and to the reality of his
resurrection (1:8, 22; 10:41; 5:31). After the imprisonment of Peter and
John and the "second Pentecost" of 4:23-31, the witnessing to the resurrection clearly meant great risk (4:33). Stephen paid for his preaching
with his life (7:54-60), so that, although he was not one of the twelve,
Paul calls him the Lord's witness (22:20). Here the meaning of
"witness" has developed from that of a testifier to events to that of
"martyr." Now if it was the power of the Holy Spirit that enabled the
apostles to bear witness (1:8; 4:29-33)—illustrated by introducing Peter's
testimony before the Sanhedrin by the words, "Then Peter, filled with
the Holy Spirit, spoke up. . ." (4:8)—this is equally true of the witness
of martyrdom. Stephen at the moment of his martyrdom is "filled with
the Holy Spirit" and granted a vision of the Son of Man in glory (7:55-
56). Luke differs from Mark in his understanding of Christian martyrdom. The passion of Jesus for Mark is all darkness. On the cross Jesus
experiences no light but only abandonment (Mk 15:34). By implication

Mark seems to be telling his readers that they should expect nothing more than to be able to pass through the trial by the power of the Holy Spirit (Mk 13:11-13). But for Luke, Jesus' last moment is one of great trust, even an experience of the presence of God (Lk 23:46). And so it is with Stephen, the account of whose martyrdom is patterned on that of Jesus (cf. esp. Acts 7:60 and Lk 23:34). If the Holy Spirit is the consoler (Acts 9:31), no one experiences his consolation more powerfully than the martyr. This is a supreme way in which the power of the Holy Spirit is given to witness (Acts 1:8). Even short of martyrdom, however, it appears from Acts that persecution and beating from without evokes an overbounding joy from within (5:41) and this is a special effect of the Holy Spirit (13:52).

The Holy Spirit and the Passion of Paul

We have seen repeatedly how Luke in his gospel presents Jesus as a prophet, that is, as a man endowed with the Spirit. We have also seen how dear to him is the image of the promised prophet-like-Moses of Deut 18:15, for in Jesus' resurrection, this prophet was "raised up" as promised. We have seen too how Jesus is presented as the new Moses who ascends to God in order to bring the Spirit to the new covenant community assembled in Jerusalem, successor to Mount Sinai. And the gift of the Spirit makes the community a community of prophets (Acts 2). Now it is most interesting to see how Paul fits this picture. Luke is aware that he is not one of the twelve. Although he has seen the risen Lord (Acts 9:1-19; 22:1-21; 26:1-23), he was not with Jesus from the time of John the Baptist, and this presents a major difficulty for Luke's theology of the new Israel. But he resolves it not only by showing abundantly that Paul's vocation was due to an intervention of the risen Lord himself but also by showing that the prophetic mission of Jesus himself was completed in Paul.

It is in the third account of Paul's conversion that this becomes clear (26:1-23). In vss. 16-18 Paul introduces and applies to himself a cluster of Old Testament texts that describe the calls of prophets:

". . . 16. Get up now and stand on your feet. I have appeared to you to designate you as my servant and as a witness to what you have seen of me and what you will see of me. 17. I have delivered you from this people and from the nations, 18. to open the eyes of those to whom I am sending you, to turn them from darkness to light. . ." (NAB)

The words, "Get up and stand on your feet" come straight from Ez 2:1-2, words addressed by the Lord to Ezekiel at the prophet's inaugural call. "To open their eyes . . . to turn them from darkness to light" (vs. 18) evokes what was said of the prophet-servant of the Lord in Is 42:7, 16, and the expression, "I have delivered you" recalls the inaugural vision of Jeremiah (1:7-8). In Luke's eyes, then, Paul is a prophet and indeed the one in whom the prophecies made of the Servant of Yahweh concerning the gentiles are fulfilled. This is confirmed when we compare Luke 4:18-19 with Mt 12:18-21. Both texts concern the mission of the servant upon whom the Spirit of the Lord rests. Matthew quotes Is 42:1-4, which mentions a mission to the gentiles. Luke selects instead a different text of Isaiah (61:1-2), one which omits mention of the gentiles. Luke is aware that it was not Jesus himself but only the apostolic church that actually brought the mission to the gentiles. The text Matthew used Luke does finally use but only in Acts *where he applies it to Paul.* Behind all this is a delicate Lukan subtlety. The Jerusalem church elaborated its understanding of Jesus in terms of the Servant of Yahweh (Acts 3:13; 4:30). Very well, Luke says; but there is one element about the prophecies of the Servant which was not fulfilled in Jesus and was fulfilled in Paul: the actual bringing of the good news of salvation to the gentiles. Paul is thus associated with Jesus most intimately, even though he is not one of the twelve. Jesus cannot be the Servant of Yahweh bringing salvation to the gentiles, nor can the church be his prophetic successor, without Paul. Paul's work is not therefore deviation: it is fulfillment.

In the closing chapters of the Acts Luke not only wants to show how the good news, as promised, reached "the ends of the earth," namely, Rome, capital of the empire (Acts 1:8). He also wishes to close the enormous circle which began in Jerusalem and encompassed Asia and Europe. In Paul's concluding return to Jerusalem Luke sees a thematic consummation and the supreme demonstration of Paul's continuity both with Jesus and with the Pentecostal Jerusalem church. Paul's final return to Jerusalem after his third missionary journey is marked at its beginning by a plot hatched against him by some Jews (20:3) shortly before the feast of the Unleavened Bread (20:6). Is Luke hinting that there is a parallel here of Paul with Jesus? Other elements suggest this. On the journey to Jerusalem there is a triple prediction of his coming sufferings (20:22-23; 21:4, 10-14), just as there was of Jesus in the gospel. In the last of these, Paul says, "I am ready not only to be imprisoned but even to die at Jerusalem for the name of the Lord Jesus!" (21:13). Now Luke, who knows well that Paul will not die in Jerusalem, must have had some reason for connecting the prospect of Paul's death with Jerusalem by including this saying. The most obvious explanation is the parallelism he wishes to draw between Paul and Jesus—and the contrast with pre-Pentecostal discipleship represented by Peter who, prior to Jesus' passion, says the same thing: "Lord, at your side I am prepared to face imprisonment and even death itself" (Lk 22:33). Peter's boast is followed at once by Jesus' prediction of Peter's denial, which is in fact reported at the trial scene. No such failure on Paul's part is expected or reported—suggesting that Paul will demonstrate the principle that now with the gift of the Holy Spirit, the disciple can witness faithfully in Jerusalem or at the "ends of the earth" (Acts 1:8). Instead of infidelity, the disciple's total identification with the Jesus of the Passion is confirmed by the next verse: "Since he [Paul] would not be dissuaded, we said nothing further except, 'The Lord's will be done' " (Acts 21:14), which recalls Jesus' similar submission to the Father's will (Lk 22:42).

But Jerusalem also represents the Jewish origin of the church and the place of the original outpouring of the Spirit on the first Christian Pentecost. Paul's return there for the feast of Pentecost would, for Luke, complete the circle and show the deep continuity of Paul's gentile mission with that first outpouring. It is not unlikely, then, that Luke is trying to make just this point when he records that Paul bypassed Ephesus "for he was eager to get to Jerusalem by the feast of Pentecost if at all possible" (20:16).

If Paul is to suffer in Jerusalem on or about the feast of Pentecost, as Jesus did on or about the feast of Passover (cf. Lk 22:1-2), it will demonstrate, toward the end of Acts, the truth of Jesus' words at the beginning, that the Holy Spirit, received on Pentecost, would make the disciples his witnesses (1:8), for witnessing is exactly what Paul does in Jerusalem (23:11). As a matter of fact, Luke's first mention of Paul's coming passion puts the journey under the seal of the Holy Spirit: "But now, as you see, I am on my way to Jerusalem, *compelled by the Spirit*. . ." (20:22). The word here translated *compelled* is literally, "chained, bound." Paul is going to be able to do what Jesus did in Jerusalem, because he has Jesus' Spirit and this Spirit has him literally "bound" for Jerusalem.

The other warnings along the way also come from the Holy Spirit. After Agabus prophesies by the Holy Spirit the fate that awaits Paul, the people of Caesarea try to keep him from going to Jerusalem (21:10-12). Earlier, at Tyre, the text even indicates that the attempt was inspired by the Spirit (probably through prophecy): "Under the Spirit's prompting, they tried to tell Paul that he should not go up to Jerusalem" (21:4). Paul is not dissuaded. Here is an illustration of the need for prophecy to be discerned, even when it apparently comes from the Holy

Spirit (1 Cor 14:29; 1 Thes 5:21). It must also be interpreted in the light
of Paul's earlier judgment that it is precisely the Holy Spirit that is leading him bound to Jerusalem (20:22). Paul sticks by his first judgment,
that he is being led to his passion by the Holy Spirit.

As events turn out, Jerusalem is indeed the place where Paul is
chained (22:33) and his life is endangered by the mob (22:30-36). Like
Jesus, he is brought before high priest and Sanhedrin (22:30), where his
life is again endangered (23:10). But Paul is not killed there. Instead, to
Paul's surprise, the Lord appears to him at night and says, "Keep up
your courage! Just as you have borne witness to me here in Jerusalem,
so must you do in Rome!" (23:11). Thus, for all his description of Paul's
ascent to Jerusalem in passion terms, Luke is faithful to the course of
events.

The Acts do not describe Paul's death in Rome. Some take this as
an indication that Luke finished his work before Paul's Roman martyrdom. This is hard to demonstrate, and it may just as well be that the
suffering in Jerusalem lent itself to greater parallels with that of Jesus
and that Luke was satisfied that once Paul arrives in Rome the plan of
the Acts was completed: by the power of the Holy Spirit, the witnesses
have testified in Jerusalem, Samaria, and now at the "ends of the earth"
(1:8).

Conclusion

So rich has been the pneumatology of Luke that as we draw these
three chapters to a close it would be irreverent to suggest they could be
briefly summarized. Suffice it to recall that Luke, more than any of the
evangelists, considers the age of salvation to be the age of the Spirit.
This appears first in the emphatic role he gives to the Holy Spirit in the
life and ministry of Jesus, in which he alone enjoys the Spirit, and then in
the church which receives that same Spirit after Jesus' ascension and
lives by it while Jesus is in heaven. Christian discipleship involves, in addition to other traditional elements, an entering into the prayer of Jesus
through the power of the Holy Spirit. The disciples are endowed with
Jesus' own charismatic power. But the seal of the Spirit upon the authenticity of discipleship in Luke, as in Mark, is the power to witness to
Jesus even unto death.

The Christian community is therefore primarily a prophetic community, and the Spirit is the spirit of prophecy, taken in its widest sense.
If Jesus is the Spirit-anointed servant of Isaiah 61 who opens the age of

salvation, the church is the community of the Spirit foretold by Joel. The Jewish feast of Pentecost offered Luke rich motifs which he exploited for interpreting what the gift of the Spirit means for the church. It is the new covenant of the Spirit given from the heavenly Sinai in tongues that proclaim in a single message intelligible to all the nations of the earth the saving event of Jesus Christ and the end of the curse of Babel.

24
The Discreet Pneumatology
of Matthew

Though Matthew comes first in the present order of our New Testament, it is highly unlikely that the gospel in its present form was written first. On the contrary, in its present form it is best understood as an artistic masterpiece written around the 80's of our era by a man who had at his disposition some version of Mark, plus a wealth of the sayings of Jesus (a source also available to Luke and called by the specialists 'Q' after the German *Quelle*, "source"), plus some materials to which Matthew alone seems to have had access. To make room for the abundant "sayings" of Jesus, Matthew often pares Mark's narrative detail to a minimum, focusing only on the essential and, in the narrative material, often highlighting the dialogue between Jesus and others in order to portray a lesson about faith or discipleship or even about Jesus himself.

The gospel as a whole, and its particular teaching on the Spirit, gain perspective if we have some idea of what was happening in Matthew's church. The gospel was, more than any other, a response to a crisis. The Christian Jewish community was no longer enjoying the halcyon days of which Luke had glowingly written, when the first Christians were held in esteem by their fellow Jews (Acts 2:27) and the church throughout Judea, Galilee and Samaria was at peace (Acts 9:31). The Romans had come and destroyed the temple in 70 A.D. and with it successfully dissolved every Jewish group except the Pharisees—and the Christians, but these could hardly be called a "Jewish" group any longer. Under the leadership of the rabbis, Pharisaic Judaism was determined to rid itself of any Christian ties. One simply could not be, in their minds, a Jew and a Christian. Jews who professed to be Christians were denied admittance to the synagogue—and this meant more than exclusion from a given building on the sabbath. It also meant for many that a decision had to be made between family loyalties and belief in Jesus. For those who chose Jesus, it also involved other social pressures and economic ones as well. Christian discipleship became a costly thing, the pearl of great price (Mt 13:45-46).

These outward pressures were not without their effects within Matthew's church, which was divided in its prophetic leadership (7:15; 24:11), confused about how really compelling the high moral teaching of Jesus was (5:20; 7:21-23) and paralyzed by polarization and even mutual betrayal (10:21). Matthew's community seems to have experienced the fulfillment of Jesus' prophecy, related only by Matthew, that "because of the increase of evil, the charity of many will grow cold" (24:13). In the midst of all this, many of the "little ones," Matthew's term for Christian believers, were going astray (18:13-14).

In responding to this crisis Matthew does several things. First, his gospel is a clarion call back to the basics—and the basics are the *words* of Jesus, the only solid foundation on which the Church can build (7:24-27). These words of Jesus are the fulfillment of the Old Law (5:17-18), which still has its validity (5:18; 23:2-3; 24:20) but only according to the interpretation Jesus gives it. This interpretation differs radically from that of the scribes and the Pharisees (23:1-39). It insists on the primacy of charity, on which the whole Law depends (7:12; 9:13; 12:7; 19:19; 22:39-40) and at times goes beyond the Old Law (5:21-48). Jesus' words are, in fact, the New Law, a command which is final (28:20).

Secondly, since the words of Jesus need to be proclaimed and interpreted afresh for the new situation, Matthew calls for a recognition of the authority of the first disciples and their successors. They are given the power to bind and to loose (16:19; 18:18), that is, to decide authoritatively for the community. The rock on which the church is founded is not only the word of Jesus (7:24-27) but Peter himself to whom the keys of the kingdom are delivered (16:18-19). If Peter was in fact dead at the time Matthew wrote his gospel, then Matthew's reason for giving so much importance to this passage must have been the need for agreement about post-Petrine authority in the church. At any rate, Matthew is concerned to protect the early disciples from any suspicion of misunderstanding the teaching of Jesus, for while he does not hesitate to portray their weak faith at times (8:26; 14:31; 17:20), he insists on their clear understanding (Mt 13:11, 51). These early disciples and their successors were the teachers in the Matthean church and, as we shall see, in the midst of much false prophecy it was important to buttress the authority of the early witnesses close to the historical Jesus and the apostolic tradition they handed on.

Thirdly, in response to creeping laxism, Matthew holds up the righteousness that must exceed that of the scribes and Pharisees (5:20), the love that must extend even to enemies (5:43-48), the importance of avoiding scandal (18:5-10) and the command of fraternal correction (18:15-18).

On the other hand, and fourthly, against those rigorists who, shocked at the weaknesses of their fellow Christians, wanted to make the church such a society of the perfect that there would be no room for sinners, Matthew incorporated two parables not found in Mark or Luke —that of the weeds among the wheat (13:24-30, 36-43) and that of the net (13:47-50), both of which urged leaving the final judgment of sinners to God and the angels at the end of time.

The Spirit and Jesus

We are finally in a position to understand Matthew's interpretation of the tradition about the Spirit, and it should cause little surprise to find it fitting into the pattern we have just seen. It causes Matthew no embarrassment to present Jesus in his traditional relationship to the Spirit. Conceived by the Holy Spirit (1:18, 20), he is announced by John as the one who will baptize with the Holy Spirit (3:11). He is overshadowed by the Spirit of God at his baptism (3:16) and is led into the desert by the Spirit to be tempted by the devil (4:1). Like Mark and Luke, Matthew presents Jesus' ministry not only as preaching and teaching but also healing and delivering (4:23; 9:35). If, on the other hand, Matthew takes Mark's simple report that Jesus teaches with authority (Mk 1:22) and illustrates it by the entire Sermon on the Mount (cf. Mt 7:28-29), he is even clearer than Mark in paralleling Jesus' words with deeds, framing the whole complex of chapters 5-9 with the note: "And he went about . . . teaching in their synagogues and preaching the gospel of the kingdom and healing every disease and every infirmity. . ." (4:23; 9:35). Elsewhere Matthew follows the healing traditions of Mark and Q (14:36; 15:29-31), which point to Jesus' fulfillment of Old Testament prophecies (11:2-6), omitting the cure of the deaf-mute with spittle (Mk 7:31-37) and of the blind man in stages (8:22-26) in order to stress instead the power of Jesus' word in the healing process (8:16) and the immediacy of its effect (15:28; 21:19). One significant point at which Matthew departs from the tradition is at 21:14. Neither Mark nor Luke describes any cure worked by Jesus in Jerusalem, for reasons we have seen above. But Matthew, after describing Jesus' cleansing of the temple, immediately adds:

14. The blind and the lame came to him in the temple and he cured them. 15. The chief priests and the scribes became indignant when they observed the wonders that he worked, and how the children were shouting out in the temple precincts, "Ho-

sanna to the Son of David!" 16. "Do you hear what they are saying?" they asked him. Jesus said to them, "Of course I do! Did you never read this, 'From the speech of infants and children you have framed a hymn of praise'?" (21:14-16 NAB)

The "blind and the lame" were excluded by Lev 21:18 from the priesthood and hence from any ministry in the temple. The money changers, who had carried on their business with the priests' blessing, are now replaced by persons the Law excluded from ministry. In 2 Sam 5:6-8, the blind and the lame are said to be excluded from the house (of the Lord, LXX) because they supposedly had opposed David's taking of Jerusalem and thus incurred his hatred. Here, however, the Son of David acclaimed by the children shows his superiority to his father David not only by admitting the blind and the lame to the house of the Lord but by reinstating them to health and thus to a right to full participation in the community of the Lord.

While Mark and Luke apparently considered Jerusalem as a whole unworthy of signs because of its lack of faith, Matthew carefully distinguishes. Jesus does work signs there—in the midst of the temple—and the faithful response of children only serves to contrast more blatantly the blindness of the chief priests and the scribes—a point to which we shall return when considering Matthew's understanding of the blasphemy against the Holy Spirit.

The one proper Matthean text which introduces the Spirit occurs in 12:15-21:

15. Jesus, aware of this, withdrew from there. And many followed him, and he healed them all, 16. and ordered them not to make him known. 17. This was to fulfill what was spoken by the prophet Isaiah:

18. "Behold, my servant whom I have chosen,
    my beloved with whom my soul is well pleased.
    I will put my Spirit upon him,
    and he shall proclaim justice to the Gentiles.
19. He will not wrangle or cry aloud,
    nor will any one hear his voice in the streets;
20. he will not break a bruised reed
    or quench a smoldering wick,
    till he brings justice to victory;
21. and in his name will the Gentiles hope." (RSV)

Matthew has drastically reduced the material which he found in Mark here (Mk 3:7-12), eliminating entirely the exorcisms and the confession by the unclean spirits, "You are the Son of God." He limits the charismatic description to healings and he is concerned to explain, as Mark does not, why Jesus suppressed notoriety about his mighty deeds. Matthew finds the reason for this in the text from Isaiah (freely translated from the Hebrew) which describes a gentle and not a noisy Messiah. The text's inclusion of the words, "I will put my Spirit upon him" should not therefore be pressed, because it was simply part of the text Matthew used, a text we already know from 3:17. On the other hand, in showing Jesus as endowed by the Spirit, the Matthean text prepares the reader in a way that Mark and Luke do not, for the next section about the spirit by which Jesus expels demons (12:22-30) and the blasphemy against the Holy Spirit (12:31-32). If Matthew's central theme is the kingdom, then 12:28 has a central thematic purpose in the gospel: "If it is by the Spirit of God that I cast out demons, then the kingdom of God has come upon you." The sense here is that the exorcisms and the healings (both combined in the *healing* of the *demoniac* which precipitates the controversy, 12:22) bring the kingdom to visibility (as Paul also said of the charisms which he called *manifestations* of the Spirit, 1 Cor 12:7). The Son of Man, in his humility and suffering, may be misunderstood, and rejection of him is forgivable (12:32), but to resist the obvious work of the Spirit is to sin against the light, and this sin is unforgivable (12:32) because as long as one sins against the light he never asks forgiveness.

Is this a reference to the resistance of the Pharisees to the signs Jesus worked during his ministry, or to the signs the disciples work after the resurrection? The more obvious meaning of the text is the former, but the latter is surely not excluded. For Matthew habitually superimposes postresurrectional situations of the church upon the life-time of Jesus (see especially chapter 10). The point for Matthew's church thus seems to be: healings and exorcisms done by the Spirit of God are signs of the inbreaking of God's kingdom. To attribute these, whether worked by Jesus or by his disciples in his name, to Satan is to sin against the Holy Spirit. Matthew's judgment apparently is that this is what the Pharisees of Jesus' day were doing—and even more so those of Matthew's day—with the result that there was no longer any hope of winning them over. This would give excellent sense to the saying interposed in 12:30: "He who is not with me is against me, and he who does not gather with me scatters"—a far cry from Mark's conciliatory, "He that is not against us is for us" (Mk 9:40) said of the strange exorcist, a story which Matthew omits. One can no longer belong to the Pharisees and to

Jesus. Nor can one harbor any other loyalties at the expense of his loyalty to Jesus, because, given the already obvious manifestations of the Spirit, one must either align with Jesus and the Holy Spirit or with the Pharisees who oppose the Holy Spirit.

The sequence about the sign of Jonah (12:38-42) and the return of the unclean spirit (12:43-45) simply pursues the same theme of the disbelief of "this generation" and heightens the likelihood that Matthew is envisaging the sin against the Spirit as the disbelief of the Jewish nation after the resurrection. For if Jesus' ministry was the casting out of the evil spirit from Israel by the Spirit of God, the return of the evil spirit through disbelief after the resurrection renders the state of the disbelieving generation worse than before.

The Spirit and the Church

Up to this point it has been clear that Matthew understands the Spirit to be linked to the person and ministry of Jesus. What about the disciples? Do they receive his Spirit in the way they do, for example, in Acts? In Mt 10:1-8 Jesus gives the disciples authority (*exousia*) to proclaim the kingdom, cure and deliver exactly as he did, and after the resurrection this authority is extended to teaching (28:19-20). There is no mention of a conveying of the Spirit in this commissioning. The word of Jesus apparently suffices in both cases. There is, curiously, no account of the return of the disciples from this mission, so that there is no report of their charismatic success—as there is in Luke 10:17-20. This is quite possibly due to the fact that Matthew knows, at the time of his writing, that the church's mission to Israel failed. In any case the result is that Matthew's focus never really leaves Jesus, who continues to be the unique wonderworker and teacher throughout. Moreover, though full authority and understanding is given the disciples, by asserting their constant need for faith, and periodically showing their weakness in faith and their resultant lack of charismatic success (8:26; 14:31; 16:8; 17:20), Matthew succeeds in keeping the figure of Jesus central as the unique charismatic wonderworker. Thus, while it is said that Jesus casts out devils by the Spirit of God (12:28), such a statement is never made of the disciples. Instead, they exorcise in the name of *Jesus* (7:22). The only place where the Spirit is said to work in the disciples is in the guarantee that when they are called to witness before rulers and kings "the Spirit of your Father will be speaking in you" (10:20).

What, then, can we say of Matthew's ecclesial pneumatology? In place of Luke's emphasis on the presence and power of the Holy Spirit we have the presence and power of the risen Lord Jesus himself living and acting in his church. It is significant that there is no ascension nor Pentecost related by Matthew. Instead there is only the appearance of Jesus to his disciples on the mountain in Galilee, an appearance without any conclusion or departure. The glorious, risen Lord virtually merges with the disciples being missioned, for he does not say, "I give *you* authority" (as he had said in 10:1) but rather, "Full authority has been given to *me* . . . go, therefore, and make disciples. . ." (28:18-19). The mission of the disciples is simply the execution of the full authority of the risen Lord. Moreover, the final words are, "I am with you until the end of the world" (28:20).

What appears explicitly here at the end of the gospel is projected earlier throughout it in many ways, especially by the fact that Jesus' disciples address him from early in his ministry as "Lord" (8:21, 25, etc.). Jesus himself is wherever his disciples gather in his name (18:20). The crowds celebrate not only Jesus' forgiving and healing power but the power given to *men*, the disciples, to do such wonderful things (9:8).

To put the case extremely: Jesus does not need the Holy Spirit to mediate his presence to the church, for he never really left it. To explain: Matthew no doubt knew of the tradition of the Holy Spirit as the gift of the risen Lord. But he also knew that for the Spirit of Jesus to be in the church was simply for Jesus himself to be there in a way as real as his physical presence among his disciples. Since in the tradition the Spirit's presence and Jesus' spiritual presence were interchangeable concepts, Matthew opted for the personal presence of the risen Lord himself, and he says nothing about the Spirit mediating that presence.

Why? The reason is not difficult to find. Matthew was writing for a divided community, a community in turmoil. There was much false prophecy abroad, and the false prophets, doubtless like those of Jeremiah's time, claimed to be moved by the Spirit of God. So the mere claim to the Spirit was insufficient to discern true prophecy from false. What signs of discernment, then, were there?

Discerning the Spirit in a Divided Community

Matthew's central discerning sign is Jesus himself. It is upon him that the Spirit rests (3:16; 12:18). If the church has the Spirit, it is only because she has Jesus. Or, to put it another way, it is not because of the Spirit that she has Jesus (Luke's view) but because of Jesus that she has the Spirit. Now this may seem a stuffy academic distinction, but it will appear less so if we recall the crisis of false prophecy Matthew had to deal with and the probability that some Christians were, under pretense of inspiration by the Holy Spirit, promoting a relaxation of the ethic of Jesus while others urged a retreat from Jesus back to the leadership of the Pharisees. Rooting the Spirit totally in Jesus was a way of excluding any possibility of meaningful charismatic activity outside the community that is gathered around Jesus as Lord. Matthew's omission of the story about the exorcist who casts out devils in Jesus' name but does not belong to the company of the disciples (Mk 9:38-41; Lk 9:49-50) is a tacit attempt to solidify the ranks of the church in a time of chaos.

But it is especially in dealing with prophecy that Matthew's concern reveals itself. The community was one in which prophecy was not only widely exercised but had become an identifiable office, both for service within the community and for missionary work too (10:41; 23:34). However, there were either pretenders to the office or abusers of it. The warning about false prophets concerns not only the final times (24:11, 24) but even the present: "Beware of false prophets who come to you in sheep's clothing but inwardly they are ravenous wolves" (7:15). The fact that they are Christians (they wear sheep's clothing) is not sufficient to discern their true nature. Thus Matthew must introduce another touchstone of discernment, and this he does with the passage immediately added: "By their fruits you will know them . . ." (7:16-20). The same passage that appears in Luke as a general teaching is applied in Matthew specifically to prophecy. What is meant by "their fruits" is clarified in the sequence:

21. "Not everyone who says to me, 'Lord, Lord,' shall enter the kingdom of heaven, but he who does the will of my Father in heaven. 22. On that day many will say to me, 'Lord, Lord, did we not prophesy in your name, and cast out demons in your name, and do many mighty works in your name?' 23. And then will I declare to them, 'I never knew you; depart from me, you evildoers.' " (7:21-23 RSV)

Thus authentic charismatic activity bears the seal of ethical holiness about it. Prophecy and healing and exorcising even in the name of Jesus can be carried on without paying any attention to the ethical demands of Jesus as given in the Sermon on the Mount immediately preceding this passage. But the Christian charismatic is authenticated by a life of personal holiness. For Matthew the authentic prophet is, like the authentic disciple, also a just man (10:40-42; 13:17). If the result of false prophecy is that the charity of many grows cold (24:12), we may infer that the role of true prophecy is to build up the community in love—a point on which Matthew would agree with Paul.

We may conclude that Matthew's pneumatology is very much conditioned by his historical situation. On the positive side he emphasizes Jesus' possession of the Spirit manifested in his charismatic activity. This power is given to the disciples but not explicitly as the Holy Spirit but as *authority* (10:1). At the very end of the gospel the disciples are commanded to baptize in the name of the Father and of the Son and of the Holy Spirit (28:19). This formula comes as a surprise, because the trinitarian direction in which it points could not at all be suspected from the rest of the gospel. It reflects an advanced liturgical tradition beyond the simple practice of baptizing in the name of Jesus (Acts 2:38; 8:12; 19:5). But it is no less authentically biblical. It shows an incipient realization of the personhood and equality of the Holy Spirit in a way that no other New Testament text does. We would like to know where this formula originated and what it meant concretely for the church's understanding of the Holy Spirit at that time. The Holy Spirit is connected with the sacrament and there is no explicit indication of an expectation of charismatic manifestation (as there is in Luke-Acts). The manifestation of authentic discipleship is rather in observing all that Jesus has commanded (28:20). While Matthew's community is demonstrably charismatic, there is need, in the present crisis, to discern and regulate charismatic activity by the norms of the confession of Jesus combined with ethical holiness and the promotion of charity. Matthew is thus related to the charismatic tradition preceding him much the same way as the book of Deuteronomy was related to the Deuteronomic history which it prefaced—the primacy of the word of God and the ethical will of God in Deuteronomy provided a discerning norm for the more ambiguous charismatic activity in the Deuteronomic history.

Beyond that, Matthew is so convinced of the presence of the risen Lord in his church that he avoids cluttering the purity of that insight by presenting the Spirit as the medium of that presence. If Jesus' presence in his church is mediated, it is rather through his word and through the teaching authority of the chosen disciples, which, like his own presence, will continue to the end of the world (5:17; 24:35; 10:40; 16:18-19; 18:18).

25
The Spirit in James, Jude, 1 and 2 Peter and Hebrews

These letters are being considered together because they are the only remaining literature of the New Testament to be examined before scaling the two final peaks of Revelation and John. Moreover, their pastoral concerns are not so diverse among themselves as to make this cluster without common interest.

The Letter of James

In the letter of James there is only one passage in which the word *pneuma* appears. In 4:5, speaking of the Christian's separation from worldly desires, James writes: "Whoever wishes to be a friend of the world makes himself an enemy of God. Or do you suppose it is in vain that the Scripture says, 'He yearns jealously over the spirit which he has made to dwell in us'?" (4:4-5 RSV). The NAB translates the latter phrase differently: " 'The spirit he has implanted in us tends toward jealousy.' " Gramatically this is possible, but the better sense is that God loves the spirit of life (and of grace too, no doubt) which he has planted in us, and he does not want it to be shared with false gods or values. No one has been able to identify conclusively the origin of the quotation from "Scripture." It is possibly a lost variant from a Greek version of the Old Testament, or it could be a citation from an apocryphal work.

The Letter of Jude

The short letter of Jude has likewise only one passage which mentions the Spirit, though the word *pneuma* appears there twice:

17. You must remember, beloved, the predictions of the apos-

tles of our Lord Jesus Christ; 18. they said to you, "In the last
time there will be scoffers, following their own ungodly passions." 19. It is these who set up divisions, worldly people,
devoid of the Spirit. 20. But you, beloved, build yourselves up
on your most holy faith; *pray in the Holy Spirit;* 21. keep
yourselves in the love of God; wait for the mercy of our Lord
Jesus Christ unto eternal life. (NAB)

With the exception of the word "most holy," this passage sounds
very Pauline: the identification of worldly people (*psychikoi*) as those
not having the Spirit (*pneuma*), which recalls the Apostle's classic distinction on this subject in 1 Cor 2:14-16; the tendency to work Father,
Son and Spirit into the lists of gifts or attitudes; "building up" the community on faith (Col 2:7; 1 Thes 5:11); and praying in the Spirit (1 Cor
14:15-16; Rom 8:26-27). What is significant is the close relationship here
between this "praying in the Holy Spirit" and "building yourselves up in
your holy faith." Paul in 1 Corinthians had spoken of the upbuilding
power of prayer in the Spirit (1 Cor 14:4). There he meant tongues. We
cannot be certain whether that restricted a meaning is intended here. We
can say in any case that Jude understands the building up of the community in faith to be promoted in a unique way by praying in the Holy
Spirit.

The First Letter of Peter

For our purposes we can accept the widely held position that this
letter incorporates a baptismal exhortation which may have originally
been used in the liturgy of initiation (1:3-4:11), and that the substance of
the letter comes from the apostle Peter but that he used Silvanus as a
secretary, as the letter itself suggests (5:12), so that the formal composition was the work of the latter. This Silvanus, or Silas for short, had
been a companion of Paul (1 Thes 1:1; 2 Thes 1:1; 2 Cor 1:19 and Acts
passim), a fact which may explain the large number of Pauline expressions which appear in the work.
    The letter begins with an address to its readers as the "elect" or
"chosen" (1:1), and this title is then qualified by a remarkable triadic
formula. The election was *according to* the foreknowledge of the Father,
in the sanctification by the Spirit, *for* obedience to Jesus Christ and purification with his blood (1:2). Christian initiation is called a consecrating by the Spirit. If the Father is the origin of the action and union with
Jesus Christ the goal of it, the Spirit is the agent, and his activity is

sanctification. Although the "Trinitarian" combination is new, the elements themselves already appeared in Paul, and this is as true for "sanctification by the Spirit" as for the other elements (2 Thes 2:13; 1 Cor 6:11).

In 1:11 the Spirit of the Old Testament prophets is identified as the Spirit of *Christ*. Peter takes the Old Testament tradition that the prophets spoke by the spirit of God, identifies this spirit with the spirit of the coming Messiah, and says that it was this spirit of the Messiah which inspired the prophets to foretell his sufferings and his glory. This is quite a telescoping of what we have seen to be a very long development. But it also shows that in the latter third of the first century Christians had so much appropriated the Old Testament to Christ and so exalted his divine character that the Spirit belonged as much to him as to the Father, and that even those prophetic activities which preceded the incarnation and the redemption could be attributed to *his* Spirit.[1] Perhaps the theological implications of this homiletical exposition should not be pressed. It is nonetheless remarkable that in this view the Spirit of Christ appears on the stage of history before Christ does, whereas other New Testament evidence we have seen points to Christ as the giver of the Spirit. To resolve this seeming paradox it is necessary to remove the rigid chronological categories by which we sometimes try to comprehend salvation history and to adopt the view, elaborated by Paul, that Christian grace and faith were already operative in an implicit way prior to the incarnation, as the case of Abraham clearly shows (Rom 4:1-12; Gal 3:6-8). That the Old Testament prophecies were indeed the work of the Spirit of *Christ* may not have been realized when they were uttered, but that relationship is transparent now, because the proclamation of the events fulfilling those prophecies has been done in the power of the Holy Spirit sent from heaven (1:12). This is a clear allusion to the Pentecost event, interpreted by Peter as Christ's pouring out upon the church the Spirit he has received from the Father (Acts 2:33). The glorification of Jesus in his resurrection-ascension is thus the implicit link which makes it possible to say that the Spirit of God is the Spirit of Christ and to attribute all the activities of the Spirit, even Old Testament prophecy, to the Spirit of Christ. The prophetic spirit and the spirit upon the Messiah are totally identified. The continuity of the New Testament with the Old is thus assured not only because the same God speaks in both but also because the same Spirit acts in both.

---

[1]So also in 1 Clement 22:1, a quotation from Ps 34:11-17 is introduced by the words: "All these things are confirmed by faith in Christ, for he himself through the Holy Spirit encourages us as follows."

The author's treatment of the mystery of Christ's death and resurrection (3:18) reflects motifs we have seen in Paul, with a sharpening of the flesh-spirit antithesis: "Put to death in the flesh, he was given life in the spirit." The thought seems to be similar to Romans 1:4, which describes the mystery in its human element as the *flesh*, in its divine element as the *spirit*. By his resurrection Christ became life-giving Spirit (1 Cor 15:45). But the sequence in 1 Pet 3:19 has a curious phrase: "It was in the spirit also that he went to preach to the spirits in prison" (NAB) or "in which [spirit] he went and preached to the spirits in prison" (RSV). What spirits are these? The text explains: "They had disobeyed as long ago as Noah's day, while God patiently awaited until the ark was built" (3:20 NAB). Efforts to deal with this difficult text have had varied degrees of success. Some exegetes interpret these "spirits" as the souls of the sinful men of all times (sinners as far back as Noah's time), the "dead" of 4:6 to whom the gospel is preached. Hence between his death and resurrection Christ went to Hades to proclaim his victory to those imprisoned there and to liberate them. But other exegetes rightly point out that such spirits are "disobedient," that the word "proclaim" (*ekēryxen*) has no object and is different from "preaching the good news" (lit., *euēngelesthē*, "evangelized") of 4:6. They think it more likely that the "spirits" are the angelic spirits which, according to the apocryphal Book of Jubilees tempted the sons of Noah (*Jub.* 10) and according to the Book of Enoch were imprisoned in the second heaven (2 Enoch 7:1-5; 1 Enoch 21:6; 67:4). Christ, raised in the Spirit, passes them on his way to heaven and announces his triumph: "He went (same verb as in 3:19) to heaven and is at God's right hand, with angelic rulers and powers subject to him" (3:22). This seems the better interpretation, and it fits well the consolation Peter intends for his hearers—Christ by his resurrection "in the Spirit" has conquered all sin and disobedience and evil spirits.

The "dead" of 4:6 to whom the good news is preached are those Christians who, having believed it, are now dead (cf. 1 Thes 4:13ff). Though in the eyes of men they appear lost, they will experience the resurrection. Such is the meaning of the flesh-spirit contrast in this verse.

Finally, in 4:14 we read, "Happy are you when you are insulted for the name of Christ, for then the Spirit of glory and of God has come to rest upon you." According to Mt 5:11-12, those who are persecuted for Jesus' sake are blessed. The Acts describe the actual suffering as a source of joy (Acts 5:41) and the face of the martyr as already transformed by heavenly glory (6:15) because he is filled with the Holy Spirit (7:55). Here Peter borrows the language of Is 11:2 concerning the Messiah ("the Spirit of God will rest upon him," LXX) to express the same tradition. The one persecuted for the name of Christ is guaranteed not only the words with which to respond but the power and the protection of God's *shekinah* which is his own Spirit.

The pneumatology of 1 Peter is merely an enrichment of the tradition we have met elsewhere, especially in Paul. The same is true of 1 Pet 2:5: "Like living stones be yourselves built into a spiritual house, to be a holy priesthood, to offer spiritual sacrifices. . . ," which echoes 1 Cor 3:16-17 (and Eph 2:22). Peter is unique in calling the spirit of the Old Testament prophets the Spirit of Christ, and he beautifully portrays the Christian witness overshadowed by the Spirit of divine glory.

The Second Letter of Peter

One should consult the commentaries for further detail on the authorship and date of this letter. There is only one passage here concerning the Spirit but it is an important one:

> 20. . . . no prophecy of scripture is a matter of one's own interpretation, 21. because no prophecy ever came by the impulse of man, but men moved by the Holy Spirit spoke from God. (2 Pet 1:20-21 RSV)

Since this admonition introduces a warning against false prophets and teachers in the church (2:1-22) it is clearly intended to correct an abuse of Scripture texts by false teachers in the church. By the time 2 Peter was written "Scripture" meant not only the Old Testament but New Testament writings as well, such as Paul's letters, for the same abuse is referred to later when the author states: "There are certain passages [in Paul's letters] that are hard to understand. The ignorant and the unstable distort them (*just as they do the rest of Scripture*) to their own ruin" (3:16).

Now if we were in the climate of Paul to the Corinthians, we would have the principle stated something like this: "Since the prophecies of the Scripture were inspired by the Holy Spirit, you need the Holy Spirit to interpret them" (cf. 1 Cor 2:10-16). But the second half of the proposition is missing. Instead there is an exclusion of private interpretation and the author goes immediately into his warning against false teachers. Private interpretation does not have the guarantee of divine authority or of being inspired by the Holy Spirit. What does? The author does not say. However, he himself certainly speaks authoritatively concerning the false teachers (2:1-22), making ample use of Scripture. This and his commendation of apostolic authority in 1:12-18 suggests that the interpretation of Scriptural prophecy in the church is to be discerned by its conformity to the apostolic tradition and recognized apostolic authority and not simply by the individual's claim to have a gift of prophecy, interpretation or teaching. There is no doubt that this passage reflects an attempt to cope with a pneumaticism gone rampant. It comes down hard on the side of apostolic authority as the haven where, amid the storm, the church will find the Spirit.

The Letter to the Hebrews

The question of the authorship of this letter need not detain us here. Suffice it to say that it was composed by a brilliant Hellenistic Jew as an encouragement to Jewish Christians to hold fast amid persecution for their faith in Jesus Christ. That the addressees were former Jewish "priests" (cf. Acts 6:7), some of whom may have even been Essenes, has been suggested on the basis of the letter's great interest in the Old Testament cult and resemblances with the Qumran literature.

In many ways the understanding of the Spirit in Hebrews is traditional. God is once called the "Father of spirits," an expression we already met in Num 16:22; 27:16, a priestly tradition. The Old Testament is considered the voice of the Holy Spirit (3:7; 9:8; 10:15), and God who spoke in times past through the prophets has now spoken in his Son (1:1-2).

One of the major themes of the letter is the superiority of the priesthood of Jesus Christ to the priesthood and the cult of the Old Testament. The expression *ephapax*, "once for all" (7:27; 9:12; 10:10), reinforces the uniqueness of the sacrifice of Calvary. Similarly, the word "eternal" is frequently used to underline the permanent effect of that sacrifice (5:9; 6:2; 9:12, 14, 15; 13:20). It is in that connection that the author speaks of the "eternal spirit" in 9:14:

> 13. For if the blood of goats and bulls and the sprinkling of a heifer's ashes can sanctify those who are defiled so that their flesh is cleansed, 14. how much more will the blood of Christ, who through the eternal spirit offered himself up unblemished to God, cleanse our consciences from dead works to serve the living God! (NAB)

The mention of the "eternal spirit" makes one think at once of the Holy Spirit, the everlasting consolation given by the Father and the Lord

Jesus Christ (2 Thes 2:16). However, this is to read another perspective into the author's thought here. Rhetorically "the eternal spirit" here contrasts with the flesh that is cleansed by the old sacrifices (vs. 13). The contrast earthly-heavenly is at work here, just as it is in the broader view of the whole letter where the "flesh" is used to characterize Jesus' earthly life (2:14; 5:7; 10:20). The "spirit" would then characterize his risen life which he now enjoys and which is the power out of which he exercises his eternal priesthood. The "eternal spirit" would then correspond to the "power of a life that cannot be destroyed" of 7:16, which is contrasted with the levitical priesthood based on fleshly descendence. Here, the "eternal spirit" then does not mean the Holy Spirit or the self or Jesus' divine nature. It means the sphere of existence in which the exalted Jesus presents his sacrifice eternally to the Father. This identification of the risen Lord with the realm of spirit is Pauline (1 Cor 15:45; 2 Cor 3:17-18), but the application of this identification to the heavenly sacrifice is proper to the author of the letter to the Hebrews.

Let us turn now to a text explicitly mentioning the Holy Spirit. In chapter 2, after exhorting his readers not to neglect "a salvation as great as ours," the author adds:

> 3. ... Announced first by the Lord, it was confirmed to us by those who had heard him. 4. God then gave witness to it by signs, wonders, varied works of power and distribution of [the gifts of] the Holy Spirit as he willed. (NAB)

The meaning is clear. Detailing the chain of agents in the communication of the good news is simply meant to show the extent to which God went to reach "us": the preaching of Jesus, the testimony of the first witnesses, and the accompanying manifestations. These include signs and wonders (*sēmeiois te kai terasin*), terms we encountered frequently in the Acts, with works of power (*dynamesin*) making a triad of attestations God himself gave to Jesus (Acts 2:22). The triad is also claimed by Paul as the proof of the authentic apostle (2 Cor 12:12).

The last phrase is literally, "and by distributions of the Holy Spirit according to his will." The charismatic gifts are obviously meant, and the phrase reflects 1 Cor 12:4, 11: "There are different gifts but the same Spirit. . . . It is one and the same Spirit who produces all these gifts, distributing them to each as he wills." Now it is interesting that the author, who most scholars hold is a disciple of Paul, brings to the traditional list of authenticating signs the manifold gifts of the Spirit. These, no less than the others, are God's way of witnessing to the good news. Luke certainly saw the Pentecost event with tongues and prophecy as authenticating signs (Acts 2:1-21; 10:44-46; 19:6) but for reasons we discussed there, the healing and exorcising gifts were attributed to the name of Jesus rather than to the Holy Spirit. In the late Markan conclusion (Mk 16:9-20) all the signs, including tongues, are brought under the name of Jesus and there is no mention of the Holy Spirit. Paul, on the other hand, seems to understand all signs and services under the rubric of gifts of the Spirit (1 Cor 12:7-11), although he also provides, as Hebrews does here, a Trinitarian context (1 Cor 12:4-6). We can conclude that the elements of this text in Hebrews are traditional but the combination of the gifts of the Spirit with the "signs, wonders and works of power" is unique. The result is a comprehensive theological statement of the ways in which God authenticates the good news—and the gifts of the Holy Spirit are perpetually enshrined in that list.

The final teaching on the Spirit in Hebrews belongs to exhortation to perseverance in the midst of temptations to apostasy. The major text appears in 6:4-6:

> 4. For when men have once been enlightened and have tasted the heavenly gift and become sharers in the Holy Spirit, 5. when they have tasted the good word of God and the powers of the age to come, 6. and then have fallen away, it is impossible to make them repent again, since they are crucifying the Son of God for themselves and holding him up to contempt. (NAB)

The statement in vs. 6 that it is impossible for apostates to repent again should be understood in the light of what was probably the usual experience of the early church as well as the pastoral concern of the whole epistle to preserve the readers from apostasy. Hardening it into an absolute principle would limit God's will to save all men (1 Tim 2:4) and his mercy elsewhere described as patient and limitless (Jer 3:12-13; Is 55:7; Ps 136; Lk 15). Nevertheless, the Montanists and the Novatians appealed to this text of Hebrews to deny reconciliation to Christians guilty of grave sins such as apostasy, adultery or murder (cf. Tertullian, *De pudicitia* 20 and Cyprian, *Ep. X ad Antonianum*). The intention of the author is to dramatize how grievous is the sin against the light and against the gift already experienced. The same thought underlies the later identification of the Holy Spirit as "the spirit of grace":

> 28. Anyone who rejects the law of Moses is put to death without mercy. . . . 29. Do you not suppose that a much worse punishment is due the man who disdains the Son of God,

thinks the covenant blood by which he was sanctified to be ordinary, and insults the Spirit of grace? (10:28-29 NAB)

The author is thus dealing with the problem already treated by Luke in his identification of the "sin against the Holy Spirit" as that of apostasy (Lk 12:8-10). As a matter of fact, the Holy Spirit figures importantly in the four-fold description in 6:4-6 of the gift Christians have already experienced. Each of the four participles in the Greek is aorist, suggesting a once-done past event, in this case Christian initiation.

The faithful have been "enlightened." This may refer simply to the light of faith in Christ (2 Cor 4:6) or it may refer more specifically to baptism, called "enlightenment" in the Fathers as early as Justin Martyr (*Apol.* I, 61, 12; I, 65, 1). Ephesians 5:14, apparently a fragment of a baptismal hymn, also speaks of enlightenment by Christ.

The second description of the Christian experience is: "having tasted the heavenly gift." Some interpreters have taken this as referring to the Eucharist. Others object that the aorist verb indicates a once-done event, whereas the Eucharist would be repeated. This objection loses its force if we understand the verb to refer to the first "taste" of the heavenly gift. On the other hand, the influence of Psalm 34 on this text may account for both the terms "illumination" and "tasted": "Look to him and be radiant. . . Taste and see that the Lord is good" (Ps 34:5, 8). It would, in fact, go counter to the author's intention to specify too narrowly the meaning of "gift" here. The cluster of Greek words associated with *dōrea* all convey the bestowal of God's spiritual treasures, in the first place his own Son (Gal 1:4; Jn 3:16). In contrast to the law and to sin, *dōrea* expresses the total gratuity and magnificence on the part of God (Rom 5:15) and the response of loving gratitude on the part of the receiver (2 Cor 9:15). It is virtually equivalent to *charis*, grace (Gal 2:20). Qualified here as "heavenly," the gift is literally a foretaste of heaven. In the Acts this gift is identified as the Holy Spirit himself (Acts 2:38; 10:45; 11:17).

That such an identification is not far from the author's mind here appears from the very next phrase: "Become sharers of the Holy Spirit." Paul had spoken of the fellowship of the Holy Spirit, using the word *koinōnia* (Phil 2:1; 2 Cor 13:13). The author of Hebrews prefers *metochoi* to describe Christians as sharers in Christ (3:14), in the heavenly calling (3:1) and in the Holy Spirit (here). While *koinōnia* allows more emphasis on the horizontal or community sharing of the Spirit, and may even mean the community created by the Spirit, the stress here is upon the Holy Spirit as the objective gift in which the Christian shares, as is obvious from the three other parallel expressions.

The last item completes the picture: "having tasted the good word of God and the powers of the age to come." Once again the formula of tasting appears. The "good word of God" is probably the author's way of saying *eu-angelion*, the "good news," a term which he never uses. Recalling the "good words" which in the Septuagint are equivalent to the divine promises (Jos 21:45; 23:15), the expression here means that Christians have experienced the fulfillment of those promises. But not only is the past now present to them in fulfillment; the future is theirs by way of anticipation. "The powers of the world to come" are to be understood of the dynamic powers and wonders of the Holy Spirit already manifest now (2:4; Gal 3:5) which on the one hand proclaim that the messianic age has begun (Acts 2:11ff) and on the other give a real foretaste, an actual beginning of the age to come (Mt 12:32). Again the dependency on Paul is evident, for the Holy Spirit is the downpayment of the fullness to come (2 Cor 1:22; Eph 1:14). But our author goes beyond Paul in describing the experiential nature of this anticipation.

This passage, viewed in the light of the others we have examined in the letter, enables us to discern the function of the *pneuma* in the theology of the author. The raw materials with which he works are drawn from preceding tradition, particularly from Paul and Luke. However, by his use of the materials and his special vocabulary, two stresses emerge as chief. On the one hand, *pneuma* stands for the heavenly sphere where Christ has entered to stand as permanent priestly intercessor before the Father (9:14). On the other hand, the Holy Spirit belongs to the experiential dimension of the Christian life, making the Christian's entry into heaven with Christ a reality known and "tasted" even now. Later theology would speak of the gifts of the Spirit, especially wisdom, as giving an experiential knowledge of God, a foretaste of glory. As long as the gifts are understood to include the charismatic manifestations as well as the gifts of interior prayer, this insight is valid. The gifts of the Holy Spirit are God's own witness to the good news (2:4). The author of Hebrews, then, might be said to view the Christian and the Christian community as living already now penetrated to the heart by a shaft of light from heaven, a light that is sweetness and joy as much as it is power. So permanent is this gift, so keen its foretaste of glory and so assured is it by the Spirit even amid persecution and temptation, that it would be unthinkable to turn from "so great a salvation" (2:3) and from such a "spirit of grace" (10:29).

26
The Puzzling Pneumatology
of the Book of Revelation

When we turn to the Book of Revelation (or *Apocalypse* from the Greek *apokalypsis*, "revelation"), we find ourselves in a strange world of style and imagery. If we feel we are witnesses of a dream sequence, parts of which are a nightmare, we are not far from the truth. The author makes no apology that his work is precisely a revelation, abounding in visions and voices and cosmic drama that come from a rapture into the spirit-world (1:10; 4:2; 21:10). He makes clear that he is a prophet (22:9) and that his work is prophecy (1:3; 10:11; 22:7, 10, 18). Though in the early church prophecy took forms other than this, the book of Revelation is the most complete example of one of its chief forms, apocalyptic.

Why the author, who identifies himself from the outset as John (1:1, 4, 9), should have chosen apocalyptic can be understood, just as his predecessor, the author of Daniel, can be understood only in terms of the historical situation to which he is responding. The church is no longer facing mere debate or harrassment or oppression. It is facing martyrdom under the boot of Rome. Scholars debate which persecution occasioned the book. Some place it as early as the reign of Claudius (41-54 A.D.), some as late as the reign of Trajan (98-117). Others think Nero's reign more likely (54-68) while the majority, following the lead of Irenaeus, place it toward the end of the reign of Domitian (81-96). In any case, the book is a response to a very concrete historical situation and even its predictions of the future are seen in the light of the present. It should not therefore be looked upon as cryptic code containing the details of distant ages of the church such as our own, except in the general sense in which "history repeats itself" and the church stands always in need of the same message of hope.

Just as the revelatory power of dreams lies in their web of symbols, often combined in ways that are totally unexpected, so the literary power of Revelation lies for the most part in its symbolic language. Horns symbolize power, eyes mean knowledge, wings mobility, palms and crown stand for triumph and kingship, the sea symbolizes chaos, insecurity and death. The woman symbolizes a city or a people. Colors have meaning too: white symbolizes victory, purple luxury or kingship, red war, green plague, black death. Numbers too, as a rule, should not be taken literally but symbolically. Seven, Jewish number for perfection, occurs 54 times. Twelve, standing for the twelve tribes of Israel, symbolizes the people of God brought to perfection. A thousand symbolizes a large number. Three-and-a-half years (1260 days or 42 months), was the length of the persecution of the Jews by Antioches IV Epiphanes, and it becomes the symbol for the duration of the present persecution, which the author expects to be short. The number of the beast, 666, falls triply short of perfection and hence is the most evil imaginable—and, interestingly enough, is the precise total of the sum of the Hebrew letters which spell out Caesar Nero.

The author speaks of the present and the future with historical images of the past. Babylon, city to which the Jews were exiled, symbolizes Rome and the Roman empire. Michael, the serpent, the eagle, the harlot, are all Old Testament figures which have now been reintroduced into the present drama, bringing the rich train of historical reminiscences associated with each. The author is not unlike his predecessor Ezekiel, who abounded in images, allegories and numbers. And, as we might expect from such an enthusiast for Ezekielian motifs, John gives an important place to the spirit.

But there is something curiously different even about the way he treats the whole domain of the pneumatic. For one thing, he never uses the term "Holy Spirit." He often uses "spirits" in the plural, and even when he speaks of "the Spirit" in the singular we are not always sure he means exactly what the other New Testament authors mean by the Holy Spirit. Then the scenario is so complicated by angels that we have the impression of looking at the ceiling of a baroque church, in which the "pneumatic" element is dramatized by multiplicity. In the midst of all this unfamiliar terrain, the surest procedure is to begin with the more obvious and familiar and from that base to explore what is less so.

The Prophetic Spirit

One thing is certain. Prophecy occupies a central place in Revelation. Since in the Old Testament and in the parts of the New which we have explored prophecy is a chief pneumatic activity, it should provide a convenient avenue to approach John's pneumatology.

We have already noted that the author considers himself a prophet and his book prophecy. He describes himself four times as caught up in the prophetic state, twice by the simple expression, "I became in spirit" (1:10; 4:2), twice by the expression, "(the angel) carried me away in spirit" (17:3; 21:10). It is difficult at our distance to tell whether this is a mere literary device to introduce apocalyptic drama or whether he is speaking of a real psychic state. Prophecy was common in the early church, but we do not know how much rapture or ecstasy was involved during or prior to its oral delivery, and even less about the process when it involved commiting the prophecy to writing. Paul speaks about being caught up to the third heaven or paradise "whether in the body or out of the body I do not know, God knows" (2 Cor 12:3). He adds that the knowledge given him was not communicable. This surely means that for him the experience was not prophecy, since he maintains that prophecy is communicable (1 Cor 14:3) and he states explicitly that the spirits of the prophets are subject to the prophets (1 Cor 14:32). For the author of Revelation, too, prophecy is likewise communicable, whether it be vision or word.

It is likewise clear that the office of prophet was recognized in the church for which John is writing. The mysterious plan of God is revealed to his servants the prophets (10:7). While not excluding the Old Testament prophets (there is probably an allusion to Amos 3:7 here), John has primarily in mind the Christian prophets of which he speaks so much throughout his book. Prophets appear along with apostles (18:20) just as they do in 1 Cor 12:28; Eph 2:20; 3:5; 4:11. When the angel speaking to John refers to "your brothers the prophets," it is obvious that John belongs to a body of recognized ministers of the word (22:9). Because of their powerful witness to Jesus, it is the prophets who seem to be hardest hit by the Roman persecution (11:1-13; 18:24).

Up to this point the shape of prophecy does not seem much different from its appearance elsewhere in the New Testament. Things begin to get sticky, however, when we inquire into the medium of prophetic revelation. God is of course the original source (1:1). But the revelation is mediated by several agents: the Son of Man, the angel(s), the "heavenly voice" (sometimes just "a voice"), and "the spirit."

The title of the book is "A revelation by Jesus Christ. . ." (1:1) and the opening vision is that of the glorious Son of Man, identified as Jesus who died and is now living (1:9-20). Not only does he appear and speak to the prophet, he also introduces and personally dictates each of the letters to the seven churches (chs. 2-3). Then comes the vision of heavenly worship introduced by the trumpet-like voice, which identifies

the vision as coming again from the Son of Man (4:1; 1:10). In the epilogue of the book, the repeated saying, "I am coming soon!" (22:7, 12,
20) obviously comes also from the glorified Jesus.

But by and large most of the revelations, especially in the central
part of the book, are made by angels. Angels, of course, participate in
the divine drama, often as introducers of new scenes. But above all they
are commentators giving the meaning of the scenes (1:1; 5:2; 10:9;
18:21-24; 5:11-12; 7:11-12; 14:6, 8, 9, etc.). Even more importantly, the
entire book of Revelation is presented, from the opening line, as a revelation made by an angel of Jesus Christ (1:1), and the epilogue repeats the
same principle (22:16). What is especially significant is that the notions
of sending (1:1; 22:6) and witnessing (16:22), here attributed to the angel
are in other parts of the New Testament tradition said of the Spirit (1
Pet 1:12; Rom 8:16; Acts 5:32). But "the Spirit" in the singular is never
said in Revelation to be *sent*. Why is this so freely said of the angels and
not of the Spirit? We shall have to return to this problem but first let us
dispose of the third medium of revelation, the "voice."

Of course the various actors in the heavenly drama speak, often
"with a loud voice." But here we are interested in the voice which speaks
directly to the prophet. It is variously described as a voice in or from
heaven (10:4, 8; 11:12, 15; 12:10; 14:13), from the altar (9:13), from the
sanctuary (16:1) or from the throne (16:17; 19:5; 21:3) or from amid the
living creatures (6:6). Occasionally the voice is totally anonymous
(10:11; 11:1). Perhaps these voices should not be sharply distinguished
from those of angels, the anonymity of origin simply heightening the
mysterious nature of the scene.

In comparison with these other sources, "the spirit" (in the singular) has quantitatively fewer times of appearance. The expression "in
spirit" referring to John's entering the prophetic state has already been
discussed (1:10; 4:2; 17:3; 21:10). Each of the letters to the seven
churches ends with the admonition, "Let him who has ears heed what
the spirit is saying to the churches" (2:7, 11, 17, 29; 3:6, 13, 22). It is not
clear whether the spirit here is the one "Holy Spirit" which belongs to
the entire church or the angel through whom the Son of Man makes his
revelation to John. In favor of the former, one might consider the fact
that although each message is addressed to a particular church, the
refrain says that the spirit is speaking to all the churches, and hence the
common Spirit would be the more usual meaning. On the other hand,
aside from the reference to the spirit of John's prophetic state, there has
been no mention of the Spirit in the singular up to this point, whereas
the sending of the angel of revelation has been explicitly mentioned. But
this would also assume that "spirit" and "angel" are identical realities

in the language of Revelation, and that, as we shall see, can be questioned.

Another ambiguous text appears in 19:9-10:

> 9. The angel then said to me: "Write this down: Happy are they who have been invited to the wedding feast of the Lamb." The angel continued, "These words are true; they come from God." 10. I fell at his feet to worship him, but he said to me, "No, get up! I am merely a fellow servant with you and your brothers who give witness to Jesus. Worship God alone. The prophetic spirit proves itself by witnessing to Jesus." (19:9-10 NAB)

The last line of this passage has been much discussed. Literally it says, "Testimony to Jesus is the spirit of prophecy." The context is necessary for the meaning. The angel has a revealing role; he communicates prophecy to John, to be written down. The angel thus appears as the heavenly prophet to which John is his earthly counterpart. But in either case the "spirit of prophecy" is proven to be authentic by witnessing to Jesus. The angel is not to be worshipped (any more than the beast!) because he, like the prophet, is subject to the Lordship of Jesus. We are reminded of the danger of angel-worship at Colossae, which was threatening the primacy of Christ. We are also reminded of 1 Cor 12:1-3, where the Spirit can be tested by its promotion of the confession that "Jesus is Lord." Though the immediate occasion of the angel's rebuke is John's attempt to worship him, there is behind the statement a blow at false prophecy which was rampant at the time Revelation was written. The book abounds in allusions to false prophets and unclean spirits who even work prodigies and lead many to accept the power of the beast (13:13; 16:13-14; 18:2; 19:20; 20:10). The second beast in 13:11-18 is described in terms of the false prophets. The church at Thyatira was warned against the false prophetess Jezebel (2:20-25). In such an atmosphere it was no idle reminder that the spirit of prophecy could be discerned by witness to Jesus, even to death if necessary (cf. 11:1-13; 18:24). In our present text, however, the "spirit of prophecy" refers to an attitude common both to angels and to authentic prophets. The "spirit of prophecy" is not the angel himself.

More difficult to interpret is the section in the epilogue which closely resembles the one we have just analyzed:

> 6. The *angel* said to me: "These words are trustworthy and true; the Lord, *the God of prophetic spirits*, has sent his *angel*

to show his servants what must happen very soon."

7. "Remember, I am coming soon! Happy the man who heeds the prophetic message of this book!"

8. It is I, John, who heard and saw all these things, and when I heard and saw them I fell down to worship at the feet of the angel who showed them to me. 9. But he said to me: "No, get up! I am merely a *fellow servant with you and your brothers the prophets* and those who heed the message of this book. Worship God alone!" (22:6-9 NAB)

In vs. 6 the expression in the Greek is literally, "The God of the spirits of the prophets." The immediate mention of *angel* may lead one to believe that in John's view the "spirits" which move the prophets are angels, and vs. 9 could be read in a similar sense, that the angels are collaborators with the prophets. Paul had used the expression "the spirits of the prophets" (1 Cor 14:32), but there is no doubt for him that "the spirits" are movements of the one Spirit (1 Cor 12:4-11). It is not so clear in Revelation. The principle of unification of all the pneumatic activity is not the "one Spirit" but the *God* of angels and prophetic spirits and *Jesus* who sends them and speaks through them.

The Affirming and the Longing Spirit

That is not to say that John has no perception whatever of the unity of the Spirit. Two other texts show that he does. The first is 14:13:

I heard a voice from heaven say to me: "Write this down: Happy now are the dead who die in the Lord!" The Spirit added, "Yes, they shall find rest from their labors, for their good works accompany them." (NAB)

How the two sentences of this passage are grammatically connected depends on what word the Greek adverb *ap' arti*, "henceforth," is taken to modify. The RSV takes it as modifying "die" and reads, "Blessed are the dead who die in the Lord henceforth." The NAB cited above takes it as modifying "happy" and simply translates, "Happy now. . . ." The Vulgate takes it with what follows, "Henceforth, says the Spirit, they may rest from their labors. . ." For our purposes what is more important is the relationship of the saying that is attributed to the Spirit to that of the heavenly voice. Is the Spirit introduced simply to vary the style, with a meaning equivalent to the "heavenly voice"? In content the second saying affirms the first and adds the reason why it is true. The "yes" appears also in 16:7 in the sense of affirmation of what has just preceded. The text suggests, then, that the expression "the Spirit says" is not simply an equivalent to the "heavenly voice" but a prophetic voice confirming and giving further understanding of the heavenly revelation.

This confirming role of the Spirit emerges even more clearly in the epilogue:

> The Spirit and the Bride say, "Come!" Let him who hears answer, "Come!" Let him who is thirsty come forward; let all who desire it accept the gift of life-giving water. (22:17 NAB)

There can be no doubt here that just as the Bride is one, so the Spirit is one. The Spirit here however is likewise the Spirit of prophecy we have met throughout. It speaks primarily through the prophets, so that the combined expression, "The Spirit and the Bride," is equivalent to "the prophets and the saints." The prophets inspired by the Spirit cry out to the Lord Jesus to come. Their "Come!" is echoed by the whole body of believers, described in the preceding chapters as the Bride of the Lamb. Their chorus in turn is an invitation to all who are listening to the reading of this book in their churches (cf. 1:3) to interpose at this point their own "Come!" The Spirit of prophecy bears witness to Jesus not only in worshipping him alone (cf. 19:10) but also in the cry for him to return.

The Seven Spirits of God

We have found some difficulty in adjusting the very fluid pneumatology of Revelation to our familiar Trinitarian concepts which derive from later theological reflection. It is important to respect the primitive terrain on which we have been moving. There are two further areas in Revelation which may shed further light on the continuing question we have about the relation of the Spirit to the Godhead. The first is John's opening greeting to the seven churches of Asia:

> 4. John to the seven churches that are in Asia: Grace to you and peace from him who is and who was and who is to come, and *from the seven spirits who are before his throne*, and from Jesus Christ the faithful witness, the first-born of the dead, and the ruler of kings on earth. (1:4-5 RSV)

The surprising element in this greeting is that the seven spirits are mentioned immediately after the eternal one and before Jesus Christ. So unusual is this expression that R. H. Charles thought it was introduced into the text by a foreign hand, and others, in the interest of Trinitarian orthodoxy, have interpreted it as a reference to the one Spirit in his seven-fold gifts of powers as foretold in the Greek text of Isaiah 11:2.

The most natural interpretation would be to take these seven spirits as the seven angels corresponding to the seven churches just mentioned in 1:4a. But if we look at other places where these seven spirits are mentioned, we may be pointed in another direction. In 4:5 John sees burning "before the throne . . . seven torches of fire, which are the seven spirits of God." Then, later on in the second half of the same vision John sees the Lamb, who is Jesus the Davidic Messiah victorious through his suffering and death, as endowed "with seven horns and with seven eyes, which are the seven spirits of God sent out into all the earth" (5:6). This is an allusion to Zechariah's vision of the lampstand with seven lamps which he explains as "the eyes of the Lord, which range throughout the whole earth." Zechariah may have been transferring Persian royal imagery to the court of Yahweh, for court emissaries of the Persian empire were popularly known as the "king's eyes." In any case, John is here transferring the eyes of Yahweh and the seven spirits to the risen Lord Jesus himself. Likewise in 3:1, the risen Christ is the one who "has the seven spirits of God." The "seven spirits of God" belong therefore both to God and to the risen Christ. They are different from the stars which are the angels of the seven churches (1:16, 20; 3:1). That "spirit" should not automatically be identified with "angel" appears from Acts 23:8, 9 where "spirit" and "angel" are clearly distinguished.

Can we then say that the unusual expression "the seven spirits of God" or "the seven spirits before the throne" mean the one Spirit symbolized by the seven torches (4:5) and the seven eyes (5:6)? Many scholars think so, and there are good reasons. Although in other contexts as we have seen, John uses "the Spirit" in the singular, he prefers Old Testament imagery when it is available to him as it was here in the text from Zechariah. Moreover, the number seven suggests perfection and totality and lends itself as well to the subsequent "division" of the Spirit into various gifts and ministries, especially prophecy. Nevertheless, we must admit that for John, in this text at least, the multiple functions of pneumatic activity are more important than their unity. Or, to put it another way, the unity of pneumatic activity is rooted elsewhere than in the "one Spirit."

The Unifying Principle

The discovery that the agents of revelation can be so many in Revelation (the Son of Man, the angel(s), the voice, the Spirit) may lead us to overlook the fact that the same revelation may at times be attributed to more than one of the agents. Thus, while the Son of Man dictates the letters in chapters 2-3, each letter is also said to be a revelation of the Spirit to the churches. Equivalently, the whole of the revelation is the work of the angel Jesus sends (1:1; 22:6, 16). And twice the author tells us that his prophetic rapture was due to an *angel* carrying him away in the *spirit* (17:3; 21:10). Where then are all these pneumatic activities brought together? Not in affirming that there is one spirit of which all of these are diverse manifestations (as Paul did it in 1 Cor 12:4-7), but simply by bringing all pneumatic activity (angelic and terrestrial as well) under God and Jesus the Lord. It is almost as if the concept of "one Spirit" were too confining to John and would lend itself poorly to the explosive drama he wished to stage. He does speak of "the Spirit" in the singular but not in any polemic way to the diminishment of the many spirits and angels who populate his heavenly choreography.

Now in giving angels a place in his pneumatology, John is not totally alone in the New Testament. In Luke-Acts especially, identical activity is at times attributed to angels and to the spirit (Acts 8:26, 39; 23:9). The Lord may be said to send his angel in the same language as sending his Spirit (Lk 24:49; Acts 12:11; Gal 4:6). And Paul, otherwise so strong in his affirmation of the one Spirit, in speaking of a woman engaged in the pneumatic activity of praying or prophesying (1 Cor 11:5) says that she should have a sign of power on her head "because of the angels" (1 Cor 11:10)—namely because in praying and prophesying she is participating directly in angelic activity.

The ambiguity and fluidity of these modes of revelation is really not so new at all. Often in the Old Testament revelations were made by angels, some of them to the prophets themselves (see our discussion of Is 63:10-14), and often it was not possible to distinguish between "the angel" and "the Lord" himself in the revelation (Gen 21:17-19; 16:7-16; 22:11-18; 31:11-13; Ex 3:2-14; Jgs 6:11-24). What is most interesting to note is that as we are coming into the final phase of New Testament revelation, the Johannine tradition, there is a return to a very primitive mixing of angelology and pneumatology. We are being prepared for the gospel of John where the confusing relationship between the two will be clarified to the enrichment of the understanding of the Holy Spirit.

For those who have been looking for a greater theology of the "person" of the Holy Spirit in the book of Revelation, these results may appear disappointing. While holding out the hope that they are preparing us for a new insight in the gospel of John, we should not forget that all the texts we have examined here so far have had to do with the Spirit of *prophecy.* Even the "seven spirits of God" seem to be seven because of their divisibility into prophetic ministries. Is the Spirit in Revelation nothing else but the prophetic Spirit?

No, there is more. But to find it we must leave the word "spirit" and turn to John's favorite teaching device, the symbol.

The River of Life-Giving Water

1. The angel then showed me the river of life-giving water, clear as crystal, which issued from the throne of God and of the Lamb 2. and flowed down the middle of the streets. On either side of the river grew the trees of life which produce fruit twelve times a year, once each month; their leaves serve as medicine for the nations.

3. Nothing deserving a curse shall be found there. The throne of God and of the Lamb shall be there, and his servants shall serve him faithfully. 4. They shall see him face to face and bear his name on their foreheads. 5. The night shall be no more. They will need no light from lamps or the sun, for the Lord God shall give them light, and they shall reign forever. (22:1-5 NAB)

Though this section is followed by an epilogue, it is really the grand finale of the book of Revelation. The final, glorious vision of the New Jerusalem begun at 21:17 climaxes in these lines. The imagery is taken from the prophetic descriptions of the New Jerusalem, especially those of Ezekiel (47:1-12) and Third Isaiah (60:20). The promise of face-to-face vision echoes the New Testament tradition elsewhere (Mt 5:8; 1 Cor 13:12; 1 Jn 3:2). The common throne of God and the Lamb symbolizes the eternal reign of Jesus in glory with the Father. But what is this river that flows jointly from God and the Lamb and gives abundant life, fruitfulness and healing to the city? The basic image is taken from Ez 47:1-12, the prophet's vision of the water flowing from the temple, growing into a mighty river. The river's waters are life-giving, the trees that grow there bear fruit monthly, and their leaves serve for medicine. John has joined to the vision of Ezekiel other motifs. Whereas Ezekiel has spoken simply of trees, John speaks of trees *of life*, clearly alluding to the tree of life intended for man but forfeited by sin (Gen 2:9; 3:22). Pluralized here, the image suggests the superabundant eschatological fulfillment—not one tree but many trees of life. The river then evokes also the river that watered the garden of Eden (Gen 2:10-14), and per-

haps also the stream that gladdens the city of God in Ps 46:5. Joel too
had promised that a fountain would issue from the house of the Lord
(Joel 3:18), waters that Zechariah said would be life-giving (Zech 14:8).
In Jer 2:13 the Lord had identified himself as the fountain of living
water. In Rev 7:17, the Lamb leads his faithful to the springs of life-giving water. And in 21:6 the One who sits on the throne says, "To anyone
who thirsts I will give to drink without cost from the spring of life-giving
water," a promise repeated by way of invitation in 22:17. The expression
"without cost" alludes to the promise of Is 55:1.

But is there any justification for identifying this river of life-giving
water with the Spirit? The image of "pouring out" the Spirit first appeared in Is 32:15, where it is the source of fruitfulness for the land. And
this image is picked up and sharpened in Is 44:3, as we saw:

> I will pour out water upon the thirsty ground,
>   and streams upon the dry land;
> I will pour out my spirit upon your offspring,
>   and my blessing upon your descendants. (NAB)

There was, then, surely sufficient Old Testament background for John
to have meant this river to be an image of the Spirit. But was he, in fact,
thinking of the Spirit? Fortunately, there is evidence within the Johannine writings themselves which help us decide that he was. If, as is held
by the majority of scholars, the book of Revelation stands within the
Johannine tradition, we are justified in calling on the Gospel of John to
help us understand the Christian symbolism of this fountain of water. In
Jn 7:38-39 the rivers of living water are identified as the Spirit to be
given upon the glorification of Jesus. Incorporating this interpretation
gives perhaps the most profound image of the Spirit in the New Testament. It is no longer the prophetic Spirit but the Spirit of life. And the
Spirit flows jointly from God and the Lamb into the city of God. Later
Trinitarian theology will develop this image in terms of the Spirit pro-
ceeding from the Father and the Son. Even as it stands, however, in its
utter primitive beauty, the figure incorporates the Scriptural promise
that the Spirit would be sent by the Father (Lk 24:29; Acts 1:4; Gal 4:6)
and by the risen Lord Jesus now glorified at the Father's right hand
(Acts 2:33). If the prophetic Spirit in Revelation is never said to be *sent*,
the same cannot be said of the life-giving Spirit, the river that flows
from God and the Lamb.

The book of Revelation has enriched our understanding of prophetic inspiration in the New Testament. It has shown us that in the primitive stage which Revelation represents there was often no clear distinc-

tion whether an inspiration or revelation came from the Son of Man, the Spirit, a heavenly voice or an angel. But it has also introduced us into a profound understanding of the Spirit of life in the image of the river flowing from the throne of God and the Lamb. In so doing, it has given us a taste of the theology of the gospel and the letters of John, to which we now turn.

27
The Rich Pneumatology
of John

The relationship of the fourth gospel and the letters of John to the New Testament literature we have seen thus far is still not settled to everyone's satisfaction, but a strong emerging position among New Testament scholars is that the gospel of John represents an independent tradition going back in some cases even earlier than Mark, that this tradition developed during the oral period around the apostle John, whose preaching and teaching it embodies, and that the final edition of the gospel, which we have today, is the work of a disciple-editor who completed the work of his predecessor(s). And what of the three letters also traditionally attributed to John? They reveal many similarities when compared with the gospel, so that there is unanimity in holding that they belong to the Johannine tradition. The difference of perspective and less refined theology, which is nonetheless evident, is attributed by some scholars to their being written earlier than the gospel by the same author, by others to their being written by another disciple of John who brings a slightly different perspective to the tradition we find in the gospel. Among the differences we may note that the first letter of John is concerned with the second Coming of the Lord in a way that the gospel is not. For the gospel, though Jesus is expected to return, there is much greater focus on "realized eschatology," the belief that the promised future goods are already possessed in Jesus. Likewise the vocabulary concerning the Father, the Word and the Spirit is less developed in the letters than in the gospel.

However this critical question is resolved, as far as the doctrine of the Spirit is concerned, the letters reflect a more primitive stage of development, and for that reason we shall look at them first, in order to conclude with the major texts of the gospel, which represent the summit of New Testament pneumatology.

1 John 2:20, 27: The Anointing from the Holy One

20. But you have the anointing that comes from the Holy One,
    so that all knowledge is yours.

26. I have written you these things
    about those who try to deceive you.
27. As for you,
    the anointing you received from him
    remains in your hearts.
    This means you have no need
    for anyone to teach you.
    Rather, as his anointing teaches you about all things
    and is true—free from any lie—
    remain in him
    as that anointing taught you. (NAB)

The Holy Spirit is not explicitly mentioned in this passage. Some scholars therefore think the anointing refers metaphorically to the word of truth, the gospel, accepted by faith. However, because of the long biblical association of anointing with the coming of the Spirit (from Samuel's anointing of Saul in 10:1ff. through Jesus' reference to his own anointing by the Spirit in Luke 4:18 to the baptismal reference in 2 Cor 1:21) most interpreters have understood the anointing to be an allusion to the Holy Spirit. In either case, the author seems to be recalling the moment of Christian initiation, since the aorist verb forms refer to a single past moment at which the anointing took place.

To begin with which is most certain, let us note first the surrounding context, all of which concerns the need to be preserved from false teaching. Verses 21-25 (which we have omitted above) are a warning against the anti-Christs who deny that Jesus is the Messiah. The effect of the anointing of the faithful is that "all knowledge is yours" (vs. 20) and "you have no need for anyone to teach you" (vs. 27). This latter expression has sometimes been invoked to show that there is no need of external teaching in the church, yet if that were the case John would not be writing his letter instructing his readers and warning them against anti-Christs and false teachers. Nevertheless, it is significant that John bases his hopes for their preservation not upon the external teaching they have received but upon the *anointing*. This anointing is not the action once performed (*chrisis*) but the abiding effect (*chrisma*), and, as vs. 27 makes clear, it is interior. It came "from the Holy One." Though it is possible that the "Holy One" here is the Father, it is more likely that it is Christ ("the Holy One of God," Mk 1:24). In that case the Greek word chosen for "from" (*apo* instead of *para*) would in no way exclude the mediation of that anointing by the church, for in John *apo* is used to suggest the ultimate source while allowing intermediaries. The sense would be, then, that Jesus is the origin and foundation of this anointing which they received when they became Christians.

There is every reason to believe, then, that the primary meaning of anointing here is the inner teaching or inner word accepted by faith and now abiding in the Christian. Compare this "anointing which abides" and assures Christians that they "know the truth" (vs. 21) with similar expressions in the Johannine literature said of the *word* or of the *truth*: "The word of God abides in you, and you have conquered the evil one" (1 Jn 2:14); "The truth abides in us and will be with us forever" (2 Jn 2) "If you abide in my word . . . you shall know the truth" (Jn 8:21-32); and ". . . all who have known the truth, for the sake of the truth which abides in us" (2 Jn 1-2). In our text, the anointing *teaches* (vs. 27)! Thus the teaching function of the anointing seems to be primary.

But surely anyone so steeped in the Christian tradition as John is could not fail to have seen this anointing, which we have described as divine teaching interiorly assimilated, as an effect of the Spirit. In Paul, as well as in the Acts, the Spirit has the role of making God's word intelligible and meaningful and bringing about the assent of faith (cf. 1 Cor 2:10; 1 Thes 1:6; 2 Cor 1:21). If Paul stressed the role of the Spirit in the initial Christian experience, John here focuses upon the role of the Spirit in the ongoing teaching of the Christian. It will be stated even more clearly in the gospel: "The Holy Spirit . . . will teach you in everything. . ." (Jn 14:26). Here the anointing teaches. For John, then, the word revealed and the Spirit revealing are not separate realities, but necessary complements of one act of revelation, whether that act be considered as originating in God, as initiating the Christian, or as teaching him along his journey and preserving him from error. It is given to every Christian and not just to the Church's official teachers.

One may still ask, however, why John should choose the word *anointing* for this purpose. In the Old Testament the anointing of the king made it unthinkable that one should do violence to him: "The Lord forbid that I should do such a thing to my master, the Lord's anointed, as to lay a hand on him, for he is the Lord's anointed" (1 Sam 24:7). Paul saw Christian initiation as an anointing of the faithful with Christ, the Anointed one, in which God himself strengthened them with divine certainty (2 Cor 1:21). The sense of preservation and certitude given the

Christian underlies this text in John, and the symbol of anointing may very well have been suggested to John by the baptismal rite itself.

1 John 4:1-6: Testing the Spirits

1. Beloved, do not trust every spirit, but put the spirits to a test to see if they belong to God, because many false prophets have appeared in the world. 2. This is how you can recognize God's Spirit: every spirit that acknowledges Jesus Christ come in the flesh belongs to God, 3. while every spirit that fails to acknowledge him does not belong to God. Such is the spirit of the antichrist which, as you have heard, is to come; in fact, it is in the world already. 4. You are of God, you little ones, and thus you have conquered the false prophets. For there is One greater in you than there is in the world. 5. Those others belong to the world; that is why theirs is the language of the world and why the world listens to them. 6. We belong to God and anyone who has knowledge of God gives us a hearing, while anyone who is not of God refuses to hear us. Thus do we distinguish the spirit of truth from the spirit of deception. (NAB)

The first lines of this passage put us in touch with the problem of false prophecy which apparently plagued the Johannine church as much as it did the Matthean. John recurs here to traditional teaching. The spirits must be tested (cf. 1 Thes 5:21; 1 Cor 12:10). And the first norm of testing is conformity to the traditional faith. For Paul this was basically confession of the Lordship of Jesus (1 Cor 12:1-3); John's formula is similar, but it stresses the incarnation more than the resurrection, no doubt because that is the point being challenged by false prophets. There is much dispute as to the exact identity of these false teachers. It appears clear however that an incipient Docetism was threatening the doctrine of Jesus-come-in-the-flesh (cf. 2 Jn 7-11). Cerinthus, toward the end of the first century, held that Jesus was possessed by the "Christ" only at his baptism and the Christ left him at the time of the passion. Is this perhaps alluded to in those Greek manuscripts which read, in vs. 3, "Every spirit that dissolves him. . ."?

In vs. 4 we have something similar to the "anointing" passage above. Christians who confess Jesus as the Christ in the flesh are "of God" and have within them One greater than all worldly powers. In the concluding vs. 6 we find an expression identical to that found in *The*

Testament of Judah known at Qumran: "Know, therefore, my children, that two spirits wait upon man—the spirit of truth and the spirit of deception" (20:1).

1 John 4:13: The Spirit and the Divine Indwelling

12. No one has ever seen God.
    Yet if we love one another
    God dwells in us,
    and his love is brought to perfection in us.
13. The way we know we remain in him
    and he in us
    is that he has given us of his Spirit. (NAB)

One of the major pre-occupations of the letters and the gospel of John is the divine indwelling. Our verse 13 is found imbedded in the long discourse on divine love. One of the conditions for the divine indwelling is fraternal love (vs. 12). Another is the confession that Jesus is the Son of God (vs. 15). Between these John has the statement that the indwelling of God is known as a reality because of the gift of his Spirit (vs. 13). Paul had often appealed to the Spirit as proof of the power of the Gospel (1 Thes 1:6; Gal 3:5) and as proof of the divine sonship (Rom 8:16). John prefers to speak of the divine indwelling, and he attributes the experiential nature of it to the Spirit.

1 John 5:6-10: The Spirit, the Water and the Blood

6. Jesus Christ it is who came through water and blood—
   not in water only,
   but in water and in blood.
   It is the Spirit who testifies to this,
   and the Spirit is truth.
7. Thus there are three that testify,
8. the Spirit and the water and the blood—
   and these three are of one accord.
9. Do we not accept human testimony?
   The testimony of God is much greater:
   it is the testimony God has given
   on his own Son's behalf.

10. Whoever believes in the Son of God
    possesses that testimony within his heart. (NAB)

This passage makes best sense if we recall the picture given in John
19:34-35, where the beloved disciple saw the side of Jesus pierced and
blood and water flow out. There John sees, in the water at least, a symbol of the Spirit. The blood is the blood of his sacrifice. That he came
not in water alone means that his baptism by John was not the only
moment in which the Spirit was manifested, for his baptism was also to
be a baptism of blood (cf. Mk 10:38). The Spirit which was shown to
"abide" upon Jesus in his baptism (Jn 1:53) was made available to the
church through his death (Jn 19:30, 34). The supreme witness to Jesus is
the Spirit (Jn 15:26), and we already know him as the "Spirit of Truth"
(1 Jn 4:2, 6; cf. Jn 15:26). The Spirit bore witness to Jesus at the baptism in the Jordan in the form of a dove (Jn 1:33-34) and upon the cross
in the mysterious symbolism of blood and water (Jn 19:34-35). Two witnesses were necessary to confirm any claim (Deut 17:6; 19:15); here
there are three. Verse 9 may be considered as referring to what immediately precedes: the Spirit, the water and the blood were God's testimony
to his Son. The believer receives God's own witness, that is, the witness
of the Spirit, manifested in the water and the blood, in his heart (vs. 10).
Early Christians no doubt saw in "water" and "blood" also a reference
to baptism and the Eucharist.

The Spirit in the Gospel of John

In the Gospel of John, as in the synoptics, Jesus is the anointed one
on whom the Spirit rests from the beginning of his ministry (1:33). But
the resulting conflict with the demonic powers appears in a different
way. In the synoptics, Jesus is led by the Spirit into the desert to do battle with Satan. There is no such temptation account in John. There is
not a single exorcism related by John, nor any resulting dispute about
the Spirit by which Jesus casts out demons. Jesus is accused of being
possessed, but the occasion for the accusation is not an exorcism but
rather his claims to divine status as God's son (8:48-59). The "casting
out" of the "Prince of this world" occurs not in exorcisms but uniquely
in the saving death and glorification of Jesus (12:31-32; 16:11). This subtle transfer of all exorcising power to the "lifting up" of Jesus shows
that for John the greatest grip of Satan upon the world is not sickness or
dementia but the sin of disbelief in Jesus and failure to recognize who he
is (cf. especially 16:8-11). The movement from the charismatic period of

Jesus' activity to the period of martyrdom, which we observed already in Mark, reappears in John, but the conquest of Satan is shifted in the latter from the first period to the second. Thus the death-glorification of Jesus appears not as an alternative way of salvation and deliverance that was humanly unplanned and unforeseen (as the synoptics might allow one to conclude) but as the unique, all-encompassing and fore-ordained act of deliverance from the power of Satan.

John's treatment of the healing and miracle traditions reveals a similar interest. He reduces them to seven and calls them *signs*. Upon examination they appear not merely as manifestations of Jesus' supernatural power but as parables in action which provide symbolic commentary on the meaning of Jesus' death-resurrection. Thus, for example, the miraculous change of water to wine at Cana (2:1-11) is an anticipation of Jesus' "hour" (2:4:13:1)—and there are many other motifs in the story which relate it to Jesus' glorification. The multiplication of loaves is an anticipation of the Eucharist (ch. 6). The healing of the man born blind (ch. 9) is a catechetical interpretation of the meaning of discipleship in the post-resurrectional church. And the raising of Lazarus, the last and supreme sign (ch. 11) not only shows Jesus to be the resurrection and the life (11:25-26) but also precipitates, paradoxically, Jesus' own life-giving death and resurrection (11:45-54).

The effect of this approach is to center all Jesus' charismatic power, more clearly than in the synoptics, upon the paschal mystery of his death-resurrection. Moreover it brings to the forefront the issue of Jesus' divine identity and portrays faith less as a tapping of charismatic power than as a personal commitment to Jesus as the Son of God. That is not to say that Jesus is stripped of charismatic power. On the contrary, some aspects of his charismatic activity, especially his supernatural knowledge of persons and events, appear even stronger in John than in the synoptics. But each of the signs is directed in some way toward the question of who Jesus is and faith in his person. Petitioning faith in Jesus' power appears in three of the signs (Cana, 2:3; the centurion, 4:49; the raising of Lazarus, 11:21-22). In the others Jesus takes the initiative. But in every case the significant issue is the faith that follows the sign, a faith in Jesus' divine person (2:11; 5:36; 14:11).

Jesus promises charismatic power to his disciples so great that the works they do will be even greater than his (14:12). But there is no sending of the disciples out during Jesus' own lifetime. The solemn missioning is reserved for Easter day, where it is described, as we shall see in detail later, as the power to forgive or hold men's sins (20:21-23).

Having drawn these rapid parallels and contrasts with the synoptic tradition, we must now go into more depth with those passages and themes that are more peculiar to John and are more immediately concerned with the Holy Spirit.

John 1:24-34: Jesus' Superiority to John the Baptist

24. Those whom the Pharisees had sent 25. proceeded to question him further: "If you are not the Messiah, nor Elijah, nor the Prophet, why do you baptize?" 26. John answered them: "I baptize with water. There is one among you whom you do not recognize— 27. the one who is to come after me—the strap of whose sandal I am not worthy to unfasten."
　　28. This happened in Bethany, across the Jordan, where John was baptizing.
　　29. The next day, when John caught sight of Jesus coming toward him, he exclaimed: "Look! There is the Lamb of God who takes away the sin of the world! 30. It is he of whom I said: 'After me is to come a man who ranks ahead of me, because he was before me.' 31. I confess I did not recognize him, though the very reason I came baptizing with water was that he might be revealed to Israel." 32. John gave this testimony also: "I saw the Spirit descend like a dove from the sky, and it came to rest on him. 33. But I did not recognize him. The one who sent me to baptize with water told me 'When you see the Spirit descend and rest on someone, it is he who is to baptize with the Holy Spirit.' 34. Now I have seen for myself and have testified, 'This is God's chosen one.' " (NAB)

The fourth gospel does not give an actual description of Jesus' baptism by John, as do the synoptics. In the development of the gospel tradition, there is a progressive tendency to deal with the theological difficulty that Jesus' submission to the baptism by John entailed, namely, that it seems to subordinate Jesus to John and make Jesus' reception of the Spirit dependent upon his baptism by John. Mark's way of relating the baptism shows no great concern for the problem. The Spirit descends on Jesus "immediately" as he comes up from the water (Mk 1:10). Luke avoids mentioning John as the baptizer and assumes that the water-rite is completed and that Jesus is praying when the Spirit descends (Lk 3:21), but the present participle "praying" (*proseuchomenou*) is still tied to the preceding aorist verb "baptized" (*baptisthentos*) by a co-ordinate "and" (*kai*), which hardly justifies a strict separation of the two moments. Matthew is even more apologetic for Jesus' baptism by

John and reports John's own protest (Mt 3:14-15), yet the descent of the Spirit is linked in the closest sequence to the baptism, though clearly as the more important and climactic of the two events. *The Gospel according to the Hebrews*, in a text reported by Jerome (*Contra Pelag. III, 2*), carries this even further. The fourth gospel eliminates the description of the baptism completely—though it retains the traditional setting for the Spirit's descent in the report that it was in the course of John's baptizing (mentioned twice) that John encountered Jesus. Another way in which the fourth evangelist has dealt with the difficulty is by avoiding any mention of John's baptism being a baptism of repentance, by making John's baptism a preparation for the one to come (1:26, 31) and by making the forgiveness of sins uniquely the gift of the Lamb of God whom the Baptist points out (1:29).

The way John describes the Spirit upon Jesus reveals a further interest of John's theology. The Spirit comes *to rest* upon Jesus (1:32, 33). The Greek verb *menein*, which John uses twice here, meaning "to rest, remain, abide," is one of his favorite terms. Jesus possesses the Spirit in a permanent way. Not only does this show Jesus' superiority to John and the fulfillment of the Messanic prophecy of Is 11:2, but the note of permanence prepares us for the later statements about Jesus' gift of the Spirit after his glorification (3:5, 34; 7:38-39; 14:15-18; 26; 15:26; 16:7-16; 20:22). The Spirit he will later give is the same Jesus alone enjoys during his ministry. The centrality of the Spirit upon Jesus is further confirmed by the fact that after the Baptist mentions that he has come to baptize with water (vs. 26), the mention of the superior role of Jesus as baptizer with the Spirit, which the synoptic accounts would lead us to expect immediately, is delayed until vs. 33, in order to focus upon Jesus himself as the one who is to come (vs. 27), the Lamb of God (vs. 29) and the one on whom the Spirit rests (vss. 32, 33).

John 3:5-8: Begotten of Water and Spirit

> 5. . . . "I solemnly assure you, no one can enter God's kingdom without being begotten of water and Spirit. 6. Flesh begets flesh, Spirit begets spirit. 7. Do not be surprised that I tell you you must be born from above. 8. The wind blows where it will. You hear the sound it makes but you do not know where it comes from, or where it goes. So it is with everyone begotten of the Spirit." (NAB)

This celebrated passage, in which Nicodemus, representative of the curious and half-believing element among the Pharisees, dialogues with Jesus, speaks more clearly than any other in the New Testament of a divine begetting through the Spirit. The idea of the Spirit as the agent of renewal appeared often in the Old Testament texts we examined, especially in Ezekiel. The idea of a spiritual, adoptive "begetting" was used as part of the enthronement ritual of the new king: "You are my son, this day have I begotten you" (Ps 2:7). And the Anointed king to come was to be endowed with the spirit (Is 11:2). But nowhere in the Old Testament were the two themes explicitly joined in the sense of the spirit mediating the sonship. Only in late prophetic literature was messianic Israel described as the result of a new birth in a passage that is obviously metaphorical (Is 66:7-9). Israel was indeed said to be son to the Lord by an adoptive relationship which began in the call out of Egypt (Hos 11:1). The idea of a new birth did not become a widespread image for the coming age of salvation probably because as an image it did not respect the already existing relationship of Israel as Yahweh's son. Why should someone who is already a son need to be reborn? In telling Nicodemus that he must be reborn if he would enter the kingdom, Jesus is challenging the adequacy of Nicodemus' approach—through study and observance—to achieve the kind of conversion needed for the kingdom. Paul had spoken of sonship in terms of adoption (Gal 4:6), and Titus 3:5 had spoken of the "bath of regeneration and renewal by the Holy Spirit" but even there the relationship between the Spirit and regeneration is not crystal clear. For John there is no doubt. He speaks of the Christian as begotten by God (1:13; 1 Jn 3:9; 5:1, 18), even going so far as to say that God's *seed* abides in him (1 Jn 3:9). Here, the begetting is the work of the Spirit.

The evangelist arrives at that affirmation progressively. Jesus first states that one must be born *anōthen*—a Greek word which can mean either "from above" or "again" (3:3). Both senses are probably meant by John. Then, to Nicodemus' inquiry, Jesus explains that this means being begotten "of water and Spirit" (3:5). The article does not appear before either "water" or "Spirit" here, so that the meaning is very general. "Spirit" here has the primary meaning of spirit in contrast to flesh, as the next verse explains. "Water" of course could conceivably be an image of the Spirit, for it is often so used in the Old Testament, as we have seen. However, "to be born of water" would indeed be a strange figure, and we would be hard put to explain why it is introduced into the "begetting" imagery if it were just another way of saying "Spirit". Thus most commentators, even those who think "water" entered the text at a very late stage in the gospel development, understand the phrase as a reference to baptism. Interpreters have discussed at great length how "water" and "Spirit" are related here: Are there two begettings, one of water and the other of the Spirit? Or is there only one begetting through two co-ordinate factors, water and the Spirit—or is one factor subordinate to the other? We cannot resolve all these questions here. Suffice it to point out how difficult it would be to affirm two begettings theologically, and that both "water" and "Spirit" are gramatically governed by the same Greek preposition *ex*, indicating the closest unity of the two. John does not therefore seem to envisage two "moments" of begetting but two necessary elements of one and the same act.

Jesus goes on to explain that the mysterious nature of this birth should not, after all, surprise Nicodemus, since the wind in the natural order is itself a mystery. *Pneuma* in the Greek means both "wind" and "spirit." The Spirit, like the wind, "blows where it will." On the level of pneumatology the phrase affirms that absolute freedom with which God's spirit moves and implicitly, therefore, the fact that the Spirit is gift (cf. Jn 4:10). And the Spirit, like the wind, is surprising in its approach and its destiny. It cannot be "caught" and possessed. Rather one is possessed or moved by it.

"So it is with everyone begotten of the Spirit" (vs. 8). Here the definite article is used with "Spirit," bringing to a climax the progressive development. While *pneuma,* when first introduced, meant primarily the realm of the spirit contrasted with the realm of the flesh, and at the beginning of vs. 8 meant simply the wind, here it is clearly the Holy Spirit, gift of the risen Lord, that is meant. Jesus, as portrayed by John, has progressively introduced us to the mystery of the Holy Spirit, agent of the new life by which man is reborn.

John 3:34: The Spirit Given without Measure

> For the one whom God has sent
> speaks the words of God;
> he does not ration his gift of the Spirit. (3:34 NAB)

This verse belongs to the conclusion of chapter 3, which is probably meant to conclude not only the final witness by John the Baptist (3:22-30) but the whole of chapter three, including the Nicodemus material. For our purposes it does not matter greatly whether the speaker of these verses is John the Baptist, Jesus, or the Evangelist. The "one God has sent" could conceivably refer to the Baptist, the man "sent by God" (1:6), but the context and the whole gospel would seem to require that it refer here to Jesus. One thing unclear about the verse is whether he who gives the Spirit without limits is the Father or Jesus. "He" could refer to either. The parallelism with vs. 35, "The Father loves the Son and has given everything over to him" would favor it being the Father who gives the Spirit without measure to the Son. In the Pauline letters, charismatic grace is said to be measured out (Eph 4:7; cf. 1 Cor 12), whereas the grace that saves "abounds beyond measure" (2 Cor 9:14; Eph 2:7; Rom 5:17). No such distinction is made by John in this passage. Jesus is not a prophet who receives periodic movements of the Spirit in order to speak the words of God. The Spirit, as we have seen, "abides" upon him (1:32, 33). This text adds to the note of permanence that of unlimited abundance. It is also significant that *word* and *Spirit* are again joined here. For John, as we have already seen, the teaching of Jesus and the Holy Spirit are simply two complementary aspects of the same revelatory process. The Spirit, we shall see later, gives the disciples an understanding of Jesus' words (14:25-26). Here Jesus speaks the words of God because the Spirit is given to him without measure.

Jesus, Source of Living Water

> 10. Jesus answered her, "If you knew the gift of God, and who it is that is saying to you, 'Give me a drink,' you would have asked him, and he would have given you living water." 11. The woman said to him, "Sir, you have nothing to draw with, and the well is deep; where do you get that living water? 12. Are you greater than our father Jacob, who gave us the well, and drank from it himself, and his sons, and his cattle?" 13. Jesus said to her, "Every one who drinks of this water will thirst again, 14. but whoever drinks of the water that I shall give him will never thirst; the water that I shall give him will become in him a spring of water welling up to eternal life." (4:10-14 RSV)

> 37. On the last and greatest day of the festival, Jesus stood up and cried out: "If anyone thirsts, let him come to me; let him drink 38. who believes in me. Scripture has it: 'From within him rivers of living water shall flow.' " 39. (Here he was referring to the Spirit, whom those that came to believe in him were to receive. There was, of course, no Spirit as yet, since Jesus had not yet been glorified.) (7:37-39 NAB)

> 33. When they came to Jesus and saw that he was already

dead, they did not break his legs. 34. One of the soldiers thrust
a lance into his side, and immediately blood and water flowed
out. (19:33-34 NAB)

These three texts are closely inter-related. The first belongs to the
encounter with the Samaritan woman, a scene which, like the one with
Nicodemus, proceeds from a mysterious statement by Jesus through
misunderstanding and questioning by the listener to a deeper self-revela-
tion of Jesus. As is often the case in John, there are several levels of
meaning operating at once. The *gift of God* in vs. 10 could conceivably
refer to the Torah, the Pentateuch, which in Judaism was regarded as
the supreme gift of God (*Gen R*. 6.7). Though the Samaritans rejected
the prophets and the other writings, they did consider the Pentateuch as
their inspired Scripture. If this were the sense, it could mean, "If you really knew the revelation contained in the Torah. . ." However, it is obvious from the sequence of the story that the gift of God is the living
water Jesus offers, for in vss. 10b and 13, the verb *give* is used twice with
Jesus as subject.

What, then does Jesus mean by living water here? "Living water"
has the double meaning of flowing, spring water on the one hand, and
the water of life on the other. Here Jesus is obviously using it in a symbolic sense. What concretely is symbolized? If we read ahead to chapter
7, we would conclude at once that it is the Holy Spirit. However, John
refrains from making that identification at this point, and the reason
may be that he would like to have the reader recall other Old Testament
texts in which "living water" was used, and to allow these, even when
they do not explicitly refer to the Holy Spirit, to come to rest upon
Jesus. Now while water is associated with the Old Testament imagery of
the Spirit, it is more often used for the law, instruction or wisdom. "The
teaching of the wise is a fountain of life" (Prov 13:14). "The fountain of
wisdom is a flowing brook" (Prov 18:4). Isaiah 55:1, written in the wisdom style, reads, "All you who are thirsty, come to the water." And in
Sir 24:21 Wisdom sings: "He who eats of me will hunger still; he who
drinks of me will thirst for more." Sirach describes the Torah as filling
men with wisdom like rivers overflowing their banks (24:23-31). The sectarians at Qumran used "the Well" (CD 6:4; 3:16) and even the more
precise expression "living water" (CD 19:34) to describe the Law. Thus
for a first-century Jew, and probably even for a Samaritan of the times,
the image would probably evoke first divine teaching or wisdom.

On the other hand, there were several Old Testament texts that associated water imagery with the Spirit (Gen 1:2; Isa 32:15; 44:3), and a
Qumran text reads: "Like purifying waters he will sprinkle upon him the

spirit of truth" (1 QS 4:21). The discourse with the Samaritan woman leads up to a discussion about the Spirit (4:23-24), and in 7:37-39 the rivers of living water are explicitly identified as the Spirit Jesus will give. Identifying the gift of God, through the imagery of living water, with the Holy Spirit corresponds to a Christian tradition we have met elsewhere in Acts (2:38; 8:20; 10:45; 11:17), Hebrews (6:4) and Paul (where the image of "pouring out" is connected with the gift of the Spirit, Rom 5:5).

If we try to choose between these two meanings we are probably falling into a typically modern tendency to dismember two complementary aspects of a single mystery. We have seen repeatedly in both the Old and the New Testament texts, that God communicates himself in two principal ways—through his word and through his spirit. Sometimes one element is stressed, sometimes another, and sometimes both are closely paralleled. This same tendency appears in John, where the Spirit and the revelation of God are intimately united: "The One whom God has sent speaks the *words* of God, for he does not ration his gift of the *Spirit*" (3:34). "It is the *spirit* that gives life; the flesh is useless. The *words* I spoke to you are *spirit* and life" (6:63). This relationship appears even more lucidly in the discourse at the last supper, as we shall see. For the revelation of God cannot be understood without the Spirit, and the Spirit's function is to testify to the revelation of Jesus and to illuminate it.

This same intimate relationship seems to underlie the expression later in the same exchange with the Samaritan woman:

> 23. "Yet an hour is coming, and is already here, when authentic worshipers will worship the Father in Spirit and truth. Indeed, it is just such worshipers the Father seeks. 24. God is Spirit, and those who worship him must worship in Spirit and truth." (4:23-24 NAB)

Jesus is not contrasting purely exterior worship with authentic interior worship. Certainly he is speaking about the replacement of such institutions as the Jerusalem temple and Mount Gerizim. But even this replacement has involved an external entry of God's revelation into time and space, in the person of Jesus himself (1:17). Later Jesus identifies himself as the "truth" (14:6); he reveals God's truth to men (8:45; 18:37). But complementary to this "truth" who is Jesus himself is the Spirit who is the Spirit of truth (14:17; 15:26) just as he is the Spirit of Jesus (7:37-39). The expression "Spirit and truth" then summarizes the new and authentic worship Jesus brings. It is a worship centered in him and vivified by the Spirit.

To return then for a moment to the "living water" image, we can say that John has seen in it the most intimate union of revelation (or word, or teaching) and the Spirit. He really goes back beyond the more recent Old Testament texts, some of which concerned teaching and some the spirit, to their more primitive root, in which the "fountain of living water" was the Lord himself (Jer 2:13; 17:13; Ps 36:9). Word and Spirit are simply two modes by which the same God communicates himself.

One peculiarly Johannine trait about this fountain of water is that it *leaps* (4:14—"welling up" RSV). The verb is used in the Greek Old Testament for the "spirit of God" as it falls on Samson, Saul and David (cf. above). The leaping of the lame would be one of the signs of the messianic age (Is 35:6), and we recall how Luke saw this fulfilled in the lame man cured at the Beautiful Gate of the temple, who was walking and leaping and praising God (Acts 3:8). In John the water leaps up to eternal life.

The second major text of John given above, that of 7:37-39, situates the saying of Jesus on the "last and greatest day" of the feast of Tabernacles. Originally a feast celebrating the conclusion of the harvest (Ex 23:16) accompanied by music and dancing and the drinking of new wine (cf. 1 Sam 1:14-15), it later became associated with the memories of the desert, when the Israelites sojourned in tents, and very early it had a relationship with the temple, because Solomon dedicated the temple on this feast (1 Kgs 8:2). In the later prophetic period the feast became associated with Judaism's hopes for the future. Zechariah 11-14 describes the coming "day of the Lord" in the setting of the feast of Tabernacles. Not only does the Lord pour out a spirit of compassion and supplication on Jerusalem (12:10; cf. above), but he opens a fountain for the house of David to cleanse Jerusalem (13:1) and living waters flow out from Jerusalem to the Mediterranean and the Dead Sea (14:8). Now water had an important role to play in the liturgical celebration of this feast, and this fact explains some of the references in Zechariah. Though the feast was originally one which primarily looked back in thanksgiving upon the harvest season, it also looked *forward* to the future agricultural year, and early rains falling during the feast were considered a specially good sign of divine blessing upon the season to come. To this end, prayers for rain became part of the celebration, as we see reflected in Zech 10:1 and 14:17. Each day of the week-long celebration, a procession made its way to the fountain of Gihon, the spring which fed into the pool of Siloam, and there a priest would draw water in a golden pitcher as the choir

chanted Is 12:3, "With joy you will draw water at the fountain of salvation and say on that day: Give thanks to the Lord, acclaim his
name. . . ." The procession would then return through the Water Gate
to the temple and upon arriving there would process around the altar of
holocausts to the chanting of Ps 118:25: "O Lord, grant salvation! O
Lord, grant prosperity!" On the last and greatest day of the feast the
procession circled the altar seven times. The priest would then pour out
the water on the southwest corner of the altar, the direction from which
rain-bringing winds came.

It is in the midst of all this imagery that John situates the saying of
Jesus inviting the thirsty to come to him and drink. The commentaries
discuss the question of how the text here should be punctuated. One
way, it would read as in the RSV, "If any one thirst, let him come to me
and drink. He who believes in me, as the scripture has said, 'Out of his
heart shall flow rivers of living water.' " This would have the rivers of
water flowing from within the believer. The other way of punctuating is
followed by the NAB, the translation we have chosen, with the meaning
that the rivers of living water flow from Jesus. The latter reading seems
preferable, though obviously the first is not contrary to John's thought
either, inasmuch as the fountain of water Jesus promises is one that
functions within the believer (4:14).

But what Scripture text is cited in vs. 38? As it stands, it does not
correspond exactly to any text of the Hebrew or the Greek Old Testament. It must therefore be an allusion to a more specific text, or a citation of an Aramaic commentary on a text (targum), or a fusion of
texts. Those who take the rivers as flowing from within the believer
often cite Prov 18:4; Is 58:11; Sir 24:28-31 and in the Scrolls, 1 QH
8:16. Those who take the rivers as flowing from the Messiah adduce the
more frequent allusions to the rock in the desert, which we know became in the early Church a type for Christ (1 Cor 10:4). Assuming that
John 7:37-39 is related to Rev 22, then it seems that the background of
both is Ezekiel's vision of the water's flowing from the temple (Ez 47:1-
11) and Zechariah's vision of *living* waters flowing from Jerusalem (Zech
14:8). Jesus would then be presenting himself not simply as the desert
rock (the view of Paul in 1 Cor 10:4) but as the *temple* rock from which
according to the view of Ezekiel and Zechariah, living waters would
flow.

Whatever the Old Testament background, John has not left us in
doubt as to the meaning of the symbol: it is the Spirit whom the risen
Lord Jesus will give to the believer. John is careful, however, to note that
at this moment, in the feast of Tabernacles in Jesus' public ministry, the
word was only promise. It would be fulfilled only upon Jesus' glorification.

That leads us to the third text, the scene of Calvary, when Jesus' side is opened. Most students of John agree that the evangelist is interested in more than the simple physiological fact. Whatever symbolism lies behind the blood, there can be little doubt that John sees in the water coming from Jesus' side a fulfillment of the prophecy of 7:37-39. As Moses struck the rock in the desert and water flowed (Num 20:11), so Jesus' side is pierced and from it flows the water, symbol of the Spirit. It is very interesting to note that according to the Jewish midrash on Ex 4:9 (*Midrash Rab.* 3:13) Moses struck the rock twice, first bringing forth blood and then water. For John, Jesus' glorification begins with the cross (12:23-24). While the evangelist does not think it necessary to state explicitly that this event is symbolic of the gift of the Spirit, he surely sees it as fulfilling prophecy, as he triumphantly adds, "This testimony has been given by an eyewitness, and his testimony is true. He tells what he knows is true, so that you may believe" (19:35). And John's way of describing the death of Jesus a few lines earlier, "Jesus gave over the spirit" (19:30), is a word-play meaning not only "he breathed his last" but "he delivered the Spirit (*sci.* to the church)."

We may conclude that John understands the Holy Spirit, just as Paul did, to come from the glorified Lord Jesus. He uses many of the Old Testament images Paul used, especially that of the rock from which the waters flow. He differs from Paul in that he dramatizes his theology more fully in the context of Jewish liturgy and so unites Jesus' death with his resurrection in one mystery of glorification that the Spirit can be seen coming directly from the crucified Jesus as the final gift of his mortal life (his last breath was the Spirit) or as the waters of life coming from his side once he had bowed his head in death.

The Paraclete

Let us now turn to the way in which John stands out as unique in his presentation of the Holy Spirit, his use of the term *Paraclete*. The fact that this term appears, in the gospel, only in Jesus' farewell discourse already suggests a close relationship between the Paraclete and the departure of Jesus.

John 14:15-18, 25-26: Another Paraclete, the Spirit of Truth

15. "If you love me
    and obey the commands I give you,

16. I will ask the Father
    and he will give you another Paraclete—
    to be with you always:
17. the Spirit of truth,
    whom the world cannot accept
    since it neither sees him nor recognizes him;
    but you can recognize him
    because he remains with you
    and will be within you.
18. I will not leave you orphaned;
    I will come back to you.

25. This much have I told you while I was still with you;
26. The Paraclete, the Holy Spirit
    whom the Father will send in my name,
    will instruct you in everything,
    and remind you of all that I told you." (NAB)

The opening line of this section is unusual in a passage that will speak of the gift of the Spirit, for it seems to make that gift conditional upon the disciples' love of Jesus and adherence to his commands. But this is covenant language reminiscent of the great "if" of Ex 19:5 ("If you hearken to my voice and keep my covenant, you will be my special possession, dearer to me than all other people. . .") and the long series of blessings in Deut 28 which are all conditioned thus: "If you heed the voice of the Lord, your God, and are careful to observe all his commandments" (Deut 28:1). The gift of the Spirit cannot be given, because it cannot be received, in one who does not love Jesus and live according to his word. In a single stroke the evangelist states what Paul had said in other ways, that the new covenant of the Spirit is available only through adherence to Jesus and acceptance of his ethic.

The Spirit given is nonetheless a gift, and he is given by the Father on the Son's request (vs. 16). And here for the first time the Spirit is called "another Paraclete". Both words are important and each bears examination.

The English word *Paraclete* is a rendering of the Greek *paraklētos* which in turn is derived from the verb *para-kalein* meaning literally "to call to one's side." Thus in the most radical sense of the word a paraclete is an advocate, a helper or spokesman or more precisely a lawyer who will plead on one's behalf. In Paul and in the Acts, the verb *parakalein* often means to exhort, encourage, less frequently to comfort.

In what sense does John use the noun paraclete here? It would be helpful if there were some Hebrew or Aramaic word from which the Greek term were certainly derived, but so far none has been clearly identified. In fact, it may well be that the Jews simply used a transliteration of the Greek word, for it appears as such in the *Pirqe Aboth* 4:11. To discover the special sense in which John uses the term, perhaps it is best to leave the reader at this point with the general orientations given above and study the passages in which the word appears, hoping to draw some conclusions at the end of our quest.

The first clue given is that the Paraclete is *another* paraclete. This assumes that Jesus has been a paraclete for his disciples. Jesus is in fact called a paraclete in 1 Jn 2:1. There the title means a heavenly intercessor. Here the allusion is to what the earthly Jesus has been. Jesus has kept and cared for his disciples and spoken in their behalf (cf. the whole of chapter 17). If the Holy Spirit is another paraclete, we may assume that he will do permanently what Jesus has done for the disciples. Unlike the earthly Jesus, whose departure was necessary (to take up his permanent role of Paraclete before the Father, 1 Jn 2:1; cf. Jn 1:1), this Paraclete once given the disciples, will never leave. Since Jesus only "pitched his tent" among us (Jn 1:14), it is through the Spirit that the promise of Isaiah 7:14, "God-with-us," will be realized.

In vs. 17 we learn that this Paraclete is the "Spirit of truth." Truth here does not mean abstract or philosophical truth. Neither does it mean the moral virtue of veracity. Opposed as it is here to the "world" which cannot receive it, the term suggests something much more akin to the view of the Qumran covenanters, for whom it meant God's revealed way of life triumphant in the final battle over all his enemies. It is likewise only in the Qumran literature that the term "spirit of truth" appears prior to the New Testament. The "spirit of truth" is an angelic spirit helping the sons of light in their struggle against the powers of darkness led by the spirit of falsehood. All the "spirits of truth" are under the dominion of the "Prince of Light," whom God has appointed to bring "the company of thy Truth" to "a destiny of Light according to thy Truth" (1 QM 13). The Prince of Light is elsewhere called the Angel of Truth (1 QS 3:24-25, 38-39). This Prince of Light is probably Michael (1 QM 17).

This background of the term raises more acutely the question we met in discussing the book of Revelation concerning the relationship of pneumatology to angelology. We shall return to it after examining the various paraclete texts. Suffice it for the moment to note that as John understands the "Spirit of Truth" here, it is opposed to the world and therefore on the side of the disciples, and yet more than a spirit battling alongside the disciples. Rather, as vs. 17 affirms, this Spirit abides within. The immediate addition of the words, "I will not leave you orphaned; I will come back to you" (vs. 18) indicates that, at least on the level of the final redaction of these words of Jesus, his coming back and his not leaving them orphans was understood to have occurred through the gift of the permanent Paraclete, though originally they may have been understood of the post-resurrection appearances of Jesus.

In vs. 26 the Paraclete, expressly identified for the first time as the Holy Spirit, is said to be *sent* by the Father in Jesus' name as he was promised in vs. 16 to be given by the Father at Jesus' bidding. He will teach the disciples all they need to know. The implication, suggested by Jesus' introduction, "This much have I told you while I was still with you," is that he has not been able to teach them everything. Above all he has not been able to give them understanding of his words (cf. 2:21-22). The Paraclete will teach them "all things." Lest the expression "all things" be interpreted as discontinuous with the teaching of Jesus, the phrase is immediately added, "and remind you of all that I told you." The church's memory of Jesus and his word is the particular work of the Holy Spirit.

John 15:26-27: The Paraclete, the Witnessing Spirit

26. "When the Paraclete comes,
    the Spirit of truth who comes from the Father—
    and whom I myself will send from the Father—
    he will bear witness on my behalf.
27. You must bear witness as well,
    for you have been with me from the beginning." (NAB)

There are three new elements in this text about the Paraclete. First, he is said to "come forth from the Father." The Greek verb *ekporeuesthai* is the same one used in Rev 22:1 for the river of the water of life which comes forth from the throne of God and from the Lamb. The same verb was used in the creedal statements of the fourth century to describe the eternal procession of the Holy Spirit from the Father. However, parallel here to "I will send from the Father" the term describes the "temporal mission" of the Holy Spirit.

Secondly, Jesus is here said to send the Holy Spirit. In 14:16, 26 the giving and the sending was the work of the Father. Since Jesus and the Father are one (10:30), the sending can be attributed to one without excluding the other.

Thirdly, the role of the "Spirit of Truth" is to witness on behalf of

Jesus. We have already met, in the synoptic tradition and Acts, the notion of the disciples as witnesses and the role of the Holy Spirit in that witness before the world: "You will receive power when the Holy Spirit comes down on you; and you will be my witnesses . . . even to the ends of the earth" (Acts 1:8). We have also noted in Paul the role of the Spirit as the inward witness of the divine sonship (Rom 8:16). The notion of witness varies considerably, from that of preaching the good news, to that of testifying before courts, to that of martyrdom. All three meanings are found in the Acts, and the last two in the synoptics. Here in John an even more powerful expression is used: "He will bear witness." Witness here has the broadest possible sense. It describes the whole role of the Spirit *vis-à-vis* Jesus and the world, and the Spirit himself is the first to witness. Obviously, he will do this through the disciples, who are particularly qualified because they have been with Jesus from the beginning (vs. 27). As the result of their witnessing, or of the Spirit's witnessing through them, the hostility of the world gets worse (16:1-4a). This leads to the final Paraclete text.

John 16:4-11: The Paraclete, in the Physical Absence
of Jesus, Prosecutes the World

4. . . . "I did not speak of this with you from the beginning
   because I was with you.
5. Now that I go back to him who sent me,
   not one of you asks me, 'Where are you going?'
6. Because I have had all this to say to you,
   you are overcome with grief.
7. Yet I tell you the sober truth:
   It is much better for you that I go.
   If I fail to go,
   the Paraclete will never come to you,
   whereas if I go,
   I will send him to you.
8. When he comes
   he will prove the world wrong
   about sin
   about justice
   about condemnation
9. About sin—
   in that they refuse to believe in me;

10. about justice—
    from the fact that I go to the Father
    and you can see me no more;
11. about condemnation—
    for the prince of this world has been condemned. (NAB)

This, the last of the Paraclete texts, resumes much that has already been said and carries it further. That of which Jesus did not speak from the beginning of his ministry (vs. 4) was the persecution in store for the disciples, just described in 16:1-4a. The reason given for this silence is not that Jesus wanted to spare them discouragement at the start but rather that during his public life Jesus himself was with his disciples, and he could, by his physical presence in their midst, be their support and defense. But now that physical presence is being withdrawn from them, because Jesus is going to the Father (Jesus' habitual way of referring to his death in the farewell discourse). But the "sober truth" is that it is actually better for the disciples that Jesus go, because if he does not, the Paraclete will never come to them (vs. 7). The negative way in which this is stated is intentionally emphatic. This phrase gives us the key to John's notion of the Paraclete: he is the replacement for the physical presence of Jesus while Jesus is with the Father. The Paraclete will indeed mediate the presence of Jesus to his disciples (cf. 14:18 above), but that presence will no longer be physical as during the public ministry. It will nonetheless be visible and experiential, but not because Jesus is palpably present in their midst. Rather the Paraclete will continue to work in and through the disciples in such a way that they will know the spiritual presence of Jesus.

In vss. 8-11 we have detailed the principal function of the Paraclete as envisaged by John. The Spirit not only enables the disciples to make the proper defense before courts (synoptics), not only acts in a way unacceptable to the world (14:17), not only witnesses to Jesus and empowers the disciples to witness (Acts 1:8; Jn 15:26-27); he prosecutes and condemns the world for its sin. The verb *elenchein peri* can be understood in several ways. It can have the general sense of "bring to light, expose," applicable both to good and evil, or the more restricted sense "to convict of a crime." In neither case is the convincing and conversion of the erring party implied. In the case of the world's sin the latter meaning is the better. The world's sin is its disbelief in Jesus (vs. 9). This categorical statement crystalizes the ethics of John throughout his gospel. John shows no interest in catalogues of virtues and vices such as we find in the epistles or in Mark 7:21-22. For him there is only one attitude on which judgment takes place: acceptance or rejection of Jesus.

The world's sin is its rejection of the light offered in Jesus Christ (3:19; 12:37; 15:22-24; 9:41).

Concerning "justice" and "condemnation" the other sense of "bringing to light" or "showing who is right and who is wrong" seems to fit better. "Justice" in this context does not mean the righteousness that is given to the disciples but the act of God whereby he fulfills his covenant promise to save his people. The idea is very close to that of Paul's "justice of God" in Romans, which develops the notion of the "saving justice" of God broached by Second Isaiah and the Psalms. What shows that Jesus' trial and death was in fact the mighty saving act of God in fulfillment of his covenant promises is that Jesus has returned in glory to the Father (vs. 10). What the Sanhedrin claimed was "justice" was indeed "justice" but God's justice, not theirs. And, although part of the glorification of Jesus is his absence from the sight of the disciples (vs. 10), the prosecuting Spirit uses even this to demonstrate the truth of Jesus' glorification, because the Spirit given by the Father and Jesus upon that glorification is known and experienced as abiding within them (14:17).

The final element that is brought to light and put in proper focus is "condemnation." The Greek word *krisis* is sometimes translated "judgment," but the subjective ring of that word in English (for example, the expression "in my judgment" often simply means "in my opinion") often obscures its originally forensic meaning, which is that of a sentence handed down by a judge or court without appeal. Here too there is a surprising reversal of the decision of the court that condemned Jesus. Jesus' death may have seemed to his judges good riddance, one man dying rather than the whole people perishing (11:50). To the disciples it may have seemed the supreme hour of the powers of darkness (Lk 22:53). But in fact, the death of Jesus was his final triumphant encounter with the Prince of this world (12:31; 14:30). Whatever may be said elsewhere about the power of Satan still operative in the world (1 Jn 5:19; Eph 2:2; 6:12), he has no further power over the disciples for he has already been condemned (vs. 11). The Paraclete makes this triumph obvious to the disciples.

In this description of the Holy Spirit as the prosecuting Paraclete we have touched on an element that is most proper to John's pneumatology. Were there any forerunners to this view in the Old Testament or late Judaism or elsewhere in the New Testament?

There is no doubt that the prophets often brought to light hidden sins. Nathan exposed David's sin (2 Sam 11-12), and Jesus did the same with the Samaritan woman (4:18). But in both cases this surfacing of sin led to the conversion and repentance of the sinner. Such is not the picture we have in John of the prosecuting Spirit. It is more like Daniel's vindication of Susanna that led to the condemnation of the wicked elders (Dan 13), except that the stage is now cosmic. It is the Holy War carried into an eschatological Christian context, with the Paraclete prosecuting and winning the condemnation of the Prince of this world.

The most helpful light on this development is found, as we have previously intimated, in the angelology of the Old Testament and its developments in later Judaism. We have already noted the various roles ascribed to the "angel of the Lord (or of God)" in early texts of the Old Testament. The angel appears as a friendly messenger from God (2 Sam 14:17, 20; 1 Sam 29:10), in whom one may confide (2 Sam 19:28). He inspires and helps the prophet (2 Kgs 1:3, 15; 1 Kgs 19:7), announces the birth of a hero (Jgs 13:3-23), commissions leaders (Jgs 6:11-24) and fights for Israel against her enemies and protects her (Ex 14:19; 2 Kgs 19:35). It is the latter aspect of conquest that interests us here.

Under the impact of Persian dualism the life of God's faithful ones was dramatized as a conflict between angelic powers, such as the accuser, Satan, and the defending angel (Job 1:6-12; Zech 3:1-8). There are allusions in Job to an angelic mediator who defends the just man (33:23-24), a witness in heaven, a spokesman on high (16:19), who will vindicate Job after his death (19:25). This "reversal of judgment" against the accusers is exactly what the Paraclete does in relation to Jesus. Elsewhere in the apocalyptic literature the angelic figure of Michael (Dan 10:13; cf. Rev. 12:7, Jude 9) is the great champion of God's people in their eschatological contests. And so important was he for the Qumran convenanters that they referred to themselves as the "kingdom of Michael" (cf. 1 QM *passim*). In the *Testament of Judah*, a text dear to the Dead Sea sectarians, the "spirit of truth" is an angel who tugs at man as does the spirit of falsehood.

Notice how in the following text there is a close relationship between this "spirit of truth" and the revelation of what is in man's heart:

> 1. Know, therefore, my children, that two spirits wait upon man—the spirit of truth and the spirit of deceit. . . . 3. And the works of truth and the works of deceit are written upon the hearts of men, and each one of them the Lord knoweth. 4. And there is no time at which the works of men can be hid; for on the heart itself have they been written down before the Lord. 5. *And the spirit of truth testifieth all things and accuseth all;* and the sinner is burnt up by his own heart, and cannot raise his face to the judge. (Test. Judah 20:1-5; trans. R. H. Charles, italics ours)

But, as we have seen in a previous chapter, the spirits of truth and false-hood are also something within man (cf. 1 QS 4:23-24), and the spirit of truth at Qumran is often called the holy spirit. So too in the *Book of Jubilees* God is asked to create a holy spirit within his people so that they may not succumb to the accusations of the spirit of Beliar (*Jub.* 1:20-23).

It is clear then that John has used motifs from angelology to express certain aspects about the Holy Spirit inadequately conveyed in previous biblical images of the Spirit. These aspects appear as two: per-sonality and militancy. Images like wind and water suggest mystery and movement; breath suggests life and personhood but more in the source of the breath than in the breath itself. The word *pneuma* is neuter in Greek and thus does not easily lend itself to personality. In the latest de-velopment on the "holy spirit" represented by the Wisdom of Solomon, personification is stretched to the limits, and the spirit of the Lord pur-sues wickedness and condemns it (Wis 1:7-9). But all these texts still be-tray monotheistic Judaism's reluctance to attribute autonomy and per-sonhood to the Spirit of the Lord. On the other hand, the concept of "angel" was readily at hand, and there was no danger attributing per-sonality to a being whose creaturehood was equally affirmed. Now John, by identifying the Holy Spirit as Paraclete, and more specifically as another Paraclete like Jesus, makes the bold step which previous au-thors, even those of the New Testament, did not make. The personhood of the Holy Spirit is assured in a way that previous Wisdom texts could only affirm metaphorically and other New Testament texts only at best imply. And to the Holy Spirit John draws all that previous tradition had said about the militant "spirit of truth" who prosecutes the world in favor of God's chosen ones.

However, the Paraclete in John is not an angel. An angelic function has simply been transferred to him. Is this transfer of angelic function to the Holy Spirit original with John, or was there some biblical precedent for it? We think there is an Old Testament text which not only justifies the transfer but was more than likely in John's mind as he set down these words of Jesus. It is one of the very rare Old Testament texts in which the precise term "holy spirit" appears—Isaiah 63:9-14. The reader may wish to refresh his memory from our earlier analysis of this text. To build on what was discovered there, let us recall that this text echoes Exodus 33, Moses' dissatisfaction with the Lord's offer to send his angel to lead the Israelites and the Lord's final agreement to go with Moses in person (*panim*, "face," "presence"). We saw that the "holy spirit" is so closely associated in Is 63:9-10 and Ps 51:13 (cf. also Ps 104:29; 139:7) with the divine presence "in person" as to be practically

equivalent, and in the Isaian text in intentional contrast with angelic in-
strumentality. "His holy spirit" is therefore not an angel but the Lord
himself in his leading, caring, saving activity.

Now we can carry this further than our previous analysis of Is 63
permitted. In Is 63:11 we read:

> Where is he who brought up out of the sea
>   the shepherd of his flock?
> Where is he who put his holy spirit in their midst. . . ? (NAB)

The shepherd, just mentioned in the preceding verse, is Moses. The Lord
brought this shepherd of his flock out of the sea in the Exodus. And
notice how this is followed immediately by the gift of "his holy spirit."
That this text provides a background for understanding the role of the
Holy Spirit in John appears from the following considerations:
(1) This is one of only four passages in the Old Testament where
the term "holy spirit" appears (the others: Ps 51:13; Wis 1:5; 9:17). The
early Christian community and John himself surely knew the passage.
(2) John not only knows the tradition about Jesus as the shepherd (Mk
6:34; Mt 9:36; 26:31; Mk 14:27; Lk 15:3-7; Mt 18:12-13; Jn 16:32) but he
has a long allegory about the Good Shepherd (Jn 10) which the other
gospels do not. (3) The expression "brought up" in the Greek of Is 63:11
is the causative form of the same verb *anabainō* used elsewhere in the
New Testament for the ascension of Jesus (Acts 2:34; Rom 10:6; Eph 4:8)
and particularly by John to describe Jesus' glorification (1:51; 3:13; 6:62;
20:17). Though John does not describe the ascension as Luke does, he has
a deep theological understanding of it. (4) While the Hebrew text of Is
63:11 reads, "brought up *out of the sea*," the better Septuagint Greek
reading is "*out of the earth*." It is not surprising then that Christians
should think of this scripture passage as fulfilled in the resurrection of
Jesus, as indeed the author of Hebrews did: "The God of peace, who
brought up from the dead the great Shepherd of the sheep. . ." (Heb
13:20). And Eph 4:9-10 relates the ascension to a previous descent into
the earth and a subsequent outpouring of the Spirit. (5) As the difference between the angel and "his holy spirit" was that the latter was given
"in their midst" (Is 63:11), so a major difference of the Holy Spirit from
the heavenly defending angel is that he abides *within* the disciples (Jn
14:17). (6) The role of guiding is common both to the Spirit of the Lord
in Is 63:14 and to the Spirit of Truth in Jn 16:13.

We believe, then, that John not only knew of the Is 63 tradition and
its Christian interpretation (witnessed by Heb 13:20) but that in identifying the Paraclete as the Holy Spirit he did with the militant angelology

of late Judaism exactly what the author of Is 63 did with the exodus angel tradition. He took from it all that was attributed to the angel and transferred it to the Lord's "holy spirit." The term *paraclete* emphasizes the personhood and the militant activity of the Holy Spirit inadequately conveyed by previous images. And yet, just as the "holy spirit" was in Is 63 an alternate way of saying "the Lord himself" or "the Lord's face," so the Holy Spirit is the real and active presence of the Father whose face was revealed in Jesus (Jn 14:9) and now of Jesus himself while he is with the Father. The presence of the Holy Spirit means that Jesus has not orphaned his disciples and the gift of the Spirit is Jesus himself coming to them (14:18).

If we seem to have reached a point of confusion, in which we do not know whether the Holy Spirit is really a distinct person or whether he is in reality the presence and activity of the Father and the Son, it means that we have reached the summit of New Testament pneumatology and have touched the mystery itself. The Paraclete is a living, personal presence given by the Father and Jesus glorified to supply for Jesus' physical absence until his return. The Spirit is both a person and the personal, spiritual presence of the Father and the Son. That is where the mystery lies.

John 16:12-15: The Paraclete—Teaching and Prophetic Spirit

12: I have much more to tell you
    but you cannot bear it now.
13. When he comes, however,
    being the Spirit of truth,
    he will guide you to all truth.
    He will not speak on his own,
    but will speak only what he hears,
    and will announce to you the things to come.
14. In doing this he will give glory to me,
    because he will have received from me
    what he will announce to you.
15. All that the Father has belongs to me.
    That is why I said that what he will announce to you
    he will have from me (NAB)

This text we have separated from the preceding one only to be able to bring it closer to the commentary. It is still part of the Paraclete passage, as is evident from the use of "the Spirit of Truth" in vs. 13. The difference lies only in the fact that the focus is upon the Paraclete's relation not to the external world but to the disciples.

Gramatically, the "more" that Jesus has to tell his disciples (vs. 12) may refer to additional content or simply to further explanation of what has already been said. That they could not "bear" it may indicate that Jesus had more to tell them about persecution; or it may simply mean that they would not understand the "more" that he would tell them. This text has frequently been cited in the discussion of whether there is new revelation to be given by the Spirit which was not given by Jesus. Though the text might at first seem to point in this direction, it must be heard in balance with other Johannine texts such as 15:15, "I have made known to you all that I heard from my Father," and the statement in this very passage we are examining that whatever the Spirit announces he will have from Jesus (16:14-15). It is a favorite theme of John's gospel that after the resurrection the disciples will be given full understanding of Jesus' deeds and words (2:22; 12:16; 13:7), and thus it is likely that this fuller understanding is what is meant by the "more" which Jesus cannot communicate now.

For the third time the Paraclete is called "the Spirit of truth" (14:17; 15:26). The function of the Spirit as guide has already appeared in several Old Testament texts we have examined (Is 63:14; Ps 143:10). In Rev 7:17 the same verb is used to describe the Lamb guiding the saints to the spring of life-giving water. But there is some question here whether "all truth" is the goal of the direction (some important manuscripts read "into all truth") or the kind of guidance that is given (a meaning suggested by other manuscripts which read "*in* all truth"). In 8:31-32 Jesus had said, "If you live according to my teaching, you are truly my disciples; then you will know the truth, and the truth will set you free." In our text we are told how that promise is to be fulfilled, namely through the Paraclete. The verb suggests that the knowledge is one of gradual unfolding, as happens when one is led along a path. The picture in the Acts, as well as in Paul's letters, shows that the apostles were not given all knowledge and all solutions to future problems in advance. But they were able, with the enlightenment of the Holy Spirit, to respond to each new situation as it arose (e.g. Acts 6:1-6; 10; 15). Even here, however, continuity with Jesus is surely involved, since Jesus is identified as the truth itself as well as the way (14:6). In fact, the same disappropriation in transmission which Jesus had maintained of himself —"The word you hear is not my own," 14:24; "The Son can do nothing of himself but only what he sees the Father doing" (5:19)—is characteristic of the Spirit: "He will not speak on his own, but will speak only what he hears" (vs. 13).

But what is the meaning of the phrase, "and will announce to you the things to come"? The phrase is similar to that which appears several times in the book of Revelation: "to show [his servants] what is soon to come to pass" (Rev. 1:1, 19; 4:1; 22:6, 16), an expression borrowed from Dan 2:29, 45. It would be natural to conclude that here the evangelist reflects the apocalyptic tradition in which the Spirit or an angel (here the Paraclete) prophetically reveals future historical events. We must reckon seriously with this meaning, for the book of Revelation belongs to the Johannine literature and a cross-influence of the tradition at this point is possible. However, it is equally obvious that John's gospel is singularly lacking in apocalyptic visions and, on the contrary, is strong in its emphasis on realized eschatology, that is, that in Jesus himself the whole meaning of all prophetic symbols, the future, and even life itself is contained (1:12; 3:19; 17:3).

Does the word "announce" (Greek *anangellein*) shed any light on the meaning of the phrase? In its classical sense the verb means to "report back" or to repeat what has already been said. A case can be made for the latter meaning in four other appearances of the verb in John but not in 4:25 where it clearly means to announce or to declare for the first time. In the Greek of Isaiah, where it appears fifty-seven times, it frequently means to *foretell*. In Dan 10:21 the angel tells (*anangellō*) what is written in the Book of Truth. The Book of Truth is not the scripture but, metaphorically, God's sure knowledge of the past and the future. On the other hand, when we read that Daniel will "declare" the king's dream (Dan 2:2, 4, 7), the meaning is the *interpretation* of a dream that has already been experienced, though its fulfillment has not yet occurred. If this is the nuance of the verb here in John, then the sense could be that the Paraclete will interpret for the disciples the ongoing events of their lives, with special reference perhaps to the persecution Jesus has already foretold.

It does not seem possible to settle the precise meaning decisively. Obviously, some orientation to the future, and not just to the past, is intended. In any case, to be faithful to the immediate context and to the gospel's overall theology, this role of the Spirit must be seen in the closest continuity with the work of Jesus. It is a continuity not just with the Jesus of the historical ministry but with the Jesus glorified in the presence of the Father. The Jesus of the Farewell Discourse has no difficulty affirming that the works of the disciples will be even greater than the ones he has done in his public ministry, since they will be done by the power of Jesus who is at the Father's side (14:12). Similarly, what the Spirit will announce or interpret about the future he will receive from Jesus, and the purpose of the revelation is to glorify Jesus (vs. 15). And, since all that the Father has belongs to Jesus (vs. 15), in interpreting Jesus to men, the Paraclete will also be interpreting the Father.

John 20:20-23: The Disciples Receive the Spirit

20. . . . At the sight of the Lord the disciples rejoiced.
21. "Peace be with you," he said again.
    "As the Father has sent me, so I send you."
22. Then he breathed on them and said:
    "Receive the Holy Spirit.
23. If you forgive men's sins, they are forgiven them;
    if you hold them bound, they are held bound." (NAB)

The resurrection appearance to the disciples causes them to rejoice, as Jesus had foretold (16:22). Jesus' first words assure them that his *shalom* is now given to them in a permanent way. The word is not simply the equivalent of the "Fear not" traditionally part of supernatural appearances but, as "peace" sums up all good things, life and prosperity as well as inner well-being, it really means the communication of all that the gospel has promised as coming from Jesus. As Paul listed joy and peace among the first fruits of the Spirit (Gal 5:22; Rom 14:17), so the Spirit is communicated in fulfillment of the *shalom* manifested in Jesus' word. If Trito-Isaiah has foretold that a river of peace would descend upon Jerusalem (Is 66:12) and Jesus had promised that rivers of living water would flow from him, it is at this moment that the prophecy is fulfilled as far as the disciples' reception of the gift is concerned.

John reserves the sending of the disciples to this moment. Matthew, too, has the commissioning scene as the climax of his gospel (Mt 28:19), but he had related a sending of the disciples during the ministry—even though he gave plenty of indications that the full mission took place only after Jesus' resurrection. By attaching the reference to the Holy Spirit immediately to the mission, John intends to show that more was involved than simply a verbal authorization (an impression we might have gotten from the synoptic "mission" passages). What is really happening is a new creation. For the action of breathing upon the disciples evokes Gen 2:7 and other texts built on it such as Ez 37:9 and Wis 15:11 describing God's creation of man by the inbreathing of his spirit. Paul had described the risen Jesus as the Second Adam superior to the first because he was "life-giving spirit" (1 Cor 15:45). In John we have the actual dramatization of this relationship. Jesus breathes upon his disciples and in this gesture communicates the Holy Spirit. Since this is the moment of the fulfillment of the promise of the last discourse, in which Jesus can send the Spirit only once he is glorified in the Father's presence (16:7) we can conclude that although Jesus appears in the upper room to his disciples on earth, he is already at the Father's right hand and that the Father is sending the Spirit co-ordinately with Jesus. It seems then that in 20:17 Jesus is already thought of as ascended to the Father on Easter morning. What the ascension dramatizes for John is the new relationship of the disciples with God now made possible by Jesus' glorification: "I ascend to my Father and to your Father, to my God and your God" (20:17).

We must not therefore try to seek a facile synchronization of John with Luke concerning the relationship of the resurrection and the ascension. We remember from our study of the Acts that Passover, the feast of the Unleavened Bread, was understood to be a feast of fifty days' duration concluding with Pentecost. Luke uses the rich Sinai covenant background of Pentecost to elaborate the meaning of the gift of the Spirit, and he stresses its charismatic manifestation. The Spirit is given, in Acts, as much as in John, by the glorified Jesus (Acts 2:33). But John's picture makes more visible Jesus' real presence and agency in the communicating of the Spirit. Likewise, John joins the moment of the giving of the Spirit to the moment of the missioning word of Jesus, thus showing the theological inter-relationship once more of word and Spirit. Moreover while Luke is interested in the charismatic explosion of the Spirit in tongues, prophecy and healing, John is more interested in the relation of the Spirit to the power over sin. This power was, in Matthew, founded in a word of Jesus to the disciples (16:19; 18:18; 9:8). In John it is founded both in a word of Jesus and in the gift of the Spirit.

The expression translated "they are forgiven them" is in the perfect passive form of the Greek verb. The passive is simply a characteristic Jewish way of avoiding a direct mention of the divine name. The perfect indicates the unaltered effects of the action, so that the meaning is: "Whenever you forgive men's sins, God forgives them and they remain forgiven; whenever you withhold them, God withholds them and they remain withheld."

There are many other questions that may be put to this text. The absence of the article before "Holy Spirit" leads some to translate "a holy spirit" or simply "divine breath." But it is hardly conceivable John could mean anything less than the person of the Paraclete whom he has identified as the Holy Spirit in 14:26. Furthermore, the term "Holy

Spirit" is used without the article in Acts 2:4, where it certainly means more than "a holy spirit" or "divine breath." We may assume, however, that John omitted the article here to suggest the connection of this communication of the Holy Spirit with the creative act of Gen 2:7.

One may ask also whether in John's understanding the power to forgive sins through the Holy Spirit is given to the eleven as symbolic of the apostolic authority which continued in the community or whether it was given to them as representative of the community as such. This question as well as the more intricate one about the specific scope of the forgiving power is discussed at length by Father Raymond Brown in his Anchor Bible Commentary on this passage. It is much too involved to fit the limits of our study. What interests us here is that the Holy Spirit is associated, in a way nowhere else so clearly in the New Testament, with this power over sin.

Conclusion

If we contrast John with Luke-Acts, it becomes clear that John has stressed the life-giving function of the Spirit over against its charismatic-prophetic function. This appears chiefly in the image of water used of "the Spirit whom those that came to believe in him were to receive" (7:39). Associating the Spirit with the rebirth in baptism and with the forgiveness of sins by the authority of the disciples also tends to domesticate the Spirit to the structural and sacramental side of the church, although the missioning aspect is not absent (20:21-22).

If we miss the Lukan way of depicting the spirit of prophecy, we must not overlook the fact that in John too the Spirit is the Spirit of revelation. But the intimate relation of the Spirit to the revealing word of Jesus indicates that John is more in the wisdom tradition than in the prophetic. For while in the prophetic tradition the Spirit's coming is manifested in ecstatic praise or proclaiming, in the Wisdom tradition, wisdom pours out her own spirit upon the listeners so that they may comprehend her words (Prov 1:23). Although it is merely a matter of emphasis, we can say that John's understanding of the Spirit in this regard is more contemplative, more concerned with the inward nourishment of the believer and the community than with its outward mission.

The Spirit does, nevertheless, have an important function toward the outside. When men are not open to the forgiveness of their sins offered in the power of the Holy Spirit (20:21-23), the outward function is expressed in the term *Paraclete*, a term proper to John. The Paraclete is not the converter but the prosecutor of the world that refuses to believe in Jesus. In the process of using this term and its angelic associations from the tradition, John has etched more clearly the traits of distinct personality in the Holy Spirit. And yet, by insisting that the Spirit is sent by the Father and by Jesus, revealing only what he has heard, and by exploiting to the full the image of water flowing from the rock who is Jesus, John balances distinctiveness with derivativeness. Thus all the elements are here which will lead to the more precise Trinitarian formulations of the fourth century and the later theological explanations of the divine persons as "subsistent relations."

The View from
the Mountain-Top

The climb has been long but we have at last reached the top. As we rest from the journey, our eyes can gently trace the long path whose beginnings are almost now lost from view.

In the earliest documents, the spirit first appeared as the breath of life, God's own breath breathed into man. But very soon we also saw men and women moved in an unusual way that was attributed to a special visitation of the divine spirit. This spirit was not really other than a way of saying that God himself was moving those whom he touched.

Because the prophets were spokesmen whose message came not from study or mere empirical observation but from inspiration, they were called "men of the spirit." With the classical prophets the spirit of the Lord began to be understood not just as charismatic power but as an ethical force bringing purification and judgment but also salvation. Because many in Israel did not understand the ethical role of the spirit, there was a tendency in the pre-exilic prophets, especially in Jeremiah, to replace "spirit" with "word" as the unambiguous instrument of divine revelation.

But during the exile, when the nation was apparently dead, Ezekiel revived the notion of the prophetic spirit and spoke of the rebirth of the people and the renewal of the covenant in terms of a new spirit. Second Isaiah saw the return from exile as a new creation wrought by both the Lord's spirit and his word, and the priestly tradition extended this historical understanding to cosmic dimensions in its magnificent description of cosmic creation in Genesis 1. While the post-exilic prophets spoke of the spirit as the power by which the temple would be rebuilt, Israel's poets sang of the spirit, even of the Lord's "holy spirit," as the holy inward presence of God's renewing grace enabling them to live as he would desire. In a special way the "holy spirit" given to man is related to God's face or personal presence.

In the apocalyptic development, the absence of the spirit in the present age was keenly felt, and the gift of the spirit was seen to be the special mark of the age to come. Glimpses of that future age were often mediated to seers by angels. The wisdom tradition dealt more acceptingly with man's present life experience and came to see the way of wisdom as God's way of living, combining at length the revelational with the empirical, though the former was more and more understood to be the written Torah. Nevertheless, this way was understood not only to be a word but a spirit poured out by lady wisdom herself, that her words might be tasted in the heart and lived with grace.

The rabbis, however, expected the "holy spirit" to be given only in the age to come, and in the present age all that the holiest of men could do is to merit that they be awarded the spirit in the age to come. At Qumran the best of Old Testament piety about the holy spirit was incorporated, along with a dualism of the good and the evil spirit and the angelic spirit leading the final holy war of the sons of light against the sons of darkness.

While already with Isaiah the Messiah was said to be bearer of the spirit, it was nowhere said that he would bestow the spirit upon others. Thus, while the tradition affirmed the spirit as the eschatological gift, on the one hand to the Messiah and on the other hand to the people, the interrelation of these two was never addressed until John the Baptist heralded the arrival of the Baptizer in the Holy Spirit.

When we turned to the New Testament, beginning with the letters of Paul, we suddenly found the "Holy Spirit" everywhere—in prophetic speech, in the preaching and the receiving of the word, in tongues and signs and wonders, in a holy ethic, so liberating that Paul could say that the law was now bypassed. The gift of the Holy Spirit meant God's love poured into men's hearts and carrying them through all counter-forces, even death itself, to the glory destined for God's sons. The community in which all this took place considered itself to have been created by the new covenant of the Spirit.

But what was most startling was the fact that this intense and ubiquitous activity of the Spirit was held to be rooted, without exception, in the resurrection of Jesus Christ, the "break-through" event which enabled the Spirit to be given. This was the great surprise, for it could not have been suspected from the Old Testament sign-posts. In Paul, the same truth appeared in his rooting the Spirit in the body of the risen Lord. Jesus, in turn, as the gospels detailed, was the Messiah-Servant-Son upon whom the Holy Spirit was manifested in the Jordan baptism and throughout his charismatic ministry.

But the door through which the Holy Spirit upon Jesus could pass to his community was not just the resurrection. It was the mysterious and paradoxical death that preceded. Not only was this unforeseen by any contemporary interpretations of the Old Testament. Even the disciples of Jesus never suspected, or when they did suspect they resisted, the idea that Jesus' baptism of them in the Holy Spirit could happen only through his own baptism by fire, the cross.

If Mark showed the manner of Jesus' death to be the supreme revelation of his divine sonship, John showed that even the gift of the Spirit in some way flowed from that death.

For Luke, on the other hand, it is the Holy Spirit that guarantees the continuity of the period of the church with the period of Jesus, for the same Spirit is operative in both, as can be seen in the many parallels of the early community with the experiences of Jesus. For Luke, the Holy Spirit is primarily the prophetic Spirit.

For Matthew, the Spirit is upon Jesus, but Matthew softens the role of the Spirit in the church not only because of the currency of false prophecy but because he wishes to focus on the enduring presence of Jesus himself in the church.

In the book of Revelation the Spirit is primarily the prophetic spirit, and only under the image of the river flowing from the throne and from the Lamb does the Spirit appear as the Spirit of life. In John's gospel, the Holy Spirit is primarily the Spirit of life, the spring or river of living water that flows from the glorified Jesus. But it is also the spirit of revelation, closely mated with the word of truth that Jesus brings.

In a special way the Holy Spirit in John is the *Paraclete*, the prosecutor who condemns the "prince of this world" by showing where truth really lay in the trial and death of Jesus and where it now lies in the ongoing trial of the disciples. In this way the role of the Spirit as a distinct person emerges more clearly, without however losing the radical sense it had from the beginning of being the breath of God himself.

If this leads us, as mountain-climbing tends to do, to a limitless horizon, it is the horizon of the mystery of God himself. But it is also the mystery of life, for, if we may attempt a biblical pleasantry, the view is less breath-taking than it is breath-giving for him who would have it so. Or, to be even more biblical, the gift of God is now available to whoever accepts Jesus (Jn 14:15-16) and, recognizing his own thirst (Is 55:1; Rev 22:17), asks him for the water of life (Jn 4:10).

Index

Adam: Christ as second, 141ff., 243, 262, 362f.
Administration: gift of, 161; office, 13.
Adoption, 209.
Almsgiving: gift of, 214.
Angel: accusing, 356; and Paraclete, 356ff.; and spirit of truth, 120; and spirits in man, 118; defending, 367; leads Israel 56ff.; medium of revelation, 80; role for Israel, 56.
Angelology: and pneumatology, 315ff., 356ff.
Angels: agents of prophecy, 324ff., and revelation, 329, 366f.; and the Spirit, 351ff.; minister to Jesus, 243; worship of, 218.
Anger: and love, 167; and Spirit of God, 20f.
Anointing: 32, 157, 185f., 334f.; and knowledge 334f.; and the spirit, 18-21, 53f., 335; teaches, 335; and truth, 335.
Apocalyptic tradition, 84ff.
Apostles: 159; authority of, 292; office of 291f.; and the mystery, 224.
Ascension of Jesus: and gift of Spirit, 286f., 358, 363; and spiritual gifts, 226.
Authority: and Holy Spirit, 272; apostolic, over sin, 363f.; given disciples, 307, 310; in discernment, 155; in Matthean community, 303; in scriptural interpretation, 315f.; of Paul, 182f.; role of, 184; to exorcise, 254.

Babel: reversed at Pentecost, 282.
Baptism: and anointing, 185f.; Christian, 242; fluidity of rites, 295; and gift of the Spirit, 292ff.; and the Spirit, 139f., 230ff., 287; in the Holy Spirit, 238f., 272f., and water, 157; in name of Trinity, 310; of Jesus, 239ff., 340f.; of blood, 338; Jesus' suffering as, 249; sealing with the Spirit, 221; successor to circumcision, 221.
Begetting: of water and Spirit, 341ff.
Berakah: form of Ephesians, 221.
Birth: of water and spirit, 342f.
Body: Christ's, source of Spirit, 142f.; as

Church, 156; and spirit, 112f., 134ff., 156f.; spirit and soul, 130; spiritual, 141f.; temple of Spirit, 140f.
Breath of Life: 95f., 97f., 101f.; Spirit as, 366.
Building (up): 162; role of Spirit, 77ff.
Burden and spirit, 15.

Chaos: and spirit, 66f.
Charism: and office, 161f., 214.
Charismatic: activity in early church, 289ff.; power promised disciples, 339; Spirit, 366.
Charity (see Love): applauds good, 168; contrasted with eros, 171; a way, 163.
Christ (see Jesus): primacy of, 218; and Spirit, 190, 208, 223, 265; spiritual rock, 144.
Church (see Ecclesiology): expansion by Holy Spirit, 289ff.; and image of God, 190; of sinners, 304; and the Spirit, 145ff., 307f.; unity of, 157f.
Cleansing (see Purification): and the spirit, 46f., 59f., 119f., 122, 139, 260.
Combat: spiritual, 227.
Comforting: 53.
Community: support of spirit, 72; work of Spirit, 187.
Confession of Jesus: and the Spirit, 260ff.
Cosmos: and Spirit, 61ff.
Conception of Jesus: by Holy Spirit, 265f.
Consolation: purpose of prophecy, 175.
Counsel: 41.
Covenant: renewal, 51; and Spirit, 45ff., 77f.
Covenant, New: given on Pentecost, 281; and the Spirit, 185ff., 188, 366f.
Creation: Spirit's role, 64ff., 70ff.; and wisdom, 50.
Creation, New: 50, 241, 364.
Cross (see Death, Passion of Jesus): 249f.; and Spirit, 194, 237ff.
Crucifixion: with Christ, 200f.

David: inspired by Spirit, 69f.
Day of the Lord: and the Spirit, 85ff.
Death of Jesus (see Cross): and revelation,

Transfiguration of Jesus, 266.
Transformation: by the Spirit, 190f.
Truth: Jesus as, 346; and love, 168f.; spirit of, 346, 349ff., 357, 359ff.

Understanding: 40f.; growth in, 217.
Union with Christ: 200f.
Unity: of Church, 157f.; of community, 138; at Pentecost, 277; of Spirit, 225.
Upbuilding: and praying in Spirit, 312; purpose of prophecy, 175.

Visions: of false prophets, 42; of Jeremiah, 43; medium of prophecy, 45.
Voice: agent of prophecy, 324.

Water: living, meaning, 345, 347; leaping up, 347; image of Spirit, 51, 158, 330ff., 338f., 341ff., 344ff., 364, 368; symbol of wisdom, 345.
Way: of the Lord, 163f.
Will of God: and spirit, 74.
Wind: image of spirit, 38f., 105, 343; and judgment, 43; of purification, 239; as vanity, 97.

Wine: symbol of Spirit, 227, 282f.
Wisdom: 40f.; ethical, 104; gift of the Spirit, 13, 16, 96, 105f.; of God, 50; and history, 109f.; identified with Jesus, 150; identified with Law, 99; and insight, 217; inspired, 96; and prophecy, 110; a spirit, 103ff.; spirit of, 62, 221; of the Spirit, 136ff.; spiritual, 217; traits of, 106ff.; as water, 345; as woman, 95, 367; word of, 149ff.
Wisdom tradition: 83f., 366f.; and the Spirit, 91ff.; in John 364.
Witness: apostolic, and Spirit, 296ff.; Paraclete as, 352f.; prophetic, to Jesus, 325; Spirit as, 338.
Word: discerns spirit, 30f., 310; replaces spirit, 30; and spirit, 34f., 42f., 45, 50, 60, 66f., 70, 227, 241, 344, 346, 364.
Word of God: 49f.; in Hosea, 34f.; in Micah, 35; institutionalized, 64; inward, 31; received in Spirit, 127; sword of the Spirit, 227.
Word of Jesus: heals, 304f.
Words of Jesus: basis for discernment, 303.
World: prosecuted by Paraclete, 353ff.
Worship: and Spirit, 346f.